THE
LITTLE
VICTIMS

THE
LITTLE
VICTIMS

How America Treats Its Children

Howard James

David McKay Company, Inc.

NEW YORK

010074

The Little Victims

Copyright © 1975 by Howard James

Library of Congress Cataloging in Publication Data

James, Howard, 1935-
    The little victims.

    Includes index.
    1. Children—Institutional care—United States.
I. Title.
HV741.J3   362.7'32'0973   74-14020
ISBN 0-679-50524-5

HV
741
.J3
1975

Manufactured in the United States of America

To Judy—colleague, wife, mother of my children, and so much more.

Contents

Introduction

Even in the quiet of a New Hampshire night, with the snow piling up evenly on the pine boughs outside my window, I hear, deep in the recesses of my mind, the children crying. Though I press my face deep into the pillow, and reach out for the warmth of my wife beside me, their voices will not be still.

And then I see them in their cells, or crowded into drab dormatory rooms, or standing in filth in slum hovels—asking me, sometimes without words, why they are being treated in this way.

I know the American people better than most who live in our nation. I have been in every city of size, and hundreds of small towns too. I know Pie Town, New Mexico, Hot Coffee, Mississippi, and Sugar Hill, New Hampshire, as well as La Push, Washington, Rock Hill, South Carolina, Blackduck, Minnesota, Mission, Texas, Browning, Montana, Skowhegan, Maine, Steamboat Springs, Colorado, Fernandina Beach, Florida, and Oxnard, California, and have been in most more than once.

My own children, traveling with me, have played with the retarded and inmates of mental hospitals in many states. As I moved about the nation in my large camper, these institutions have been home, briefly, during two summer vacations. And during one trip from New Hampshire to California, and then north to Seattle, my expectant wife was carrying our youngest son—putting up with the hardships of the road with incredibly good spirit.

And sometimes late at night, when I awaken, remembering what I have seen and heard and smelled, I quietly leave my wife's side and cross the dark room to my desk, and stare out at the small New England village that is scattered in the valley and wonder how one can move a nation, change a culture, and help the children. I know that I cannot do it alone.

It was to this end that this book was written: to tell my friends and neighbors across America what I have seen and felt, hoping that some will join in my concern and demand change.

In a sense this is not my book. It belongs to the children, and to the hundreds of child-care professionals I have met through the years. I served largely as a stenographer, taking down their words, telling their story. And because this book has been so long in the making, I know that some have taken new jobs and a few have even died, some without my knowledge. Few who dedicated their lives to children make the *New York Times* obituary page or the columns of other major papers.

Others may have changed their views since last we talked (or had them changed by political threats), and still others, lacking access to the notebooks that I have carefully kept, may feel that I have misinterpreted their words. I can only ask their forgiveness and explain that that is a hazard of a book of this magnitude.

Steve Antoniotti, who, although assisting me less than a year, gave much of himself to this project, both in the field of retardation and in helping me organize the mass of material we acquired, is among those deserving praise.

Without the enthusiastic support (and firm prodding) of James O'Shea Wade of David McKay this book might never have been published. I also thank the many others at McKay who have been patient and support-ive—especially the sales staff, the men who must convince the book-sellers that this book is worthy of their shelves.

And finally my thanks (accompanied by hugs) to my wife, Judy, and to the children: Mark, Eric, Paul, Heidi, Katie, Steve, and Jon. Their love and understanding gave strength to my work and happiness to the months and years on the road and hunched over my typewriter.

PART
I
The Little Victims

1

All in the Family

I remember a warm summer evening in Iowa when I was small. We were outdoors, listening to the radio. My mother and father sat on the steps. A bedroom window was open so that we could hear my little brother if he cried. I scrubbed a stick on the sidewalk, slowly wearing it down, listening to Charlie McCarthy and Fibber McGee and Molly. My mother leaned against my father, her eyes closed. The sweet scent of clover drifted into the yard from the field behind the house. Fireflies blinked. Then something happened. Perhaps I was told to go to bed. Now, more than thirty years later, I can only remember running off into the darkness, throwing myself down on the grass to cry.

After a while my father came to find me. When I heard him coming I sobbed loudly so that he could find me in the darkness. Soon he was stretched out on his back beside me, his hands behind his head, asking me to look at the stars. We talked for a long time. When we went back to the house my mother didn't say anything, she just sang an extra hymn as she tucked me into bed.

My childhood is filled with memories of picnics with my parents and with a great-aunt who lived next door; of my grandmother's freshly baked bread with real butter melting on it; and walks on the university campus with my father—one of the few married students in college then. He would take me to the art building, or the music practice hall, where I could absorb the sounds and sights and smells, or he might stop to show me a small animal or bird in a hedge, or to crush flowers on a bush because they smelled like strawberries. My mother and I gathered berries, hazel nuts, hickory and walnuts, and my grandmother would hold a heavy flat stone in her lap and crack the nuts with a hammer, the shells falling into her apron. I would put the nutmeats in a tin cup to be used for desserts. Each July we would visit cousins who grew melons, and sometimes we would break them open out in the field and only eat the rich watermelon hearts, and we always returned home with the car trunk loaded with them, and until our family grew too large (we were riding with relatives) we filled the back seat as well.

I remember Christmas Eve in Illinois in 1943. We were sitting in the living room. The fireplace was crackling and the tree threw pine-needle shadows on the wall. My aunt and cousin were there, along with my mother, grandmother, and two younger brothers. We were singing Christmas carols before going to bed.

My father was off fighting somewhere in the Pacific, and no matter how hard I tried, I couldn't fight back the tears. When I was smaller my father, a tall, strong man, had held me on his lap on Christmas Eve and I could feel his voice come rumbling from his chest when he sang. But on this night only women and children were singing, and the carols seemed high and screechy. I felt small and alone. Then my mother began to cry. Soon nobody could sing, and we all ran off to bed feeling miserable. I felt better in the morning until my grandmother scolded me for spoiling Christmas.

During that same period I earned spending money selling radishes and rhubarb from the garden, and my grandmother crocheted hotpads and started African violets in sand for me to sell in the winter months.

After the war we moved from Illinois to Elkhart, Indiana, but we still couldn't afford a car. The whole family went on outings and even to church on bicycles. My mother earned extra money running the popcorn concession at basketball games, and my father, an art teacher, took tickets and made posters and signs for the school.

We didn't have much money, but we had a strong family unit. My mother was always at home after school, and so were my grandmother and my great-aunt. When I needed him, my father was available, and he was always willing to take me places and let me work with him on projects. I grew up happy—feeling loved and needed. It was a comfortable and certain world that I lived in.

Years later, when I began interviewing slum families, and then delinquent children in some forty states for my book *Children in Trouble* (McKay, 1970), I often asked myself if my own childhood was unusual. Could I only remember the pleasant events? Did I unconsciously reject the pain I felt? I also compared my life to that of the children I was studying.

What if I had been born a girl instead of a boy? How would my childhood experiences—and my life as an adult—have differed? What if I had been born black, Indian, Mexican-American, or into some other minority group? Would I be the same person if my parents had neglected or abused me? What if my parents had been separated or divorced? What if I had been born out of wedlock? Would I have been a different person if I had been adopted or placed in a foster home? How important was it to have my grandmother and great-aunt in the home, and other relatives living in the area? What if I had been hauled into juvenile court, jailed, or committed to an institution? What if my father had been a highly paid executive, always on the road? Or a gas station attendant or factory worker, rather than an artist who encouraged creativity and intellectual activity? What if my mother had worked, so that I would come home from school to an empty house? How important was it to know that I was a *wanted* child, and that my parents loved me deeply?

My parents always had an extra place at the table for a dirty or hungry child, and we shared Christmas and other holidays with a schoolmate of mine whose mother was dead and whose father was an alcoholic. My father liked people and people liked him. He counted janitors, policemen, farmers, doctors, and lawyers among his friends. What does this mean to me now? How important was it to live safely in cities of modest size, in an area where I could bicycle, fish, go camping, swim, hike, collect spiders, snakes, butterflies, and moth cocoons to hang on a screened porch to hatch out in the spring?

Although we lived in three midwestern cities during my first eighteen years, I was able to put down roots, get to know the neighbors, walk through the alleys to collect treasures (broken umbrellas and alarm clocks), dig holes in vacant lots, build tree houses, and fly kites. I had friends, a paper route, safety, freedom of movement, health, and the opportunity to attend a school far better than many in America.

In writing this book, I have considered these things and more. For I have seen thousands of retarded children locked in cold institutions around this nation. I have visited the schools for the deaf and blind in several states, along with mental hospitals scattered across the country. In the decades that have passed since I was a child, vandalism and shoplifting have become national problems. More than a million children are processed by our juvenile courts each year, according to one federal study. Another government report suggests that between 500,000 and a million youngsters run away from home each year—some never to return.

Every community, large or small, has been plagued with drug abuse and teen-age alcoholism. Why?

How important are the schools? Do they cause or prevent problems? What impact has television had on our society? Who sells drugs to our children? Why? How important are parents? What happens to children who are reared by babysitters, day-care centers, schools, street gangs, drug pushers, the drug culture, social workers, television producers and entertainers, disc jockeys, foster parents, mental health workers, and others, like Little League coaches?

What has pushed the rate of child abuse to record highs? What is child abuse? Does it hurt a teen-age girl to have sexual relations with her father? Should a twelve-year-old be given the pill? At what age or stage of experience should a boy or girl freely engage in sexual intercourse? What should one do if a child runs away? Why do mental health officials report record rates of instability? Should highly active children be calmed with drugs administered by a school official? What impact has the sudden increase of working mothers had on our nation? Or the three decades of movement to urban areas? Are the suburbs really the best place to rear children?

Interviews with hundreds of children in reform schools show that children congregate at parentless homes after school and at other times to use drugs, drink alcohol, engage in sexual activities, or read books and magazines banned in their own homes. Many of the girls I interviewed in reform schools reported that they first experienced sexual intercourse in their own beds, before their mothers arrived home from work or bridge club. Yet schools continue to lock their gyms and playgrounds; there are, in suburbs and cities, few vacant lots to play in, few trees to climb, and little loose lumber for building club houses. And where are the clean streams to wade or fish in?

Even when mothers remain at home, millions of American children sit staring at television sets for hours. Many of these children live in a kind of isolation unknown in an earlier generation. Later they become bored, listless, aimless. They take death and violence for granted. They have seen adults depicted as bumbling fools.

Since World War II the divorce rate has steadily climbed, and now claims one marriage in three and sometimes one in two. During this same period Americans have been on the move. Each year some 7 million of us move to a new state, according to the U.S. Department of Commerce, while 6 million more move to a new community in the same state. During the 1940s and the '50s and '60s, a million persons a year (and more) moved from farms to towns and urban areas. (In 1940 more than 30 million Americans lived on farms. By 1971 the number dropped to 9.6

million on farms, even while the nation's total population grew by more than 75 million persons during the three decades.)

Writing in the September 1974 *Fortune*, Lionel Tiger, a Rutgers University professor of anthropology, says: "Have the managers of companies promoting their executives from one side of this continent to another forgotten the tumults of their own childhoods, when they moved into a new house or a new town? Are they aware of the problems of children who must establish themselves in a new school, with new friends, new bullies, new teams, new loyalties and new challenges? Are the large numbers of affluent dropouts, the children of the most privileged members of the community, rebelling in part against a special form of deprivation—of continuity and stability? Are they reflecting an unwillingness to be exiles in their own country?"

And what of women going to work? The number of mothers working outside the home has been soaring. In 1972 there were some 30 million mothers with children under the age of eighteen; of these, 7.3 million worked full time, while 5.5 million worked half time or more. The total number who worked at least part of the year hit 15.5 million—over half of all mothers with children under eighteen, according to the U.S. Bureau of the Census.

Children (and their parent or parents) receiving welfare checks under the Aid to Dependent Children program climbed from 2.2 million in 1955 to 10.6 million in 1971, according to figures released by the Department of Health, Education, and Welfare. Reasons vary.

Illegitimate births soared from 89,500 in 1940 to 339,200 in 1968 (the latest figures available as this is written). Nearly half of the illegitimate babies were born to mothers between the ages of fifteen and nineteen, and 7,700 were born to mothers under the age of fifteen. In fact, of all children born in 1968, a total of 9.7 percent were illegitimate, according to figures supplied by the U.S. National Center for Health Statistics. In the 1970s (and earlier) many parents began giving teen-age daughters birth control pills and other contraceptive devices, and even the federal government began dispensing contraceptives, often with or without permission of the girl's parents.

I am not trying to glamorize the "good-old days" and wring my hands over the age we are living in. On one corner of our farm, under two ancient pines, a row of thin and weathered gravestones show that long ago nine children from a single family died on what is now our land— some within weeks of one another. When I stop by the fence to stare at those gray stones, I can feel the pain those pioneer parents must have felt as the rocky earth was shoveled in on their children's bodies.

Perhaps today's heartbreak is different, but it is just as painful. Ask any mother whose child is in jail, or imprisoned by the narcotic needle, or who has run away, never to be heard from again.

Further, my study of American children does not only include the grim side, for I found many strong, happy children living with solid, salt-of-the-earth families. Perhaps the largest numbers still live on family farms in the Midwest and South, but others can be found in New England, the Southwest, Pacific Northwest, and other corners of the country. There were happy children in the city and suburbs too, although I feel more live hollow lives there than in small towns and rural areas. And I often found more love and warmth in the black ghettos than in expensive suburban homes, as well as more pain.

As I will point out in subsequent chapters, many factors influence the quality of life our children lead. For example, it seems that millions of parents are afraid of their children, perhaps because they have read or misread Dr. Spock and other popular writers who specialize in child-rearing. Studies show that separating mothers from their babies during the first few hours of life seems to have a life-long impact on the children. Bottle feeding too—especially when the child engages in it alone in a playpen or crib—also may have an impact. Neglect and abuse take their psychological toll, and children who are mistreated when they are young often grow up to mistreat their own children.

Few subjects of such importance are more neglected in America. We too often assume that parents—like robins and rabbits—will automatically do the right things for their offspring. We also believe, erroneously, that if the natural parents fail or damage their children, the benevolent state will step in and meet their needs as a surrogate parent. But as this book will show, state agencies and institutions can be more damaging than the poor parents.

No community meets the needs of even a fraction of our unwanted and handicapped children. Billions of dollars are being squandered on schools, institutions, agencies, and programs destined to fail. Nor do the professionals have the answers either. That is why Karl Menninger, the eminent psychiatrist who has devoted his lifetime to problems of people and children, told me that the best hope lies—to his mind—in The Villages, started in Topeka, Kansas. The Villages are really strong foster homes, built in a cluster, with wholesome and intelligent foster parents, using normal community facilities.

Dr. Menninger will not permit psychiatrists or policemen on the grounds; his whole program centers on building a strong family unit for children who do not have adequate families of their own. He gives them shelter, food, love, and stability. But even Dr. Karl has not been able to get others to accept his plan and spread it across the nation.

Perhaps too few people care.

2

Children Are Chattels

Throughout history children have been looked upon as chattels—possessions, property—to be used, disposed of, or cared for as the parents (or the church or state) saw fit.

Adam Smith, the great English economist, observed in 1776: "The value of children is the greatest of all encouragements to marriage. We cannot, therefore, wonder that the people in North America should generally marry very young. Notwithstanding, the continued complaint of the scarcity of hands in North America. The demand for labourers, the funds destined for maintaining them, increase, it seems, still faster than they can find labourers to employ" *(The Wealth of Nations,* Dutton & Co.).

Earlier, in 1619, the Virginia Company in America wrote the mayor and aldermen of London, thanking them for the one hundred children of the poor sent in 1618, "which by the goodness of God there safely arrived (save such as died in the way). . . . " The colonists then asked for a hundred more youngsters.

"Our desire is that we may have them of twelve years old and upward with allowances of three pounds apiece for their transportation and forty shillings apiece for their apparel as was formerly granted. They shall be apprentices, the boys till they come to twenty-one years of age, the girls till the like age or till they be married, and afterwards they shall be placed as tenants upon the public land with the best conditions where they shall have houses with stock of corn and cattle to begin with, and afterwards the moiety of all increases and profit whatsoever" *(Children and Youth in America,* Vol. I, p. 7, Harvard University Press, 1970).

In 1620 the Virginia Company wrote again, asking London officials for another "one hundred children, out of the multitudes that swarm that place." Two years later the Rev. John Donne, dean of London's St. Paul's Cathedral, preached a sermon praising the Virginia Company, suggesting that: "It shall sweep your streets, and wash your doors, from idle persons, and the children of idle persons, and employ them. . . ."

Perhaps the children shipped to the New Land were better off. Both the English and the Dutch stored unwanted children, including orphans and paupers, in almshouses—poorhouses—where they lived wretched lives with vagrants, drunks, petty thieves, the retarded, the insane, and the unwanted and homeless elderly. Historians report that this practice dates back to the tenth century and possibly earlier.

Other children were "spirited" away against their will, and during this era, child-stealing was reported in England, as people earned their livings filling quotas requested by American settlers. Because the quota-fillers were paid a fee for each child sent, kidnapping was inevitable.

This part of our history we have largely forgotten. We are far more familiar with the selling of black African children in our southern Colonies. The Portuguese brought the first African slaves to Europe in 1442, and in 1502 the new Spanish governor of Haiti brought black slaves, born in Seville, with him. More than a hundred years later, in 1620, a Dutch ship sold a cargo of blacks to tobacco planters on the mainland, at Jamestown, Virginia. By then thousands had been carried to Haiti, Cuba, Jamaica, and Puerto Rico. By 1786 more than 2 million black slaves had been sold in British-held islands and mainland colonies.

Inhuman treatment of young black slaves, the separation of families, and the extreme forms of abuse are well known in the nation today since the civil rights battles of the South of the 1960s brought about the teaching of black history in the seventies.

Indenture was another, less severe, form of slavery. The indentured servant or worker eventually earned his freedom. Under Maryland law, in 1638, males "under the age of eighteen years transported into this province at the charge and adventure of some other person shall serve such a person . . . until such person or persons so transported shall be of the full age of four and twenty years. . . . " Girls under twelve served seven years for their transportation to America. The length of the indenture varied and grew less in time, but practices varied also, and some children were indentured ten years and more.

The same Maryland law required masters to give girls, after they had completed their servitude, "one new petticoat and waistcoat, one new smock, one pair of new shoes, one pair of new stockings and the clothes belonging to the servant. . . . " Boys got a new suit, a shirt, stockings, pair of shoes, and a "new monmouth cap." Both boys and girls also received "three barrels of corn, a hilling how and a weeding how and a felling axe . . . " *(Children and Youth in America*, Vol. 1).

Not only was indenture used to pay for the passage of an adult or child from Europe, Asia, or elsewhere but it also was a way to pay for the keep of orphans and the children of the poor.

While indentured children and slaves were worked hard and often maltreated, many children were badly treated by their own parents and by those who took them in as apprentices. Sometimes whole families went to work when sickness, death, an Indian massacre, or some other mishap left pioneer women and children without support. Some worked as a unit, while others were farmed out to whoever would take them.

Grace Abbott writes in *The Child and the State* (University of Chicago Press, 1938): " . . . dependent families were frequently auctioned off to the lowest bidders, sometimes with the provision in the contract that the children were to have the privilege of going to school in the winter."

In Colonial America severe punishment of children was considered proper and normal, just as it was in the days of Plato and Socrates. In her book *Child Life in Colonial Days* (Macmillan, 1899), Alice Morse Earle writes: "Parents, teachers, and ministers chanted in solemn and unceasing chorus, 'Foolishness is bound up in the heart of a child,' and they believed the only cure for that foolishness was in stern repression and sharp correction—above all in the rod. They found abundant support for this belief in the Bible, their constant guide."

She uses as an example an essay by the Pilgrim preacher John Robinson, who called for the "beating and breaking down" of children. She contends this approach had been considered normal and proper for centuries. As evidence she quotes a letter from Agnes Paston in 1457 to the London schoolmaster hired to teach her son. The letter urges the schoolmaster to "belash" the boy if he did poorly, and told of how she beat her daughter every week, sometimes twice a day, and with result that she had "her head broken in two or three places."

School books from the seventeenth, eighteenth, and nineteenth centuries picture the schoolmaster with a rod or birch twigs in his hand. Similar implements were used on children who fell asleep during the long sermons in churches of that era. Peddlers sold birch rods for whipping children and some children in boarding schools were forced to pay for the birch from their already meager spending money.

"Many ingenious punishments were invented," Mrs. Earle writes. "A specially insulting one was to send the pupil out to cut a small branch from a tree. A split was made by the teacher at the severed end of the branch, and the culprit's nose was placed in the cleft end. Then he was forced to stand, painfully pinched, an object of ridicule."

For children who whispered in school, wooden gags were devised. Made of small boards, they were held in the child's mouth much as a bit is held in a horse's mouth. In some schools children who misbehaved were put in stocks, wore wooden shackles, or were hung in a sack.

Despite the maltreatment, which was normal and accepted for thousands of years of human history, children had little difficulty knowing they were needed and useful. Families in early America were large, with ten or twelve children quite common. Many, of course, died at birth, during epidemics that swept the country, or from a wide variety of diseases. Sometimes several children would die in a single family in a single day.

Children were needed for the survival of the family, and the family was the basic unit of society. Before the industrial revolution, which began roughly in 1750 with the harnessing of steam power and the development of textile looms, everyone depended upon the work of his hands to survive—whether craftsmen or farmers. Children as young as five or six were expected to work in the fields from "can to can't"—from the time the sun rose until it set—and in the barns, their homes, and their fathers' shops and stores.

The culture, based to a large extent upon Puritanical religious teachings, called for hard work. It was the key to salvation, and it was believed that idle hands would be used by the devil.

In 1790, when the first census was taken, less than 4 million persons lived in the United States. Land was everywhere and was available to anyone who was willing to work hard, clear, and plant it. Hired hands were hard to find, and so children were more valuable than money.

"It was the child's duty to work, the father's legal obligation to prepare him for a useful occupation, and the responsibility of the magistrates to provide work for the poor and to punish the idle," the book *Children and Youth in America* (Vol. 1) reports.

Cities also were growing during the early years of America, and with the arrival of the industrial revolution the infamous sweat shops developed. Children as young as five and six worked twelve hours a day. Orphans and paupers in England received only room and board in exchange for their labor.

In 1790 the first experimental cotton mill in America opened in Rhode Island, and nine children from seven to twelve years of age were put to work. This was considered a good use of children. In Beverly, Massachusetts, those pushing for a cotton mill there at about the same time argued that it would "afford employment to a great number of women and children, many of whom will be otherwise useless, if not burdensome to society."

Our forebears found other ways to make these children useful. During the nineteenth century they worked in coal mines, lumber mills, shoe and glass factories, cigar factories, and in many other forms of manufacturing. If they were paid at all, children received pennies a day, and seldom over $2 or $3 a week. The plant owners starved some, whipped them, dunked them in tubs of cold water when they dozed off, and stunted them through overwork and malnutrition.

The census of 1900 shows 1,750,178 children between the ages of ten and fifteen at work in industry in America. By 1910 the number climbed by another 200,000.

With many mothers working, young children were cared for by other children, by neighbors, elderly relatives, and on "baby farms." According to the 1910 edition of the *Encyclopaedia Britannica*, these were notoriously evil places, especially in England, where large numbers of children perished.

"It had become the practice for factory operatives and mill-hands to place out their children by the day, and since in many cases the children were looked upon as a burden and a drain on their parents' resources, too particular inquiry was not always made as to the mode in which the children were cared for," the *Britannica* states. Baby farms also were used as places to dump illegitimate children, and those who ran them were paid lump sums when the children were delivered. This resulted in many deaths because the shorter the child's life span the more profitable it was for those running the farms.

In 1871 the House of Commons grew so concerned that it appointed a committee "to inquire as the best means of preventing the destruction of the lives of infants put out to nurse for hire by their parents," The committee reported, among other things, that "improper and insufficient food, opiates, drugs, crowded rooms, bad air, want of cleanliness, and wilful neglect are sure to be followed in a few months by diarrhoea, convulsions and wasting away." The following year baby farms were licensed, but when this did not solve the problem an act was passed in 1897 that required local authorities to oversee their operation.

In the United States orphanages were growing in number and many infants, getting little or no attention and poor care, died in their cribs. Almshouses still existed, and again children were badly treated, but studies of that era show that a child nursed by his mother in an almshouse, no matter how bad, was better off than the orphan who was not held, loved, or properly cared for in an institution.

Even while cruelty to children reached new highs during the industrial revolution, reform and change was taking place. Puritanical churches, with their theory of "beating the devil" out of children, were losing ground to more humane religions. Philosophers such as John Locke helped lead the way. Charles Dickens, Sir Walter Sesant, Dorothea Dix, Charles Loring Brace, Jane Addams, Sigmund and Anna Freud, John Dewey, Maria Montessori, John Bowlby, A. S. Neill, and Jean Piaget all have been credited with bringing about reform.

But there were other factors contributing to a spirit of reform. Growing affluence and the use of children in new ways—that is, as a kind of adornment or extension of the parents, to be nurtured and coddled—also came into being.

In America public education has been mandated for all children except the retarded, insane, delinquent, and others deemed worthless or useless. This also helped bring about change in treatment of children, although even today corporal punishment is still permitted and even encouraged in schools in a number of states.

The first White House Conference on Children was called in 1910, and in 1912 the Children's Bureau was established by Congress and was not dismantled until the Nixon administration took control of government.

States began regulating child labor at the turn of the century, and some even earlier. Federal child labor laws were enacted in 1916 and 1919, but were struck down by the Supreme Court in 1918 and 1922. Finally, in 1938, the Federal Fair Labor Standard Act was passed, and it was amended in 1950.

It seems certain that these laws would not have been enacted had not the nature of our need or use for children changed drastically in the early years of this century. No longer do we need children to help clear our forests, plow our land, or work in our mills. The arrival of the internal combustion engine and gasoline as a fuel, automobiles, tractors, electricity, and other sources of power and motion, and modern production techniques all reduced the need for hand labor.

At home, rural electrification, home appliances, the extension of the day with modern lights, all helped change the lot of children. Housewives did not need as much help. At least in cities women with small families had time to think more about themselves and their children. Comparisons were made. The ability to climb socially extended to more and more families. The use of money to make money grew more important. Sending a child to Harvard or Yale could move him up the social ladder several notches in one generation. Our children were needed for something new, and many were being pampered, cared for, and groomed for a pleasant life.

While many American children were spoiled in the 1920s, the depression in the 1930s and World War II in the 1940s resulted in a more serious, severe life. But Americans made up for the hardships in the 1950s, and again the middle class broadened. The postwar baby boom not only replaced persons lost in the war, but created a surge of children and an increase in taxes to pay for schools.

In the late 1950s emphasis on childhood education to achieve the good life suddenly shifted again. We were well along in the cold war with Russia by then, but we also were scoffing at Russian claims of inventing almost everything from electric light bulbs to the telephone and the jet engine. Hatred for communism, as well as fear, was building all through the decade, in part stoked by Senator Joseph McCarthy, who held the now infamous hearings in Washington in 1953 and 1954.

The competition with Russia came to a head on October 4, 1957, when the USSR launched Sputnik I—the first man-made earth satellite. While the Eisenhower administration knew well in advance that Russia would launch a satellite, it had not prepared the American people for the event. Suddenly the scoffing at Russian technology stopped. Our national pride was momentarily crushed. And we searched for a scapegoat. Instead of turning on President Eisenhower, war hero and father symbol, we turned on our children.

Suddenly we had a new national use for our youngsters. If the Russians could build rockets, then they must be superior in the scientific and technological fields. To be superior they obviously needed a better educational system. Clearly it was tougher than ours. Therefore, we concluded, the best way to catch up with the Russians was to tighten the screws on our children in school.

It is not just coincidence that our delinquency rates started to soar at this point, or that eventually our children would rebel, taking over the universities and disrupting the high schools. Children who were being indulged at home were suddenly placed under a great deal of pressure at school. Individuals who could not keep up, and who also were having problems at home and with their peers, and who did not fit the national need, got into trouble. Dropouts became a national issue, for going to school and being bright was "the American way." Even the brighter students objected to what was happening to them in our schools and universities and in society in general. As we teach in science courses, applying heat and pressure to a volatile substance can be explosive. Trouble finally broke out in the 1960s.

3

We Dislike the Deviant

"Peter's cross-eyed! Peter's cross-eyed! Peter's cross-eyed!" The taunts rattle across the playground.

Seven-year-old Peter stands by a swing set, gripping a metal post until his knuckles turn white, fighting off tears, trying to turn away from his rollicking tormenters, who point, giggle, and snatch at his clothing.

Life can be living hell for children who are different. Deviance, even in minor forms, is seldom tolerated in our society. Almost any sensitive person who spends a few hours on a busy playground or in the halls of an elementary or junior high school will find more than one child being teased because he is fat, thin, crippled, ugly, retarded, or otherwise different. Sissified boys are favorite targets.

Nor is our national intolerance of deviance limited to persons with physical or mental handicaps. A high-powered Washington lawyer sitting before a microphone at a Senate hearing in 1973 was heard to mutter the words "little Jap" when referring in anger to a senator from Hawaii. Polish-Americans have been the butt of many jokes, as were the Germans and Irish a few generations earlier. In Michigan's Upper Peninsula I found Finnish-Americans substituted for Poles. French Canadians have been ridiculed in New England. Jews have been hated here, just as in other parts of the world. Our history includes three centuries of inhumane treatment of blacks, American Indians, and citizens with Spanish surnames. Even today we hurt Spanish-Americans. In 1973 California officials ordered schools there to use only the English language in teaching, even when only Spanish-speaking students are involved. In time this may help these children survive in our intolerant, competitive society. But edicts of this sort, when issued without sufficient care, make Spanish-speaking children feel inferior.

Insensitivity is a national trait. Or perhaps more accurately, a human trait. Sympathy is a newcomer to the human scene. Our jokes (and sometimes our joy) often center on the misfortunes of others. Retribution remains, for many, the highest sense of justice. Our ancestors considered public executions social events. Motion pictures and television shows depict violence and death. Blood spurting from a wounded man's vein is shown in color close-ups. On urban expressways we slow down to stare at mangled cars and broken bodies, creating traffic jams that stretch for miles.

Our people are paradoxical. Millions of Americans could shrug off bombing and napalming Vietnam villages—even when women and children were burned, maimed, or killed.

Large numbers of young people learn to hate at home. After laws were changed in the 1950s and 1960s millions of white, middle-class Americans fled from the cities to the suburbs. When the courts ordered busing of children to maintain a racial balance in schools, ugly prejudice was seen again in our cities. Through it all, little thought has been given to how minority-group children—the victims of hatred—react.

The middle-class majority does not limit its dislike of deviance to outsiders. During the 1960s middle-class boys were thrown out of school, forced to quit athletic teams, and were ridiculed because they chose to wear long hair. Rigidity dies hard. For while most communities eventually accepted the new hair styles, a few schools still opposed them in the 1970s. In 1973 a Texas high school coach attacked long hair on boys as a "sin against God" and backed his views by quoting obscure Biblical passages in an article he wrote for a national magazine.

While boys were in trouble because of their hair styles, girls who wore jeans, took off their bras, or ignored the dress code in other ways also were thrown out of schools. Girls who wore "granny dresses" which covered them from chin to ankles were excluded in several suburban schools near Chicago. In the spring of 1973 an Arizona girl was not permitted to take part in her eighth grade graduation exercises because her mother made her a flowered dress and the school had called for dresses without patterns. The little girl fled the school in tears.

Forcing all to play the game by the majority's rules, or not at all, is a strange concept in a country founded on individual freedom and the right to do as one pleases as long as it hurts no one else.

A few people, beyond those working for underground newspapers or speaking to members of the counterculture, have been disturbed by our intolerance of deviance. One of these is Dr. Burton Blatt, director of the Division of Special Education and Rehabilitation and the Center on Human Policy at Syracuse University.

"It is characteristic of the American culture to segregate and stigmatize people," he contends. "We turn away from cerebral palsy. We flinch when we see someone having a seizure. We are embarrassed before anyone who is blind, black, different or even pregnant."

Dr. Blatt is often attacked for his views, and if his words have an angry ring it is because he has seen what I have seen, and his pain is deep and real. It is hard to be calm, to speak with a measured voice, after visiting a state mental hospital, institution for the retarded, jail, or reform school.

Dr. Blatt asks why, if we are a gentle, compassionate, law-abiding people, "have I seen children nude and bruised, sitting, sleeping and eating with moist and dried feces covering them? Why have I seen children lying on filthy beds, uncovered, flies crawling all over them? Why have I seen a state school director of nursing leave suddenly on a three-day vacation without assigning additional staff or someone to succeed him in his absence during the midst of a hepatitis epidemic? In one building alone 27 of 71 patients were diagnosed as having this dreaded disease. Why have I seen two young women in one solitary cell at the state school, lying nude in a corner, their feces smeared on the walls, ceiling and floor—two bodies huddled in the darkness, without understanding the wrongs they have committed or those committed against them?"

It is, Dr. Blatt believes, in part because "artists distort reality to present reality" and so "many of us distort reality to preserve it." Or to put it another way, we see only what we want to see and ignore that which disturbs or offends us. We make our own reality.

We can drive past a mental hospital, reform school, school for the deaf, or institution for the retarded and never see it, never hear the cries of the children inside. We do not want to see them. We write them off because they are different, deformed, subhuman, unworthy of attention, too unpleasant to think about, or better off hidden out of sight, away from people who would tease, abuse, or ignore their needs.

But I am ahead of myself. This chapter is about our intolerance of deviance. I am writing it to lay the foundation for an understanding of the conditions I found in the kinds of institutions that upset Dr. Blatt. Before we can face what we do to these children we must understand why we do it to them.

One person with answers: Leslie T. Wilkins, visiting professor of

Criminology at the University of California at Berkeley, author of the book *Social Deviance* (Prentice-Hall, 1965). In the book he notes that when we think of deviance we usually think of bad behavior. But when a genius, reformer, or religious leader appears in society his behavior is deviant—yet *good*. (In that context, cynics might say an honest politician in Washington also is a deviant).

Our attitude toward deviant behavior largely depends upon what we have grown up believing to be normal. But it also is tied to our sense of security and the extent of the deviance. If the behavior makes us afraid, we demand one course of action, while if it makes us laugh, we shrug it off.

A newspaper headline warns that a "madman" has escaped from a mental hospital and has stabbed four persons. We lock our doors against all strangers and fear those labeled as "disturbed," even when they are harmless children.

"In earlier times the young and the old were continuously in touch with each other; youth was aware of the problems of age, and age was aware of the problems of youth. The village was aware of the problems of mental deficiency—each village had its village idiot who was a part of the total culture," Wilkins explains. "Everybody knew 'Jack' who stood at the corner of the cross-roads and drooled. The newcomer to the village might feel threatened by Jack's behavior, but immediately he spoke with a member of the village culture [and] he would be assured, 'Oh! Jack's all right, he's just a little weak in the head—he was dropped on it when a baby.' "

But, Wilkins adds, we do not get this direct, face-to-face information, so readily available in a rural village, when we live in urban areas. Because of this, "in urban societies the isolation of deviants has become institutionalized."

Hundreds of thousands of "different" Americans, many of them under the age of sixteen, are locked up. Reasons for locking them up vary widely. Delinquent behavior is used as a reason for removing unwanted or unmanageable children from the community. For years, until controlling drugs were found, those were severe cases of epilepsy were institutionalized, and some of those inmates remain in institutions. We also too often have provided warehouse-like institutions for children without parents, or for those who have been abused or neglected. And there are large facilities for emotionally disturbed Americans and those who are retarded, as well as institutions for the deaf, blind, and some that are crippled. Millions have been shuffled from one foster home to another.

Institutionalization, Wilkins says, is our response to poor information, our fear of those who are different, and our lack of direct contact with those we deem deviant. How can we make people understand what it feels like to be taken from the community, from family, friends, familiar neighborhood, and a sense of belonging, to live in a limbo for months or years? Who can show the citizens of this country the damage done, help them feel the pain experienced by these children, even in the best institutions? How can we show taxpayers the high cost of present methods, and convince them there are better ways?

In traveling across the country, I constantly hear reports of communities fighting small group homes for children. Neighborhood groups hiring lawyers, petitions being passed around, calls to city councilmen, groups attending meetings in blocks to fight change—all doing their bit to hurt children.

Take the case of the institution for the mentally retarded in Denton, Texas—the Denton State School. Richard Day, the assistant superintendent, says every effort is being made to help children return to the community, to eliminate them as tax burdens and convert them to self-supporting taxpayers.

Ron was one of these young retardates. Denton officials worked hard to prepare him for the community. His table manners became acceptable. He learned to wear clothing appropriate for the occasion. If colors weren't a perfect match no one cared. At least he was properly dressed. He learned to handle money, clean his own room, to cross streets, and to live in the community. In time, they found him a job with a car dealer in a small town. He seemed to be making it on his own.

And then one day Ron was emptying trash behind his place of employment and noticed two young girls playing nearby in a yard. He forgot himself and let his mouth droop, and he stared a few seconds too long. The girls' mother looked out of her kitchen window, saw him and panicked. Running out of the house, she screamed at Ron, and he took off as fast as he could run. The police were called. They packed his suitcase and had him out of town before the sun had set. They delivered him to Denton's doorstep and told officials that Ron could not return.

He had done nothing wrong. Ron was hardly dangerous. His childlike mind could not grasp what had happened. Denton officials felt there was little they could do but take him back. No one knew, with this blot on his record, how soon Ron would have another chance.

One can dismiss this incident as just another example of hysteria or small-town Texas justice. Ron didn't have a hearing. No one checked his side of the story. They just ran him out of town. But the fact that Texas is ahead of many states in caring for children is important. More money is now being spent and more effort is being made to help both disturbed and retarded youngsters there than almost anywhere else.

One researcher, John L. Tringo, of the University of Kentucky, questioned 455 persons on their attitudes toward the handicapped. His goal was to determine the social acceptance of handicapped persons. The sample of those interviewed included high school students, college students, graduate students, and those assigned to work with the handicapped—the rehabilitation workers.

In his study of "social distance," as reported in the January/February 1972 issue of *Human Behavior,* he found that ulcers and arthritis are the most accepted handicaps, while mental illness, alcoholism, and criminal behavior are the least accepted. Here is his list, ranking handicaps people may have:

	Ranking	Disability	Ranking by Men	Ranking by Women
Most acceptable disabilities	1	Ulcer	1	2
	2	Arthritis	2	3
	3	Asthma	4	1
	4	Diabetes	3	4
	5	Heart disease	6	5
	6	Amputee	5	9
	7	Blindness	7	8
	8	Deafness	8	6
	9	Stroke	9	7
	10	Cancer	10	10
	11	Old age	11	11
	12	Paraplegic	13	13
	13	Epilepsy	14	12
	14	Dwarf	12	15
	15	Cerebral palsy	15	14
	16	Hunchback	16	6
	17	Tuberculosis	17	17
	18	Ex-convict	18	18
Least acceptable disabilities	19	Mental retardation	19	18
	20	Alcoholism	20	21
	21	Mental illness	21	20

We can speculate on why, in the last quarter of the twentieth century, old age, epilepsy, alcoholism, and tuberculosis appear so far down the list of acceptability. Or why hunchbacks and dwarfs are so disliked.

It is worth noting that except for alcoholics those we banish to institutions show up on the bottom of the list, while handicapped persons who move fairly freely through out society are deemed more acceptable.

I learned this anew in the spring of 1974 when I met Elwyn (Ellie) Mann, a thirty-nine-year-old accountant and graduate student at the State University of New York at Binghamton. As an infant he had what he describes as a "mild case of cerebral palsy." His mind is better than most persons', but he speaks and walks oddly—in a way that many mistake for drunkenness. In fact he was once jailed while stone sober.

My wife and I spent three days with Mr. Mann on the Binghamton campus and in the city and a neighboring community, visiting a church, shopping center, restaurants, and professionals in child-caring fields. Even with my wide exposure to the handicapped and their problems I was shocked to see the revulsion and hostility displayed toward Mr. Mann —even by some professionals and by supposedly intelligent and highly educated people.

I watched facial expressions change from smiling "how-do-you-do" masks to anger, at worst, and to the kind of disapproval one sees from churchgoers when a child passes gas loudly during a service. People stepped back from him, turned away, acted as if he was drunk, and avoided him. Two women—in their forties or fifties—sitting in a car in a shopping-center parking lot made crude remarks.

Mr. Mann, who is kind, intelligent, and normal in every way except appearance and speech, suffers from intense emotional pain beyond that ever experienced by most of us. Perhaps only blacks and other minority groups, or other handicapped persons who try to live and support themselves in the world, can really understand. We talked at length about his problems. Mr. Mann says that he is most deeply scarred by the lack of love. It is not just that people react in negative ways. Rather, it is nearly impossible for Mr. Mann to experience normal warmth and love from other adults.

"My family always told me that I'd find a nice girl with cerebral palsy and we would fall in love and get married," he says. "But it hasn't worked that way. When I was younger I was too busy learing to compete in school and in the business world. But after I went to work [for IBM] I had the feelings everyone else has. I wanted to love and be loved. But even when I dated, girls were never interested in getting serious with me. I have fallen in love with women, but they have never loved me."

Even low-visibility handicaps present those who have them with problems. For example, deaf persons are often encouraged to date and marry others who are deaf.

We are willing to spend millions to hide these unwanted people in institutions that may be far from their homes. And by doing this, millions of children face searing pain, rejection, and abnormal lives. The same is true of those like Ellie Mann, who refuse to be a burden to taxpayers. Instead of rewarding him for his effort we make him miserable.

We must give more thought to our attitudes toward deviance.

4

The Hard-boiled
Egg Syndrome

Karen sat sobbing softly on the edge of her bed in the group home in a northeastern Indiana city. I put my arm around her shoulders and tried to comfort her. After several minutes Karen caught her breath and began to talk.

"My mother killed her," she said, starting to cry again.

"Whom did she kill?"

"My sister. She killed my sister."

"When?" I asked as gently as possible. "When did she do it? How did she do it?"

There was little doubt that Karen's words were sincere. But she found it difficult to talk because the memory of her sister dying brought fresh pain.

"They took three of the kids away from Mom a long time ago," she said. "She couldn't take care of them, and welfare took them away. But nobody wanted my sister, Beverly. She looked funny and she wasn't right in the head, you know. She was retarded. Real bad. She couldn't go to school or anything and nobody'd take her."

"But what makes you think your mother killed her, Karen?"

"I know she did. I was there. Mom kept sayin' how much trouble Beverly was. She looked different, you know. And she had to have braces on her legs. Kids would tease her an' everything and she'd get real mad. Mom said Beverly didn't need to be in this world. She said she was nothin' but trouble—more than the rest of us put together. After she killed her, Mom said that Beverly wasn't worth buyin' a tombstone for. She was my sister!"

Karen began to cry again and I waited for several minutes to see if she wanted to talk more about the incident. While I do not assume the role of therapist when researching, children often want to talk to me. I hold no power over them, am nonthreatening, and I am willing to listen. So, often, children tell me things they tell few others.

"She killed her with pizza," Karen said. "Beverly's mouth wasn't right, you know. She couldn't swallow right. The doctor told Mom never to give her anything like pizza. He said it might kill her. But Mom said Beverly was too much trouble.

"I didn't see her give Beverly the pizza, but my brother did. He came runnin' out into the yard and told me. I went in an' Beverly was chokin' and cryin' and couldn't breathe. I tried to help her but Mom told me to 'get the hell out' or she'd kill *me*. There wasn't nothin' I could do."

The records show that Karen is now mildly disturbed. She blames herself, in part, for what happened to her sister. Local officials confirm that her sister died by choking, and they tend to believe her story. Karen is in a group home because she had been abused physically, sexually, and emotionally. I saw the scars on the back of her legs where she was beaten with an electrical extension cord. The fingernails on both hands dropped off (but have since regrown) when her mother, angered by a poor school report, told Karen to put both hands flat on a table. Then she pounded Karen's hands with her fists. Not only has a stepfather used Karen sexually but he apparently used her retarded sister, as well, before she died.

The story is grim, but it is hardly unusual—although pizza is not the most common instrument of death. Dry hard-boiled egg yolks can be fast and effective, according to institutional workers and others who work with retarded children. It is hard to prove that death is anything but accidental.

Killing unwanted children may not be the favorite topic at parties or at the breakfast table. But it happens, and no one knows how many unwanted children die each year. In February of 1974 newspapers across the country carried the story of a Portland, Maine, baby—born without a left eye or an ear canal, and other defects. The hospital sued the parents after they rejected corrective surgery when they were told that the baby might be blind, deaf, profoundly retarded, and handicapped in other ways—whatever the outcome of the operation. A judge ordered the operation, ruling that to withhold treatment violated the baby's constitutional right to life.

In the October 23, 1973, edition of *The New England Journal of*

Medicine a doctor at the Yale–New Haven Hospital brought this often hidden subject out into the open. The article was summarized in the following abstract:

"Of 299 consecutive deaths occurring in a special-care nursery, 43 [14 percent] were related to withholding treatment. In this group were 15 with multiple anomalies, eight with trisomy, eight with cardiopulmonary disease, seven with meningomyelocele, three with other central nervous system disorders, and two with short-bowel syndrome. After careful consideration of each of these 43 infants, parents and physicians in a group decision concluded that prognosis for meaningful life was extremely poor or hopeless, and therefore rejected further treatment. The awesome finality of these decisions, combined with a potential for error in prognosis, made the choice agonizing for families and health professionals. Nevertheless, the issue has to be faced, for not to decide is an arbitrary and potentially devastating decision of default."

Yet this does not tell the whole story. I have met too many people who believe that death is the best answer for profoundly retarded children. Those who run institutions tell me that many doctors are poorly informed, and are quick to suggest, if not death, at least institutionalization before parents "get too attached to the child."

Infanticide—the killing of retarded, deformed, crippled, bastard, and other unwanted or useless children—has been with us throughout human history.

For thousands of years young girls were strangled or drowned by parents with "too many" children. In ancient Sparta and in other early Greek and Roman cities the law required all newborn babies to be brought before a committee for examination. Sickly and deformed babies were destroyed. This custom was approved both by Plato and Aristotle in the idealistic political systems they developed. Seneca the Elder (54 B.C.–39 A.D.), an influential teacher and theoretician in the early Roman Empire, wrote:

"Monstrous offspring we destroy; children too, if weak and unnaturally formed from birth, we drown. It is not anger, but reason, thus to separate the *useless* from the sound." (Italics are mine.)

Two well-known Bible stories tell of infanticide. One, in Exodus, tells how a new Egyptian king, concerned at the rapidly growing number of Hebrews in his country, fearful that they would join forces with his enemies, ordered all male Hebrew babies to be killed at birth. One was saved: young Moses.

Later we read that King Herod was told a new king had been born. Herod sent three astrologers to find the infant Jesus. When the three did not return, Herod ordered "all of the children that were in Bethlehem, and in the coasts thereof, from two years and under" to be killed.

Certain Eskimo and Indian tribes buried the infant with the mother who died in childbirth. For centuries, children born deformed in Oriental countries were destroyed at birth. Ancient Arabs buried most female children alive. In India the Rajputs could not permit daughters to marry below their caste; it was dishonorable for the girl to remain unmarried; and the cost to the bride's father was so great that a man with several daughters faced financial ruin. Thus it was common in India to smear poison on the mother's breast, to give the infant poisoned tobacco, or to drown the baby in milk. Many plastered the baby's nose and mouth shut with cow dung before the child could draw its first breath. In other parts of India children were thrown into the sacred river Ganges, and the alligators that ate them were worshiped by the mothers of the children.

It has been reported that in Hawaii all children after the third or fourth were strangled. Overcrowding in Polynesia resulted in the practice of infanticide by people of all levels. Darwin told of a Fuegian who dashed his child's brains out for upsetting a basket of fish. Tasmanians saw the birth of a child as good fortune, for they practiced cannibalism, as did tribes in Africa and elsewhere. In war it has been common to kill the children of one's enemies. Margaret Mead tells of how in New Guinea children were taught to kill by stabbing a young captive from a neighboring tribe who was caught for this purpose. In South America and elsewhere children were thrown into rivers to assure good harvests. For centuries, and until less than a hundred years ago, overlaying—smothering a child with a blanket, pillow, or the mother's body—was common. So was "sacking" unwanted children, i.e., placing them in a bag weighted by stones and throwing them into a river.

Even today, with easy contraception and legal abortion (which can be considered infanticide at the earliest stage of life), children are sometimes found floating in gas station toilets, in sewers, and in garbage cans.

In the book *The Battered Child* (University of Chicago Press, 1968) a contributor, Dr. Samuel X. Radbill, lists six major causes of infanticide: (1) population control, (2) illegitimacy and the problems related to it, (3) greed, in which those hired to care for children and paid lump sums take the money and kill the youngsters, (4) superstition, (5) deformity, and (6) ritual.

Unwanted children have been disposed of in many other ways. One of the more common methods was called *exposure*. Today we call it abandonment. The tale of Hansel and Gretel, and the story of their escape, must have been reassuring to European children who saw children left in the forest or along roads and in towns to be used by the finder (including so-called witches) as he or she saw fit.

Seneca wrote of the common practice of beggars taking children exposed by their mothers and maiming them so that they would have shortened limbs, club feet, broken joints, and other grotesque features. The beggars then used the children to gain sympathy—and coins—from the compassionate. Up until the start of this century, exposure remained common in many so-called civilized countries, including much of Europe. Illegitimate children and the offspring of the poor were most often the victims. Even today the practice continues in the United States and abroad. Dr. Thomas Reichelderfer, chief of pediatrics at the Washington, D.C., General Hospital, says 100 or more are abandoned there each year, and that hundreds of children are abandoned in other cities across the country.

"About half of them were products of our own nursery and were delivered in this hospital," he told me in a filmed report I was preparing for the 1970 White House Conference on Children. "Others came from the Department of Public Health, Department of Public Welfare, the Metropolitan Police Department, and a small number came from various Catholic charities and their hospitals. We have had children left on doorsteps, pulled from sewers, and one was found in the jaws of a dog."

5

The American Way

It was a rainy February day when I met Debbie, a very pretty eighteen-year-old living in a state institution for girls in Atlanta. Petite, with blonde hair, blue eyes, and freckles, it was hard to believe she was over fourteen. There was little hint in her face that she had been through a hellish childhood.

The records show that Debbie's father died when she was four. Her troubled mother couldn't care for her three children. An aunt tried, but the youngsters were too much for her and she sent them away. Eventually Debbie, her brother, and her sister were taken to a church-sponsored children's home. As can be expected, some private facilities are good, but others aren't. In the church-supported institution Debbie was treated harshly.

"The people they hired weren't trained," Debbie, by now an expert on institutional living, says. "They talked all the time about God. They preached a lot, but I don't think they believed it 'cause they beat you when you cried, and for everything else they didn't like. I ran away enough times so they had to take me to court. But the judge didn't know what to do.

"Between the fifth and eighth grades the welfare put me in four different foster homes. But none of them worked out. It was my fault, but I didn't know it then. I resented those ladies pretending to be my mother. I wanted my real mother and I kept running away from them like I did at the children's home, looking for her. When I got to the eighth grade they finally let me go home.

"It was pretty much of a shock. My mother wasn't what I thought she was. I had this idea of a nice lady who would love me and hug me and take care of me. She was completely different from what I had expected. She was—you know—an alcoholic. My mother was married again and had five children I didn't even know about, and she didn't take care of them very well 'cause she was drunk all the time. At first I had to stay home and help take care of them. Then my mother made me quit school and take a job.

"My mother was sleeping with a lot of different men too. One time my stepfather and I looked for her for five straight days. I found her in bed with a man in a hotel room and I felt awful. I stayed with my mother eight months and then I met a fellow and ran away with him. He was nineteen and I was fourteen. He was more or less a hippy and didn't work. First we lived with his mother, and she knew we weren't married, but she didn't say anything. After a while he started running around with a bunch of hippies down near Peachtree [street], and we moved into their place.

"There were fifteen boys and eight of us girls—and sometimes ten. None of the boys worked. They had us get money for food and rent and things by hustling. After seven months I was pregnant, and I caught a disease besides. So I turned myself in to a court worker, because I couldn't hustle anymore, and my boyfriend was mad. The people at the court helped me get rid of the disease and I lost my baby.

"I couldn't go back home to my mother and I didn't want to go to another foster home. I wasn't quite fifteen, so I couldn't be on my own. The court sent me here [to a reform school]. I thought it was going to be a bad place, but it isn't that bad. You get nice clothes, a lot of understanding, and a lot of patience and love."

[Debbie was more fortunate than many girls sent to institutions. Too often they live grim lives, learn to hate themselves, and may develop into hardened criminals.]

"If I hadn't come here three years ago I'd probably have killed myself. What good is somebody when they feel not loved, not respected, not wanted? When you're little, somebody's got to help you."

Debbie admits that several agencies and institutions—public and private—tried to help her. But no one could give her what she wanted and needed, a love-filled, secure home. Her mother used her as sort of a slave, her stepfather used her to search for her mother, and her boyfriend and his pals used her sexually for their own pleasure, and to earn money so they wouldn't have to work. When Debbie became pregnant she was no longer useful to them.

There are millions of "useless" children in America. While some were conceived by accident, others were produced when their mothers got pregnant to "catch a man." In most instances using children to promote marriage fails, and the woman finds she is stuck with an unhappy husband as well as a baby. Yet I found, through hundreds of interviews with delinquent girls, that many want babies so that *someone* will love them. They learn too late that infants *take*, rather than *give* love—and that babies are not puppies that lick your hand and lie at your feet. Further, some women discover the feminist movement *after* they have children, and then feel frustrated, or neglect their youngsters when they go looking for ways to be "fulfilled." They no longer have a use for their children.

We do not like to think about using children. The idea somehow seems crass, shoddy, inhuman. Even the suggestion makes some people, who do not want to believe that they use others, angry. But all children are used. Throughout history they have been used, if only to perpetuate the species and to carry on ideals, traditions, and the lifeblood of a culture.

The educated and affluent in our society, knowing at least subconsciously that we use children—most often for egocentric reasons—try to cleanse their feelings of guilt by giving their children the best of everything. And why not, if our children are little extensions of ourselves?

As individuals and as a nation we tend to meet the physical needs of children, at least those we find useful. Except for several million children of the poor, we have the healthiest, best-fed, best-clothed, most-pampered children in human history. In America today a garbage collector's son can live better than the offspring of royalty born a few centuries ago. Even institutionalized children usually are offered food prepared under the supervision of college graduates in nutrition. We care, but not enough.

In some ways even unwanted children are valuable. For nearly a century small towns across America bid for institutions. A state legislator was pleased when he won an institution for his home district. Institutions have been considered to be a major industry, and the children sent to them the raw products to be watched over and "treated." When young men and women finish high school in such a community, and do not plan to go on to college, they apply at the local "people factory" for work. During the 1950s institutions were filling up with unwanted children, creating more jobs and a building boom. By 1960 it was decided that inmates should be given therapeutic treatment, and many of the old institutional farms and workshops were phased out. The universities produced more social workers, special education teachers, industrial arts teachers, psychiatrists, psychologists, and other specialists. New sub-divisions were developed to provide housing for the professionals. And the institutions needed janitors, cooks, attendants, diaper-changers, car-penters, electricians—a whole range of skills and services. If the majority of Americans did not know of this booming business, those who lived in the small towns near the institutions did, and were prospering as never before. Food and clothing sold well. Merchants and contractors smiled a lot. There were long waiting lists at the institutions for the retarded. Reform schools shuffled children in and out in what some called the revolving-door program. As the police arrived with a fresh carload of children at the front door, attendants searched their lists for children to discharge so that there would be enough beds to go around.

Later, in the 1960s, the federal government spent billions to fight poverty, curb delinquency, and eliminate slums. For a while it looked as if the human services field would, in time, rival the military-industrial complex, or the highway builder, oil company, auto-maker in their ability to reach out for and grasp tax dollars. It all seemed so logical. Take useless and unwanted children—boys and girls like Debbie and millions of others, particularly members of minority groups—and jerk and shove and haul them, kicking and screaming, into the high-spending, credit-using, hell-bent-to-get-more-of-everything middle class. As these useless lower classes of people became more affluent they would also become better consumers. A new, untapped market. The economy would soar!

But the theory didn't really work. The programs developed by so-called experts provided jobs for middle Americans and those on the upper level of the lower class, but it didn't do enough for the hard-core poor, the truly unwanted, and the handicapped. The poor stayed poor and became welfare-dependent. The handicapped, when they were rehabilitated, couldn't find jobs. And too many troubled children got worse instead of better in the hands of professionals.

The answer seemed to be to pour more good money after bad, but then a new administration took control in Washington, Vietnam was already draining the economy, and the taxpapers were angry because of the big bites taken from their paychecks for "deviants and loafers." Sadly, the politicians and professionals of the sixties had made promises they couldn't keep.

Other factors also were at work. For decades, tough, skilled indus-trialists, with the help of their advertising agencies, had been teaching us to discard all that is useless, defective, or obsolete. Trade in last year's car and buy the newest, the latest, the greatest, the finest, the happiest, the sexiest automobile ever produced by man, they told us. Replace those drab, outdated fashions with new and exciting clothing. Trim off unprofitable portions of the business. Cut out the deadwood in the office. Keep inspectors busy on production lines rejecting defective parts. Throw away yesterday's newspaper, empty packages, cans and bottles, vintage battleships, excess food, tired toys, cars that still run, clothing, and even buildings. Call it urban renewal. Bulldoze them down. It is cheaper and smarter to build new ones than to repair old ones. And when you build a new apartment building put in a trash compactor so that we can discard more with less effort.

It isn't exactly a giant step from discarding unwanted and unproductive *things* to discarding useless people, young or old. When elderly parents get feeble or sick we send them off to a nursing home to die. Husbands get tired of wives, or wives of husbands, and dump their mates for someone who better meets their needs. Older workers are put out to pasture. And why did the euphemism for killing the enemy (and sometimes women and children) in Vietnam become "wasting" them? With all of this, it only seems logical that we should cull out and throw away defective and unwanted children.

Strangely, many Americans do not really understand that we do this to youngsters. We drive by institutions hardly aware that children are there, and if we think about them at all, convince ourselves it is all for the best.

We pride ourselves in being a nation of practical people. Our schools are expected to turn out "useful, productive citizens." Those on welfare and drifting, long-haired Americans, are "useless bums." Ask almost anyone and he will tell you that the *useful* person holds down a job and pays his own way, and spends his wages on food, housing, clothing and having a little fun.

It was not until the early part of this century that we truly became a society of consumers. And not until the end of World War II that children were seen as a major market. During the depression years there was too little money available to young people for that.

Several events coincided to produce the change. First, labor unions helped lift millions of Americans into the middle class. Wartime technology made it possible to produce more goods for more people at lower cost. Higher productivity and a society built on the consumption of consumer goods gave more people more leisure time. Add to this chemistry the catalyst of the larger, more sophisticated advertising agency, the arrival of television, and improved marketing systems, and throw in a political philosophy that believes "more is better" and that endless economic growth is possible, and it seems only natural that we would, sooner or later, turn to children as a market. Comic-book publishers, cereal, candy and soft-drink manufacturers, and toy- and movie-makers were the first to rake in millions, and then billions, by seeing children as consumers. Many other groups were not far behind.

My view on this is hardly original. In the early 1950s Dr. David Riesman suggested, correctly, that "Today the future occupation of all moppets is to be skilled consumers." And many who came after him agreed.

Perhaps parents, educators, and child-care workers weren't listening. Even today many refuse to accept the fact that children are used in this way. But the manufacturers and advertising agencies were tuned in to the times. As Vance Packard pointed out in his bestseller *The Hidden Persuaders* (McKay, 1957), it was the talk of industry. An ad in the trade magazine *Printers Ink* also told the story rather clearly: "Eager minds can be molded to want your products! In grade schools throughout America are nearly 23,000,000 young girls and boys. These children eat food, wear out clothes, use soap. They are consumers today and will be buyers tomorrow. Here is a vast market for your products. Sell these children on your brand name and they will insist that their parents buy no other."

Mr. Packard discusses our *use* of children as consumers, but he does not carry it far enough—to point out that nonconsumers are not terribly valuable to those with power in our society. Nor did he fully explore the philosophy of life, the value system, that our mass merchants and advertising men were peddling, although he touched on it and raised important questions about the morality of what the advertising men were doing.

Mr. Packard told us that businessmen believed that man was created to be used, manipulated, sold. That is why, for example, advertising men could rationalize that inducing anxiety and fear to sell face creams and lotions is actually beneficial. And why they explained away other misdeeds in an economy built on consumerism. The idea is that all business is good business, for that's what keeps the economy alive and growing.

The book was written in 1957, and Mr. Packard could still tell us: "We still have a strong defense available against such persuaders: we can choose not to be persuaded. In virtually all situations we still have the choice, and we cannot be too seriously manipulated if we know what is going on."

That was his view when television was still young and growing. Mr. Packard could not know that there would be little choice for millions of young Americans. He could not foresee that in the 1960s and 1970s television would become baby-sitter, parent, and teacher—pouring out what seems to be reality to millions of children by the hour, week after week, year in and year out.

Peer, surrogate parent, preacher, teacher—television is fed by the mass merchandisers and their advertising agencies. It has brought about the most drastic change in our culture in this century. Television produced the revitalization of a long-lost system of ethics, a system that has had a small group of followers through the centuries, but was nearly choked out by the Puritans. This system of ethics or philosophy of life is egocentric hedonism—or more accurately today, *sensual consumerism.*

Sensual consumerism has been sold to us day and night on television, radio, and in print. It has made advertisers rich and created new empires of wealth. Hugh Hefner saw the potential of sensual consumerism to build his Playboy Enterprises. So did Helen Gurley Brown. And the more blatant pornographers. But the new philosophy of our culture was not limited to the more obvious sexual subjects.

Strictly defined, egocentric hedonism is self-centered pleasure-seeking. It is not the hedonism of Hume, Bentham, and Mill, the nineteenth-century English philosophers who helped shape our thinking in more modest ways. For these men rejected egocentric hedonism and turned to utilitarianism—a doctrine that preaches that moral conduct is good when it promotes the "greatest happiness of the greatest number of people."

Superficially it would appear that is what we have now achieved through mass merchandising and advertising. But such is not the case. Hume assumed that benevolence is the supreme virtue, and says that the central point of benevolence is to make others happy. One individual being nice to other individuals. Bentham's basic goal in life was law reform, and saw "the greatest happiness" concept as the method of separating good from bad law. John Stuart Mill arrived in an age when the emotion of sympathy was current and so he saw pleasure in compassion. He also made a clear distinction between the higher pleasures of the mind and the lower pleasures of the body.

Our advertising is directed to the greatest possible number of people, but it urges them to seek pleasure individually and selfishly. The appeal is not for the good of mankind. It is for instant gratification, and it is almost always an appeal to sensual or bodily satisfaction. Hence sensual consumerism.

(There are those who say that times have changed—that with the recession of 1973–1975, high energy costs, inflation, the end of the baby boom, and the food shortages, sensual consumerism is on the way out. Yet they seem to forget that, even at the height of the economic crisis, in the seventies yachts and expensive cars have continued to sell, along with perfume, jewelry, and other luxury items. If we experienced the beginnings of a back-to-the-earth movement in the sixties, it would seem that the seventies have brought us back to luxuries—no matter what certain pundits are saying.)

Sensual consumerism has become as much the basis of our present culture as austere Puritanism was the basis of the culture established by our founding fathers. Sensual consumerism rejects the basic tenets of Christianity, which urges giving up all worldly goods and requires followers to love their neighbors.

"Do not store up for yourselves treasure on earth, where it grows rusty and moth-eaten, and thieves break in to steal it," Jesus preached (the New English Bible: Matthew 6:19). "Store up treasure in heaven, where there is no moth and no rust to spoil it, no thieves to break in and steal. For where your treasure is, there will your heart be also.

"No servant can be the slave of two masters; for either he will hate the first and love the second, or he will be devoted to the first and think nothing of the second. You cannot serve God and Money.

"Therefore I bid you put away anxious thoughts about food and drink to keep you alive, and clothes to cover your body. Surely life is more than food, the body more than clothes."

Talk like that continues to be heresy to the businessmen and advertising executives of twentieth-century America. As one car dealer recently told me, it is "un-American."

If there is an element of unselfishness in sensual consumerism it is the concept that "anything goes as long as it doesn't infringe upon the rights of others." But even this is followed only by the more mature and moralistic members of our culture.

Sensual consumerism is most closely aligned with the earliest and, until now, most extreme form of hedonism—the hedonism of the Cyrenaics.

Cyrenaic hedonism is a system of ethics devised by the Greek teacher Aristippus (435–356 B.C.), a pupil of Socrates and a native of Cyrene, Greece.

Socrates believed virtue to be the only human good, but he also concluded that happiness would be the end result of moral, virtuous behavior. His pupil Aristippus dismissed virtue and insisted that the pursuit of happiness or pleasure was the purpose of life. He ignored both logic and physical science, and he believed in living for the pleasure of the moment. Only bodily sensations are real of valid, whether they be painful, pleasant, or somewhere in between, he added.

Since some momentary pleasures later produce pain, this established the difference between right and wrong in the view of Aristippus. Yet Aristippus stopped short of sensual consumerism. He insisted that true pleasure belongs only to those who are self-controlled, the masters of themselves. He could not foresee our modern psychology, based as it is upon mass production and mass consumption of goods that promote the end of pain and the beginning of self-centered pleasure. Nor did he anticipate a credit economy that frowns on self-control in the race for happiness.

It is appropriate that quarterback Joe Namath, apparently the perfect American, now pitches products on television. We invented Paul Bunyan, John Henry, and Pecos Bill in an earlier age to illustrate the muscular can-do strength of the Americans of that era. If we had not found a Joe Namath we would have had to invent another man as the symbol of the super-consumer. His injured knee in this age of self-centeredness is as important to us as an axe was to Paul Bunyan or a hammer to John Henry.

American children are products of our culture. They watch television, listen to us talk, notice the magazines we read, see how we treat our fellow men, emulate our national idols, and imitate our behavior—sometimes in exaggerated form. They tend to use others as we use them.

6

The System

It is possible for the U.S. Department of Agriculture to count the nation's cows. The Department of Commerce knows how much we spend on beans, barley, booze, books, and bananas—or so they say. And we know how many board feet of timber we can cut from vast forests scattered across the continent.

But it is far more difficult to determine how many delinquents there are in a city like Chicago, or how many children can't read at grade level in New Jersey. Nor do we know the number of creative youngsters in America who see their creative sparks extinguished before they reach the age of ten, or how many children run away from home each year, or how much child neglect or abuse exists in California.

The problems of children are hidden. But it is important to know that few people ask for such figures. If there were more requests, it is quite possible we would work harder to get answers.

Some educated guesses have been made. A congressional committee looking into the problem of runaways was told that between 500,000 and 1,000,000 youngsters take off each year.

In 1967, the President's Commission on Law Enforcement and the Administration of Justice reported that 95 percent of all children in the United States commit acts that would put them in jail, and they added that "one in every nine children will be referred to juvenile court for an act of delinquency before his eighteenth birthday."

Since 1967, millions of children have engaged in drug abuse or in the heavy use of alcohol. There have been changes in the sexual behavior of girls—and some parents have become more tolerant of this and other forms of behavior once considered delinquent.

The U.S. Department of Health, Education, and Welfare has estimated that 126,000 retarded babies are born each year, while the National Association for Retarded Children puts the annual figure at between 100,000 and 200,000. When the birth rate is down, the number of retarded born should go down, but physicians now save more multihandicapped children than in the past. Child-battering apparently is climbing, and neglect and abuse cause retardation. So accurate figures are hard to come by. Most authorities agree that roughly 3 percent of the total population is retarded. That sets the figure at about 6.5 million retarded persons of all ages in this country. And up to 200,000 live in institutions or group homes.

Less is known about mental health. Some experts say that one in ten children "needs help" and has some degree of emotional disturbance.

Even with community mental health centers scattered across the country, more states are building children's psychiatric units on state hospital grounds—both to get children out of adult wards and because some officials believe there is more mental illness than in the past. As our society grows more complex, as more families split up, as mothers go to work, and schools become less responsive to the needs of inner-city children, many expect the number of disturbed children to soar. The number already is believed to be in the millions.

Child abuse is an enigma. Records show that it is growing at a tremendous rate. But reporting methods have been improved. Dr. David Gil, of Brandeis University, headed a study that looked at 13,000 child-abuse reports. He estimates that up to 2.5 million children are battered and abused each year in America.

Dr. Vincent DeFrancis, of the American Humane Association, also an expert on child abuse and neglect, studies sexual abuse of children in New York City and elsewhere. He believes that sexual abuse is 50 to 100 times more common than physical abuse—but he is not using Dr. Gil's figures as his base. Most of the children involved are girls, the victims of their fathers, stepfathers, other relatives, and family friends.

No one is able to produce accurate figures on the number of children who are the victims of deprivation or neglect. But again, there must be millions of such children.

It is estimated that 1 out of every 1,000 children is born deaf. With an average of 3 million (or more) live births each year, some 3,000 or more deaf children arrive annually.

The number of those born blind is lower, but blind children are more noticeable than many with other handicaps.

In much of America the divorce rate has hit one in three marriages, and in some cities one in two homes break up. Millions of children—treated as property by parents and the courts—become the little victims of these breakups.

Youthful suicides increase, and the age of those who take their own lives keeps dropping.

The high mobility of families means fewer roots for children, and less contact with grandparents and others who offer warmth and understanding. Parents who have not felt love do not know how to give it, so the modern American tends to give *things* to their children instead. Our economic system reinforces this, and we are taught that we are poor parents if we fail to offer children whatever they want. Some studies show that lack of love and warmth has a negative impact on a child's emotional and mental development. It is possible that unless we turn this trend around mankind will change for the worse.

We know that millions of children still live in abject poverty in this country. While some spin out of their environment, many do not. They remain to raise their own children in poverty.

Many schools are in turmoil and children are being hurt. But no one can say for sure how many are damaged each year.

Minority groups have made substantial gains in recent years, but they have lost ground in some areas. The love and warmth that once characterized the black family has too often been replaced with anger and hostility. "Soul" may be dying as blacks grow more like whites.

And what of the children of the middle class and the rich? How many are damaged by uncaring, indulgent adults? How many fail to reach their full potential because of poor parenting? Even in this age of the computer and of federal meddling in every aspect of our lives we have few answers. Too many children with problems are hidden away or ignored. And too many who are detected are hurt more than they are helped. For the systems we have designed to meet the needs of children are badly flawed.

The System

When parents cannot meet the needs of their children, *the system* takes over. At least in theory, if not in fact. It can be difficult to see the system, and even harder to understand it. That is because it is so vast, and consists of many sub-systems. And because, like crabgrass, it scatters its seeds quietly and spreads its roots unnoticed.

Most of us have grown up with the system. It is part of us and we are part of it. We have grown accustomed to the system in the same way we have become comfortable with our faces. It is something we were born with, have grown up in, and support with our money. We may not always be happy with it, but we tend to defend it as ours. In this, we should remember that we view the system from a vantage point different from those caught up in it.

One further point should be made. Unlike some looking at America today, I do not suggest that we should tear the system down and start over. Rather, my feeling is that we should try to make it work—changing only those parts of it that do not. I am reminded of the man who was asked about the merits of living a "Christian life." He replied that there might be much value in it, but that we won't know until someone actually tries it.

It is possible that the system fails because it lacks leadership, or because of the people who work in it, or because we have never really given it a chance to work.

The system is made up of many sub-systems.

To see it in logical sequence, we must begin with the American method of mating. Does our mating system bring together people who are suited and trained to be parents? If so, why do we have so many neglected, battered, and disturbed children in America? After we have resolved the mating question, we must move on to contraception, abortion, and prenatal care. Then we must discuss mothering and fathering—the parenting system (or systems) that offer warmth, security, and love to small children, and independence, self-discipline, and happiness to older youngsters. Studies show there is a direct relationship between the skill of the parents and the quality of the adult produced.

In addition to the family system, we also must look at the alternative systems developed for children whose parents are killed, for victims of divorce, abuse, neglect, for unwanted children, for those born to parents who live in poverty, or born to parents who cannot care for a handicapped child. The child born out of wedlock also falls into this category.

Other sub-systems are local in nature, while some are run by states or the federal government. The list includes the school system, welfare system, and the mental health system. In addition, we have the juvenile justice system, the day-care system, the religious system, the special education system, the system designed to care for retarded youngsters, the parks and recreation system, systems designed to meet the needs of blind, deaf, or crippled children, the health-care system, and others.

If these systems were properly designed, and if they functioned in a logical or orderly way, one might compare the total system to an orchestra—with a conductor, various sections, and an orderly plan to follow (the musical score). The result would be harmonious because each player would know his part, all would be in tune, and the conductor would see that all worked together to achieve the results desired.

But the system that deals with children is not an orchestra. There is no conductor, and no general or overall plan. Each sub-system, from the family to the prison, fiddles its own tune with its own instruments, paying no attention either to harmony or rhythm. This results in discord and damaged children, crime, mental illness, and much pain.

The system is like a giant squid. With many tentacles reaching out, *the system* grabs some children and misses others. (Often one tentacle doesn't know what the others are doing.) And when attacked, the system, like the squid, ejects dark clouds so that it may escape in the confusion.

It costs billions of dollars each year to keep the system running. Many institutions, for example, require from $10,000 to $30,000 to care for one child for one year. And yet the system does not promise to produce results. Moreover, many children caught up in it get worse instead of better, as this book will show.

Beyond the high cost, weaknesses of the system include a poor method of selection of those to be dealt with; the lack of meaningful diagnosis; poorly conceived therapeutic treatment programs; the lack of research into the impact such programs have on children; a shortage of alternatives for those who find that therapeutic treatment programs fail to achieve desired results; the lack of standards for those who work in the system; and no system of accountability.

To put it another way, the system hurts many children, but few Americans know this. Even if they found out how damaging the system is, and even if they cared, they would not know what to do about the problem.

We have already seen the public reaction to the soaring costs of public welfare. But citizen anger has not changed the system—partly because the American people do not know how to exercise power, but also because no valid alternatives to the welfare system have been offered.

Selecting Children for the System

One of the weakest links in the child-caring (or child-hurting) system is the method of selection used.

Most often it depends upon who first finds the child for the system. If it is a policeman, the child may go to jail. Should mental health officials spot the child, the youngster may get outpatient therapeutic treatment, and when that fails, he may then go to a mental hospital. Welfare officials tend to take children from their parents and put them in foster homes. A pediatrician most often is concerned with health care, and may ignore the child's other needs (even while other pieces of the system ignore health needs). The school system may funnel the child into another system, simply kick him out, or put him in a special education program. Youngsters who find themselves caught up in the juvenile justice system may be put on probation, sent to a reform school, or be shoved into another system. Some children are dumped on the courts by parents who cannot cope with them.

The important point about selection is that many different things may happen to the *same child*—depending upon who first finds and labels him.

It is difficult to separate diagnosis from the selection, for in some cases the diagnostic process takes only a split second.

Take the diagnostic work done by policemen. Equipped with a rule book and a knowledge of the law, the policeman does not take much time to diagnose the child walking down the street after curfew, for in many states a child must be off the streets by 10 or 11 P.M. and is delinquent in the eyes of the law if he is not.

The little girl picked up as a runaway is selected and diagnosed quickly. Seldom does anyone bother to find out *why* she has run. But if the system provided a better method of diagnosis, it would change the treatment process.

The girl who has run may be the victim of her own father. Take the case of one girl I met. Her father began using her sexually when she was nine, and demanded that she submit to intercourse two or three times a week. At thirteen she could take it no longer, ran away from home, was jailed, and returned to her own home with a warning from a judge. When she ran again she was put on probation. The third time the judge sent her to reform school.

Because the selection system looks at symptoms, and no further diagnosis may be made, children are damaged by the system for life.

I met one boy in prison who was born with eye trouble. No one discovered the problem, and so when he reached third or fourth grade he was labeled as "slow" or slightly retarded, and as a poor reader. Children made fun of him, teachers were critical and some found him a bother because he slowed down the class. By the time he reached the ninth grade he was an angry child, and eventually struck a teacher. This made him eligible for selection by the system.

The school did not hesitate to select him, and the boy was diagnosed as "a troublemaker who needs to be taught a lesson." Since the state and the local school board approved of corporal punishment, the therapeutic treatment given was a sound paddling. Beating the child didn't help solve his (eye) problem. His parents had already tried that, so he was used to it. When the boy misbehaved again, and seemed to be acting oddly, he was selected for mental health treatment. The worker assigned diagnosed the problem during a series of weekly interviews and began discussing his sexual feelings about his mother, as well as other feelings that he might have.

But that didn't help solve his (eye) problem either.

So the school selected him again for therapeutic treatment, and began putting pressure on the boy. They made it clear he wasn't liked and that he didn't belong in school.

When the boy became truant he was selected by the juvenile court, diagnosed by a probation officer and a judge, and was assigned to the probation officer for therapeutic treatment. Twice a week the boy reported to the courthouse, and twice a week he was told that if he didn't shape up he would go to reform school. The threat-treatment program failed to help his (eye) problem, and in time he punched out a teacher who ridiculed him in front of the class.

The judge was livid, lectured to the boy on how much everyone in the system had done to help him, diagnosed the boy as being "very delinquent and ungrateful," and sent him to reform school.

At the reform school the boy lived with other youngsters who had been selected by the system for therapeutic treatment. While the young man didn't get much help from the staff, he did learn from the other boys how to steal cars, rob stores, break into buildings, shoot up heroin, and commit other crimes. For the first time in his life the boy was accepted by his peers. And that made him feel good.

The reform school released the youngster after nine months of therapeutic treatment, and he quickly began to steal cars, break into homes, and soon he acquired a gun.

Perhaps the system did not properly select and diagnose the child at the outset, and the treatment programs may have failed at first, but at last the diagnosis coincided with the facts. There is little question that he is delinquent, and his eye problem is now of little importance.

Since therapeutic treatment programs in the criminal justice system fail far more often than they succeed, and because the boy will probably mate with a girl who also is delinquent, and because they will produce several children, the family will be a burden to the taxpayers for many years. It also is likely that his children will need services from various parts of the system.

Thus, by borrowing a technique from the American corporate system, the child-caring (or child-hurting) system assures itself of an ever-expanding market.

The Birth of the System

While it may seem that the system—like death, taxes and the poor—has always been with us, this is only partly true. The school system may have been invented by the Greeks and Romans, but it was late in the last century and early in this one that school attendance was made mandatory in all of the states. When children labored in sweat shops and on farms early in this century, attending school was often a privilege.

Until the nineteenth century, children over the age of seven were processed and dealt with in the same way as adult criminals. In 1825 New York established a "House of Refuge" so that young offenders could be separated from adults, and children were to receive corrective treatment instead of punishment. Massachusetts built the first reform school in 1847. Juvenile courts were unknown until the mayor of Chicago was given the right to appoint a commissioner to hear minor charges against boys six to seventeen years old. That was in 1861. And in 1870 a juvenile court was established in Massachusetts.

Welfare, as it has come to be known through newspaper headlines, dates back to the poor laws of England and to the beggars of ancient times. America decided to deal with the problem by building poorhouses, orphanages, and other institutions. Because this system was cruel, and it "pauperized the poor," settlement houses were established, public aid grants were made available, and the "social worker" was invented.

The Great Depression of the 1930s helped pave the way for the present bloated welfare system. But it all really was made possible through the passage of the Sixteenth Amendment to the Constitution, ratified in 1913. The Sixteenth Amendment gave the federal government the power to collect an income tax.

In an effort to streamline the system, as well as cut administrative costs, welfare now is divided into two divisions—one that doles out money, and another that provides "services" to children, the aged, and others. One such service is designed to protect children from the system. It doesn't work very well.

Public health nursing began in 1885 when a nurse was paid to call on the poor in their homes. The funds to pay for these services were raised by voluntary contributions.

Mental health care is a slightly older concept, although for centuries the insane and retarded roamed the streets begging, or were thrown into prison or poorhouses. Although the first insane asylum opened in Virginia in 1752, the Quakers of Pennsylvania and the people of Rhode Island tried to provide care before that.

Many institutions for the retarded were first used to detain epileptics. State institutions for the deaf and the blind are late arrivals, historically speaking. Special education has just arrived on the scene. The term "learning disability" is so new that most psychiatrists and many psychologists deny that it exists, or defy educators to define it.

The professionals are often at odds, speak different professional languages, and hardly speak to one another at all.

At no time in history has there been a coordinated effort to meet the needs or resolve the problems of children—or adults, for that matter. Throughout recorded history men have sought ways to rid their streets of those best described as useless and unwanted—whether lepers, lunatics, idiots, the poor, cripples, or those unable or unwilling to work.

In a sense, the system is the product of social evolution. It exists through changing moods, growing affluence, the work of reformers, a growing population, the ability of physicians to save children who once died, and the arrival of the graduated income tax, which pays the bills for the system. A few states have legitimatized the system by establishing all-encompassing departments of human resources and services. But no state has come close to developing a system that helps all children in need, while hurting none.

Much more can (and will) be said about the system. But perhaps it is enough to point out that it exists. But why? What is there in the American way of life, in our family and child-rearing pattern, in our diverse society, that requires such a huge, overlapping, often damaging system to exist? If we can find the answer to this question perhaps we can begin to solve the problems of our children—and even those of our nation.

7

Doing Many Things

You can't do just one thing.

This phrase, so simple at first glance, has profound meaning in any discussion of unwanted children. For in it lies the concept of chain reaction—so often ignored by Americans—which has an immense impact on our lives.

The idea that you "can't do just one thing" comes from the ecology movement. Garrett Hardin, a California biologist, is credited with originating the phrase. It is used to explain, for example, that it is impossible just to dig coal from the hills of West Virginia. By digging the coal you level hills, leave large holes, heap up waste material, kill off trees and shrubs, change water tables and watersheds, pollute streams with residue, drive away birds and animals, destroy their breeding and nesting grounds, provide industry with a fuel that pollutes the air, and more.

The things you do aren't all bad, of course. And it is possible, in time, to rebuild hills, fill holes, create lakes, replant grass and forests, clean streams, filter the chimneys of industry, and restore the balance of nature.

But restoration of human beings is not that easy, as psychologists, social workers, and correction officials will tell you.

Why is the phrase "you can't do just one thing" so significant? Take the man and woman who try to do one thing: make love without a contraceptive. They risk unwanted pregnancy. This, in turn, leads to a choice between abortion and birth—the birth of an unwanted child.

Further, it can cause financial hardship, force two people who do not care that much about each other to marry, or increase the welfare rolls.

To follow this single and simple act to an extreme, but factual end, it could start a chain of events that would change the course of history. Another Hitler, or Stalin could be born, or another George Washington or Abraham Lincoln.

To explain the phrase in another way, a self-centered or emotionally unstable parent can't just neglect or abuse a child. In time the impact may be felt by the child's peers, teachers, the police, welfare department, mental health officials, taxpayers, and eventually the abused or neglected child's own children.

A teacher who fails the child in school may well do more than that. A policeman can't just put a youngster in jail. A mother can't just go to work or on welfare. Nor can a National Guardsman just fire a rifle into a crowd of students on a university campus. Television hucksters can't just sell toys or cereal to children. And legislatures can't just lower taxes by cutting the budget for schools, mental health, or welfare.

The Swiss understand the importance of the concept. When a Swiss family or firm wants to construct a house or office building, they buy the land, hire an architect, and then—with lumber or steel—construct the outline of the building on the site and leave it there for all to see for weeks. During the waiting period all citizens have the right to comment. If the building will spoil the view for some who live or work in the area, they have the right to say so. If the design is out of step with the character of the neighborhood, residents and other property owners may complain. Should parents or school officials feel the building will create a traffic problem, endangering children, they will comment. If someone feels it will shade a sunny playground or garden, that will be considered. If there are enough complaints, a hearing will be held. If the complaints are found to be valid, the structure cannot be built.

The Swiss also consider the impact of other actions. They understand that when families damage children, all of society can be hurt. They recognize emotional as well as physical neglect and abuse of children.

I know of one Swiss girl whose father was considered to be a spendthrift. He did not use his money wisely, and so could not provide adequate food, clothing and shelter, and other basics for his family. Nor could his wife do anything about the problem.

When canton (state) officials learned of this the man was hauled into court. He promised to do better, but failed. They took him to court again, and told him he had one more chance. But again he was unable to handle money as he should.

Swiss officials, knowing that a child who lacks food and other basics can be harmed, and may, in turn, harm others, appointed a family acquaintance as guardian. Each payday the father turns his paycheck over to the guardian, who sees that bills are met and that the money is budgeted wisely.

Some self-centered, I'll-do-as-I-damn-please Americans may see this as an incredible infringement on the father's rights. Unlike Americans, who tend to think largely of themselves, the Swiss also are concerned with the rights of children. And parents are free to do as they please—as long as children are not hurt.

The same approach is used when a Swiss child exhibits delinquent behavior, begins to fail in school, or has other problems. When a father cannot control or help his child a guardian is appointed. All citizens are expected to accept the role of guardian if asked by the court, and it is done in the same spirit that Americans express when asked to serve on a jury. It is a responsibility that cannot be taken lightly.

Two words come to mind when thinking of the Swiss approach to problems: responsibility and accountability. Think what impact this might have in America. Consider the alcoholic parent, the mother who runs off with another man, the man who fathers a child and refuses to pay for its support, the couple that abuses or neglects their children, or the parents of a young shoplifter or burglar.

And what if we carried the concept of accountability even further and actually held teachers, social workers, judges, mental health professionals, juvenile court judges, city planners, institutional workers and administrators, and others responsible for their actions?

What if, instead of blaming the child, parents, teachers and mental health workers were held accountable for the child who doesn't learn?

What if the juvenile court judge who sends a child to reform school was held responsible. along with corrections officials, for impact the institution had on the child?

What if a social worker who shuffles a child from one foster home to another, were held accountable for the impact this has on a child?

What if auto makers where held accountable for not building a theft-proof car, and the owner of the auto for not locking it, instead of arresting the child for joy-riding?

What if city planners were held responsible for unsafe streets, or for failing to put a park and wading pool in every neighborhood?

What if legislators were truly held accountable for the bills they pass, or for the expenditure (and waste) of funds they authorize in the budgets they pass on?

What if policemen were held responsible for children killed in high-speed chases, or for the impact on a child of a night in jail?

It remains doubtful that we will ever be able to hold parents, teachers, or others who come in contact with children accountable for their actions in America. But at least we can help them understand that what they do has a lasting impact on our children, and on our society. It is, as the man said, impossible to do just one thing.

PART

II

The System Unmasked

8

Love Story—The American
Mating System

This is a report on the American Mating System (AMS).

The camera zooms in on Doris. We see that she is a freshly scrubbed, seventeen-year-old virgin. We know she has experienced a long, painful wait, for she began developing sexually when she was eleven, and the tension has slowly been building for six years. Doris is buxom. Fertile. Sexually hungry. Eager. Worried. Anxious. Wondering. Willing. Waiting.

The camera cuts to Bill. He is eighteen and about to graduate from high school. Tall. Athletic. Cool. Handsome. We know that he has been around just enough to know. Has his own car. Sexually hungry. On the prowl. Sensual. Anxious. Willing. Hunting.

Bill notices Doris. Doris notices that Bill notices her.

Wham. Bam. Crash! Emotions merge! Zam! Yeow! Hug! Kiss!! Pet!!! Wow! Yeow! We must be in love!! Kiss!! Hug!! Pet!!! Pet!!!!! Sex!!!!!! Nice! Yeah! We are in love!! Yeah!!! Kiss!! Hug!! Pet!!!! Sex!!!!! Sex!!!!! Sex!!!!! Pregnancy? Marriage?? Yes! Okay! Responsibility!!! Money problems!!!! Disappointment!!!! Two strangers living together!! Anger!!! Complaints!!!! Conflict!!!! Retribution!!!!! Hatred!!!!! Divorce!

Time passes.

The camera zooms in on Doris. She is sitting in a bar. We see that she is a slightly weary twenty-five-year-old. The mother of two children.

Cut to Jack as he enters the bar. He is twenty-nine and divorced too. On the prowl. Lonely. Jack notices Doris. Doris notices Jack noticing her.

She suddenly feels younger. Alive. Interested. Eager! Wham! Bam! Crash!! Emotions merge! Zam!! Yeow!! Kiss!!! Hug!!! etc., etc., etc.

Exaggerated? For some, perhaps. But for thousands of Americans the scene is all too true. And not only for the poor or undereducated. It is the pattern for many young people who come from what we call "good" (or financially comfortable) homes.

No long ago I interviewed a young college graduate living with (and, in fact, supporting) a boy who had graduated from the same school. She also was sleeping with a second youth, and was interested in expanding her circle of experience.

"God, it's great!" she said in reply to a question. "Now I know what my body is for!"

In a study of teen-age girls in the early 1970s it was found that at least 14 percent of the fifteen-year-olds and 44 percent of the nineteen-year-olds had experienced sexual intercourse. Yet only 20 percent of the girls reported using contraceptives, and fewer than half could tell researchers at what time of the month they were most likely to become pregnant.

Sex is not the only reason for mating, of course. I have talked to many mature and intelligent women with children in school who bitterly complain that they married too young and for the wrong reasons—and not only because of sex. Some wanted desperately to get out of their parents' homes. And others were afraid of becoming spinsters and said yes because they were sure no one as good as "Joe" or Dick" would ask them to marry.

Parents who should know better push their children to date early, to attend dances, to mature too soon. Some of these parents are bitter and shriveled and live out their lives vicariously through their children. Others unselfishly want their offspring to enjoy life more than they did when they were young.

Guilt also plays a role in the American Mating System. Some young people marry because they feel they must, after succumbing to the temptation to engage in intercourse (or, to use the euphemism, after "making love," as if it could be manufactured).

Most Americans mate (to include the new life-styles, I deliberately do not use the word *marry*) in time, and at a much earlier age than in many cultures. In its report *Population and the American Future,* the U.S. Commission on Population Growth and the American Future says: "Our average age at first marriage is the lowest of any advanced country in the world. The great divide in the orientation to marriage seems to have come in the 1890s, when age at marriage started a long downward movement that lasted, with only minor fluctuations, until the 1960s. In 1959 the median age at first marriage was 22.5 for men and 20.2 for women; by 1970, these averages had reached 23.2 and 20.8 respectively. . . .

"Nearly universal marriage and early marriage in our society would possibly not be so prevalent had not circumstances made marriage less of an economic and social commitment and less of an irreversible step. . . . Formerly it was required that the man be able to provide adequate support for the family before marriage. Many men, therefore, had to delay marriage and some had to forego it altogether. Today, however, the proportion of women in the work force has increased markedly; and the willingness of women to work after marriage, with or without children, has encouraged many young people to decide they could 'afford' to marry. . . . "

The Commission also attributes the change in mating habits to improved contraception, the growing respectability and ease of divorce and remarriage, and such practices as federal subsidization of home ownership, unemployment compensation, veterans benefits, college housing for married students, as well as "parental willingness to continue supporting offspring after they are married." And the Commission sees the changing attitudes toward abortion, keeping a child born out of wedlock without stigma, and the women's liberation movement as having an impact on mating, marriage, and the American family.

They could have said (but did not) that there is little of such great significance in one's lifetime so completely ignored by the American people as careful thought about mating. Mating can be as casual as jumping in and out of bed.

In Japan and some other nations marriages are still arranged. In the United States mating is the outcome of dating, and dating is casual and sexual in nature. If in parts of Europe separation for six months or a year is still a test of true love, in America living together—learning whether a couple can tolerate one another under varied circumstances—is a common practice.

It is easier to understand why this is so when you consider it in terms of the economy. For generations, producing children was thought to be good for America. Manufacturers were overjoyed at the thought of an ever-growing market and said so in speeches and magazine articles; economists (paying little attention to natural resources in a large and wealthy land) echoed the idea and showed that it was necessary to pay farmers *not* to grow crops; and politicians—responsive to business interests—pushed the idea of "the more the merrier."

Churches and minority groups also have seen large numbers of children as the best method of retaining their rights, and rapid breeding has been encouraged.

Those attitudes have been dumped in the 1970s with warnings of shortages and overcrowding. Urban growth has spawned crime and a host of other problems that seen incurable. Hedonistic consumerism, which has hurt children in so many ways, has helped reduce the number of children a couple has. It is too hard to find baby-sitters and too tempting to enjoy the good life. Who wants to drag children along, either to parties, bowling allies, the golf course, or to Europe?

Nothing has had such an impact on population growth as has easy contraception, legalized abortions, education, and the women's movement. And yet too many young people produce too many unwanted children. And too few are taught about how to select a mate. We are quite busy producing books and reports on the results of the American Mating System. But few Americans—politicians, scholars, researchers, or writers—address themselves to the system itself.

As I pointed out earlier, it is impossible to do just one thing, and that includes mating. It is here—in the mate-selection process—that the problems of the American child begin.

Children need strong families. A strong family exists when two emotionally healthy, happy, mature, intelligent, and giving persons unite and when those two people work together to meet their needs as individuals and as a couple. Being a good parent is hardly the same as being a good sex partner. And yet it is the sexual aspect of mating that is so heavily stressed in our culture.

Too often two immature, self-centered youngsters are drawn together because they want to copulate—and as a result they have children. But the youngsters are incidental (especially to the man) or accidental (44 percent of all births in America are unplanned), or parents who want children have little understanding of child-rearing practices that will help rather than hurt youngsters. Then, because it is hard to sustain sexual excitement, or because of money problems, or old-fashioned incompatibility, they separate.

Some couples who hate in silence, and stay together for the sake of the children, do a poor job of hiding their frustration and antagonism, and damage not only their own lives but the lives of the children as well. Those who divorce without thinking of the children also risk long-term damage to the youngsters.

In all of this I am hardly opposed to the pleasant experience of "falling in love." Nor am I passing judgment on the pleasure of sexual relations, or suggesting that the sexual urge is either unnatural or anything less than biological. All I am suggesting is that sexual attraction and satisfaction have little to do with the ability to rear children and are a poor basis for the American Mating System.

Studies, surveys, and statistics on premarital sexual relations, divorce, unwanted pregnancies, the importance of the female orgasm, the absent father and nonsupport of children all say this is so.

The success of *Playboy* magazine and similar publications, of books like *Sex and the Single Girl, The Joy of Sex, The Sensuous Woman* (which, under the heading "The Hazards of Sex," notes in a single sentence that "Carelessness can cause an unwanted pregnancy," and makes no other mention of the subject in 192 pages) further illustrates the point. Or consider the explicit sexual scenes in films, novels like *Valley of the Dolls* and those cranked out by Harold Robbins, and even the debate over trial marriages.

Surely some, perhaps many Americans marry for intellectual compatibility, out of loneliness, for money, social status, security, or to get away from home. But how many mate (and eventually produce children) because the partner will be a good mother or father to their offspring? In fact, what *is* a good father or mother? Few Americans know.

But complaining of the problems produced by the American Mating System isn't enough, either. Sex is a normal, healthy, biological urge. We ask adolescents to ignore that urge until their late teens, or even until they are in their twenties.

Under the law, the age of sexual consent (that is, the age at which a girl may say yes to intercourse without being delinquent, and without her partner being charged with statutory rape) varies from state to state. In California and Georgia the age is fourteen, while in Tennessee it is twenty-one. Twenty-five states have set the age at sixteen, two at seventeen, while nineteen states say eighteen is the proper age, and in one state it is nineteen.

Perhaps it is possible to repress sexual feelings, just as it is possible to repress the urge to kill or steal. Many healthy adults either consciously or unconsciously curb the urge to engage in sexual relations with co-workers, family friends, and perhaps even strangers. One can hardly imagine the impact it would have on our society if every person acted upon every urge to have relations with every person he found attractive. But what can we do about the problem of teen-agers in an age of easy contraception?

I wish there were easy answers.

Our divorce patterns, the practice of polygamy and polyandry, widespread infidelity and promiscuity, and the history of prostitution suggest, at least to some persons, that monogyny is not the only "normal" form of relationship. In fact throughout history, dating back to before Biblical days, polygamy has been practiced in parts of Asia, the Middle East, and Africa, as well as in other portions of the world.

There is reason to believe that, biologically, men and women could have almost daily relationships with different partners. Whether or not this is emotionally possible is another question, but it might be answered by a long-term study of a few of the swinging singles apartment complexes scattered across America.

When religion is widely practiced (and it is not today) people are kept in check partly by being taught that sexual permissiveness is sinful. Some historians suggest that promiscuity and related forms of selfish behavior have coincided with the downfall of civilizations. Preachers frequently warn of this.

Jewish law condemned adultery, and the Christian ethic, as developed in the New Testament, took a similarly strong position. Jesus is quoted as saying that even looking at another person lustfully is wrong. Even while taking a compassionate attitude toward a woman being stoned for adultery, he is reported to have said to "go and sin no more," while Paul, in his first letter to the Corinthians, and elsewhere, attacks fornication (unmarried sex), asserting that not only does it defile the body but that those who engage in it cannot "inherit the Kingdom of God."

This does not seem to have kept even our Puritanical forebears from engaging in it, at least as long as it led to marriage. Thomas P. Monahan, in a paper delivered to the American Sociological Association in Chicago in 1959 on premarital pregnancy in the United States, notes that "even though sexual relations out of wedlock were severely frowned upon by early Colonial churchmen and leaders, according to the records of the time such practice was quite common. The community was generally tolerant, providing marriage was forthcoming, especially if there were a child; and one's spiritual salvation could be restored if a public confession were sincerely given. During a period marked by a 'moral reawakening,' one-third of the couples in one church who were admitted to communion made such a confession."

The U.S. Commission on Population Growth and the American Future adds this footnote in its 1972 report: "Until modern times, high rates of reproduction were necessary to offset high mortality—especially high among infants and children. In agricultural societies, children had an economic value. More hands were an asset in a home-centered economy. Also, before care of the aged became institutionalized, parents had to rely upon children for care in their old age; and large numbers of children were advantageous."

Before the arrival of modern means of warfare, large numbers of people also were needed for national defense. So again a high production rate of children was needed.

During the 1950s manufacturers, advertising men, and economists were pleased with with an ever-climbing population, for it was seen as a stimulation to the economy and an ever-growing market. Little thought was given to depletion of *other* natural resources, although even then a few persons, including those quoted by Vance Packard in his ahead-of-the-times book *The Waste Makers* (McKay, 1960) were issuing warnings. It was not until the late 1960s and 1970s that we began to realize that more did not always mean better. Thus we live in a society that has just begun to put the brakes on population growth—and at a time when sexual freedom has hit new heights.

There are some who believe that with easy contraception and abortion we can have it all—a utopia with sexual license, a falling population (or at least leveling off), a strong economy, sufficient military might, and ever-higher living standards. This may cause euphoria for adults who support sensual consumerism as a way of life, but is does not address itself to the problems of teen-age sexuality in a society obsessed with sexual matters. Nor does the grand plan that is envisioned come to grips with the problem of children who lack love, attention, and the right kind of family.

Lacking a better answer, some may suggest that we encourage young people to put off marriage until their late twenties; begin educational programs on mate selection in the early grades, if not at home; reduce the level of sexual stimulation (pornography, films, books with graphic accounts or pictures of sexual acts); and keep children busy with other things.

Among the alternatives suggested: encourage masturbation; or find creative alternatives that reduce sexual tensions; or accept sexual freedom outside of marriage with contraception and establish a severe penalty for producing out-of-wedlock children; or permit young people to marry earlier, subsidize the marriages, and insist upon contraception.

If out-of-wedlock births, divorce, and poor homes hurt children—and who can deny that they do—something must be done to prevent these problems if we really care about youngsters.

It is probably true that many people who read this book are happily married, faithful spouses, who waited to engage in sex until they were married, planned all of their children, and are excellent parents. It is even possible that the majority of Americans are like that. Yet several hundred thousand children are born out of wedlock each year, and thousands more are born to parents who are too young, too selfish, too unstable, too poor, or otherwise incapable of meeting the nutritional, physical, and emotional needs of the children they produce.

According to the U.S. population study, "Unwanted fertility is highest among those whose levels of education and income are the lowest. For example, in 1970, women with no high school education reported that 31 percent of their births in the preceding five years were unwanted at the time they were conceived; the figure for women college graduates was 7 percent. . . . Not all unwanted births become unwanted children. Many, perhaps most, are eventually accepted and loved indistinguishably from earlier births that were deliberately planned. But many are not, and the costs to them, to their siblings and parents, and to society at large are considerable, though not easy to measure. And the costs are not only financial. The social, health, and psychological costs must be enormous. . . ."

It is this last fact that concerns me most about our mating system for I have seen too many battered children in hospital wards, and neglected youngsters in courts, mental hospitals, foster homes, institutions for the retarded, and the reform schools.

My concept of the ideal basis for mate selection, marriage, and parenting is based on healthy, mature love—a love that is based on giving, sharing, caring, and accepting. In his book *The Art of Loving*, Eric Fromm suggests that, "Giving is more joyous than receiving, not because it is a deprivation, but because in the act of giving lies the expression of aliveness."

Few who marry find their mate the same after five or ten years of marriage, and the change is not always for the better. But those who marry for reasons other than sexual pleasure, and who can gain from giving, will hopefully be mature enough to meet the needs of their children.

What takes place in the privacy of one's bedroom is no concern of mine—at least, not until a child is conceived. Then, because of the nature of our society, it becomes the concern of all of us. Not because of big brotherism, or a desire to meddle in the affairs of others. Rather, because when a child is conceived, and the parents do a poor job, both the child and society suffer.

If we wish to curb crime, mental illness, and other handicaps, then our first concern must be the American Mating System. For that's where the trouble begins.

9

Making Babies—
The Production System

A Princeton University study shows that two groups of women—teen-agers and those over thirty-five—have the largest number of unwanted children. Most were unwanted at the time of conception. These two groups also produce more mentally and physically handicapped children than mothers between the ages of twenty and thirty-four, and more of their babies are born dead, or die shortly after birth.

Researchers also report that teen-agers have more premature babies, and women over thirty-five have more babies suffering from Down's Syndrome (Mongolism) and more with hereditary diseases than women twenty to thirty-four years of age.

It is difficult to interpret these studies in the context of this book. There is the strong temptation to draw conclusions that may or may not be valid. And there is so little really solid research in this area that the statistics produced often raise more questions than they answer.

For example, is it true, as some persons say, that children born to teen-age mothers and to women over thirty-five are more likely to be neglected or abused? Do more of these children become delinquent, emotionally disturbed, or welfare statistics? How many unwanted children are born to mothers on welfare? Of the healthy, but unwanted children born, what is their "success" rate in society? What kind of mothers are these women? Do they meet the basic needs of their off-spring in terms of love, attention, stimulation, and care? As more women use contraceptives and seek abortions will the number of unwanted, diseased, and handicapped children go down? Or are women who produce unwanted children emotionally incapable of preventing or aborting children? Will easy contraception and abortion wipe out crime,

61

mental illness, and welfare in America? Are unwanted children more or less likely to produce unwanted, disturbed, neglected, battered, or handicapped children when they reach child-bearing age? What do we know, or should we know about the fathers of these children? Why is the infant mortality rate higher for teen-agers and women over thirty-five? Is the reason physiological, psychological, or both? What about prenatal care? And what is the relationship between a mother-to-be's mental state and the mental and physical health of the child produced?

While we have too few answers to extremely important questions, most experts agree that we can no longer wait until a youngster has been born to begin meeting its needs. The first step is to consider the mother-to-be's health and habits at the time of conception.

Only in recent years have we really begun to understand the importance of prenatal care. Before the 1950s most doctors believed that the unborn child was a kind of parasite that took what it needed from the mother's body, regardless of the mother's state of health. Now we consider the unborn child to be at risk if a pregnant woman is a drug addict, an alcoholic, chain smoker, user of certain prescription or nonprescription drugs, is on a diet, is living in poverty, has (or catches) certain diseases, or if she had other problems at the time of conception.

One only need remember the terrible story of the expectant mothers who were using the sedative thalidomide in the early 1960s to understand. I remember it well because, when the news broke, I was writing for the *Chicago Tribune*, and I was assigned to the story. It was grim—a series of reports on children with missing limbs, grotesque bodies, and other unthinkable malformations.

In Germany, where gross deformities were first tied to the drug, it was found that more that 90 percent of the children with the kinds of anomalies associated with the drug had mothers who had taken thalidomide, while less than 1 percent of the mothers with normal infants reported they had used it, according to a report in the July 1970 *Pediatric News*.

While visiting institutions in the course of researching this book, I saw young people living out vegetable-like lives, said to be the victims of the drug. I also have been exposed to the awful sight of newborn infants in hospital wards suffering from withdrawal symptoms because their mothers were heroin addicts.

Medical researchers report that women who have rubella (German measles) during early pregnancy may produce children that are deaf, retarded, or otherwise handicapped. Poor nutrition during pregnancy also is blamed by physicians for physical, mental, and neurological handicaps. Babies born to mothers who are chain smokers are said to be underweight, and may suffer from other problems.

At the University of Washington's medical school in Seattle a team of researchers found that alcoholic mothers produce babies that average two-thirds the normal weight at birth, that are 20 percent shorter than normal babies in length, and will never catch up—even with proper nutrition and care in a foster home or hospital.

At the end of a year, for example, the average weight gain is only 38 percent of that experienced by normal children, and height increase is only 65 percent of normal, according to the report. The researchers also found that the children of alcoholic mothers often have a smaller than normal head size, congenital heart defects, underdeveloped jaws, joint defects, and other problems.

Malnutrition, which often accompanies chronic drinking, was discounted as the cause. The difference between babies of malnourished, alcoholic mothers and those of alcoholic mothers who ate properly was found to be insignificant. Researchers concluded that the alcohol itself, one of the chemical by-products of liquor, or a toxic substance in the alcohol, was to blame.

Whether or not moderate drinking during pregnancy has an impact on unborn children is uncertain, but the possibility cannot be overlooked. And it is significant that there are a million or more women alcoholics of child-bearing age in the United States, and many are capable of producing several children.

Just as little has been known about the impact alcohol and tobacco have on the unborn, even less is known about the thousands of chemical compounds an expectant mother may take. What if she uses marijuana or LSD? What impact does coffee, tea, or aspirin have on the fetus? And what of nonprescription drugs, or those prescribed by doctors? Do these account for the growing numbers of children with learning disabilities, who are hyperactive, emotionally unstable, or otherwise handicapped?

We simply don't know.

Take the case of aminopterin, a drug taken by some women to induce a miscarriage chemically. In Cincinnati General Hospital a few years ago a woman who had taken the drug for the purpose delivered a baby with an oversized head, no bones in the cranium, a small body, a webbed neck, peculiar eyes, low-set ears, club feet, and a cleft palate. A few other children have been born with a similar combination of defects under similar circumstances.

Not only is there limited information about the impact of the mother's physical health and habits on the unborn child but we know even less about the impact of the mother's mental state. What does it mean when a mother hates the unborn child she is carrying? No one knows.

The whole area of mental health and how it relates to one's physical well-being is under study. We are told that the relationship between the mother's body and the fetus is highly significant. If then, a woman's mental state affects her body, it is quite possible it also has an important impact on the unborn child.

Doctors agree that stress, fear, and other factors trigger physiological responses that range from a sudden burst of strength to ulcers. Old wives' tales have it that a woman frightened by a black cat will produce a deformed baby. While we scoff at this, it is possible that under certain conditions chemical changes related to the mother's mental state could have an impact on the fetus.

Studies show that loneliness, deep-seated mental illness, and a feeling of rejection may produce what we call hypochondria. Researchers at the Kaiser-Permanente medical complex in San Francisco say that though the pains patients feel seem to have no physiological basis, the patients really do feel aches and pains. What of the mother-to-be who feels rejected or is disturbed?

Whether or not it can be shown that the unborn is effected, experts have turned their attention to the newborn. Dr. Lee Salk, director of the Division of Pediatric Psychology at the New York Hospital, and professor of psychology and pediatrics at Cornell University Medical College, writes in his book *What Every Child Would Like His Parents to Know* (McKay, 1972): "Clearly, if adult personality is markedly influenced by an individuals earliest experiences, we should concentrate preventive efforts on the very young. While most professionals in the mental health field recognize this, relatively little effort is directed toward assisting those who are primarily responsible for the personality development of infants and young children—their parents." He also notes that half of the hospital beds in the United States are occupied by people suffering from some form of mental illness.

My point is this: If it is true, as the Princeton study shows (a study conducted in 1970 for the Office of Population Research), that 15 percent of all children that are born are unwanted (and 44 percent of all births were unplanned at conception), and if the largest percentage of unwanted children are born to teen-agers and to women over thirty-five, and if these two groups of women produce the highest percentage of babies who are premature, and physically, emotionally, and mentally handicapped, then should we not develop a full-blown study of the impact these unwanted children have on our society?

I believe there may be a direct relationship between unwanted children and our crime rate, the number of people who enter mental hospitals, and even welfare statistics. Yet no one seems to be looking at this possibility—even though, if true, it could have a significant impact on our society and the way it deals with social problems.

If we are truly concerned with crime, child abuse, mental illness, retardation, welfare, and many other problems we face, we should begin studying the lives of unwanted children. Surely some future generation of Americans will stand incredulous at the barbarity of their twentieth-century ancestors, who ignored the child-production system and dealt with the problems created by that system by building more jails and prisons, more mental hospitals and mental health centers, and institutions for the retarded and for other handicapped children. They will be startled to find that we ignored the child-production and child-rearing systems and invested in more guns, police cars, and policemen, more social and mental health workers, and handed out more and larger doles of money to so-called welfare mothers who produced more and more unwanted children.

It seems certain that they will believe our systems were *designed* to produce pain—and an ever-increasing number of children with problems.The fact that during the same period Americans were obsessed with sex and lived in an age of high sexual stimulation will only add weight to their conviction that we were either barbaric or—as a society—emotionally unstable.

Even now it is clear to some Americans that the solution does not lie in the warehousing or therapeutic treatment of society's unwanted children and misfits. Nor does it rest with big-brotherism screening and control of the mating, child-producing, and child-rearing systems, although these might have some impact on the problem.

Rather, the answer lies in instilling in every American a sense of responsibility toward children; in changing the present method of mate selection; in educational programs that teach all Americans about contraception; in training all young persons basic child-rearing principles; and in holding all parents accountable for their offspring.

There are some who understand this. Germain Greer, in *The Female Eunuch* (McGraw-Hill, 1971), writes: "If women could regard childbearing not as a duty or an inescapable destiny but as a privilege to be worked for, the way a man might work for the right to have a family, children might grow up without the burden of gratitude for the gift of life which they never asked for." (I certainly cannot agree with all Ms. Greer says in her chapter on the family, and yet she is more concerned with children than many in the women's movement.)

Historically women have been considered most valuable in their function as producers of children. But why must a woman who does not want to be a wife and mother feel that she is either abnormal or a "bad" person? Should she not have the right to make a choice that is thoughtful and intelligent?

Both parents and would-be-parents must understand the impact children have on their lives.

The Cost of a Child

In 1969 it cost nearly $100,000 to rear a child from birth through college, according to a study made by Ritchie H. Reed and Susan McIntosh for the U.S. Commission on Population Growth and the American Future. They came up with the $100,000 figure by adding up the cost of the doctor and hospital, child-rearing costs, college expenses, wages lost had the mother worked, and the interest that would have been earned if the money spent on the child had been invested.

Today the sum is far higher, not only because of inflation and higher interest rates but because most women have greater earning power than in the past. Cost of a second or third child would be less, of course, since the mother's wages lost stays the same regardless of the number of children. But even an additional financial drain on a family of $1,000 or $2,000 a year per child can have a stifling effect on the pleasure a couple may get out of life. And when the unspeakable happens, that is, when a child is diseased, handicapped or seriously injured, the cost to parents can be astronomical.

Studies also show that the younger the couple (or mother) at the time the child is born, the less lifetime earning power the couple can expect to have, and the more problems the children face. A women who gives birth to a child while very young is likely to produce one, two, or three more in rapid succession. Both parents are less likely to achieve educational and career goals. And they can expect to live in poorer housing, have older cars, eat lower quality food, and have less opportunity to travel.

The working mother who provides her child with minimally good day care may have little to show for her labor financially, unless she is a professional person with a comfortable salary. And regardless of rationalization and arguments to the contrary, it is growing increasingly clear that the mother who truly cares about her children (and does not consider them as pets) will work sparingly during the child's first six years, and will be home before and after school until her youngsters are grown.

I say this assuming that the mother is emotionally stable and is capable of caring for her children. If the mother is unstable, incompetent, and thus hardly deserving to be a mother, the children may well be better off with a baby-sitter or in a day-care center or even an institution, if it is small and meets basic needs.

Fathers also must play a larger role in the lives of their children—or choose not to have them.

From my studies of the mental health and delinquency problems of our children, and after having interviewed hundreds of professionals who work with problem children, I can only conclude that good parenting is more critical to child-rearing than good management is to business and industry. For that reason it is clear that American parents—if they are to be parents and not pet-keepers—must expect to sacrifice substantially if they have children. And the costs are not in dollars alone.

Physical Costs of Parenting

Dr. Fitzhugh Dodson, in his book *How to Parent* (Nash, 1970), begins with a rather obvious, but sometimes overlooked fact: "When you become a mother, you join the ranks of an absolutely unique, twenty-four-hours-a-day profession: a parent."

It is the twenty-four-hours-a-day aspect of the job, and the need, in our complex society, to have something close to professional skill, that most Americans contemplating parenthood overlook. It seems certain that if more people did understand this—and took it seriously—we would have less crime and delinquency, better mental health, and far fewer social problems. Or fewer children.

But as I have said, Americans do not always understand that you "can't do just one thing."

I know a couple who moved to the country because they wanted to own horses. It had been the childhood dream of the wife, and when they could afford it she talked her husband into it. Once they purchased the horses their entire life-style changed. Not because they enjoyed prancing through luxuriant fields and down picturesque roads. Rather, it changed because they found that without fail horses must be fed, groomed, and exercised. That meant no more leisurely dinners in the city, with the theater and an evening with friends afterward. And it became much harder to go away on long weekends, even to take vacation trips. Horses, children, and other living things require humane care and attention. Especially children.

Like any other kind of work experience, owning children (and how else would you put it under our present legal system) is pleasant if you are really skilled at it, and if you like the work. Unfortunately, many Americans are poorly trained, have little natural aptitude, and only limited interest in child-rearing. Unlike the couple with the horses, couples who have children cannot sell them and return to their old life-styles.

But some try.

Americans dump thousands of toddlers into beds and playpens for hours—paying little attention to them beyond changing their diapers. Or we go to the other extreme, and toss them about and play with and overprotect them until they are spoiled. I know of parents who prevent toddlers from exploring the world because it is too much bother. We slap their hands and tell them they are bad when the reach for adult bric-a-brac that we carelessly leave around. We rear children in sterile apartment buildings where they seldom feel the wind in their faces, grass under their bare feet, and sand, stones, branches, and water with their hands.

Until a child is five or six, parents need enormous energy and great patience. Both mothers and fathers must be able to go without sleep from time to time. Demands on parents of handicapped children can sometimes be multiplied a hundredfold, and stretched out over twenty, thirty or more years. Some parents die still worrying about basic care of their handicapped child, although that "child" may be forty or fifty years old.

Emotional Costs

When emotionally mature, happy parents have a happy, healthy, vigorous child. And when they love children and child caring, the emotional reward can be great. What is more pleasant than seeing a child develop and grow and respond? A proud parent, exhausted at the end of a day of child caring, may still take time to tell her spouse about the progress made, or to call or write a grandparent to tell of the accomplishments of the children.

There is little that is more draining and defeating than having to put up with soiled diapers, crying, complaining, discipline problems or temper tantrums and other routine difficulties when one is not really suited for child rearing. It is even worse when one is not happily married.

One must really love children and be emotionally strong to meet the needs of a retarded, disturbed, or otherwise handicapped youngster. And some parents find themselves angry, resentful, filled with hate because producing an imperfect child seems so ego shattering, so unfair. But rearing normal children can produce pain as well.

Older children tend to rebel during adolescence. They talk back, get into trouble, ignore parents' questions and statements, fail to achieve as they should in school, experiment with drugs or alcohol or sex, and create conflicts between parents and other members of the household.

Not all teen-agers are at war with their parents. In families where flexibility, openness, and understanding are the rule, where parents have the maturity to cope with minor conflicts without bringing on bigger battles, the teen years can—most of the time—be as rewarding as any. But too few families seem to pass through this period without pain.

Improving the Production System

In industry we can slow down a production line, cull out imperfect parts, or design better ones. It just isn't that easy in the child-production system.

Changes are taking place. The birth rate is down, due in part to improved methods of contraception. There is less pressure today on couples to have children. The high cost of rearing a family and the opportunity for mothers to follow new careers, once open only to men, also has made a difference.

But many mature Americans still want to become grandparents, and urge their children to have children. Girls still grow up believing they are not "whole" until they have had a baby. As Dr. Walter Menninger, of Topeka, Kansas, has said, "for most of us our immortality is our children."

We live in a society saturated by sex. While contraception is more effective and more readily available now than at any time in history, no method is fully sure. Thus every sexual encounter involves a risk. Thousands of girls, rejected by their parents, feeling unloved, take risks daily. Some want babies, just to "have someone love me." Other young people take pleasure in their children. They like to watch them, play with them, feed them, care for them. Children give meaning to life. But often, children are little more than pets.

One wonders if this should be the destiny of children. We have not lived long enough with affluence to know how best to use children, but we are too far removed from the age of the working child to understand the changes that have taken place.

I cannot imagine a world without children, wide-eyed and full of life, swinging and jumping rope, throwing balls, hiding behind trees and jumping out, giggling, teasing, playing on the beach or pretending a small sandbox is beside the shore, reaching out to show you worms and spiders and beatles, sliding down snow-covered slopes, or bringing in May flowers for mother.

I feel most alive when I am with my children. We have, for weekend and summer use, a farm with old barns, fields and forests, trails to follow and hills to climb. The children plant a garden, dig holes, climb trees, and throw stones in the brook. When all seven (some are adopted) are packed into our camper and we are bouncing along a country road, singing or playing an on-the-road game, life is good. Sometimes we drive up to the Wild River, a cold, boulder-filled mountain stream, and jump in to cool off. Children are an important part of my life.

But there are those who do not want children. Until the 1970s those couples were either stuck with the child, or they would have to give it up for adoption, or risk an illegal abortion. Now, at least under the law, that has changed. Ads appear in newspapers across the country like this one in New York City:

> Bronx Community
> Abortion Clinic
> A Modern Facility, Expert Care
> Relaxed Atmosphere, Non-Profit,
> Hospital Affiliate. Call for an
> Appointment in Confidence. Up to
> 12 Weeks. Total Cost $125.
> Medicaid Accepted
> 212-920-4088

The classified ads come complete with area codes for reluctant mothers-to-be from out-of-town or out-of-state. Women of all ages flock to the clinics by the thousands and, apparently with great relief and peace of mind, rid themselves of the unwanted fetus.

Few topics pose more problems for me—an advocate for the rights of children—than abortion. I have heard the many arguments, both rational and emotional:

—An unwanted child is better off unborn.

—Women should control their own bodies.

—You are worried about a "small, inert piece of meat." (Or, as one woman put it, "All the anti-abortion furor is about a chemical fusion that is benign only when it is timely.")

—We must do it at least for women who cannot emotionally handle a pregnancy.

—It is safe, easy, and simple. Far easier than extracting a tooth or removing one's tonsils.

— "My God, how could any enlightened person be against abortion in this age?"

— The embryo cannot be classified as human in any ordinary sense.

— This is a democracy, where majority opinions must be respected and minority rights protected. Most women favor abortion. And what right does the state have to tell her what she can or cannot do, or what she should or should not believe?

— It is the only solution to out-of-wedlock births.

— Like all other medical matters, abortion is a private decision between a patient and her doctor.

— If we don't provide abortions to minority groups and the poor they'll soon outnumber us. Educated women have fewer children.

— You and your wife do what you want, but keep you nose out of our business.

— Abortion should be mandatory for girls under eighteen unless they can show they are able to care for the baby.

I know there are other, perhaps more rational, more compelling reasons for abortion. But no matter how strong the argument, I have a difficult time accepting it.

First, it is difficult for me to weigh the rights of two people, the mother of the unwanted child and the unborn infant, against one another. I say this understanding that many people feel that the fetus is not a child, and that no matter how logical or sound my arguments may be, I cannot change the minds of those who favor abortion.

Nor is it enough to know that an unborn child has at least inheritance rights and other legal standing.

I am inclined to agree with two doctors who wrote (in my view) eloquent defenses of the fetus in letters to the editor of the *Wall Street Journal* a few years ago. One, Dr. F. D. Foley of San Antonio, Texas, examines the remains of unborn children after abortions are performed. He said:

"You may be correct in assuming that the majority of Americans hold a pro-abortion position but I think many would alter their opinions if the abortus were visualized rather than considered in the 'abstract.'

"Having received hundreds of fetal bodies or parts thereof to examine, I've experienced no difficulty in determining whether a given fetus was human or not. The products of spontaneous miscarriage or an induced abortion are similar and characteristic in every respect and are easily distinguished from fetuses of other species much earlier than the 20 weeks originally recommended by the state medical society or the 16-18 weeks proposed by Governor Rockefeller.

"To deny that a human form with integrated circulatory and respiratory activity is alive seems incredible, particularly when we require the absence of these spontaneous vital functions to make an accurate diagnosis of death. Your position might be less ambiguous as a direct, rather than a distant observer."

The second physician, Dr. Thomas E. Nix, Jr., argues that tracing life to the moment of conception is hardly "abstract or ambiguous" if one relies on biological fact—rather than "speculation, subjectives or faith." In the letter he explains that:

"When a living sperm unites with a living ovum a new cell is produced which has every feature unanimously agreed upon by biologists as being characteristic of life (as opposed to an inanimate chemical system). It grows by repeatedly budding into more cells; it respires; it utilizes nutrients and discharges waste products; it is capable of a continuum of growth, maturation and development. The human conceptus is 'living' by any definition of science.

"Living beings are classified into species by biologists. Species classifications of plants and animals are made on the basis of their form, appearance, behavior and other traits. The traits of an individual are to a large extent determined by its genetic composition, the amazingly complex and specific programming code within the chromosomes of each cell of a plant or animal. These DNA codons are locked into each cell of an individual at the moment of fertilization of the egg by the sperm and they are physical determinants of that individual (conditioned by environment) until he dies. The genetic code for each species is highly specific and the code for each individual within the species is also unique and specific. Thus, the human conceptus has the hereditary makeup, the genes, that characterize it as belonging to homo sapiens, and to no other species, neither orangutan, salamander, nor artichoke.

"Human traits develop continuously in successive stages; heart action at 25 days from conception, brain activity at about 6 weeks, heart wall closures and lung expansion at birth, first tooth development 6-12 months after birth, sexual maturation at age 12, etc. Human life consists of overlapping and progressive stages of development beginning at conception and ending in old age and death.

"It appears that ambiguity and arbitrariness depend not so much on positing human life in the conceptus as in trying to say that one day, one week, sixteen weeks, twenty-six weeks, etc., constitutes the difference between 'human' life and 'non-human' life. Such 'reasoning' might be acceptable if biologic facts didn't shout as loudly as they do."

Beyond this, one must consider other factors. If abortion is proper, then what about infanticide—especially in the case of handicapped infants? And should we change our views then on euthanasia? Should we be more concerned with prolonging the life of a person diagnosed as suffering from an incurable disease than with saving the life of an unborn child whose prognosis is life and health?

My concern is not out of lack of sympathy for the mothers of the unwanted child. Freedom of choice is important in our society. But the freedom of each individual is protected from the excesses of others. And death to the unborn child, when balanced against the needs of the expectant mother, often seems an excessive exercise of the woman's rights.

Call it idealism or worse, but it seems to me contraception and adoption are far better answers. Thousands of couples unable to have children would welcome them into their homes.

Risking the wrath of thousands of modern women, I still must suggest that they might better battle against sexual license and support sexual responsibility.

This is not to excuse the American male, although there are those who believe he is too weak to control his sexual appetite, or is culturally programmed to play the role of the super-stud.

To place the total blame on the present crop of parents is unfair, for they are what they are because of training they received as children. But to shift the total blame to the culture is a cop-out. The culture is *us*—and we have either helped shape it or have apathetically accepted it.

If we are truly civilized, and not barbarian, we will—as individuals and as a nation—change our culture and life-styles so that we will go down in history as a child-loving, not a child-destroying, society.

10

"Train up a child . . ."
—The Child-rearing System

Violent crime. Shoplifting. Alcoholism. Drug abuse. Vandalism. Runaways. Abortion. Divorce. Welfare. Neglect and abuse of children. Mental illness. Political corruption at the highest levels. Dishonest policemen. Shyster lawyers. Apathy. Waste. Promiscuity. Pornography. White-collar crime. Racial intolerance. Loneliness. Hatred.

What's wrong with America?

What can we do about it?

I suppose if you are genetically or biologically oriented you might believe that the American gene pool has, along with everything else, become grossly polluted. That calls for one set of solutions. We might even find it necessary, if we buy the genetic theory wholesale, to resort to mass sterilization of incompetents and criminals and other undesirables.

However, if you believe that the causes of crime, mental illness, and other problems are, to a large extent, environmental, then we must look elsewhere for answers. The logical starting point is the home and the first six years of life—that crucial period before the schools take over.

We have learned that children left in their cribs without human attention or affection during the first months of life may die or suffer from a form of retardation.

Nutrition also is seen as important.

There has been a long-standing debate going on between those who favor "permissiveness" and those who believe in stern punishment and firm control of children.

Richard H. Blum, Stanford University psychologist, produced a study in 1972 that suggested that overly permissive parents encourage drug use and other social ills. And Dr. Spock, sometimes called the "father of permissiveness," recently called for more discipline, and says he has been misunderstood and misquoted.

Dr. David Rosenthal, a researcher for the National Institute of Mental Health, reported in 1970 that while it has long been believed that between 7 and 17 percent of the children of parents hospitalized for schizophrenia would suffer from the mental illness, if the offspring of a schizophrenic parent is given up for adoption, few will develop the symptoms.

Other studies suggest that delinquent behavior is learned at home—or is the "normal" reaction to an "abnormal" family. This also seems to be the thrust of the book *Sanity, Madness and the Family* (Tavistock Publications, 1964) by two English psychiatrists, Doctors R. D. Laing and A. Esterson. They suggest that "madness" may really be the struggle to cope or live in "an unlivable situation."

Parenting begins early. A mother's relationship to her baby minutes after birth is seen by a growing number of pediatricians, psychologists, and psychiatrists as crucial. Mothers, often under heavy sedation or recovering from a difficult delivery, may be separated from their babies for hours. Yet Dr. Lee Salk suggests that the mother-child "bond" is weakened if they are not together during the critical period immediately after birth. He attributes the mother-child bond to "an intricate set of biochemical factors, developed in the course of evolution," and says that when the mother and infant are together it will "trigger built-in behavior patterns."

Young children must be held, cuddled, and touched. Lack of warmth and touching may well contribute to certain forms of learning disabilities, mental illness, and delinquence, as well as adult immaturity.

Yet children also can be "spoiled" when given the wrong kind of attention at the wrong time for the wrong reasons. The nineteenth-century philosopher and historian, Thomas Carlyle, said that "When parents spoil their children, it is less to please them than to please themselves. It is the egotism of parental love."

Professionals working with deaf, blind, and retarded children complain that most are either neglected or overprotected by their parents during the early years. These children, when improperly parented, must first overcome emotional problems before they can learn to cope with their handicaps.

Dr. Joan R. Hebeler, of the University of Texas Medical Branch, Galveston, reports that rejection, loathing, revulsion, and shame are normal parental reactions to the birth of a multiply handicapped child. Most families of the multiply handicapped need counseling, she adds.

So-called "normal" children also need help. The forum concerned with creativity at the 1970 While House Conference on Children concluded that every child has creative potential, but creativity is stifled at an early age in many youngsters.

Dr. Earl S. Patterson, who runs a nonprofit psychiatric clinic for young people in Meriden, Connecticut, notes that "Children deprived of a culturally rich environment tend to lag behind those who are more fortunate."

And what of child abuse? Wayne Holder, a bright young welfare official in Albuquerque, New Mexico, told me that workers on his staff assigned to protect children from their parents and other adults are "overwhelmed—they can't sleep at night." I have heard the same story the country over. One social work supervisor in the State of New York wiped tears from his eyes as he told me what is happening to children in his community, and how little is being spent on protective services. He says he is actively seeking a job in another field—the burden is too great.

Each year 10,000 children die in unexplained crib deaths. In 70 to 80 percent of these deaths no autopsy is performed, and parents are left with deep feelings of guilt.

The United States has a greater rate of infant mortality than Sweden, the Netherlands, Finland, Norway, Japan, Denmark, Switzerland, Australia, New Zealand, Great Britian, East Germany, and France. And yet more than 90 percent of our children are born in hospitals, and 97 percent are attended by a physician.

The death rate of children under one year of age exceeds that of persons fifty-five to sixty-four years of age in America.

Many, but not all states, have tried to warn parents that lead-based paint in old houses can cause brain damage or death in children who pick up flakes and eat it—as many toddlers do.

Some 15,000 children under the age of fifteen die from accidents each year, and 19 million more are severely enough injured to seek medical care or to restrict their usual activity. Of these accidents, 10 million occur in the home and 3 million in school.

Of the accidental deaths of children one to four years of age, 33 percent are the result of motor vehicle accidents, and 22 percent from fires or explosions, 14 percent drown, and 13 percent are attributed to "inhalation and ingestion," poisoning kills 6 percent, while falls and other causes destroy 12 percent of the children who die accidentally.

There are some 10 million children (roughly 6 million white and 4 million black) living in families with an annual income that is below the poverty level. Roughly 80 percent of all Indian children live in poverty.

More than half of all preschool children in America get too little Vitamin A, and large numbers lack other basic nutrients. While many children still get milk and hot lunches at school, there is no hot-lunch program during the most crucial years—the first six years of life. It is estimated that a child's brain grows at the rate of 1 or 2 milligrams a minute after birth, and this rapid growth actually pushes the skull out from the inside, enlarging it. When growth is inhibited by malnutrition, even for brief periods, the child's intellectual capability is impaired, according to medical researchers.

Ninety percent of all public elementary schools in America report that there are children attending with severe reading problems. Yet not all schools provide remedial programs for children. Between 12 and 20 percent of all school-age children have what is called a "learning disability."

One out of 12 children (nearly 2 million) between the ages of six and eleven has a speech defect, 1 in 9 has a defective vision (2.6 million children), while 1 in 4 between the ages of five and fourteen has never seen a dentist.

Only about 5 percent of all children in need of psychiatric care in America get it. It has been estimated that 1 out of 3 children living in poverty has serious emotional problems.

Roughly 100,000 children under the age of nineteen contract gonorrhea each year.

In 1950 fewer than 300,000 children were victims of divorce, but twenty years later the number had more than doubled, and the divorce rate, like the crime rate, climbs unchecked.

The number of persons under twenty-one with epilepsy climbed from 350,000 in 1960 to 450,000 in 1970. Cerebral palsy victims under the age of twenty-one increased from 370,000 to 465,000 in the same period.

More than 10 million children are on the welfare rolls. But no effort is made to determine whether or not the children are being properly cared for, or that the money is even being spent for their care.

What do these statistics, collected from reports issued by federal agencies and private and child-care groups, prove? That as a society we seem to forget that all children are dependent and defenseless. Born naked and largely hairless, without teeth and unable to walk or crawl, the human child is dependent for years. Dropping a week-old baby into a snowbank, or even leaving it alone in a flower-filled meadow on a warm day would assure its death. Nor can many children eight or nine survive without adult care. Most teen-agers dropped by helicopter into a wilderness area could not survive.

While all children are dependent, some are more dependent than others. The retarded child is slower to stand, walk, or talk. Those classified as profoundly retarded may lie in the fetal position, diapered, whimpering, and infant-like even after their bodies are fully developed. I have seen hundreds of infantile retarded adults in their fifties and sixties in the nation's institutions.

Disturbed children may live in a fantasy world, or they may feel crushing spasms of depression, live in terror and confusion, or strike out with uncontrollable anger.

Deaf children often do not realize that they are different from other children until they are seven or eight. Nor can they understand why their mothers spanked them. Most have no concept of language. Someone must protect them from traffic and other danger. The same is true of the blind child.

The dependency of the crippled child is more obvious and better understood, at least by some parents. But others do not always know how to deal with the physically impaired youngster and may treat the child as if he were unintelligent.

Battered and neglected children may never grow up emotionally. Those who have been given too little love remain dependent—sometimes seeking love through sex, or hurting others as they have been hurt. They also tend to be more self-destructive than children reared in warm, loving homes.

As a nation we must come to realize that a child must grow mentally. He does not think as an adult does—even in his teen years.

The eminent Swiss psychologist Jean Piaget, who has devoted a lifetime to studying children, explains in his book *The Child and Reality* (Grossman, 1973) that childhood (or the period of vulnerability) lasts longer for a child than a kitten or chick because "the human infant has more to learn."

He uses proportional relationships as one example of how, over a period of time, a child develops new concepts. In an experiment in which children are given two balls of clay equal in size and substance, a fairly young child will understand that both balls of clay are very similar in "volume, weight, everything." But keep one ball round and have the child flatten the other, or roll it into a sausage shape, and the ability to understand that they are still the same depends upon the age of the child, he reports.

The young child does not understand that the amount of material in the round ball and the sausage-shaped (or flattened) piece of clay remains the same. The small child believes the long sausage or wide pancake has more clay in it than the ball—even after he has flattened or rolled out the ball himself.

The average age for understanding that no change has taken place in volume is eight, Dr. Piaget says. While the eight-year-old does understand this, unless he has been taught he cannot understand that they also remain the same in weight. Ask him which is heavier, and he will say the sausage. Not until he is about ten does he seem to know automatically that the weight also remains the same. Then two years more must pass before he can answer a third question correctly: What will happen if he drops the round clay ball into a glass of water and the pancake or sausage-shaped clay in another glass of the same size containing the same amount of water. The typical child under the age of twelve will assume that one or the other will make the water deeper.

Just as the adult fails to understand that a child's ability to grasp abstract ideas is a growth process, so the twelve-year-old forgets that just a few weeks or months earlier he could not answer the questions correctly. In fact, he may consider the responses of younger brothers and sisters, when tested with the clay, silly, and the answer obvious.

(For those who want to experiment with their own children, Dr. Piaget stresses that the ages are average, but adds that results were similar when made in several different countries in different parts of the world.)

We all forget—as adults—that children see the world differently. We forget even the most simple things.

During my early school years (until the end of the sixth grade) I lived in a house on a hill in Moline, Illinois. When we moved to Indiana I was quite short, and I did not return to our former house in Moline until I was in my late twenties, and over six feet tall.

For years, when I thought of our former house I remembered the high bank in front of the house, with the long flight of steps from the street to the front door, and how hard it was to find a ball or toy lost in the vast thicket of barberry bushes that covered the towering bank. I will never forget visiting the house shortly after my twenty-eighth birthday. I was actually stunned to find that the bank was not nearly as high as I had remembered it.

I learned the same lesson in many other ways. One of my children had an eye condition that seemed to hinder his motor control, and he was frustrated by the inability to express himself with paints and crayons. So I purchased an inexpensive camera for him to use. When the first roll of film came back I saw the world as my young child saw it. Adults were grotesque giants—all legs, feet, bodies, and faceless chins. Chairs were major barriers and tables like one-story houses.

Dr. Piaget also discusses how infants of five or six months have little concept of the permanency of objects, and how a baby's life is like a slide show, filled with objects without permanence, substance, or "localization." He shows that this is so by putting the infant's bottle in plain sight. If hungry, the baby will reach for it. But hide the bottle under a diaper and he does not know he should look under the diaper. It is as if a magician has made the bottle disappear, and it no longer exists.

Time is another difficult concept for children. A rainy afternoon can last forever, a northern winter may seem to stay for years, and waiting for a friend or relative to arrive for ten or fifteen minutes may provoke two dozen questions of "When will they get here?" Discussing distances will not help. But tell a child she must be in bed in a half hour and she may begin to fuss about "never being able to do anything."

Childhood is a time of myths. Many believe in the Easter Bunny, a Santa that flies, and Tinker Bell, Peter Pan, and Captain Hook. One of our children, when three, decided he was a chicken and hid raw eggs throughout the house, just as the chickens did down on a farm we own. My wife, fortunately, has a good sense of humor. She needed it when she stuffed clean clothing into the drier and then, after she turned it on, discovered he had hidden two eggs inside.

Childhood can also be frightening. Dr. Benjamin Spock warns that children of three or four may be afraid of "the dark, of dogs, or fire engines, of death, of cripples." "The child's imagination has now developed to the stage where he can put himself in other people's shoes and picture the dangers he hasn't actually experienced," the good doctor continues. Childhood is the world of play and toys, and of imitation. Even small children emulate parents and older siblings. One of my older children was a well-behaved child until, when he was three, a friend visited with a seven-year-old daughter. The seven-year-old didn't get her way, threw a tantrum, and our three-year-old watched. That night at bedtime he kicked and screamed and threw himself around for the first time.

A. S. Neill of England's Summerhill fame, admitted that his wards insisted on playing with toy guns, and lacking those, shot at each other with their fingers, sticks of wood, or other substitutes. A child builds a sand castle on the beach, and if another child kicks the lump of sand, the builder's house has really been wrecked in his or her mind.

An inquisitive toddler wants to touch and taste everything—the telephone, pine needles, marbles, a kitten, mud tracked in by older children, the ironing cord, and the electrical outlet. But in a year or two it may be impossible to get the same child to taste unfamiliar food.

A six-year-old who has mastered language may ask questions until parents find it unbearable. Older children put down answers that cannot be proven through the senses, logic, or on the basis of what they see as fair and just. A few years earlier the child may have drawn unreasonable conclusions—and argued just as firmly then as later.

It is not possible to discuss in a few pages or single chapter the vast amount of knowledge that has been acquired on child development. Or, conversely, to explain how little we truly know about children.

Perhaps it is enough to say that children are not only physically dependent, they must have the opportunity to know and understand the world around them. If their view of the world is warped, it is only natural that their behavoir should be deviant.

Oliver Twist, one of the more popular Dickens characters, was out of step with his peers when he lived in an environment that rewarded stealing. As more than one slum mother has told me, their children learn to steal, roll drunks, and snatch purses just as easily as suburban children learn to pitch, bat, and catch in the Little League. In the slum, crime and delinquency are too often the norm, not unusual behavior.

It is easy to understand the physical dependence of a small child, or to see that the child views the world from knee-high, and must have time to learn about it. But too few of us really understand a child's emotional needs, or how to be sure our children grow up mentally healthy.

Perhaps that is why parents who feed and clothe their children well, buy them toys, and seek out the best schools, pay so little attention to their offspring when they contemplate getting a divorce, or when mother decides she will go to work, or have more children, or when dad decides to accept a corporate transfer.

"What possible impact could it have on the children," we say to ourselves, forgetting that they need roots, reassurance, friends, consistency, familiarity.

How many children suffer emotional damage in the school my children have attended here in New Hampshire is hard to say. But it is a fact that new arrivals are picked on and tormented—with little interference from the teachers. Dad may have the excitement of a new job, and mother of decorating a new house or making new friends. And children may adjust easily to a move, especially if they are in their early teens, but not always.

A mother may believe her husband is the world's worst father, and convince herself that the children will gain as much as she will from a divorce. And yet after years of interviewing children in mental hospitals and reform schools I remain amazed at how many deeply love even cruel or neglecting parents. The younger the child the more certain this is to be true. Very seldom do I find a child under the age of fourteen who takes a divorce in stride, although older children may say they hate one or both parents.

Contrary to what a variety of experts or members of the women's liberation movement may say, I can recall very few children who seemed happy their mothers were working, or pleased that their fathers took a second job to provide the family with a "higher standard of living." In fact, I cannot, at the moment, think of a single child who would put financial gain ahead of love, attention, and time with this parents. Often children have shrugged and said they "guessed Mom had to work"— otherwise she wouldn't do it.

I have met working mothers who managed well. But the number is exceedingly small—although many *thought* they were doing a good job with their children. Those who balance work and child rearing effectively have flexible hours and enormous energy. Evenings and weekends are devoted to parenting. One woman, a New York City social worker, told me that every Friday after work, rain or shine, she put her children in the family car and drove into the country to hike, climb, or swim. Few of us are able to give that much of ourselves to the children after a hard week in the office. Maturity involves, among other things, putting first things first.

Like other traits, maturity is learned or developed in the home. It is lack of maturity, in part, that causes delinquency—if we relate immaturity to gross selfishness—while more mature persons know how to give and share. (Can it be true that the greedy businessman has never really grown up, and is obsessed with "getting?")

Obviously the newborn child is the most immature human. He is hardly aware that others exist. Soon he learns that someone out there feeds and diapers him, and when that happens he feels better. Each day the infant grows in his understanding of relationships with others.

Then—the time varies from child to child—the infant begins to understand that two persons separate from himself can interact. Mother and sister, or mother and dad, have a separate, distinct relationship, and he is not part of it! Until that time the child is fully egocentric, believing the world is focused on him and on no one else. In time the normal child grows in maturity, and understands that those around him have many different relationships with many people—the clerk in the store, the paper boy, other motorists on the street, teachers, relatives, neighbors, strangers.

If the delinquent (or criminal) is different from the rest of us, it may well be in this area. Most delinquents are egocentric. He can think only of himself, of gratifying his own needs. He may give no thought at all to what he is doing to others, and he may have little or no remorse for his victims. He lacks empathy. This is why one finds both severely deprived children and those who are badly spoiled in trouble with the law. Neither has learned to share or to give.

The place to learn to care is in a strong, happy home. Caring (which I relate to maturity) is learned and mastered through constant practice and correction. I feel that emotional neglect is as damaging as physical neglect—and often results in innocent members of society being hurt.

Even the way the mother holds or handles a child has an impact on the infant's emotional growth. "A mother's feeling that either she or the baby is inadequate will translate itself into the way she handles him," says Dr. Lee Salk in *How to Raise a Human Being*. This will "affect the way he experiences the world, both now and in later life."

He also contends that research shows us that children are extremely vulnerable during the first days of life, and perhaps even before birth. And he is not alone in this.

The widely admired Erik H. Erikson suggests that the Russian custom of swaddling babies—that is, binding them up to the neck in almost rigid bundles—for their first nine months has much to do with the Russian temperament. The Russians believe "you must swaddle the infant to protect him against himself; this causes violent vasomotor needs in him; he must remain emotionally swaddled in order not to fall victim to wild emotion. This, in turn, helps to establish a basic, a preverbal indoctrination, according to which people, for their own good, must be rigidly restrained, while being offered, now and then, ways of discharging compressed emotion," Erikson writes in *Childhood and Society* (Norton, 1950).

Child-rearing practices have a great deal to do with the kind of culture that develops. And the kind of culture that a nation has is closely tied to the nation's economic system. That is why it is only logical that in an era when advertising agencies and manufacturers want to promote hedonistic consumerism, permissiveness (or child spoiling) is pushed as the ideal method of child rearing.

(It must be pointed out here that there is a great deal of difference between giving a child proper care and love and catering to every whim and need. Dr. Spock *has* been misunderstood.)

We live in a complex, confusing world, and child rearing is no easy task. Just as it is not my role to tell others whom to marry, or whether or not to have children, so it must be up to each set of parents to determine *how* to rear their children.

The key to successful child rearing lies in meeting all of a child's needs—physical, mental, and emotional. (Those who would have me add the word "spiritual" will be heartened, perhaps, to know that I assume that that is part of meeting one's mental and emotional needs.)

As concerned citizens, living in this world shoulder to shoulder with others, we have—if only for selfish reasons—the need to grow more concerned about child-rearing practices. What we teach our youngsters, directly or indirectly, has a major impact on the quality of life. In fact, it has everything to do with our ability to walk the streets in safety. Perhaps making all parents responsible for properly rearing their children is a radical suggestion in the last quarter of the twentieth century. But somehow it must be done.

It is my feeling that all children should be assured of:

1. *Being wanted.* If not by their own parents, then by adoptive parents. Call it love, or by some other name, but children who are to develop into whole individuals must have it from the moment they arrive in the world. And better yet, from the moment of conception.

2. *Saneness.* Perhaps it is asking too much, but children need mentally healthy parents. If they had them, mental illness could be reduced within two or three generations, if not wiped out entirely.

3. *Roots.* Children need a sense of home and community. A feeling of belonging. U-Haul children too often are troubled children.

4. *Protection.* Children should grow up free from fear. They are not little adults who can fend for themselves. They are highly dependent in a difficult and often dangerous world.

5. *Nutrition.* How can a nation that spends more than $19 billion on alcoholic beverages annually, $12 billion each year on cigarettes, or $23 billion on advertising let children suffer from malnutrition?

6. *Discipline.* Every child must learn self-discipline to survive in our culture. This is true of creative persons as well as those who must work at hum-drum jobs.

7. *Freedom.* A child must have room to grow mentally, physically, and emotionally.

8. *Sensitivity.* The child who cannot feel what others feel will not grow up caring about others. Selfishness is, in the end, self-destructive.

9. *Laughter.* A child who cannot laugh is already partly dead. It is joy that proves life is worth living.

10. *Stimulation.* By this I mean "aliveness"—being a fully participating person in the world. Even the smallest infants need to be stimulated.

11. *Peacefulness.* Many city children and chronic television watchers have little peace. It is needed. We must somehow instill more calmness into our hectic lives.

12. *Integrity.* If a child is to grow up honest he needs honest parents and an honest world. This may be pie-in-the-sky idealism, but it is worth working for.

13. *Otherness.* To be mature a child must be aware of and care about others. Those who are egocentric lead limited lives.

14. *Uniqueness.* The world is large, and each individual has different

talents, interests, and ideas. Every child needs to know that he is an individual—worthwhile, unique, and of great value.

15. *Purposefulness.* It is not enough simply to live. A human being must have meaning or purpose in his life, and a child should be helped to find that purpose. A whole child lives for more than self-gratification.

16. *Creativity.* Self-expression is important to personal growth.

17. *Talent.* Every child has some talent or skill, but it must be uncovered. This is true of those who are retarded as well as all other youngsters.

18. *Dignity.* A child is a person, not a number, statistic, or pin in a map. He has, in America, equality with all other beings. Not in theory, but in fact.

In closing this chapter a point should be made: Child rearing, in the last quarter of the twentieth century, is not easy, but it is extremely important—both to the child and to our society.

11

"I'll mash your face in the sidewalk"

The winter sun streams into my third-floor study, past the green and flowering plants that line the window sill, reflecting from the cluttered white and gold counter top that serves as my desk, nearly touching the shelves of brightly colored books, warming the pine-paneled walls.

When I look up from my typewriter to stare out of the window at the snow-covered New Hampshire mountains, the world seems to be at peace. And yet when I stop to think about it (and I seldom do), I know that beneath the birches and maples, the spruce and pines, constant battle for survival goes on. Birds, small animals, and larger creatures live out a brutal, food-chain existence in the mountains.

In shutting out the violence of nature I use the same mental mechanism that wipes away the grim memories of institutions, jails, courthouses, homes, hospital emergency rooms, courtrooms, children's jails, probation offices, schools, clinics, back wards, and cruelty to children in city streets and along the back roads of America. To constantly remember what I have seen would produce too much pain. Yet to help these children I must somehow paint word-pictures that will touch the hearts and the consciences of middle-class Americans.

It is with this in mind that I write on, knowing that if the scenes are too vivid I will lose the more sensitive readers. Yet, unless my words are clear and strong, too many will miss the point that must be made. So I strive for a balance, hoping to help you feel the sense of urgency that presses down on me, yet also working to bring the optimism that I also feel. I remain confident that if the people of America understand the problems of unwanted children, and if they sense the direction our nation must go, they will find the push needed to produce change.

Having said that, I mentally depart from my mountain view and sun-filled study to plunge again into the cesspool world of unwanted children, promising—if you will follow—to resurface soon into the sunlight most of us live in.

Three-year-old Kevin died not long ago in his sobbing mother's arms. The young Connecticut divorcée beat the child to death with a shoe in a moment of overwhelming rage and frustration. State officials say they have fairly strong evidence against her, inasmuch as a neighbor tape recorded the thudding blows and screams through a thin apartment wall. But the neighbor did not intervene, nor did she call the police until after the child was dead. It was not the first time she had heard the child being abused. The records also show that Kevin had been returned to the mother a few weeks earlier by a Massachusetts welfare agency.

Another Connecticut child, a girl of eleven, died of strangulation. Her enraged mother forced a bar of soap down her throat, knocking the little girl's teeth out in the process. Earlier a sixth-grade teacher had noticed bruises on the girl's face and arms and had talked to the school principal. But no preventive action had been taken.

In Yakima, Washington, a woman told a welfare worker that her six-year-old niece had cigarette burns on her hands, arms, and the bottoms of both feet. A social worker sought state custody, got it, and placed the child in a foster home.

When a nine-month-old baby, left in the desert sun for hours near Tucson, Arizona, died, the mother—on a drug trip—buried the infant in the sand. A girl, also using drugs, made the report.

A private agency in Tucson was asked to care for an eighteen-month-old girl after she was forced to swallow a bottle of hot sauce by a father high on marijuana. The child's mother, fearing worse harm, asked the agency to take the baby for safekeeping.

In western Illinois a mother of four moved into a public housing project when her own parents left the city. A few months later a fifth child was born. At first the child's father paid support, but then lost his job. The baby's mother asked the welfare department for more money. The check was mailed after the woman filled out the required forms, but no social worker visited the home. Later, when the infant's father stopped by to see the child he found it locked in a dirty, cluttered room. The baby was malnourished and was suffering from a bleeding skin condition because no one had changed the diaper in days. The infant died in a hospital.

Welfare officials in western Oregon report that a fourteen-year-old girl asked to be put in a foster home. A social worker found that the mother believed that her daughter was "insane," and as a cure was forcing the child to take twenty vitamin capsules each day. Because of an overdose of the vitamin the girl's face was constantly flushed, she vomited frequently and suffered in other ways, according to the social worker who handled the case. When the mother refused to stop giving the girl the "cure" the court removed her from her home and placed her with a relative.

I met seven children in a group home in Indiana. All but one had been either neglected or abused, according to official records. But they were in the group home because they were "delinquent."

A child arrived at school in Connecticut with a black eye. When the police began checking, the father complained of harassment and the mother said the girl hurt herself during a "temper tantrum." It was found that the family had fled Massachusetts to avoid child-abuse charges. Before Connecticut officials could act, the family moved again—this time to Pennsylvania.

In Texas, a man running a children's home who was also a minister with a large radio following, openly admitted beating youngsters. When asked why, he quoted from the Bible. State officials have at last taken steps to close the children's home.

A Florida woman dipped a child's foot into a pan of boiling water when the child misbehaved.

These are not unusual reports. One finds abuse in the nation's largest cities, in the suburbs, and along rural roads of the North, South, East, and West. Some children die. Many are scarred or crippled for life. Millions suffer emotional scars.

Those who have studied the problem find many battered children are only a few days old. Much abuse takes place in the first three years, when children cannot communicate and find it hard to follow instructions. Parents call them "stubborn, unresponsive, difficult, or chronic criers." Many are considered below average in intelligence, but it isn't clear whether the child's mental problems existed before the battering began. Some studies show delayed language development, neurological damage, and other handicaps. Abused children also have been called "fearful, unappealing, apathetic" and lacking in interest in food or human contact.

Dr. Arthur H. Green, who studied sixty abused, thirty neglected, and thirty "normal" children in the New York City area, found both abused and neglected children had a higher level of anxiety, greater depression, more impairment of the thought processes, impairment of aggressive-impulse control, and more impairment of "overall ego competency" than children from the "normal" group. The damaged children also had poorer self-concepts, and experienced, in varying degrees, "impairment of reality testing, impairment of object relationships, impairment of defensive functioning impairment of body image, and organic impairment." Both neglected and abused children thought more about self-destruction than normal children, with the abused children the most likely to think about it.

One who reads such a report can quickly understand why so many abused and neglected children find their way into juvenile court, jail, reform schools, and mental hospitals. It is not so easy to understand why so many Americans suggest more punishment as the cure.

As I pointed out in an earlier chapter, child abuse has been a constant part of human history. Until the nineteenth century most parents apparently believed that beating children was God-ordained, and that it was the only way to rid them of evil. While most Americans scoff at quaint religious theories such as that, it is a fact that physical abuse is handed down from one generation to another.

It is difficult to prepare a profile of the battering parent. It can be either the mother or father. Some are rich, others are poor, but many fall somewhere in between. They are both young and old; educated or ignorant; married, unwed, or divorced; black, white, brown, or red; Catholic, Protestant, members of smaller groups or irreligious; and such parents may have large families or a single child.

Dr. John D. Madden, a pediatrician on the University of Chicago Medical School and Clinical Director of Pediatrics at Weiler Children's Hospital, believes that most abuse can be attributed to three basic factors: (1) emotional immaturity of the parent, (2) a family in crisis, or (3) parents who believe sparing the rod will spoil the child.

It is the emotionally immature parent (regardless of age) who most often severely injures or kills a child, Dr. Madden says. But he also believes that more affluent parents tend to have resources (baby-sitters, nannys, and other help that permits them to escape to the country club to hit golf balls rather than the children) available to them. The ability of a parent who feels uptight to get away from the children reduces child abuse, he adds.

Most experts agree that *all* parents are capable of abusing their children. Few children grow up without being spanked too hard or otherwise hurt one or more times. Is it so easy to be tense today (traffic, noise pollution, urban crowding, stock market problems, marital difficulties, employment problems, periods of political upheaval, street crime, or just a bad day at work) that most parents lose control now and then.

It also is true that many of us find it difficult to face up to our own flaws, or admit that we have abused our children. Like incest, abuse causes such great guilt that few will admit it—even to themselves. Yet, until we can face up to child abuse it is doubtful that we can do much to prevent it.

Nor are parents alone guilty. Children are abused by school teachers, principals, policemen, correctional workers, employees in other kinds of institutions, foster parents, baby-sitters, and by other children.

Dr. Vincent DeFrancis, Director of the Children's Division of the Denver-based American Humane Assocation, has found that while the traditional hairbrush is one of the more common implements used to batter children, adults also use "bare fists, straps, electric cords, TV aerials, ropes, rubber hoses, fan belts, sticks, wooden spoons, pool cues, bottles, broom handles, baseball bats, chair legs, and [in one case] a sculling oar. Less imaginative, but equally effective, was plain kicking with street shoes or heavy work shoes."

Dr. DeFrancis, a lawyer, also found in his studies that children had their extremities—hands, arms and feet—burned in open flames as from gas burners or cigarette lighters. Others bore burn wounds inflicted on their bodies by lighted cigarettes, electric irons or hot pokers. Still others were scalded by hot liquids. Some children were strangled or suffocated by pillows held over their mouths or plastic bags thrown over their heads. A number were drowned in bathtubs, and one child was buried alive, according to his findings.

"To complete the list, children were stabbed, bitten, shot, subjected to electrical shock, were thrown violently to the floor or against a wall, were stomped on, and one child had pepper thrown down his throat," he writes.

Another highly respected researcher, Dr. David Gil of Brandeis University believes after the analysis of some 13,000 child-abuse reports, that much abuse takes place because the use of physical force in dealing with children is so widely accepted in our culture. He suggests that as many as 2 million children are abused each year, although he adds that it is impossible to produce accurate statistics.

Of the 13,000 incidents investigated by his research team, well over half were clearly the result of angry adults punishing children in "response to actual or perceived misconduct," Dr. Gil reports. A related study conducted by the National Opinion Research Center at the University of Chicago indicates that hitting children, while not condoned in all cultures in the world, is widely approved of in present-day America.

"Rarely, if ever, is corporal punishment administered for the benefit of the attacked child," Dr. Gil says. "For usually it serves the immediate needs of the attacking adult who is seeking relief from his uncontrollable anger and stress."

My own findings support this, and I believe that this also helps explain why so many children have, through the years, been locked up in jail, reform schools, mental hospitals, institutions for the retarded and similar institutions. Not only do we seek relief from our anger and frustration by physically punishing children but we also find relief by sending the children away. It is worth noting that each year thousands of children are turned over to the court voluntarily by parents who see them as stubborn, ungovernable, or in need of supervision.

Fifteen years ago child abuse was a hidden problem in America. Early researchers depended upon infrequent accounts of abuse as a source of their data. This was in the early 1960s. Dr. DeFrancis and a handful of others brought the issue before the people of the nation and forced them to talk about it. Now new legislation has been passed in all fifty states, the District of Columbia, the Virgin Islands, and Guam.

But Dr. DeFrancis, Dr. Ray E. Helfer, Dr. Henry Kempe, and other pioneers found great resistance on the part of doctors, hospital officials, and others who were asked to report abuse. This resistance still exists. Reasons given vary. Some doctors fear they will lose patients if they challenge them on their children's injuries. Others ignore clear-cut evidence of abuse because they cannot deal with the problem emotionally—either because they have abused children themselves, or have felt angry enough to abuse them.

"Physicians, although aware of the need to uncover and correct family situations in which children are abused, are concerned whether reporting in the absence of statutory immunity will involve them in lawsuits with outraged parents," writes Monrad G. Paulson, of the Columbia University Law School and a leader in the field of law that deals with children. (See *The Battered Child*, University of Chicago Press, 1968.)

A growing number of states have now passed laws that solve this problem, and some go a step further by making doctors and others who *fail* to report suspected abuse liable for court action. Enforcement of the reporting law is spotty, but some doctors feel more comfortable about reporting because they can now tell parents and critics that they *must* report suspected abuse or face legal problems.

In some states, among them New York, officials are now required to take colored photos of all injuries in suspected abuse cases so that the photos can be preserved as evidence in court. Bruises fade, cuts and welts heal. It can take months to deal with abuse in the courts, although most states permit welfare officials to remove children from their homes until a hearing can be held.

Trauma experts are now found in many hospitals. X-rays can be used as evidence, and experienced and trained specialists can determine beyond a doubt which injuries were caused accidentally (e.g., falling down the stairs) and which were inflicted by angry adults.

If, as Dr. Gil suggests, more than 2 million children are abused each year, and if battering results in angry, sullen, disturbed, delinquent, or brain-damaged children, it is quite possible that there is a direct relationship between abuse and the American crime rate, climbing delinquency statistics, runaway problems, drug abuse, and many other ills of our society, for nearly every child I have interviewed in a jail or reform school has been abused to some degree.

But the amount of abuse may be even greater. Dr. John Caffey of Pittsburgh tells of hidden abuse—brain injuries that come from a form of battering that leaves no bruises or marks of other telltale evidence. And yet this abuse is so common that it takes place in schools, in parking lots, shopping centers, and the waiting rooms of pediatricians. Dr. Caffey is concerned with severe, "whiplash-shaking" of children. Shaking is a common method of dealing with a disobedient or fussy youngster in America. Such shaking results in a kind of "brain banging" (my term) inside the skull. And while it leaves no bruises or marks on the child's skin, as most battering does, the practice can result in "grave permanent damage" to the child's brain and eyes, it can cause mental retardation and even death, Dr. Caffey asserts. Such shaking also may injure a standing infant's legs or knees, he adds.

In the Tenth Annual Abraham Jacobi Award Address, at the 121st annual convention of the American Medical Association, Dr. Caffey adds that damage also can result from tossing a child into the air during play, from whacking him on the back too hard while "burping" him, from bouncing a baby too vigorously on one's leg, by swinging an infant from his ankles, by getting him to somersault while very small, and through other forms of rough play.

He warns sternly against children under the age of eight riding on snowmobiles, motorcycles, or even bicycles on rough roads. And he says young children should avoid contact sports such as boxing, wrestling, and basketball, for when "indulged in repeatedly," brain injuries result.

Like adult fighters who have been in the ring too long, children can become "punch-drunk or slap-happy"—developing "severe losses of

memory and impairments of judgment with speech and gait disturbances." The fighters experience these problems from being "repeatedly
jabbed and beaten over the head during years of exposure in the boxing
ring. . . . The cumulative pathogenic effects of repeated mild or moderate
whiplash-shakings of the head, though inapparent clinically, may be far
more grave than single, even if heavy, blows or punches to the head," Dr.
Caffey says.

Although there are no final statistics, he also finds evidence that "baby
bouncers and infant jumpers, and, for younger children, the swings,
seesaws, and playslides in amusement parks, the powered vibratory
training and practice equipment in gymnasia; powered cradles and
powered rocking horses; trampolines; skateboards and sled jumping," all
can contribute to the number of injuries.

He tells of one husky "nanny," very popular among the wealthy, who
allegedly killed several infants over a period of years by shaking them or
whacking them too hard on the back while burping them. This, he
suggests, shows that "even repeated murderous whiplash-shakings can be
concealed for years without arousing the suspicions of educated parents
and well-trained pediatricians."

Children are most vulnerable when they are very small, and yet we
tend to shake the smaller children rather than spank them. We also may
hurt an infant by trying to dislodge a foreign object from the throat or
mouth, or to stop violent coughing, or prolonged crying or whining, he
adds.

The problem exists because, while we understand that infants cannot
walk until their muscles develop, we forget that inside the head the brain
also must become securely anchored, the bones of the body and the skull
hardened, and other, less obvious muscles strengthened.

He concludes that infant deaths, brain damage, and mental retardation
might be substantially reduced in this country if jerking and whiplash-
shaking of children could be prevented.

This is startling news, since so many delinquents and disturbed children have been maltreated by adults during their early years. And yet
few researchers have tried to tie abuse, maltreatment, and early injuries
(deliberate or accidental) to these problems.

As suggested earlier, the battering of children is hardly new. Our
ancestors saw it as a virtue, believing it necessary to beat the devil out
of children. Yet, if child-abuse experts are right, these beatings were (and
are) the cause of mental and emotional problems in our society. Thus we
may beat the devil *into* children.

It also is believed that parents who were maltreated as children mal-
treat their children in turn, and that abuse is passed down from father to

son and from mother to daughter. This would suggest that the damaging and abnormal practice of beating children is, in fact, the historical norm for our culture. It would follow that the "crazies" are in control, and would explain why those calling for reform are so often beaten down.

This supports the theory of Dr. Gil, who studied child abuse and concluded that it is so common because physical punishment of children is so widespread in our society.

There are other factors to consider. Dr. Madden and others suggest that there is a clear and direct relationship between the length of time a mother is separated from the infant after birth and the way the mother later treats the child. He cites the "high incidence of abuse" of premature babies—separated from the mothers for weeks—as one proof of this.

In one case, for example, the premature baby was the mother's fifth child, he reports. It weighed only two pounds at birth. Later the child suffered a parent-inflicted fracture of the arm and skull. During an interview the mother told Dr. Madden that the baby "never smiles when I'm around. When I come into the room he stops talking." When asked to characterize the youngster in a single word, the mother said "stubborn." And she admitted having great difficulty holding the child.

"There is evidence that the initial contact between the mother and child can, in some ways, be equated with animal imprinting," Dr. Madden told me. Whatever the child feels because of separation, often the mother believes the child has rejected *her*, he continues. Dr. Madden, during our interview, produced a study along these lines as reported by Dr. Clifford R. Barnett an anthropologist who works with the Stanford University School of Medicine, in California.

There they permitted some mothers of premature infants to have physical contact with the babies, but followed normal hospital procedures with others—excluding the mother for from three to twelve weeks while the child was under intensive care.

In the magazine *Pediatrics* in 1970 the Stanford group reported on their findings: "[Through history] studies suggest that the timing and duration of [an] animal mother's earliest contact with her young are crucial in determining her later behavior toward her infant." In the case of animals, separation of the mother and infant at birth can result in poor mothering later. Using this as a guide, they concluded that the same can be true of human mothers.

Their pilot study suggests that lack of contact results in a weakening of the mother's "commitment to the infant, self-confidence in the ability to mother the infant, and behavior toward the infant."

The study, in fact, raises more questions than it answers. What does it mean when considering the role of the father? Or in terms of working mothers, day-care workers, teachers, adopted children, and institutional living? Can this help explain the maltreatment of children in institutions for the retarded, mental hospitals, reform schools, and homes for dependent, neglected, and orphaned children? Or are there other, more significant factors to consider?

There seems to be more than separation involved in physical abuse of children, although little is known about the early experiences of battered children, since information is collected *after* the battering, and those asking questions may miss key areas. But a number of studies show that most parents who hurt their children physically were either neglected or battered or maltreated when *they* were small.

"Without exception in our study group of abusing parents, there is a history of having been raised in the same style which they have re-created in the pattern of rearing their own children," writes Brandt F. Steele and Carl B. Pollock of the Department of Psychiatry at the University of Colorado School of Medicine, in the book *The Battered Child* (University of Chicago Press, 1968). During the research period, which lasted more than five years, sixty families of battered children were carefully studied. "Several [battering parents] had experienced severe abuse in the form of physical beatings from either mother or father; a few reported 'never having had a hand laid on them.' All had experienced, however, a sense of intense, pervasive, continuous demand from their parents."

Further, as children, the battering parents had been expected to always be good, submissive, obedient, and never to make mistakes. They also were expected to comfort their parents when the parents were distressed, and always to approve of the actions of their parents.

These parents, when children, were expected to act like tiny adults— not children. There was much stress on what others thought about the child's behavior, and fear that improper behavior would disgrace the parents. They grew up feeling unloved, and believed that their needs, desires, and talents, were ignored, unheard, unfulfilled, and "even wrong."

The Steele–Pollack study also suggests that parents who abuse or batter their children have missed out on "basic mothering," although the mother may have "hovered over" the child. Rather than giving it love, warmth, understanding, and support, she subjects it to demands, criticism, and selfish requests.

In many instances the researchers were able to trace this behavior back to the grandparents as well. "We believe we have seen this style of child rearing or pattern of parent-child relationship existing in three successive generations. Unwittingly and unfortunately, it is transmitted from parent to child, generation after generation," they write.

Proper mothering requires a mature, capable, and self-sufficient person who understands that the child is helpless, needy, dependent, and immature. Unlike children described as neglected, the battered child, according to the study, often is clean and properly fed and clothed. While the neglecting parent tends to be immature (regardless of age) and also wants to *take* from the child rather than give to it, there are differences between the neglecting parent and the battering parent. The neglecting mother will stop caring for the child, or reduce the amount of care given to destructive levels. Those who batter their youngster tend to give it basic care, but punish it for failure, or to make it "shape up" and perform better, according to Steele and Pollack.

In the book *Violence Against Children* (Harvard University Press, 1970) Dr. Gil writes:

"Six out of ten Americans think that almost anyone could at some time physically abuse a child in his care. The majority of Americans also show a rather tolerant attitude toward perpetrators of abuse, favoring treatment and supervision for them, and rejecting punishment. They think social welfare and health agencies, rather than law enforcement agencies, should carry primary responsibility for dealing with the problem of child abuse, and that abused children should be removed from care of abusive parents only as a last resort."

Dr. Arthur H. Green, a New York City professor and physician, notes that while pediatricians and radiologists have led the way in exploring "the age-old phenomenon of child abuse," psychiatrists did not recognize it as a clinical syndrome until 1962. And even now it has been "relatively neglected by the mental health field." In fact, Dr. Green believes psychiatrists and psychologists are two decades behind the physicians in exploring this field.

He notes that while most observers agree that parents who batter their children were themselves maltreated, a "wide spectrum of behavioral characteristics and psychopathology have been attributed to abusive parents. They have been variously described as immature, depressed, isolated from family and friends, impulsive, rigid and domineering, dependent and narcissistic, chronically aggressive, and prone toward marital difficulties," he writes.

One report suggests that abusive mothers are "masculine," while their husbands are "passive," he adds. " 'Role reversal' has been described, by which the abusive parent seeks out love and approval from the child."

There is speculation and some evidence that certain children, either because of hyperactivity or for other reasons, "invite" abuse. To help find answers, Dr. Green and other researchers) weighed all of the data available and then (developed a (series of tests, interviews, and other criteria to learn more about abuse.

Among other things, he found that battering mothers lacked help in caring for the children; had poor relationships with their own parents; were having marital problems; and often had been beaten by their husbands or boyfriends.)

He found fewer differences between neglected and abused children than had been expected, but noted that "mothers of the neglected children reported the highest percentage of unplanned pregnancies; the most frequent absence of a husband or male companion at home; and the most frequent loss of a mother or maternal guardian by death or abandonment during childhood." Neglecting mothers "also were found to suffer from the highest incidence of drug addiction, alcoholism, physical abuse and psychosis."

All evidence points to the causes of abuse being environmental—that is, it is learned behavior—rather than genetic or innate. The causes also seem closely related to family problems. With the family under attack and in trouble in America, with the emphasis on changing women's roles, and a push for zero population growth, it is easy to speculate on why the abuse rate is climbing. But during this same period there has been a great deal of publicity generated, and reporting of child abuse has improved a hundredfold.

And yet, too little is known about abuse.

A friend recalls riding on a Boston bus many years ago, watching a frustrated mother try to quiet a difficult little girl. The anger welled up within the woman, and then spilled over. "Shut up or I'll mash your face in the sidewalk," the mother shouted. At the time, my friend thought that the threat was an exaggeration that bordered on being humorous. But evidence today suggests that such a threat can be real. Worse things happen every day in America.

12

Daddy's Little Girl

Slick magazines print glossy pictures of male genitals and female pubic hair. Every conceivable sexual act is shown larger than life on theater screens. Homosexuals, long in hiding, now band together and openly fight for their rights. And thousands of young men and women live together without traditional bonds of marriage. Little is hidden today.

Why then are so many people unwilling to discuss the problem of sexual abuse of children?

One man, Vincent DeFrancis, stands almost alone in the fight to bring the problem of sexual abuse to the nation's attention. He has conducted conferences on the local, state, regional, and national levels. And yet too little happens.

"I believe there is fifty times, even a hundred times more sexual abuse than physical abuse of children in this country," he says in a worried voice. "Their cry for help is unheeded—it is unheard or ignored. These children are acutely in need of services to protect them against repeated offenses and to help reduce the effects of the traumatic occurrence."

As head of the Children's Division of the American Humane Association, Dr. DeFrancis also fights in behalf of battered children. Using federal funds, he also has conducted one of the few major studies of sexual abuse of children in history. And his background is both in law and research. Thus one cannot dismiss his words quickly.

I first learned of the incest problem in 1968, while visiting institutions

98

for children in Maine. At the reform school for girls I found that a third or more of the girls locked up had been sexually used by their fathers, stepfathers, brothers, or men close to the family.

As I read case histories and interviewed hundreds of children in institutions over a period of several years, I concluded that most cases of incest are hidden, and that incest is a major cause of girls becoming what we call "delinquent." Many victims run away from home, and no one asks why they have run.

The problem is hidden for many reasons. Incest is a strong taboo in our culture, and most girls (and boys) are afraid to tell authorities they are being used. Institutional workers tend to see their wards as "bad children," and treat complaints of incest as more lies, used to excuse deviant behavior. Institutional counselors (not to mention probation officers) are poorly trained, if they are trained at all, and have no way of evaluating or dealing with such information. Even those who want to help know that there is little they can do about a child's home. And many counselors, probation officers, social workers, and other "professionals" do not want to talk about such "dirty" subjects.

If Dr. DeFrancis has made a dent, it is in the field of social work. More protective service workers are now aware that the problem of incest exists.

Some, when they begin to deal with incest, discover a small flood of cases. Take the experience of Ms. Kathleen Prescott, who works for the welfare department in Coos Bay, Oregon. In a two-week period four cases came to her attention from a single high school.

It started when a distressed thirteen-year-old, living in another town in the area covered by the Coos Bay office, complained to a school friend that her father was using her and other children. The friend urged the girl to go to the sheriff for help.

The thirteen-year-old was being used sexually by the father whenever the mother, who worked, was out of the house. He first made her engage in intercourse when she was nine. More recently he had used his sons, eight and nine years old, in homosexual acts, and then involved his six-year-old daughter. Sometimes he used them individually, and often he encouraged group sex. When the girls pleaded with the mother to help stop the sexual abuse she became angry at the girls, and she said there was nothing she could do.

When the thirteen-year-old at last went to the sheriff, all four children were interrogated more than once. Then all were given polygraph tests. These convinced the deputies the children were telling the truth. Then the children were questioned again by the district attorney.

When word got out, the "mother was angry with the children and

blamed them for the whole thing," Ms. Prescott says. "The mother said, 'See what you've done to your father—he's going to be sent up for twenty years.' " There was great pressure on the children to change their stories, to say that they had lied.

Word also traveled through the school. A few days later another girl, this one fourteen, contacted the welfare department for help. This girl's parents had been divorced when she was two, her father was given custody, and he did not remarry. In time he began treating her like a wife. Now the girl wanted out. Ms. Prescott interviewed the girl at the school and concluded the problem was real enough. It was decided court action was the only answer.

First the girl told her story to a juvenile court counselor. Then she was asked to tell it again to the district attorney. Next sheriff's deputies interrogated her with a tape recorder running. Because officials decided to press changes against the father, the girl was asked to testify before a grand jury. Again she talked of her life, this time before friends and neighbors. When an error in the grand jury report was discovered, the girl had to appear before a new grand jury for questioning. Officials also gave her a polygraph test. The missing mother was contacted, and she agreed to care for her daughter. When the father was tried, the child had to testify before a judge and jury while her father watched. And, of course, the father's lawyer attempted to trip her up during cross examination.

"This was a quiet, withdrawn, meek and mild child when she came to us," Ms. Prescott says. "Somehow she had the courage to be direct; she looked the attorneys in the eye; her answers were quiet; and she gave straight answers. But when it was over she fell apart. Seeing a girl go through all of this really hurts."

During this period two more girls in the school sought "help." There is no way to know how many others were afraid to speak out.

Sexual abuse is not limited to girls or to incest. Hardly a day goes by in a city when police do not hear of a stranger opening his pants to expose himself to girls. Every year children are raped and even murdered by men the newspapers call maniacs. Some, like the celebrated Texas murders, involve homosexual acts and many children.

Until the Texas case, homosexual abuse was a subject hardly ever discussed in polite company. And even now little is said about father-son or mother-daughter relationships. One researcher, Dr. John W. Rhinehart, writing in *Comprehensive Psychiatry* in December 1962, suggests that the subject has been ignored "because it carries a double taboo."

I met Mike in a Texas mental hospital (Mike had no ties to the infamous mass-murder case in that state in 1973–74). He had been arrested as a runaway, and also had been accused of sexually assaulting several children, one a preschool nephew. This is Mike's story, verified by official reports:

My father first asked me to have sex with him when I was eight. I was too fearful to say no, and after the first time it happened three or four times a week. It was mostly oral—with the mouth, you know. Him doin' it to me, and me to him.

It was a pretty rough thing, you know. I consider myself a Christian, and here I am doin' that with my Dad. The first time, I didn't know what was happenin', really, but I got pretty upset. It just didn't seem right. But pretty soon I got used to it, and then I liked it pretty good.

My Dad is a tough guy. He's beat me with everything from a two-by-four to hoses, and he even slapped me around the head with a plastic garbage can lid. I ran away from home fifteen or twenty times. Sometimes I was picked up by the police, and they asked me a couple of times why I ran. I never said much. I just told them I had family problems. I was scared to say anything else, so they took me home.

One time after I came back he was mad as hell. He said "You think you're a man, don't you?" And then he made me try and fight. I'm a pretty big guy now, but that was when I was little. I didn't want to fight, and I just stood there and he whipped me with his fists, and when I couldn't stand it any more and fell down he picked me up and spit in my face.

Sometimes when he beat me my stepmother would come out and try to get him to stop. He used to beat her too. Twice after he beat me up he dragged me into their bedroom and made me have sex with her.

Once, after I had run away, I was sent to a children's home. But I got in trouble tryin' to have sex with one of the little boys, and they wouldn't keep me. Then I was sent to live with an aunt, and I got in trouble with my five-year-old cousin. When my aunt found out I didn't want to live anymore and I cut my wrists. There was a lot of blood, but after a while it stopped bleedin'. I tried to kill myself when I was little too. I took a whole bottle of aspirin. Two years ago I cut my stomach open with a razor.

I guess I need to be locked up. Sometimes out on the street I feel lust, and it makes me sick. I want to be a Christian. I want to live normal, like other people. I want to love a woman and get this homosexual feeling out of my mind. If they can't help me here I know I'll kill myself. I want to be dead.

Girls also face homosexual abuse. In a New York reform school I met a fourteen-year-old black girl who said she was a homosexual. She was introduced to the gay life when she was six by her mother's older sister.

Many professionals believe sexual abuse is cultural. A mental health worker in Kentucky told me that in the eastern end of his state, and in neighboring states, "a virgin is a girl who can outrun her brothers and father."

Sexual abuse is not unusual in the black ghetto, where a girl may be used by her mother's boyfriend. It also is found among the Spanish-speaking. But there is evidence that thousands of white, lower-class families have this problem as well.

Because so little research has been done, it is difficult to know how much incest is found in middle-class homes. Some speculate a great deal—hidden because of the "silent majority" tradition of this group of Americans. Isolated cases that surface suggest that it is there. But others say that just as more affluent housewives can hire baby-sitters and take out their anger on golf balls, so middle-class men sleep with their secretaries or pickups in bars instead of with their daughters.

In his study in New York City, published in 1969 by the American Human Association ("Protecting the Child Victim of Sex Crimes Committed by Adults"), Dr. DeFrancis examined 250 families where children were sexually abused. In a list of major findings he writes:

1. The problem of sexual abuse of children is of unknown national dimensions, but findings strongly point to the probability of an enormous national incidence many times larger than the reported incidence of physical abuse of children.

2. Natural limitations, built into the process of community case-finding, tend to associate the problem of child sex victimization with minority groups and economically deprived families, but the problem is not common solely to such families.

3. Children were subjected to sexual offenses of all types varying from such molestations as indecent exposure and fondling to full intercourse in rape and incest. Included in the range of sexual acts were sodomy, carnal abuse, and impairing the morals of a minor.

4. In 41 percent of the cases the offenses were repeated, and were perpetrated over periods of time ranging from weeks to as long as seven years.

5. Offenders were predominantly males ranging in age from seventeen to sixty-eight. They tended to victimize children of their own race.

6. In 75 percent of the cases the offender was known to the child and/or the child's family.

7. Victims ranged in age from infants to under sixteen. The median age was eleven. Victims were on a ratio of 10 girls to 1 boy.

8. In 60 percent of the cases the child was coerced by direct use of force or under threat of bodily harm, while in 15 percent of the cases the child was enticed by such tangible lures as money or gifts. In 25 percent of the cases the lure was more subtle, and was based on the child's loyalty and affection for a relative or near-relative.

9. In about half of the cases, children told parents or others of the

offense either immediately after it happened or within one day. In the remainder of cases the time lapse ranged from a week to three years.

10. The offense was reported to law-enforcement agencies in 82 percent of the cases studied; the balance to public health facilities, to school authorities, or some other service. (In the study, Dr. DeFrancis relied on known cases dealt with by government.)

11. Victims generally came from families with many children. Of the 250 studied, 93 percent lived with their natural mothers; natural fathers were found in 41 percent of the homes; and both natural parents in 40 percent.

12. When the study was made in the late 1960s annual family income ranged from $3,000 or less to more than $8,500.

13. Roughly a third of the 250 families of the victims were "broken homes," that is, death, divorce, separation, or desertion removed a parent. In some instances the mother had never married, and the children were born out of wedlock.

14. Because of the large number of broken homes, about half of the families in the study were supported by public welfare funds. (Again, it should be noted that only families that agreed to be interviewed were included in the study.)

15. Many of the families had a wide variety of problems which predated the sexual abuse report. Often the complexity of the problems tended to immobilize the families, preventing them from seeking help, at least until a crisis occurred.

16. Behavior indicative of psychological disturbance was identified in 41 percent of the parents. Such behavior included parental promiscuity, gambling, excessive drinking, use of drugs, criminal acts, and hostile-aggressive behavior directed at family members or others.

17. In half the families, one or more out-of-wedlock children had been born. In a third of the families the current sexual offense was not the first such occurrence—some other family member had been either offender or victim in an earlier offense. The mothers of the victims had, themselves, been victims as children in 11 percent of the cases. Fathers had been offenders as children—largely in cases involving other family members—in 10 percent of the cases.

18. The greater the family pathology the greater the tendency for the offender to be more closely related to the family. In families with lesser pathology the offender tended to more often be a stranger.

19. Most of the sexual offenses occurred directly or indirectly as a consequence of some parental dereliction of duty. Child neglect was found to exist in 79 percent of the cases. Most common was emotional

neglect. Physical abuse was found in 11 percent of the families. In 72 percent of the cases parents contributed to the sexual molestation by acts of omission, acts of commission, or by perpetration of the offense.

20. Of the 250 homes, 64 percent of the parents (or parent) were found to be inadequate, both by failing to provide care and by ignoring protection necessary for the child's welfare and safety.

21. Roughly 70 percent of the children who were victimized lacked the degree of maturity normal to their age group. Half were judged moderately emotionally immature, while 20 percent were considered grossly immature. The immaturity was most often the by-product of cultural deprivation, the result of limited experience and limited exposure.

22. Fewer than one-third of the parents, after discovery of the offense, took action out of concern for the child.

23. Most parents were more concerned about the disruption of their own lives than they were for the child victim.

24. The least child-oriented responses occurred in cases where the offender was a member of the household, a relative not in the home, or a person known to the family.

25. The parents who were "indifferent," "immobilized," or "self-oriented" in response to the sexual abuse that took place were most often those who shared their household with the offender.

26. Two-thirds of the child victims were found to have been emotionally damaged by the experience—52 percent assessed to be mildly or moderately disturbed; 14 percent found to be severely disturbed.

27. Feeling of guilt, anxiety, fear, and rejection contributed to the emotional disturbance the children felt.

28. When an unhealthy emotional climate existed in the home prior to the offense, the probability of damage to the mental health of the victim was higher.

29. The victim's emotional disturbance was manifested in problem behavior. In 55 percent of the cases it was identified as hostile-aggressive behavior; in 19 percent, delinquent or antisocial; and in 57 percent it was identified as school problems.

30. Of the 269 child victims in the study (of 250 families), 29 girls became pregnant as a result of the offense, producing added fear, anxiety, shame, and loss of self-esteem because of the highly visible condition and the extra responsibilities imposed.

31. When parents provided assurances and emotional security, the child victim more often escaped serious emotional damage. For a majority of the children, parents failed to provide this help. In fact, many parents, because of their own needs and deficiencies, contributed to the

tension-charged climate and to the emotional damage to the children.

32. The criminal code, which considers sexual abuse of children a crime, is intended to act as a deterrent to the commission of such crimes, but does not protect the child victim from the consequences of such crimes.

33. Police methods add considerably to the stress and tensions of the victim and the family member.

34. Of the 250 cases in the study, police made 173 arrests. Of that number, 106 offenders were released on bail or recognizance, and this resulted in many problems for the child victim, especially when the offender was a member of the household and returned home.

35. With few exceptions, parents of the victim were asked to file criminal charges against the offender and to swear to the truth of the complaint. These parents were often frightened; they had guilt feelings when relatives were charged; and many expressed resentment at being pressured into signing the complaint. Of the 173 complaints filed, in 48 cases parents withdrew the complaint after having signed it.

36. In the study sample, prosecutions were not initiated in 31 percent of the cases. Decisions not to arrest or prosecute the offender occurred at a ratio of 9 to 1 in Brooklyn as against the Bronx sample because of the interventive service of the Brooklyn Society for the Prevention of Cruelty to Children.

37. More than a thousand court appearances were required for the 173 cases prosecuted. This resulted in much stress and tension for the child, an inordinate dislocation of normal activities for the parents or parent, who appeared each time with the child, and created, in parents, strong resentments against the process and the people responsible for it.

38. Of the complaints filed, 44 percent were dismissed, most often because the penal code requires corroboration of the victim's testimony. When proof is lacking, initiating a prosecution and subjecting the child and parents to the ordeal of questioning and court appearances is a futile and meaningless exercise.

39. Half of the unfavorable reactions to the court and its staff were in response to what the court and court process did to the child. Parents felt the children experienced too many pressures, too many confrontations, and too much contact with other examples of criminal behavior.

40. Only in the Brooklyn portion of the study sample did a public or a private agency provide a "buffering service" for cases to be prosecuted and protective casework when warranted by assessment of possible neglect or abuse.

41. Intervention by the Brooklyn SPCC (Society for the Prevention of

Cruelty to Children) helped identify and provide services to families with gross problems, as well as to the children going through the experience.

42. While the needs of the children in the Bronx were the same, no services were available. Child victims of sexual abuse in the Bronx were left unaided and unprotected.

My own findings make it clear that it is not only in the Bronx that the victims of sexual abuse are "left unaided and unprotected." Even when trained social workers are involved, the laws of a state and the demands of police, prosecuters, and the courts can make the experience as damaging as the actual molestation.

In Rockford, Illionois, for example, one concerned professional told me that a good defense lawyer can make the most innocent victim look like an experienced whore, and that most often a jury will decide in favor of the father or other adult.

In California, a school teacher noticed a once happy girl acting strangely in class. Winning the girl's confidence, the teacher learned that her father was using her sexually. The teacher went to the principal, who contacted school administrators. They called the police, and it was decided that when the little girl's mother left the home the girl should call the teacher, who would tip off the police, so that they could catch the father in the act. Eventually the father was caught, but the strain on the girl was, to put it mildly, great.

Most often, as the DeFrancis study indicates, mothers side with the father in cases of incest. Social workers across the country told me that this was most often their experience. In my interviews I found that these mothers most often were considered "hard," they were believed to be sexually frigid, and some seemed to welcome giving up the marital bed to a daughter. Others feared scandal, worried about going on welfare if the father went to prison, or felt they were competing with the daughter for their husband's love.

One study which sheds some light on this was conducted in the early 1950s by Dr. Irving Kaufman and others at the Judge Baker Child Guidance Center in Boston. The study, which was reported in the *American Journal of Orthopsychiatry* in April 1954, concerned eleven girls and their families. The "age at which incest began ranged from six to fourteen years."

In most cases the incestuous relationships lasted a "year or more," and in one instance "as long as six years." In two cases the mother reported the problem to authorities, and in the remaining cases it was discovered by accident when, for example, a neighbor reported child neglect.

Of the eleven girls, five had sexual relations with their natural fathers, and two other fathers were suspect. It did not seem to matter whether the act was committed with a natural father or a father substitute. All experienced a sense of "depression and guilt," and some suffered from pregnancy fantasies and other discomforts. All but one of the girls developed "specific or general learning disabilities" apparently as the result of the incestuous relationship.

Seven of the girls were given psychological tests, and all saw their mothers as "cruel, unjust, and depriving." Most also had problems with their own sexual identification.

As for their mothers and fathers, in almost every instance, both had left home at an early age to "escape their unpleasant environments." All came from "backgrounds characterized by poverty, alcoholism, little education, inadequate housing, and little warmth or understanding" from their own parents (the victims' grandparents). Most fathers worked at casual jobs and tended to be absent from their families through separation or work that took them away from home for long periods.

When researchers first interviewed the mothers they saw them as "hard, careless in dress and personal appearance, infantile, extremely dependent and intellectually dull." Other generalizations included "poor housekeepers, panicky in the face of reponsibility. . . . " And yet over a period of time the mothers "emerged as brighter than average with a potential of achievement far beyond their actual performance. They married men who were also dependent and infantile. If they married a second time, the second partner was even more irresponsible and unsuccessful than the first. This was a repetition of the pattern set by the maternal grandmothers."

The study found the maternal grandmothers of the child victims to be "hard workers and masculine in character. As a rule they assumed most of the responsibility for the support of their families and gave their children good physical care but little real warmth and understanding." The maternal grandmothers also were seen as "stern, demanding, controlling, cold and extremely hostile women, who rejected their daughters and pampered their sons."

The mothers of the victimized girls constantly wanted to return to their own mothers, hoping to "receive the love and encouragement they never felt." They also had a strong sense of "worthlessness." Many of the mothers were hostile toward women in general, and toward their own daughters when confronted with evidence of incest.

Another researcher, Dr. John W. Rhinehart, a Yale professor, writing in 1961 in *Comprehensive Psychiatry*, concluded that those caught up in cases of overt incest were "extremely immature personalities ill-equipped to adequately fill parental and responsible roles intelligently and effectively. Serious disorganization of family structure and the breakdown of social taboos ensued."

In a California study, published in *Psychiatric Quarterly* in January of 1955, researchers, headed by Dr. Karl Mr. Bowman, found the victim's mother to be "masochistic."

Often she is married to a helpless, dependent man whom she has to support, or to a strict, demanding man who permits her little individual expression. Frequently she is divorced or separated from the victim's father.

The mother is masochistic in her attitude to her daughter. She feels harassed by her daughter and unable to handle her. If she has other children, she feels closer to them. She describes her daughter's moodiness and uncooperative attitude, maintaining that her daughter is spoiled because she had been overindulged. She describes the sacrifices she makes for her daughter and her daughter's ingratitude. She complains that her daughter has a winning way with adults which conceals her real selfishness. It is not hard for the interviewer to detect jealousy of the daughter in the mother's comments.

The typical mother is at least as critical of herself as she is of her daughter. She vacillates between criticizing herself for strictness and criticizing herself for leniency. She feels that her strictness and her lack of understanding of her daughter have contributed to the child's difficulties; but, also, that she has spoiled her daughter by being too lenient. If her husband is strict and punitive toward the child, she vacillates between supporting his strict attitude and protecting the child from him.

Often, the mother is in conflict, not only about strictness and leniency, but also about her attitude toward the child's developing sexuality. She feels that she should teach her daughter more than she has taught her about sex, but cannot do so because of embarrassment. At times she feels proud of her daughter's attractive appearance and winning ways, but at other times she labels her a "flirt" or a "prima donna" and fears that the child's attractiveness will lead her into sexual difficulties in adolescence.

The child victim sometimes was caught between parents with differing sexual attitudes, according to the study. Her father might stand nude before the little girl, and the mother then expressed her disapproval. The father sometimes aroused the daughter when she was very young, by kissing her, fondling and wrestling with her. Some victims even watched parents having sexual intercourse. Mothers, in some instances, frequently warned daughters about men and the sexual consequences of getting close to them.

Even though these children can best be classified as seductive or actively involved in the events that resulted in incest, they felt guilt, and suffered from phobias, anxieties, and nightmares, according to the report.

As in the other studies, almost all of the children felt "deprived by their mothers and resentful toward them."

"Through sexual relations with adult men, they expressed their defiance of their mothers and gained a feeling of independence. At the same time they satisfied their longings for approval and attention," according to the report.

In 1961 Dr. Marvin Hersko and others at the Wisconsin School for Girls published a study of three girls and their families. The girls, according to the report in *Corrective Psychiatry and Social Therapy*, avoided female staff members and sought out male employees.

In the case of these three girls, the problem began in their early years. "All of the mothers were unable to meet their daughters' needs for dependency gratification. The girls, therefore, sought such gratification from their fathers. The fathers, because of personal inadequacies, which were further aggravated by the wives' rejections, tended to sexualize the relationships with their daughters. Each of these men, in fact, took advantage of their daughters' craving for love by making sexual activity the price for gratification of affectional needs."

All three mothers were aware that incest "had been going on for at least five years," yet "they made no attempt to inform the authorities or to obtain a divorce. The father-daughter incest seemed to relieve them of their feminine duties, give them an opportunity to rationalize some of their inadequacies as mothers, and served as a weapon they could use against their already inadequate husbands."

All three fathers, "to compensate for feelings of weakness and inadequacy," tried to put up "a powerful front, frequently acting toward their families in an aggressive manner." Often the children were brutally beaten.

There seems to be limited difference between fathers who use their children sexually and men often called "exhibitionists" or "child molesters"—the strangers who expose themselves, or friends who fondle, kiss, caress, or commit fellatio on boys or cunnilingus on girls.

Writing in the publication *Diseases of the Nervous System* (February 1962), Dr. Eugene Revitch and Dr. Rosalee G. Weiss characterized sex offenders who passed through the New Jersey State Diagnostic Center as men "who are emotionally immature, physically underdeveloped, or have mental defects," and those who "are in a state of regression such as loss of potency, alcoholic inebriation, and early senility."

Pedophilia—the erotic craving by an adult for a child of the same or opposite sex—is clearly a problem in America. But we must change our views about it and find better methods of dealing with it.

"The stereotype of the sexual offender against children is the pervert who lurks at a school yard to lure a child into his car," Dr. DeFrancis says. "This does happen. But such cases are in the minority. In 75 percent of the cases, the offender is a member of the child's own household, a relative not in the household, a neighbor, a friend or a person in the community with whom the child has frequent contact."

He also suggests that women also "may sexually exploit younger boys," but the cases are seldom reported, for the boys do not see themselves "to be victims."

It is not just the act that is reprehensible, according to most researchers. Rather, it is the emotional impact the experience has on children who are used sexually.

As a first step, we must face up to the fact that sexual abuse of children is a major problem in America. A problem that may be larger than physical abuse.

Then we must find more humane ways of dealing with it. Dragging a child through a series of interviews, hearings, and a trial may well be as destructive as the abuse itself.

13

Through a Glass Darkly

If physical and sexual abuse of children are hidden problems, consider emotional abuse. Few Americans have ever heard of it. Yet emotional abuse occurs daily in millions of homes, including many that are considered, by the community, to be "good homes."

Emotional abuse can be found in upper-middle-class families as well as in the hovels of the poor. Large numbers of teachers, principals, judges, probation officers, and other professionals also, though unwittingly, engage in it, damaging children in many ways. Through constant criticism, unreasonable demands for high levels of performance, ridicule, emotional and physical neglect, lack of early childhood stimulation, pressure always to be "good," labeling, harsh treatment, or worse, children develop poor self-concepts. Yet we live in a competitive society that demands confidence, creative ability, and a positive outlook for success.

The emotionally abused child may see himself as inadequate, unable to measure up to his parents' demands, or may believe that he is a "bad" child, or that he is stupid, inferior, or worthless. He may merely conclude that he causes family problems, or he may become fearful or hostile. The reaction to emotional abuse varies.

Many emotionally abused children simply fail to reach their full potential as adults. Others run away from home, drop out of school, escape through drugs or alcohol, become promiscuous, shoplift, assault others, or engage in vandalism or other acts frowned upon by our society. The

111

more severely abused may become delinquent, insane, or commit suicide.

Even while knowing this, it is hard to discuss emotional abuse, for our society has given it little thought. One must begin with words like neglect, dependency, deprivation, delinquency, low achievement, and insanity. For laymen and professionals alike such words can be less than precise. Differences may depend upon whether you are Freudian, Skinnerian, or something else. Or even upon whether you are a liberal or conservative. Abuse to one may be proper treatment to the other.

Most often in our society the *victim* of emotional abuse is seen as the *offender*, a person who should be punished, forced to face up to his shortcomings, sent to a reform school or mental hospital. Both professionals and laymen want to "cure" the *child*. After the cure has been administered we return the child to the same home, school, and neighborhood that produced the disorder. Then we wonder why the cure has failed.

A thirteen-year-old girl who lacks love and attention at home may become sexually involved with many boys while searching for love. But we do not understand her need. Rather, we brand her as a tramp—deserving whatever befalls her. And should she have a child out of wedlock, we curse the infant as a "bastard"—as if the baby was also at fault. And thus we transmit emotional abuse to another generation.

The child failing in school because the school cannot meet his needs is labeled "slow," "stupid," or retarded. Then when that boy seeks recognition through boisterous behavior he is seen as a troublemaker or worse and is punished or put out of school.

Delinquent children have problems at home, at school, and with their peers. But try to explain this to a woman who has had her purse snatched. She wants "justice," which means "vengeance." (One should not lack sympathy for victims of crimes. Damaged children can be dangerous. But abusing the abused is hardly a cure.)

To discuss the subject of emotional abuse we must begin by defining terms. *Dependency* is a logical starting point.

Arthur Mandelbaum, a social worker with the Menninger Foundation and clinic in Topeka, Kansas, writes:

Dependency is one of the basic characteristics of the human condition, one of the "rules of the world," an inevitable part of birth, infancy, childhood, adolescence, adulthood, old age, and yes, showing its power even in death. Throughout each stage of human growth and development, dependency needs take on new forms, new intensities, new colorations, in orderly sequence within which for each individual there may be great variation; but the pattern is basically the same for all human beings.

What is dependency? It is need, it is trust, it is reliance, it is consistency, it is cohesion, contact, interchange. It is that component in a relationship which allows two individuals to come together when they need each other, and freedom to separate when they do not. It is that component of love, that when given freely, warmly, responsively, enables each individual involved to give of himself to others to the end of his days. It is imperishable and it is prolific.

For some the poetry in Mr. Mandelbaum's definition may prevent a serious reading. But it covers much ground, stressing the fact that dependency is ongoing throughout life, but is related to such important intangibles as love, contact, and sharing.

In his popular paperback *How to Raise a Human Being* (Warner, 1973), Dr. Lee Salk uses another intangible term—trust—to help describe dependency and the impact of the care that is so much needed by children. He writes that "if an infant's earliest needs for food and comfort, contact and stimulation are gratified in the state of total dependency, he develops a sense of trust that becomes the basis for learning to move around on his own, away from his mother, at a later point in childhood."

Whether dependency is love, trust, the need for human contact, or much more, there can be little doubt that all small children are dependent, and that deprivation of their needs at this stage results in a variety of problems. What happens to the child in his first dozen years (some say six, others three) will have a major impact on the rest of his life.

Dependency is best tied to the word *need*, and that need is the same for all children. However, it also is obvious that some children are more dependent than others. The retarded child is slower to stand, walk, talk, and to care for himself. Those classified as profoundly retarded may lie in the fetal position, whimpering and infant-like, even when their bodies have long been fully developed and their hair has turned gray from old age. Others never progress beyond crawling and spend their days on the floor and in giant cribs, with stuffed animals tied to the rail. Some classified as retarded, on the other hand, can live alone in the community with minimal supervision and protection from society's sharks.

As for disturbed children, some live in a fantasy world, while others express uncontrollable anger, overwhelming fear, crippling depression, or mental confusion. Many others are simply "hard to handle."

Few persons with normal hearing comprehend the dependency of the deaf child. Yet without early help the deaf child may not understand that there is such a thing as language until he is seven or eight years old. While he can see, he cannot hear, danger. And a deaf child has no way of understanding why he is hurt or punished.

We are more sympathetic toward the child who is blind, and for many blind children overprotection is a problem. It is easy to make too much of a blind child's dependency because most of us are terrified at the thought of losing our sight.

We also understand the dependency of the crippled child, and we react with pain when we see a crippled child watching others run and play.

Until recent years, most girls were taught to be dependent and submissive. While this barrier has been broken, it has not been destroyed. Thus dependency also can be artificially maintained for cultural reasons.

The word that most logically follows dependency on the list is deprivation. And deprivation is not the same as neglect, for neglect implies indifference. Deprivation suggests a less intentional withholding of something a child needs.

Millions of American children suffer from various forms of deprivation. The premature infant kept in isolation is deprived of basic bonds to the mother. The child born in poverty may be deprived of food, clothing, adequate shelter, protection from rats and insects, and of other basics, even while getting love and attention. The child born to affluent parents may be deprived of parental love and attention, even while living with a surplus of material things.

Schools that stifle creativity deprive children of the opportunity to develop the faculty of original thought. Permissive parents who fail to set limits or refuse to give children some measure of responsibility may deprive the youngster of self-control and self-discipline—two key ingredients in a creative life.

The word that most logically follows dependency on the list is deprivation. And deprivation is not the same as neglect, for neglect implies to, or to bind up wounds—physical or emotional—suffered during the day. Highly successful executives, who live in the Amazonian villages of suburbia, may deprive their sons of the proper role models, and their daughters of the opportunity to learn of healthy male-female relationships, or to understand the masculine mind.

The children of famous men and women often are deprived of the opportunity to develop a sense of individuality, freedom, or independence. Those with rich fathers may never understand the meaning of individual achievement.

Deprivation is limiting and damaging, but it is often the result of thoughtlessness, ignorance, or other mitigating circumstances. Deprivation is more passive than active, while *neglect*, the term used by the courts when dealing with the problems of parents and children, is behavior that carries with it the force of blame. It too may be the result of ignorance, lethargy, poverty, or negative social pressures, and the results may very well be the same as deprivation.

Neglect most often refers to refusing to meet basic *physical* needs that a parent is expected to provide for his child. Because a child is dependent he must have his diaper changed, his nose wiped, a nipple thrust into his mouth, his room warmed, his bed supplied with a firm mattress and freshly washed sheets. The toddler who wanders barefoot through the snow is not just deprived, he is neglected. When a child lives in filth, is denied food through laziness of because the mother is drunk, or is left alone all day, the mother can be charged with neglect, and the child often will be removed from the home by the court.

(It is interesting to note that this has not always been so. My great-aunt, who was raising children a century ago on the Iowa prairie, did not think it unusual to leave a preschool child home alone all day in a rustic farmhouse when she went to town in a wagon for supplies, or when she was asked to care for a neighbor suffering from a contagious disease. She would put a bowl of milk and a loaf of bread on a chair and be confident the child would survive until she returned.)

Our neglect laws are based upon standards that might best be called "normal" for our culture. It is, I believe, for this reason that seldom does emotional neglect appear on the law books. Little thought is given to a child's mental or emotional needs by judges, lawyers, or legislators—unless an act involves the violation of a moral code. It is as if children existed only in body, and that their emotions or mind played no significant role in their behavior. (Perhaps one reason why there is so little concern for what children watch on television.) Stopping parents from damaging children emotionally seldom crosses the legislative or legal mind. Instead, emphasis remains on manipulating or "reforming" the deviant child.

Take Shawn, a fifteen-year-old serving time in a South Carolina reform school. A high-strung, angry child, I found him, while making a film on delinquents, in a solitary confinement cell. He needed solitary as much as an accident victim needs kicking and beating. Shawn's father abandoned the family when Shawn was small. His mother, a gray, bitter woman, was so filled with hate she could not love Shawn, and was constantly nagging him. He could do nothing right. Because of his behavior, the public school he attended often removed him from the classroom. Eventually absorbing his mother's anger, he hit a neighbor's child, showed no remorse, and the judge sent him to the reform school.

Only love and kindness will make Shawn whole. Solitary confinement only makes him harder to reach. Instead of meeting his needs, those hired by society to solve such problems locked him up. Because he ran away from the institution, he was confined in a small, blue cell hardly larger than the average bathroom. All in the name of "therapeutic treatment."

Sadly, laws make it impossible to follow Shawn's career. But surely he will join others similarly treated in prison or mental hospital, a burden to society for much of his life. How far have we come from the era that saw witches locked up, burned or drowned?

Why do we return to what can best be described as the "devil theory" when it can be shown that a child's behavior reflects his physiological and emotional state? A child who touches a hot stove may scream and jump about in a very strange way. Taken out of context, we might conclude that the child is insane or, to use the more ancient term, "possessed." Yet if we had watched him touch the hot stove we would feel his actions were normal. But we do not understand that when a child is emotionally "burned" day after day, at home or at school, that he too will react in a deviant way, or that his behavior is normal in an abnormal environment.

The ridiculed child, failing at school, rejected by his peers, mistreated at home, cannot hope to grow up open, back-slapping, friendly, enthusiastic, loving, or sensitive. And yet we demand that of him. It is not unlike demanding a crippled child to spring from his wheelchair and run, jump, and pole vault.

So many thousands, even millions, of American children are victimized emotionally. They are cursed and blamed for things done to them by adults, men and women who would never consider punishing a child for contracting measles or a heart disease.

Emotional abuse, while it must be considered, like murder, by degree, is best described as cruel and inhuman treatment of a dependent person.

Take the case of Phil, a sometime truck driver and alcoholic, who lives in Michigan. His father is an inadequate man who is intellectually bright but who has failed to gain recognition through work, and has failed to achieve the material success that he so much desires. Throughout his adult life, Phil's father has put up a phony front, spending much-needed money for clothing, parties, and booze, living in a high style while depriving his family of basics. With deep-seated emotional problems, the father cannot tolerate competition from other males—even small boys. His stock in trade is the put-down, the sarcastic remark, the cynical sneer, or blatant criticism behind the backs of other men.

Until Phil was fourteen, and passed the six-foot mark in height, his father controlled him with physical force. A strong, pleasant boy, Phil was, like many other teen-agers, a bit clumsy, struggling a bit in a rigid school, and having problems with reading and math.

It was at the time when the father could no longer control Phil by physical force that he began to call the boy "Big Stupe."

"Hey, Big Stupe, come to supper," he would say. "When are you gonna mow the lawn, Big Stupe? If you weren't so dumb, Big Stupe, I might teach you how to drive the car."

Phil's father made the name stick. His wife was too weak to stop him. Her weakness and instability added to Phil's problems.

For two years Phil suffered from constant humiliation in silence. His grades continued to drop at school, his reading ability did not improve, and he was having trouble with male teachers. It was after Phil turned fifteen, and was nearly six feet five inches tall, that he decided that he had had enough. He began running wild, drinking heavily, was arrested for assaulting other youths, and once knocked his father down and felt no remorse.

Phil's parents took him to court, and the boy was sent to an institution. The country club set felt sorry for the parents, for it all was embarrassing and too much to put up with.

Phil never finished school, is now an alcoholic, and sometimes drives the truck his guilt-ridden father helped him buy when he could find no other work. While details may differ in other cases, Phil's story is hardly unique.

Mrs. Carry Minkler, a social services caseworker and supervisor in Mendocino County in northern California, tells of a brother and sister who were damaged by emotional abuse.

John is thirteen and Liz is eleven. Their father, who could not support his family because he was disabled in an accident, died when they were ten and eight. At the time of his death their mother left the children with her parents and moved to the southern part of the state.

The grandfather is able to bring home a substantial paycheck because he often works overtime at a factory. The grandmother is a former "therapist" at a state mental hospital. The state pays them to care for the children through ADC (Aid to Dependent Children). The grandparents had three children of their own. One committed suicide, a second died in an accident, and the third is the runaway mother of John and Liz.

Both grandparents live in a "boozy haze" much of the time, says Mrs. Minkler. Although the youngsters go to school, they are confined to the house when they are not in school, and they are not permitted to play with other children in the neighborhood. The blinds are kept drawn in their house, and the feeling inside is "dark, gloomy, and depressing," she adds.

It is difficult for the grandmother to talk about anything but her troubles, and Mrs. Minkler characterizes a typical conversation with her as "morbid." "She goes to great lengths to describe in great detail the horrible events she and her family have experienced," she explains.

Several years ago, when the children were smaller, the grandmother was able to get a doctor to prescribe tranquilizers for the children because they were "hyperactive." Both are forced to take them, and are sometimes zombie-like. Much of the rest of the time the boy, John, entertains himself by tormenting his sister.

"He picks at her, pokes her, teases her," Mrs. Minkler says. "It can go on for hours at a time."

John and Liz came to the attention of the welfare department when the grandmother asked that they be cared for in a foster home while she had an operation.

Officials were forced to return the children when the grandmother recovered. And there is little that can be done for John and Liz at present, for they have adequate food, the house is clean, and they are not physically battered by the grandparents.

"Under the law all we can do is ask them if they want our services," Mrs. Minkler says. "It is rather obvious that they are being emotionally damaged. But there is nothing we can do about it when the grandparents turn down our offers to help."

One can find similar reports in every community.

A seventeen-year-old Arizona boy, whose older brother is retarded, "acts retarded" although he has an IQ of over 110. Officials are uncertain whether it is an attention-getting mechanism or whether he really believes he is retarded. The youth was neglected by his parents, who spent all of their time and energy trying to care for their retarded son.

In Albuquerque, New Mexico, Wayne Holder, an able young welfare official, told me of a five-year-old Indian boy, born out of wedlock, who was "rescued" by welfare officials at the age of two from a mother described as "immoral, living in poverty, filthy, unable to care for her son." The child was placed in a foster home, and three years later the foster parents have asked to adopt him. The mother wants him back.

"Now everybody has a lawyer," Mr. Holder says. "The boy is caught in a power struggle. The Indian community is involved, at our request. The youngster, who has known two mothers in five years, is confused."

In a tug of war, the child feels the tensions. Long court delays add to the confusion. And one attorney predicts that the case may "go all the way to the Supreme Court."

Kathy, a sixteen-year-old girl from Arlington, Virginia, ran away from home "just to get out of the house." A beautiful girl, her parents were "so afraid I'd get pregnant" they refused to let her date, attend dances or parties, or even to leave the house without an adult. When Kathy refused to return home, the judge sent her to the training school where she has had several homosexual experiences, and, by her own admission, is the "most popular girl on the grounds."

"I got everything I asked for from my parents except trust, love, and affection," Kathy told me. "I tried to hurt them and I messed up my life."

What can social workers, mental health officials, and others do to prevent neglect, emotional abuse, or mere deprivation? After talking to dozens of professionals in some forty-five states I found that few have answers. The laws may permit them to remove a child who has been battered, after the battering takes place, or when gross physical neglect can be proven. But in most states little is done for the emotionally abused child. And there is some evidence that more children then even before are becoming emotionally disturbed.

"Many children we get come from what you might call 'character disordered' families," says John Ely, who has charge of services to children for the Connecticut state welfare department. "Many of the children we see today are more damaged and face more serious problems than any I have seen in my twenty-three years with the department.

"I know one mother, a heroin user, who has been in and out of mental hospitals and prison," he says. "Her son is five and we have him in foster care. We are unable to terminate parental rights, and we haven't been able to keep her from visiting the boy. I can't begin to describe the problems that little fellow faces."

In Connecticut alone there are more than 7,000 children in foster care—private homes. The children have faced great deprivation, their own homes are extremely disorganized, their parents are so caught up in their own problems they cannot begin to meet the needs of their children. Other parents simply disappear, leaving welfare workers unable to terminate parental rights, but taking no responsibility for the child. And welfare workers fail too.

"Right now I know of eleven hundred kids who just drift along, who get few services, who have no help with the problems of rejection, no help with their identity crises, and all the other things this kind of child faces," he says. "The parents aren't interested in helping, the foster parents are largely untrained, and the children are in limbo."

If they are in limbo in Connecticut, a fairly progressive state, what is the situation in the rest of the nation? It is almost too depressing to think about. We have no accurate count of the children taken from parents who have been abandoned, temporarily dumped, or "lost" in the welfare system. But the number runs into the hundreds of thousands.

Welfare workers are too often untrained or poorly trained. They live with few guidelines and operate from need, rushing from one crisis to another, using whatever skills they have. The judges who make decisions base their decision on personal whims, on the majesty of the law, or upon resources available.

Millions of children are emotionally abused each year who never meet a welfare or mental health worker. They are hidden from the world because they still have families, and (with good reason) families are sacrosanct in America. So little is known about how to parent, and the magazine columnists and "popular" experts have done so much to confuse parents, that many have lost sight of common sense.

But why can't we at least help the most damaged children? Case-finding is a problem. And once the children are identified, what do we do with them? There are too few foster homes, and foster care is often damaging, for foster parents move away, become ill, or decide they cannot put up with a child. It is bad enough to be jerked from your own home, feeling rejected and unloved. But how must it feel to be shuffled from one foster home to another, being rejected over and over again?

Professionals do not have the magic solutions that some of them pretend to have. Institutions are not the answer. A good, small facility can cost $20,000 a year per child—and then they make no promises to undo the damage the child has experienced. Group homes are one answer. But there are poor group homes as well as good ones. And in many neighborhoods property owners fight against bringing six or eight children into the area.

Even *finding* severely damaged children is difficult. For many years social workers have believed that the only families they could help were those who *asked* for help.

"As the profession of social work began to incorporate psychoanalytical concepts into its knowledge and practice, the notion that a person's ability to ask for help was an indication of his ability to benefit from help began to hold sway," writes Annie Lee Sandusky, a consultant to the federal Department of Health, Education and Welfare in the publication *Children* (January 1960). "As a result, if an individual needed help he had to ask for it. For many years most social agencies would not reach out to offer help to people who did not request it even though their need was evident.

"The very nature of neglect problems prevents the people involved from asking for help. Being a *good parent* is one of the highest attainments and basic expectations of our culture. To admit failure in one of the most fundamental aspects of human relationships—that of parent and child—is a terrible onslaught on the ego. Most neglecting parents cannot come to a social agency and say: 'Help me—I am neglecting my child.'"

Because of the heavy load of guilt parents may carry, bolstered by our society's tendency to blame and punish, it is even harder to face the fact that you are abusing your children emotionally, sexually, or physically.

In his study of neglected and abused children, Dr. Arthur H. Green, of the Downstate Medical Center in Brooklyn, found little difference between abused and neglected children, except that the abused child gave more thought to destroying himself. He concluded that abuse and neglect are important causes of retardation, learning problems, and mental illness in this nation.

It is possible, just possible, that this also helps explain why members of minority groups continue to struggle, and find it hard to compete with white children. I have found that, like poverty-level whites, black and Spanish-surnamed children are more likely to be maltreated than middle-class youngsters.

It would seem prudent of so-called scientists who travel the country talking of how minority group members are genetically inferior to examine *all* the facts. If they bothered to look at the children as I have, they would be inclined, I believe, to pay more attention to the impact of widespread abuse and neglect on these children.

14

The Troubled Years

What qualifies a person—beyond a great deal of research—to write a book on children? Among other things, experience. I have been foster father to several children, and I still have stepchildren, adopted, and natural children at home.

My children will tell you that my finding my tools scattered across the driveway and lawn, especially in a rainstorm, may cause me to raise my voice. When children tie curtains in my camper in knots, the better to see out of the windows, I take my stand. While the late A. S. Neill may have been able to watch his wards rip apart the furniture with equanimity, I cannot. And there is a limit to the rudeness I will tolerate. Those who, in the name of child advocacy, encourage bratty, uncivil behavior or worse, are, in my view, doing a disservice both to the child and society. Children have rights, but like the rest of us, they must understand that those rights have limits.

My first experience in working with teen-agers came when I was in my twenties. My father died at a fairly early age, and soon I was asked to rear one of my five younger brothers, a lad of fourteen. Because he was a rather normal middle-class youngster, a boy struggling still with his father's death, we lived through a period of testing and rebellion.

Several years later I was amply rewarded when he wrote me a thoughtful letter, as a young college student, thanking me for both standing firm and for being patient. Watching him grow and mature, helping others along the way, also has been satisfying.

A few years later I became "father" to several girls in an institution in Maine—although we seldom saw one another. One of them, an adopted girl, had run away from home. When her adoptive parents decided they didn't want her back, she was locked up.

Three years later my wife and I played "Mom and Dad" at her high school graduation because her parents refused to attend. She was awarded a scholarship, won her release from the institution the next day, and left, carrying the luggage we gave her as a graduation present.

Less than a year later she packed that same suitcase and went to a hospital to have a baby out of wedlock—a baby she gave up for adoption, repeating the history of her own life.

Then there is the black youth that I met in the Gary, Indiana, slum, living with his nine brothers and sisters in a bug-infested three-room hovel, while I was writing a series of articles on welfare mothers. In time I found that the boy could write as easily as a bird sings. At night, at home, he worked on poetry, short stories, essays, and plays.

Not long after that, he was suspended from school for smoking on the playground, second offense. My young friend did not return to school. So I took him to my home and started to enroll him in a white suburban school where he would have the opportunity to develop his talent. But the cultural shock was too great for him, and he asked to be taken home to the slum. A Christmas card came from the family this year. Now the young black no longer tries to write. Instead he sweeps floors in a steel mill.

Another teen-ager was hiding in a closet in his parent's $80,000 home. His father had emotionally abandoned him, the boy was on drugs, and his mother asked if I would help. The youth—whose father earned at least double my salary at the time—spent the summer working in my garden and painting my house. I saw him change as we talked about what is beautiful in nature, poetry and prose, and music, and discussed whether or not there is a God who cares about young people.

I remember another boy, whose parents led such destructive lives that the court ordered them never to contact him again. He came to my home from a Michigan reform school, and not long after that was picked up by a deputy sheriff racing my nine-passenger, bus-like van 80 miles an hour in a 30-mile-an-hour zone. We both grew through that experience and others like it. Eventually he enlisted in the army and volunteered for Vietnam duty, where the danger he craved was real.

Taking responsibility for children abandoned by others is always a risk, and there is little room for carelessness, as I and many others working in the field have found out. Perhaps that is why I write this chapter with more than the usual amount of empathy.

Christina almost always could tell when Brad was about to blow, even if her husband's sudden flash of anger was a surprise to nearly everyone else. An engineer and successful executive, Brad was skilled at hiding his emotions. Most people saw him as cool, thoughtful, easygoing—a good husband and father. And he was most of the time.

It was Randy, their fifteen-year-old son, who pushed Brad's button. Long-haired, spoiled, and demanding, it seemed that for months Randy's only goal in life was to goad his father into anger. Randy worked at it constantly. And now Chris watched the countdown, as her son grew more defiant, rude, unreasonable.

She could see the slight narrowing of her husband's eyes, an almost imperceptible flaring of his nostrils, and the small motion of his jaw just below the ear as he clenched and unclenched his teeth, trying to retain control.

Hoping to head off another conflict, Chris quietly asked her son to run an errand. Anything to get him out of the house. Randy resisted and Brad grew red.

"Get your lazy butt off that chair and do what your mother says," Brad said. "Now!"

Feigning a yawn, Randy slowly lifted himself erect, stretched, and sauntered across the kitchen. It was more than Brad could take. Suddenly he was on his feet, gripping his son's shirt, shaking him.

"I said move!" He sent Randy reeling against the table.

"You stupid jerk," Randy shouted, rubbing his leg. Then, heading toward the door he turned and shouted again. "Jerk!"

His mother sat tight-lipped and numb, wondering what had happened to her family. They had been so close, so happy.

Parent-child conflict is hardly unusual during the teen years. The young person's body is changing, and most feel confusion and even emotional pain. Their parents may be bewildered and resentful. When they seek help they may be told that conflict is normal—that teenagers are going through a stage called adolescence, and like young birds they are struggling to leave the nest.

Is it really that simple? Or is there something wrong with our child-rearing system? How valid are present theories? Have we really done enough research into parent-child conflict? Some experts, like Arthur Mandelbaum, chief social worker at the Menninger Clinic in Topeka, have reservations.

"We see patterns of family conflict," he says. "But we must remain skeptical that these are scientific observations. They are incomplete, partial, ambiguous, too generalized."

What would happen if our culture could provide a rite or system for children to reach adult status without fighting their parents? Other societies have, including the American Indian, with positive results. If conflict is normal, why is it exaggerated for some, so that we place them on probation or send them to reform school, or to a mental hospital or community mental health center?

And why so much drug abuse, heavy drinking, shoplifting, promiscuity, wild driving, vandalism, aimlessness, defiance, delinquency, serious crime, mental illness, running away, even teen-age suicide?

As is the case in all areas of the children's field, we have done too little research to know for sure. It seems America is more interested in other important things to pay much attention to youngsters. But there are answers.

Over the past ten years I have interviewed several thousand young people, as well as parents, teachers, social workers, psychologists, psychiatrists, and other professionals around the country. These interviews offer strong hints of what is wrong.

1. *Isolation.* In an age of working mothers, fathers who commute long distances, marathon television-watching, widespread affluence, and individualism, few families have continuous and close ties.

Several people can sit in the same room watching television for hours and remain isolated—talking only when it is time to decide which program to watch next.

Meetings, golf, and other adult-only activities keep fathers from building relationships with their youngsters. Children belong to the Little League or just drift in packs. They also pair off and do things apart from the family. Mothers work and are busy with their own activities. Meals can, for some families, be catch as catch can. Families become groups of half-strangers—people passing one another without common ties beyond sharing the same last name. Teen-agers have too few duties. They use the family car or have their own cars to leave the home and neighborhood and travel long distances.

In an interview published in the *Christian Science Monitor,* Mrs. Eda J. LaShan said that "Children now spend much less time with adults than they ever have before in history. . . . By the time they reach adolescence and early adulthood most of their values and most of the attitudes they reflect most clearly are those of their own age group and not adults."

In many ways today's children rear each other, and are being reared by entertainers, advertising agencies, teachers, and strangers.

2. *Parental fears.* Perhaps it is because of guilt, or as a result of the pop psychology they constantly are exposed to in magazines and newspapers. Whatever the reason, many parents today act as if they were afraid of their children.

At a school parents' meeting not long ago, where the problems of parents and youth were being discussed, a husky man in his late thirties stood up and pathetically begged someone to tell him how to get respect from his son.

3. *Teen-age fears.* "Will there be a tomorrow?" The problems of the world, death without warning in an age of missiles and H-bombs, the inability to control one's own destiny because of big government, big industry, and big labor unions, and increasing crime make living only for the moment seem sensible.

Having a pet-like status in the modern family, growing up in a permissive society that sets few limits on behavior, knowing that parents are uncertain and insecure, and living in the age that worships youth and the idealistic wisdom of youth all make it more difficult to be young.

Absent fathers, working mothers, day care, baby-sitters, moving vans coming and going, impersonalization of life and death on TV, the high divorce rate, and the importance of things rather than people all add to teen-age insecurity.

There were dangers in an earlier age, but families faced problems together. Now too many people must stand alone.

4. *The need to be needed.* Everyone, to be happy, must see some purpose to life. Children treated as pets or as "things" to make a mother or adult feel good or happy or whole, do not, when they reach their teen years, like to be used in this way. Especially when parents "use" them only now and then.

Many lost and lonely young people seek ways to remind their parents that they are alive and need attention. Some youngsters who use drugs or turn to promiscuity or delinquency are shouting: "Stop me if you care! Pay attention."

Most experts agree that many teen-age suicide attempts are extreme forms of the same message. They are saying "I need to be needed."

5. *Boredom.* American children are constantly entertained by television. After ten or more years boredom sets in. But what is there to do?

In the suburbs, with their groomed lawns and landscaping, and in city apartments with keep-off-the-grass signs, how can a child entertain himself as children have for generations? Where can he find frogs' eggs to hatch into tadpoles? Where can he build a shack on a vacant lot? Where is there a clean stream stocked with fish in urban areas? Or even a tall tree to climb?

6. *Too few challenges.* Does all of life come from a television set or in kit form? How can a young person today test and challenge himself and find his adulthood? What gives life excitement?

Rock climbing is a popular sport today in rough sections of the nation

The Troubled Years 127

because young people can test themselves and feel a part of nature. There is risk, danger, and challenge.

Some youngsters bait the police just for the thrill of the chase. There are delinquent children who keep scrapbooks filled with newspaper reports of burglaries and other crimes—and beside the clippings they write "my job" or "I did that one." Shoplifting has become a national thrill-sport. Wild driving has long been a part of teen life.

Young people need a challenge. The opportunity to try something that is "adult"—beyond sex, smoking, or drinking. The more urban our society becomes the more anti-social the challenges become.

7. *Consanguinity.* Several decades ago—before disc jockeys, teen-age music stars, underground newspapers, the arrival of the drug culture, television, the high mobility of families and the impersonalization of neighborhoods, the constant availability of automobiles, excess leisure time, and the worship of youth—children did not think of themselves as a unified national or international group. They related to parents, grand-parents, adult neighbors, younger children, and others of varied ages. They were not part of "youth," they were members of a family and a community.

All that has changed. As I traveled through England, Germany, France, Denmark, Switzerland, Yugoslavia, and other nations I found young people—including Americans and Canadians—thinking of themselves as a united group the world over. The fraternity of the young is a stronger bond than either that of the family or of the nation they come from.

It was especially interesting to find young people in Yugoslavia—a communist nation, and a land that still uses hand labor and ox carts in rural areas—wearing long hair and looking and acting very much like the teen-agers in Miami, Philadelphia, Dallas, Minneapolis, or San Francisco.

8. *Homogeneity.* Children, when they band together, may reject "sameness" and claim individuality, but they hardly live it. Teen-agers are faddish, and they worry as much about what other young people think as their mothers worry about how to dress and act.

Schools also, through grading systems and teachers who look for con-formity and reward it, tend to emphasize "sameness." Children are grouped by age, ability level, and in other ways that encourage homogeneity.

Or consider the country clubs, labor unions, and the tendency to limit adult friendships to persons of the same economic and social strata. This too teaches children to band together, even while rejecting those who are not members of their group.

9. *Role models*. Children learn by copying others. Even while rejecting the beliefs of their parents, they may unconsciously buy into many aspects of the adult world that cause alienation and other problems. We live in a society that seems too often to worship money and to promote selfishness. While believing they are rejecting the false values of their parents, children sometimes substitute values that are little better.

If they reject their parents and their parents' heros (Charles Lindbergh, Admiral Robert Peary, Amelia Earhart, Babe Ruth, Red Grange, Clark Gable, and Bette Davis were admired by their grandparents) they have their own idols to pattern their lives after. Unfortunately, in recent years these idols promoted promiscuity, drug abuse, drinking, and dropping out of society.

(It also is worth noting that adults, eager to profit from the young, provided the record companies, radio stations, printing presses, and funding for the promotion of these idols.)

10. *Rebellion*. We have already discussed teen-age rebellion, pointing out that most experts feel that it is probably normal. But are we sure? And must it take such painful forms?

Not all young people feel hatred toward their parents. In fact some get along fine. They talk, interact, and work at understanding one another. In most instances the parents involved understand that their children are undergoing biological and emotional changes, and they help them along the way. They give them the right balance between support and freedom, understanding and firmness, that makes conflict minimal.

Perhaps most lacking in our society is a rite, a ceremony, test, or challenge that gives our young people a method of moving—when they are ready—from childhood to adult status. In an era when children became apprentices at thirteen or fourteen, or began doing a man's work on the farm, it was not needed. But today we prolong childhood and provide no sure method of transition.

Further, many children see little meaning to their parents' lives. Is wall-to-wall carpeting, a car or two, and all of the other things most of us work for all there is to life, they ask? And hard-driving, successful, middle-class Americans don't like being asked questions like that— especially when the questioners are their own offspring.

11. *Hedonistic consumerism*. We live in a world that demands that we trust and even love *things*, not people. One only has to watch television commercials to realize that this is true.

We hear mature adults gush about how they "love" their new cars or houses or carpets. Even their dishwashers or candlesticks.

Parents communicate their love of things and disregard for people every day. They spank John for breaking a dish or send Sally to bed without supper for tearing her new dress.

A working mother or father-on-the-go may explain that they are busy earning money for the children. Feeling guilt, they give them things instead of their time and attention.

At the same time we express anger or hatred toward others, and the television screen tells us how cheap life can be, with half a dozen bodies scattered around on an hour-long detective show.

Our economic system clearly contributes to parent-child conflict.

12. *Prolonging childhood.* Francis Bacon entered Trinity College at the age of twelve. Beethoven wrote his first compositions before he was in his teens. Michelangelo was a successful artist before he was sixteen. At the age of eighteen Joan of Arc led more than 4,000 soldiers against the English, and she was burned at the stake when she was twenty. Many of our ancestors were expected to work alongside the adults when they were seven or eight.

Our children today mature physically at an earlier age than in the past. But emotionally we keep them young until they are sixteen or eighteen or older.

Child labor laws helped reduce exploitation of children, but some contend that these same laws contribute to delinquency by denying young persons the opportunity to work. Our schools too often present a mish-mash of material that probably will have little value at any time in life. Yet children must attend school and act as if what they were being taught was important.

If we could restructure our life patterns—building in periods of schooling and experience, and extending education over a lifetime, as it became relevant—we would have fewer childhood problems. And less boredom later in life.

13. *Self-concept.* To be happy, one must feel good about himself and his life. He must know who he is (and this is more difficult for girls than boys today) and how he fits in. Unfortunately, we no longer assume the identity of our parents, as was the case for many generations. Nor do our schools help us to find out who we are, what we can do, or how to have a positive self-concept. In fact, schools often do the opposite, unless a child is academically inclined.

Entering the adult world at sixteen or eighteen or twenty can be a frightening experience. When military training was required, and when we were not at war, the army often helped us gain confidence, and it gave us more time to find ourselves. Now young people seem more confused and lost than before. Little wonder that the teen years are years of conflict.

14. *Parental immaturity.* As anyone with a little experience with the adult world knows, age has little to do with maturity. Nor do we really have a clear idea of what maturity is.

130   PART II · THE SYSTEM UNMASKED

We do talk of teen-agers and adults with "impaired ego development."
These are adults or near-adults who faced parental inconsistency and/or
emotional deprivation during their early years. There is strong evidence
that the number of persons with impaired ego development is growing.
One hardly dares guess what our society will be like in one or two
generations if this is true.

Such persons never really grow up. They struggle in vain to "manage
the realities" of their lives. They may buy compulsively, use easy credit
without the means to pay back the money, constantly blame others for
their problems, find it difficult to maintain lasting relationships with
others, and, in extreme cases, refuse to face up to their problems. Some
hide and others resort to compulsive behavior, including drug abuse and
alcoholism.

We find their children in reform schools and mental hospitals, and
many of these children suffer from abuse and neglect. It is believed that
immature parents produce children who will be, in turn, immature when
they become adults. It is interesting that such parents can be pleasant,
even charming, and outwardly give the appearance of providing "good
homes" for their children.

15. *Peer Pressure.* Many Americans concerned with children talk of the
close bonds that have been built between young people, even as family
ties fall apart. One of these is Dr. Urie Bronfenbrenner, whose studies
since the end of World War II suggest that there is a serious decrease in
"all spheres of interaction" between adults (including parents) and children. When this happens "the vacuum is filled by the age-segregated
peer group," he says.

My studies of delinquent and disturbed children in institutions
produce findings that agree with Dr. Bronfenbrenner's. And they are
supported by those who have looked at street-gang behavior, our runaway problem, crash pads, and even the renewed popularity of com-
munal living.

Lacking meaningful or satisfying relationships with their parents,
large numbers of children turn to other young people for companionship,
comfort, and support. This is not bad in itself. But it can lead to a value
system based on a very limited view of the world, bitterness, rejection of
that which is good in society, and antisocial behavior.

It is hard to say whether this can be turned around in a society that
bases its economy on hedonistic consumerism. For it requires parents to
be mature, responsible, and consistent. The tide is running the other way
at the moment. Each day there is more emphasis on egocentric satisfaction—especially for women.

Many who speak for women's liberation groups seem determined to push their followers to develop one of the worst traits of men—irresponsibility toward their children.

The less parenting parents do, the more likely it is that children will band together. We seem all too willing to encourage our youngsters to rear one another.

I do not feel I am overstating the problem when I suggest that such a course could lead to the destruction of our civilization.

15

That's the Law

The following news item ran on the Associated Press news wires in April of 1974:

JACKSONVILLE, FLA.—Ernest John Dobbert Jr. was sentenced to death in the electric chair today for the torture killing of his 9-year-old daughter.

Circuit Court Judge Hudson Olliff ignored a jury recommendation for life imprisonment, saying aggravating circumstances made this "an especially heinous, atrocious and cruel crime, more cruel than any I have known."

Olliff sentenced Dobbert to the maximum for three other convictions. He gave him 30 years for second-degree murder in the death of his son, Ryder, 7; 15 years for torture of his son, Ernest John III; and one year for child abuse of his daughter, Honore, 7.

Olliff made the sentences consecutive.

The first-degree murder conviction was in the death of Kelley Dobbert, 9.

If one wants to drive a car in America he must pass both written and road tests. The motorist who ignores a parking sign or goes a few miles over a speed limit is ticketed and fined. It is against the law to trespass on another person's property, or to peek in someone's window. One must register to vote. And in most communities if one wants to use the library, one also must apply for a library card.

Although in the 1920s and '30s there was a strong thrust to sterilize criminals, retardates, and other deviants—and 26 states still have in-

132

voluntary sterilization laws on the books—seldom are the laws used. The horror of Hitler sterilizing thousands of persons for political reaons ended that.

Today, nearly anyone, married or single, alcoholic, heroin addict, criminal, retarded, insane, or suffering from a contagious or incurable disease can have children—almost without question or governmental interference.

In fact, a man with sufficient stamina and seductive talent could sire a hundred, even a thousand children. He cannot be forced to support any of them unless he admits they are his, or unless each woman involved files a separate paternity suit for each child. Then it must be shown with scientific certainty and beyond a doubt that he and he alone could have fathered each one of them. Even when it is shown that this is true, the super-stud will be forced to pay no more than he can afford—and that depends largely on his earnings and his other financial obligations.

If a woman is unmarried, separated or divorced, and the husband missing, and if she cannot support her child or children, then the government will provide sufficient food, shelter, clothing, and medical care to assure survival until they are grown. When a man's wife disappears, he also may collect welfare benefits under the Aid to Dependent Children program if he is unable to find a compatible job and provide adequate child care.

Further, a parent has the right to do as he or she pleases with the children—short of extreme neglect, severe physical abuse, incest, prostitution, or murder—as long as the parent sends the children to school. A parent can force older children to work, and in most states the employer must turn the entire paycheck over to that parent. If the child does not obey, the parent (or parents) may use physical force or various other forms of punishment, and if that fails, may take the youngster to court to be threatened by a judge. Those who remain recalcitrant are put on probation or sent to reform school.

Should a child run away, authorities will, usually without asking questions, hold the youngster in jail and force him to return home—if the parents want the child back.

In short, a child is property. A youngster's status is very much like that of a slave or pet. Children are chattels under the law. They are owned by their parents and by society.

This may result in anguish for millions of American children. But the concept of ownership is based upon centuries of tradition, upon the common law and legislation at all levels of government, and upon Supreme Court decisions.

Having children is a sacred right in America, ranking with the ownership of other forms of private property. And yet this basic right and other rights are being challenged on many fronts. Among the key issues:

1. Whose rights are superior: a parent's or society's?
2. When is a child a *person* with the right to life and to self-determination (rather than being a thing or a pet)?
3. Whose rights are superior: the child's or the parent's?
4. Whose rights are superior: a child's or society's?
5. When do the rights of adult citizens apply to children?
6. Are there "classes" of children in our society? Are some children "more equal" than others?

The right to become a parent is a core issue. At the same time Ernest John Dobbert Jr. was torturing and murdering his children in Florida, doctors were sterilizing women in other states. At about the same time Mr. Dobbert was found guilty, Julian Bond, the southern Civil Rights leader, was sending out letters to thousands of persons asking for contributions. The letter began:

"Lucy," said Dr. Benton, "when I deliver your baby you should have your tubes tied."

"What does that mean?" asked Lucy. Her six grades in Belson County Elementary, still all black, had given her an even poorer education than the average white Tennessean.

"You don't need no more chillen, Lucy. Tying your tubes will fix that." Dr. Benton's word was usually unquestioned, but this time Lucy knew something wasn't right.

"Lucy, you want me to deliver this baby, don't you? It's due next week. My charge is $250. You ain't got that much money. Unless I let you use my office to get your Medicaid, you ain't gonna have no doctor. And unless you let me tie your tubes, I ain't gonna deliver your baby."

"But, Dr. Benton . . . "

"Look, Lucy, if you don't agree I'll get a court order and I'll see to it that your welfare is cut off."

Dear Friend:
The above is a true story. Only the names have been changed. On May 23, 1973, a white doctor performed a tubal ligation on Lucy Martin, bringing the number of coerced sterilizations this year in that one county to eighteen.

In Alabama, another white doctor made incisions in the abdomens of twelve-year-old Mary Alice Relf and her fourteen-year-old sister, Minnie Lee. Hours before their sterilization surgery, Minnie Lee had to borrow a dime from a patient in Montgomery's Professional Center Hospital to call a neighbor who would fetch the girls' mother to the phone.

That afternoon, a family planning nurse had gotten Mrs. Relf's "X" (she can't read or write) on a form authorizing the sterilization of her minor daughters, then returned her to her apartment in the Project.

"Mother, we're scared. Y'all come get us."

"Minnie, you stay down there and take those shots like they said. You know we don't have a car to come get y'all."

"They're not gonna give us shots," Minnie cried, her voice beginning to waver, "a lady in the next bed said they gonna operate on us."

"That nurse said they was gonna give y'all shots," reassured Mrs. Relf. Mary Alice and Minnie had been receiving Depoprovera injections, an experimental birth control drug, for several months. But it had recently been banned by the FDA because it produced cancer in laboratory mice. No proof existed that these children even needed birth control assistance. Little did the Relfs know they had been human guinea pigs for experimental drugs. And less did they know that when the operating room opened the next morning, their two daughters would be made forever sterile.

This is a true story. The names weren't changed, because the national press introduced this family to the nation while exposing their tragedy.

Sterilization is fine . . . but only for consenting adults.

Dr. Benton told the press he insists on sterilization of all welfare mothers with two or more children because ". . . my hard-earned taxes go to support these children." Justification for the Relf girls' sterilization was "because boys were hanging around and we could no longer give the shots."

Reports of involuntary sterilizations have been discovered throughout the South. And all have a common these. Each was obtained by coercion, threats of misrepresentation. Several women were even told their tubes would come *untied* in about two years allowing pregnancy. But, in truth, each operation is *final*.

The letter goes on to explain that the Southern Poverty Law Center filed suit to require "constitutionally acceptable guidelines for the sterilization of minors, illiterates and the mentally incompetent," and the Department of Health, Education and Welfare then issued "woefully inadequate regulations continuing its policy of illegally sterilizing the poor."

Bond says that the two children who were sterilized weren't retarded, as some had reported. And that even if one "favors sterilization for the retarded, surely adequate safeguards must be available to determine who is retarded, and whether immediate and permanent sterilization is the correct remedy."

Then he focused on a key issue:

Only the most callous have written favoring sterilization of welfare mothers. Many realize that a welfare mother is only temporarily dependent on public support. Over half are off welfare in less than two years. But more importantly, most appreciate the fact that the decision to bear children is a very personal right not lightly to be overruled by governmental planners. Sterilization of a welfare mother [or any person] might be sound medical and family planning advice. The decision, though, must be accepted with full, informed consent, and not after threats, coercion or fraud.

Sterilization is hardly a new issue in the United States. But concern died down as in the 1940s and '50s the number of persons involuntarily sterilized decreased.

The push for sterilization began in 1885, when persons who were concerned with the problems of crime, retardation, insanity, and other social ills looked at studies made by Charles Darwin and Gregory Mendel. It was Darwin who told us that a species could change over a period of several generations, and Mendel developed the concept of genetics or the inheritance of traits from parents. The 1910 *Encylopedia Britannica* concludes a report on "Mendelism" by saying: "If it is shown that the qualities of man, his body and his intellect, his immunities and his diseases, even his very virtues and vices, are dependent on unit-characters whose mode of transmission follows fixed laws, and if also man decides that his life shall be ordered in the light of this knowledge, it is obvious that the social system will have to undergo considerable changes."

It was Darwin's cousin, Sir Francis Galton, who pushed the concept of improving mankind by controlling the birthrate of those deemed "unfit" or inferior, while encouraging the breeding of those who are superior. It was hoped that as in cattle breeding, or the raising of race horses, this would improve humanity. In a book, *Human Faculty*, published in 1884, he coined the word for this concept, "eugenics," although he began pushing the idea as early as 1865.

The idea excited Americans after the turn of the century, and eugenics was practiced in a number of state institutions before the turn of the century. The United States Supreme Court endorsed the concept in 1927, and the opinion was written by no less an authority than Justice Oliver Wendell Holmes, who had been sired by a prominent American writer and physician. Justice Holmes' grandfather had been a clergyman and important historian, and his paternal grandmother was from a wealthy New York family, and was a descendent of two Massachusetts governors. On the subject of sterilization, Justice Holmes wrote:

In the view of the general declarations of the legislature and the specific findings of the Court, obviously we cannot say as a matter of law that the grounds do not exist, and if they exist they justify the result. We have seen more than once that the public welfare may call upon the best citizens for their lives. It would be strange if it could not call upon those who already sap the strength of the State for these lesser sacrifices, often not felt to be such by those concerned, in order to prevent our being swamped with incompetence. It is better for all the world, if instead of waiting to execute degenerate offspring for crime, or to let them starve for their imbecility, society can prevent those who are manifestly unfit from continuing their kind. The principle that sustains compulsory vaccination is broad enough to cover cutting the Fallopian Tubes. . . . Three generations of imbeciles are enough.

Abortion is an issue closely related to eugenics, although many Americans, perhaps for emotional reasons, refuse to admit that this is so. And abortion is closely tied to various forms of infanticide so commonly practiced for centuries, although some pro-abortionists will deny this.

Easy (and legal) abortion is a convenient method of population control, and, like contraception, can be used on minors, deviants, and minority groups with little public opposition. Further, it limits the spread of undesirables because a dead fetus will not grow up to produce more unwanted children.

In its 1972 report, the U.S. Commission on Population Growth and the American Future wrote:

In the development of western culture, the tendency has been toward a greater protection of life. At the same time, there is a deep commitment in our moral tradition to individual freedom and social justice. The commission believes that the various prohibitions against abortion throughout the United States stand as obstacles to the exercise of individual freedom; the freedom of women to make difficult moral choices based on their personal values, the freedom of women to control their own fertility, and finally, freedom from burdens of unwanted childbearing. . . . Medically safe abortions have always been available to the wealthy, to those who could afford the high costs of physicians and trips abroad; but the poor woman has been forced to risk her life and health with folk remedies and disreputable practitioners.

The Commission, which calls for population control for economic and other reasons, including something it calls "the quality of life," endorses contraception for minors, "voluntary contraceptive sterilization," and abortion. It urges that "This nation give the highest priority to research in reproductive biology and to the search for improved methods by which individuals can control their own fertility."

In addition to other population-related problems, the Commission cites "congenital deficiencies," poverty, the "inadequate distribution of and access to health, education, and welfare services; cultural and social constraints on human performance and development associated with race, ethnic origin, sex, and age; barriers to full economic and cultural participation; unequal access to environmental quality; and unequal exposure to environmental hazard."

It also states: "The relative importance of heredity and environment in shaping an individual's growth and development remains uncertain. Clearly, it is desirable to reduce the incidence of genetically related disorders in the population. The frequency of such disorders is much higher than formerly suspected. According to experts: No less than 25 percent of hospital and other institutional beds are estimated to be occupied by patients whose physical and mental illnesses or defects are under full or at least partial genetic control.

"Others estimate that one out of 15 children is born with some form of genetic defect, some so severe as to have tremendous implications in the life of the affected person and his family."

To resolve these problems the Commission called for, in addition to more research, better delivery of services to the handicapped, and better "care and treatment of persons suffering from genetically related disorders, the exploration of the ethical and moral implications of genetic technology.

"We spend billions in therapy, remedial treatment, custodial care, and repair of damage that might have been prevented by a more complete understanding of the factors governing reproduction," the report adds. But in another section it notes that "child-bearing is very highly valued in our society, and sterilization should never be undertaken without serious prior thought and knowledge of the ramifications."

While some believe that population can be controlled by "financial inducements" not to bear children, the Commission believes that "bonus payments would serve to discourage child-bearing only among the relatively few who are poorest."

These are not easy issues to deal with, at least in the last quarter of the twentieth century. In a section headed "The Quality of American Life," the Commission suggests that it is "concerned with population trends only as they impede or enhance the realization of those values and goals cherished in, by, and for American society."

Perhaps earlier cultures were, in a sense, more "practical" than we can be. The 1910 *Encylopaedia Britannica* notes that "among primitive savage races abortion is practiced to a far less extent than infanticide, which offers a simpler way of getting rid of inconvenient progeny. But it is common among the American Indians, as well as in China, Cambodia and India, although throughout Asia it generally is contrary both to law and religion. How far it was considered a crime among the civilized nations of antiquity has long been debated."

It would appear that approval and disapproval of abortion runs in cycles. Plato approves of abortion in his *Republic,* and in one of his Dialogues he has Socrates talk of it as both common and legal. While two prominent Romans, Ovid and Seneca, write that abortion was common, Cicero indicates that it was punished, at times, by death.

During the early years of Christianity, "foeticide" was a crime similar to murder of an adult, yet in seventeenth-century England it was no worse than a misdemeanor. Blackstone, the eighteenth-century jurist, wrote that "if a woman is quick with child, and by poison or otherwise killeth it in her womb, or if any one beat her, whereby the child dieth in her body, and she is delivered of a dead child, this, though not murder, was, by the ancient law, homicide or manslaughter."

In most sections of the new United States abortion was legal until the nineteenth century, but then became a criminal offence as states passed laws opposing it. California permitted abortions in 1967 for the first time and New York's law went into effect on July 1, 1970. In a 7 to 2 decision the U.S. Supreme Court legalized abortion in January of 1973. Since then many questions have been raised as to the right of an unborn child to life, the right a father may have to challenge his wife when she decides to have an abortion, and the point at which a fetus actually becomes a human being.

The High Court ruled that women are free to have abortions during the first 3 months of pregnancy, and probably should have the right until the fetus is roughly seven months old—the point when it is possible for an infant to survive, with artificial means, outside of the womb. But many who oppose abortion, and some who support it, contend that the Supreme Court has opened the door to infanticide and euthanasia. The recent decision by doctors at the Yale–New Haven Hospital to permit multiply handicapped infants to die tends to support this theory.

Decisions made on sterilization, abortion, infanticide, euthanasia, and in other civil or human rights areas have an important impact on America's children, especially those classified as the "little victims" in this book.

We are hardly consistent in the legislative and legal stands that we take, and for good reason. We are dealing with a thorny thicket of overlapping rights that are basic in America.

Obviously the rights of the Dobbert children, tortured and killed in Florida, were violated. But what of youngsters warehoused in institutions, or children used experimentally by medical researchers, psychologists, psychiatrists, and social workers? And what of youngsters held in jails and jail-like detention homes for acts that are not criminal in the usual sense, inasmuch as had adults committed the acts, it would not be considered criminal behavior. (School attendance laws, running away from home, curfew violations and similar children's [or status] crimes serve as an example.)

It is interesting that the Constitution does not single out children, minority groups, or handicapped persons to afford them special rights, liabilities, or duties, although it assures members of minority groups equal rights with others.

Roman law and English common law did establish differences between adults and children—but to protect them, not hurt them. Under Roman law a girl came of age at twelve, a boy at fourteen, although certain protections were provided until they reached the age of twenty-five.

The barbarians let young men bear arms at fifteen, and saw fit to make this the age of majority. England, greatly influenced by the barbarians, followed their lead until the middle of the seventeenth century when Charles II saw too many young men squandering their fathers' estates, and so allowed fathers to appoint guardians until their sons turned twenty-one. This coincided with the age at which a youth could become a knight, or fight duels. Peasant boys were generally of age at fifteen.

Twenty-one was accepted as the voting age of our Founding Fathers as well as the age at which one could enter into contracts. The right to drink alcoholic beverages at age twenty-one (or eighteen) came later, and the voting age was lowered to eighteen by Constitutional amendment in 1971. Long before that, persons eighteen and even younger could serve in the armed forces of the United States, although they could not be forced to serve until they turned eighteen.

Divorce decrees often require fathers to support their legitimate children until they reach eighteen or twenty-one, and sometimes until they finish college. But as we have pointed out, support laws, especially in the case of illegitimate offspring, are not enthusiastically enforced.

In theory, at least, parents have full control over their children's lives because children are both innocent and dependent. And like most social theories, this one is flawed. For who is to protect the children from their protectors—whether parents or state agencies and institutions?

If a child, at least after birth, has Constitutional rights, they certainly differ from those given adults. Strike another adult and you will be charged with assault. But parents, teachers, and others in charge of children have the right to hit children, and apparently youngsters lack the right to defend themselves, in most states.

In an earlier day children could be severely treated by parents and guardians and they had legal recourse. The same thought processes that scuttled monarchies and the feudal systems of Europe and brought about more democratic forms of government helped improve the lot of children as well. In time laws were passed to protect children from gross forms of neglect and abuse, even if the right to punish children remains. Abusive adults were to be dealt with by the judicial system.

Sadly, our system of justice is designed to deal with problems *after* they occur, and it is the obligation of the victim (with the help of a prosecutor and others) to prove the guilt of the offending party. But a child's word is seldom accepted against the word of an adult in court; offenses against children occur without witnesses in most instances since they take place within the home; and there are laws protecting one spouse from the testimony of the other in criminal court.

Even if laws were passed further protecting children's rights, it is ludicrous to believe that we could hire enough policemen (or social workers) to monitor every home in America where children might be hurt. Further, pitting a child against a parent in court defeats the very goal of most social legislation involving children—to provide him with proper care *in his own home.*

Much is being said today about children's rights, and the rights of those who are handicapped. The battle is being waged on three fronts—in the courts, through passage of legislation, and through propaganda (using that word in its best sense) that will sway the court of public opinion.

Most Americans agree that a child should have the right to grow up happy and whole. But each individual has his or her own views as to how we might best achieve this, and large numbers of persons are unwilling to give up some of their own rights—or their money—to achieve this goal. Nor have we found the means of enforcing the rights that now exist. How do we hold accountable those responsible for the care and welfare of children—the parents, teachers, social workers, mental health professionals, judges, policemen, foster parents, and those who work in and run child-caring facilities, agencies and institutions?

The government is incapable of protecting children's rights, and the rights of the deviant and handicapped—or so it seems. One has only to look at the nation's juvenile courts, probation officers, reform schools, mental hospitals, public schools, welfare offices, institutions for the retarded, community mental health centers, and even doctors and hospitals to see that this is the case.

Beyond that, as in the case of abortion, children's rights are at odds with those of adults, and sometimes the rights of other children.

If the mixing of slow or retarded children with bright youngsters at school limits the bright child's ability to learn and grow, whose rights are most important?

If a child is unpleasant to look at, drools, or walks in front of cars because he is retarded, does society really have the right to hide and thus exclude the child?

If crippled children cannot navigate curbs, cross streets, or push their wheelchairs through doors in public buildings or rest rooms, are they denied access to their freedom or rights?

If a parent follows an off-beat course in life, or believes in a form of religion unacceptable to the majority, does the parent have a right to the child, or should society take the child away?

When a child disrupts a classroom because he is emotionally disturbed does he still have a right to an education? To remain in the community?

How much of one's income can one be forced to pay through state, federal, and local taxes to support schools, institutions, and programs for children?

Does the state have the right to monitor every family's kitchen to see that children are provided with adequate nutrition? Does this also extend to the mother's body and breast feeding?

If 10 million children are suffering from emotional problems, and if most of these problems are caused by parents, can the state force parents to change?

Should we punish children for delinquent behavior if that behavior is caused by parents, schools, poverty, or other social ills?

How does the right to "liberty" apply to children? In the case of adults, the right to be free is limited only when one adult endangers others in society—at least in theory, if not in practice.

Should children have equal access to the courts, to jury trials, and due process? It is presently denied them in many ways. In many instances the same is true of the handicapped.

What about the right to earn wages and keep them? Or to own property? Or to make decisions about one's own future?

Does a person have a constitutional right to therapeutic treatment, as Alabama Federal Judge Frank Johnson has ruled? Under what conditions does society have the right to lock human beings—adults and children—in jails, prisons, reform schools, mental hospitals, institutions for the retarded, and other facilities, against their will?

These are a few of the legal questions being asked today. Our answers will have an important impact on this nation's little victims.

16

The Selling System— Mercantile Abuse

Somewhere back in the mists of memory I recall a cartoon showing a businessman telling a friend that he had found the perfect product: it could be manufactured for less than a penny, sold for a dime, was used up instantly, was habit forming—and legal.

The cartoonist was probably spoofing pills and patent medicines or cigarettes. But he could have been poking fun at the candy, soft drink, cereal, cookie, and toy businesses—the children's market.

One can hardly fault making a buck. Getting rich has long been the major theme of the American Dream. But should we put so much emphasis on making money off our children?

Toys can be dangerous. One government agency has estimated that there are 700,000 toy-related accidents each year, although some officials add that "misuse" of toys can be blamed, apparently assuming that children are rational little adults who will know there are right and wrong ways to use toys.

Many children have nutritional problems not because of poverty but because they prefer candy, soft drinks, and snack foods to wholesome meals.

Shoplifting has become a national problem in part because merchants, dependent on impulse buying, display goods in a way that makes stealing easy. Officials also say the poor, in a society that is based on hedonistic consumerism, steal because living without things in an age of instant gratification is unbearable.

Nearly all American children watch television, and they are coached daily in the catechism of what some call the state religion, hedonistic consumerism, where self-indulgence (supported by easy credit) is said to be rewarded with eternal happiness. And some parents do feel like miserable sinners when they say no to their offspring. Most of us have seen three-year-old, tantrum-throwing consumer-tyrants in supermarkets and discount stores, demanding that their mothers buy them products they have seen on television.

In the home of a friend a seven-year-old stomped around, whining and fussing, because his mother had neglected to buy him a toy that "all the kids have." The desperate mother finally promised to take him to the store after supper. A doctor's wife told me—quite seriously—at a dinner party that there is only one way to cope with modern children. Bribe them!

There are those who believe children are losing their ability to read, think, or be creative because this is a boob-tube society that has the earmarks of a nonstop puppet show or carnival, and there is always the promise of something new, free, and wonderful in every package purchased.

In my own home there is a problem of broken toys and too many toys strewn about. So one evening at dinner I decided to discuss the subject with my children—trying not to tinge the answers by offering my own views.

"What do you kids think about the toys we get you?" I asked.

"Whaddaya mean?" Mark, our thirteen-year-old, asked. Mark is old and wise enough to know that it is best to ask questions when dealing with adults. That way he can avoid trouble—and extra work assignments, like cleaning up the playroom out of turn.

"Well, you have a lot of toys around here," I suggested.

"So?"

"So what do you think about them? Toys, advertising, that kinda thing?"

"We've got too many of them," Eric, our eleven-year-old, said. Eric is past the toy stage and likes plants and animals. "It's a lot of trouble picking up all those little pieces when I clean the playroom."

Eric had suggested at a family meeting a few months earlier that each child be limited to three toys.

"The trouble with a lot of toys is they're too flimsy," Mark added, feeling safer now. "They break too easy."

"Yeah," nine-year-old Paul chimed in, "and they think they can get away with it because we're kids. If our toys fall apart the stores make more money. Right?"

"The stuff you see on TV isn't as much fun as they say after you get it," Eric said.

"I got a cash register for Christmas, and it was broken in the box," Paul complained. "Mom took it back and the new one didn't last even an hour."

Katie, our kindergartner, agreed, for she had seen both broken cash registers. "And you know those little cars?" she added. "Well, all you have to do is tug a little on one of the doors and it comes right off in your hand!"

"How do you know?" Paul quickly asked. He is collector of cars, and some were unexplainably broken.

"Because I got one for Christmas," Katie countered.

Jurg, a young house guest from Switzerland, who is living with us so he can learn English, said that in his country toys are more substantial, often made of wood, and are sometimes the kind "you can put together."

"I remember how Eric and I used to spend hours with just a few blocks and maybe some Lego and a car in the sandbox," Mark said.

"TV makes kids want to buy toys," Eric said.

"Yeah? Parents buy toys for their kids—the kids don't buy them," Mark countered. "And a lot of things parents get bore kids."

"But the kids saw the toys on TV and they asked their parents for them," Eric argued.

"Yeah," Mark said, conceding the point.

If there was a single undertone to my talks with my own children, and with other youngsters, it is that they feel they are being used by merchants trying to make a buck. And they don't like it.

Whether or not there is youthful cynicism toward hedonistic consumerism in this country is a point that can be debated. But one thing is certain. If there *is* growing cynicism, the manufacturers, merchants, and their hucksters are to blame. They may deliberately introduce children to planned obsolescence at an early age, and it may all be very, very good for the economy. But youngsters—who often have a highly developed sense of what is honest and what is dishonest—don't like being used or lied to.

In a popular book on investment, *The Money Game* (Random House, 1967), the author, a Wall Street mogul writing under the pen name Adam Smith, began the first chapter:

"The world is not the way they tell you it is.

"Unconsciously we know this because we have all been immunized by growing up in the United States. The little girl watching television asks will she really get the part in the spring play if she uses Listerine, and her good mother says no, darling, that is just a commercial."

Mr. Smith goes on to say that parents, the government, stockbrokers, and others have their own commercials, and none are especially truthful.

It is not just an accident that Mr. Smith used a child as an example of how the American people are gulled. Nor is it merely coincidence that hedonistic consumerism is referred to as our state religion. The Mr. Smith of Wall Street, while a rather lighthearted writer, as writers go, seriously suggests that no only did the original Adam Smith make himself "immortal as the first great free-market economist" but he also thought of himself as a "moral philosopher," rather than an economist.

Our Wall Street friend also reports that "Bishop Lawrence, the doyen of the Episcopal Church, really did say, 'In the long run, it is only to the man of morality that wealth comes. Godliness is in league with riches. Material prosperity makes the national character sweeter, more Christlike.' " And Mr. Smith adds that "when John D. Rockefeller was asked how he came by his vast fortune, he answered, 'God gave me my money.' "

Whether or not worship of wealth is commendable or lamentable is a matter of personal and theological speculation that dates back to the invention of commerce. But the fact that our present form of hedonistic consumerism, state religion or not, can have a negative impact on our children is difficult to deny. For it warps values, teaching that *things* are more important than people, pits children against their parents, uses youngsters for personal and corporate profit, with little thought for what is good for them, and causes frustration when parents are too poor to buy the things that children want.

Hedonistic consumerism, as it has developed in the past few decades, is a significant departure from long-standing practices of protecting children from exploitation. Forty-four states still have laws requiring a young, unmarried male to be twenty-one years old before entering into contracts without parental consent. In three states the age of majority for a male is twenty, in two it is nineteen, and in one eighteen. (Ten states permit a girl of eighteen to sign a contract legally.)

If a car dealer sells an auto to someone underage without the signature of an adult, he may well have to take the car back if the child (or parent) decided he no longer wants it (although the court may permit the dealer to charge something for the car's use).

Nor can a minor manage his own property. Instead the property must be owned by a parent, guardian, or trustee until the youth reaches majority.

Laws limit the age of sexual consent for girls—a limit set to protect them from men who would take advantage of them if they could. Marriages can be declared void or annulled in most states if one or both spouses were underage at the time of the marriage.

At least in theory, labor laws were designed to protect children from exploitation. To help enforce these laws, work permits are issued in all states except Alaska, Idaho, Maine, Mississippi, South Carolina, and Texas.

In this decade an effort has been made to protect children from dangerous toys, including those that shoot or can be thrown, or that have sharp points or edges that will cut or stab. Stuffed animals with eyes that pull off or with limbs attached with long pins, and rattles filled with small objects that might be swallowed if the rattle breaks, have been banned.

Writing in the December 1972 *McCalls* magazine, Betty Furness, once a TV pitchperson and now a consumer advocate, wrote: "Buying safe toys isn't child's play—it's more like a treasure hunt."

If toys are safer now, and fewer break than in the past, it is hardly due to self-policing of the industry. And there is, in fact, little proof that toys are stronger or safer or last longer. The assignment to clean up the toy industry was given to the U.S. Food and Drug Administration's Bureau of Product Safety. It is hoped that in time the agency will see that fewer youngsters are injured by gifts from well-meaning parents, relatives, and friends.

Toys do not provide the only hazard to children. Manufacturers are being asked to put childproof caps on containers of household products that can cause illness or death. Many (but not all) states protect children from paint that contains lead and can cause brain damage and death when peeling chips are swallowed by youngsters.

Hardly anyone considers putting the lid on an industry that sells billions of dollars of merchandise each year to children—the soft drink peddlers, cookie, candy, and snack manufacturers, and those that make chewing gum. Dentists warn that these foods cause teeth to rot, and nutritionists warn that we hurt the health of our youngsters when we provide so little control over what youngsters consume. In fact, even mentioning this problem brings surprised looks from many people.

The reaction is about the same when one questions the use of television to pitch products to youngsters, although in 1974 Canada began taking steps to curb advertising abuse, and some nations consider commercials beamed at children unthinkable.

It seems certain that the children's market is here to stay. The American economy rides the ground swells of consumer buying, and children are good customers, with billions to spend. Further, if we reduced the number of toys on the market, stopped pitching on television, built toys so they would last, or worried too much about soft drinks, candy, cereals, and other products used by children, we might knock the bottom out of business and put people out of work.

But what of areas where there is some measure of concern? Take, for example, cigarettes. It has been illegal for children to use tobacco in many states for years. The laws were passed long before the surgeon general announced that cigarette smoking can harm one's health. But the fact remains that there are vending machines almost everywhere.

Enforcement of antismoking laws is almost nonexistent. Although I am sure there are some, I can not recall a single case involving use of tobacco in a juvenile court, detention center, or jail. In many states where reform schools are otherwise repressive, young inmates are furnished with cigarettes daily. Some institutions require written approval from parents, while others consider smoking a health hazard or refuse to permit youngsters to smoke because of state laws. But tobacco is often smuggled into these institutions, or stolen from staff members, and illegal smoking then gives the institutional staff another reason to punish youngsters.

Some people also are concerned by what we call pornography. To exclude children, films are X-rated when explicit sexual scenes are shown, and sometimes when violence is severe. To attend most other films, children must be accompanied by an adult. This taboo makes pornography all the more exciting to young people. For years they have passed around dog-eared copies of pant-and-groan third-rate novels. On magazine racks in nearly every drug and grocery store one can find rows of bare breasts in living color, along with penises and pubic hair. Paperback copies of publications like *The Joy of Sex* show intercourse in its varied forms, along with many variations on the sexual theme. These and other books also can be purchased through the mail, regardless of the age of the purchaser.

In some states, contraceptives have long been available in gas station rest rooms to anyone with a quarter. Disc jockeys play popular songs that encourage free love and drug-taking.

A wide variety of drugs and alcoholic beverages is readily available to children with spending money. The sudden surge in drug abuse in the late 1960s and early '70s frightened many parents, but law-enforcement officials could do little to stop it, although they arrested many young people both as users and pushers.

If drug abuse, widespread use of cigarettes and alcohol, and sexual promiscuity among the young have taught us anything, it is (as we found out when the nation was dry) that you can't legislate problems away.

If we control our behavior at all we control it from within, and the key to self-control is early childhood training. Hedonistic consumerism preaches the opposite message. As the television commericals so often say, "Don't wait"—now and now and now is the time for self-gratification, and never consider the consequence.

Children must have fun, laughter, and stimulation. Toys, music, games, and exposure to a wide variety of experiences are beneficial. But our merchants and manufacturers do too little to help children grow. They are far more interested in making money.

In some democratic, free-enterprise countries—Switzerland, for one —the culture requires all citizens to care deeply about children. Exploitation is unacceptable. Even their festivals are usually far more wholesome than our carnivals.

Behind the Iron Curtain attitudes toward children differ from ours. In an article written by a young couple taking part in the Soviet-American cultural exchange program, published in the April 1974 *Parents'* magazine, Karen and Robert Devlin expressed their surprise at the kindness and love they found when they enrolled their three young children in day-care programs.

"What most impressed us about the staff of the nursery school were their love and gentleness," the couple wrote. "Contrary to what one might expect from a rigid and doctrinaire system, the children were treated with warmth, kindness, and respect. Care was taken to assure that each child participated in activities which held his interest. I never heard an angry voice raised against a child, nor did I see any aggressive behavior on the part of children."

While exploitation of children commercially is hardly the only reason we have problems, it is not the most attractive part of our culture. Perhaps it is little worse than repairmen and mechanics who do not repair but charge large fees, or manufacturers who produce goods designed to wear out or fall apart or become obsolete within a short period of time. Everyone socks it to the consumer, and since children now have become consumers, why spare them?

The only valid reason I can think of is that they are young, dependent, and trusting. It seems sad that they must become cynics while still in elementary school. The fun makers have taken some of the joy out of childhood.

17

Days of Drivel,
Nights of Nausea

Picture a cartoon character, the Mad Scientist, a weird little man with flying hair, eyes that roll and cross, and a mouth that contorts and smirks. Standing in his laboratory, he tinkers with a strange box. Then, suddenly, he waves his arms and shouts in a foreign accent:

"Eureka! I have done! I have done it!"

He tightens a screw and adjusts some wires and turns two or three dials, then grins sadistically.

"Igor. Igor! Come quickly. I have done it!"

Trotting obediently into the room, Igor, who looks a bit stupid and speaks with an adolescent whine, asks the Mad Scientist what he has done.

"Look, Igor. Look. See what I have done, Igor. With this machine I can control the human race. I can make people hate and I can make them love. I can make them cruel to one another and I can make them gentle. They will react in any way I want them to. Now I will have control of their minds! Everyone's mind!"

"But, but, sir, won't they try to stop you?" Igor asks.

"Ha, ha, ha! That is why my invention is so wonderful. It makes people happy. With this machine they won't even know that I am controlling them! Don't you see the power we will have, Igor? I can control people's minds and they will thank me for it! They will think I am doing them a favor!"

Just another Saturday morning television show? Well, you're half right. What most of us fail to understand is that such an invention is not the work of a mad scientist. And one or more such boxes can be found in nearly every American home. We call the invention the family TV set.

In addition to the television set we have radios, newspapers, magazines and—to a lesser degree—books and lecture platforms. But no other medium carries the impact of television.

A growing number of studies show that even brief television programs can influence human behavior—including the level of violence we express and tolerate. Given enough time, television and the rest of the media can alter our lives and the course of history. One only has to look at what happened in the 1960s. We achieved what had begun a century earlier and faltered—the freeing or at least enfranchisement of the black man in America. It never could have happened without the national news media prodding and exposing.

I was one of the writers sent to the South by the national media. I was working for the *Christian Science Monitor,* and my assignment was to be fair to all sides. My copy was to be balanced. And I did my best in what was an almost impossible task. Reporting the news requires one to write about *events.* About happenings. And in the south in the sixties the events were carefully *staged* by civil rights leaders, who believed that if the nation saw proof of white bigotry and supremacy, it would be moved.

Martin Luther King, like his idol Gandhi, was a masterful psychologist. He knew how to stage a dramatic event by putting his life on the line, and how to use the media, especially television, to stir up the public. To gain power and control.

I did not know Dr. King well. As a writer I was only on the fringes of his movement. Since I was not assigned to the South on a full-time basis as other writers were, Dr. King and his aids treated me well, but often kept me at a safe distance. Now and then I was permitted into the inner circle, briefly, especially when Dr. King was in jail in Selma, and so could observe some of the methods used.

Dr. King did not hide his methods. He publicly told all who would listen that he was "dramatizing" the problems of the black people. He was creating theater in the streets and highways of the South, using nonviolent marches in which he and young people, women and ministers, were the victims of white policemen. He knew how the police would act and react because he understood the police mentality—a bullying use of force. (Had they permitted Dr. King to walk a thousand miles without opposition, until he was bone-weary, little would have happened.)

Dr. King not only understood the police, he also understood the national media and always made sure the network cameras were near to record the drama, certain that it would enrage the nation. As a result an outraged citizenry demanded that civil rights legislation be passed. By manipulating the media Dr. King changed the lives of millions of Americans.

Similar techniques were used to end the Vietnam War. The beginning of the end came when the television networks began showing American brutality and atrocities, including the burning of villages and the killing of women and children. There was nothing new in the history of war in what the Americans did. What *was* new was television coverage for once told the *true* story of war, and Americans didn't like what they saw.

Violence surrounding student protests, both on campuses and at the 1968 Democratic convention, televised and reported in the newspapers and magazines, again changed history. And without the presence of a sympathetic press media, little of lasting importance would have happened.

I also believe that through publicity the media, especially radio and television, helped create the so-called counterculture and to spread drugs through the ranks of school children. The news media feeds on novelty and tends to glamorize unusual behavior, sometimes by acting alarmed at what is seen. When one major paper, TV network, or news wire service spots a "trend," the others rush in to report, and some cannot resist embellishing and exaggerating while seeking out fresh angles.

Perhaps San Francisco's Haight-Ashbury could have flourished without publicity, but it is doubtful so many children would have traveled so far, at least so rapidly, without the publicity given to it by the media.

We have nearly forgotten Timothy Leary (and do not remember the names of his compatriots), who got a great deal of (at first, positive) publicity in the press when he urged young people to turn to drugs. Later, when he was attacked, he became a martyr and folk hero.

Jerry Rubin (do you remember him?) in his book *Do It!* suggested that much of what happened in the sixties began with Elvis Presley and his television appearances (Ed Sullivan gave him wide exposure) and the playing of his records on radio. There is some truth in what Mr. Rubin (how strange the "Mr." sounds with that name) says.

In the thirties in Germany Adolf Hitler created events to gain publicity, to win control and alter history. He used radio, huge stadiums, the streets, newsreels, and the press. By creating events that could not be ignored, he controlled the media, and in time millions died.

Later Senator Joseph McCarthy used the media for his own purposes. Others who have used it include Franklin D. Roosevelt, John and Robert Kennedy, Richard Nixon, Spiro Agnew, and those who wanted to expose the Watergate affair. In other societies, when dictators want to gain absolute control of a nation, they silence and seize control of the media during the first days of their government.

But, consciously or unconsciously, television, newspapers, and other branches of the media do more than offer the use of their news time or space to divergent causes. For they have an important impact on what we do and think, both through advertising and by the kind of entertainment and information they bring us day after day. For this reason the media, especially television, must take some (and perhaps a great deal) of the responsibility for our high crime rate, delinquency, mental illness, family breakups, and many of the other problems that we face.

I am well aware of the arguments the media use to refute this. Among them, the fact they are only the "bearers of bad news" and not the creators of it. For years I defended the media, and argued with passion at meetings and in lecture halls in defense of a free press. Nor have I changed my mind about the importance of a free press. But I now add that with freedom goes responsibility.

It was not until I sat down to think about television, until I read reports on the impact that it has on children, considered my role and that of others from the media in the South in the sixties, looked at what is reported on the say-so of self-interest groups, publicity seekers, or the public relations man's handout, and reviewed the music of the sixties, that I started to understand.

Then I saw that I was being used, and so were (and are) a lot of other media people, who, like me, believed that we were only "reporting the news," selling products, or entertaining. That was before I really understood that you can't do just one thing.

This is especially true in the field of advertising and entertainment. You can't just create a desire for a product, or just fill theater screens, magazines, or television sets with pictures and stories of sex or violence. Because there are people—and children—out there watching and reading, and a chain reaction sets in. And, as is the case in spontaneous combustion, it can sometimes be difficult to control the blaze once it starts.

This is not to say that the media are "bad." Rather that they are sometimes unthinking. Or unaware. Unaware of the impact on people. This is especially true of television.

Two researchers, Robert M. Liebert and Rita W. Poulos, reported in *Psychology Today* on experiments they conducted in which they used films and/or television to alter the thinking of children. In one experiment they worked with eighteen pre-school children who were afraid of dogs. They split the children into two groups of nine, and one group watched a film on a rear-screen projector (to simulate television) showing how a small boy overcame his fear of dogs by watching an older youth play with one. They reported:

"After they had seen the film, eight of nine children . . . willingly approached [a] German shepherd. Less than 10 minutes of our imitation TV had helped erase long-standing fear that prevented children . . . from playing with the dog. Children in the second group did not see the film and they retained their fear."

They then used a similar film to ease fear of dental work. An eight-year-old boy "climbed fearlessly into the chair" while a little girl watched. Seeing that the boy, who had his teeth cleaned, was unhurt, she climbed, unafraid, into the chair. Both children were rewarded on the film with a large red toothbrush. When the film was shown to groups of children frightened of going to the dentist the attitudes of the children toward the dentist immediately improved, according to Mr. Liebert and Ms. Poulos.

The article also tells how brief TV or film programs have encouraged shy preschoolers to join in with a group by depicting a child who grows more confident as she interacts with other youngsters under a variety of circumstances in a nursery school.

This is hardly news to manufacturers and retailers. They have known for years that a visual and verbal message can change peoples minds on a wide variety of subjects. That's why they spend so many billions each year on advertising on television, in newspapers, in magazines, and on radio. And why they keep spending more each year. In 1950, for example, some $5.7 billion was spent on all forms of advertising. Twenty years later the sum had risen to $19.6 billion, and by 1972 it was up to $23 billion, according to the publication *Advertising Age*.

In his book, *With All Its Faults* (Little, Brown and Company, 1969), Fairfax M. Cone, of the agency Foote, Cone and Belding, tells of the great advertising campaigns he was associated with, including those with magic phrases that became part of the language after being repeated again and again in (or on) the media. Mr. Cone, whose agency came up with such classic lines as "Which twin has the Toni?," "You wonder where the yellow went," and "Does she or doesn't she? . . . only her hairdresser knows for sure," also brags that some ads have, at least in small ways, changed the way we act or live.

"What happened to Clairol when this advertising appeared, and in the dozen years since, is history," he modestly tells us. "It is enough to say here that today almost seventy percent of American women use hair coloring, happily and with no attempt to disguise the fact, and most of them use Clairol."

While Mr. Cone attributes the success of another product his firm pushed to its improved flavor and quality, he also suggests that a "lucky break" in advertising played a major role. This lucky break occurred, he says, when an art director assigned to the account passed away the time at a picture-taking session by "drawing with his finger, on a frosty pitcher of purple grape Kool-Aid, a happy, smiling face." Soon the happy face appeared on the package, in print advertising, and on television, along with the slogan "Kool-Aid tastes great" and the company (and the nation's children) have lived happily ever after.

"Added to the fact that a five-cent package made two full quarts, children found the picture irresistible," Mr. Cone tells us.

Foote, Cone, and Belding was not (and is not) the only agency exploiting children for fun and profit. One only has to watch Saturday morning TV to learn that several toy manufacturers, McDonald's, Burger King, Dairy Queen, Nestle, Sunkist, Oreo, and other soft drink, candy, cookie and snack peddlers know how to make money by pitching to children. They spend huge sums because they know they will reap huge profits. The media are aware of the impact they have on children and adults, and use psychology, humor, hard sell, and repetition to reach and convince as many as possible.

Several years ago it was estimated that Saturday morning TV advertising alone produced $90 million in revenue for the three television networks, and some predicted that the amount would keep climbing —and they were right, of course.

Individual companies spend huge sums to reach and persuade children, for short-term sales and to turn them into life-long customers. For example, it has been reported that in February of 1969 Mattel toy manufacturers purchased television time averaging more than $100,000 per Saturday. That figure was doubled in September, was up to $400,000 per Saturday in October, and topped out at more than $800,000 in November—as the firm stretched out to haul in Christmas dollars.

One national citizen's group, Action for Children's Television (ACT), with headquarters in Newtonville, Massachusetts, has been trying to alert the public on the impact TV advertising has on children. Among other things, it has filed petitions with the Federal Communications Commission and has challenged the industry's own inept policing group. One petition argued: "Children's commercials generally employ 'hard sell' tactics. They misrepresent the products advertised. They encourage children to pressure parents."

This leads to family conflict and upset parents, according to a survey by Daniel Yanelovich, Inc., which reported that mothers were disturbed over the misrepresentation, and over "manipulation of the child, stress and strain imposed upon low income mothers by the demands created by the commercials and a generally unhealthy environment."

ACT also points out that children have long had special protection from hucksters and others who would use them for personal gain. But no longer is that true. As with the old sweatshops, the business community stands to lose too much money.

"Since the beginning of law, children have enjoyed a special legal status by reason of their innocence, inexperience and credulity," the ACT petition continues. "Under the laws of most states, children may not enter into binding contracts and may not manage, purchase or dispose of property except under the supervision of a guardian. They may not purchase potentially harmful products. They are carefully protected from communications whose content is considered overstimulating.

"This special legal status is a recognition that children do not have the knowledge, experience of judgment to protect themselves. A child cannot cope with a skillful adult who is seeking to sell him something.

"A neighborhood storekeeper who enticed children into his shop with candy and proceeded to talk them out of their allowances would be universally condemned. A teacher who urged poor students to buy expensive toys would be considered unfit. Television has induced its audience to accept such practices as normal.

"There is a special cruelty and inhumanity in the ceaseless touting of expensive toys to low-income children. It is not necessary to trace the resentments of blacks or the delinquency of underprivileged youth to these television practices. It is enough to say that no publicly regulated system should tolerate them. And parents in all income strata believe that the constant sparring between children wanting their parents to buy them merchandise and parents saying 'yes' or 'no' creates an unhealthy environment and relationship."

Physical harm also can result. Peddling pills is a common TV practice, and Dr. Frederick H. Lovejoy, Jr., executive secretary of the Boston Poison Information Center, says that national statistics on child poisoning show that aspirin and vitamin pills are the most commonly ingested poisons by children under five.

A child who takes about twenty-five tablets containing iron, for example, may develop "diarrhea, blood in the stools, vomiting, and possibly shock and coma." An overdose of Vitamin A—fifty times the accepted dosage—may result in "irritability, poor appetite, structural changes in bones, and increased intra-cranial pressure." Yet these bottles, available in most supermarkets in doses of from sixty to a hundred tablets (a dangerous amount), are often colored like candy, may be shaped like TV cartoon characters, and are heavily advertised on television.

In 1972 ACT succeeded in getting three drug companies to take vitamin pill commercials off TV programs for children, but the pill pushers are still selling hard during other times, and the bottles still can be found on grocery and drugstore counters. According to Dr. Lovejoy, the public spends $350 million annually on vitamins, and yet a child, after the first year of life, who eats a normal meal receives sufficient quantities in a proper diet.

Television (and other media) sell more than products. They also push ideas—and often without parents understanding what the results may be. Dr. Isidore Ziferstein, a research psychologist at Southern California Psychoanalytic Institute, points out that television is a major part of the average child's life, and we would be wise to pay more attention to it. Federally and privately backed studies show that the typical child often spends more time watching TV than he does in school. In fact, no activity absorbs as much of his time except for sleeping.

Some contend that Dr. Ziferstein goes too far when he suggests that TV could, if it wanted to, serve as a therapist for children in need of help. But more agree with several basic points that he makes.

1. TV can provide children with wholesome fun.

2. It can increase a child's awarness of the wide world.

3. When children need an outlet for "expressing emotions that have been repressed" in an "adult, repressive world," television can help. Stifled emotions include love, hate, ambition and success, he says.

4. TV can help "heal" wounds to a child's self-esteem, can strengthen weakened egos, help overcome fear, or feel stronger.

5. By watching a program about a painful real-life situation a child can "re-experience" that situation and—because he can look more objectively at it on TV—perhaps resolve the problem.

6. Television gives children the opportunity to identify with a "hero" and to absorb the hero's values.

7. When an adult wants to help a child with problems the adult can watch the youngster's reaction to "certain situations presented on the screen" and use this information to assist the child.

8. Television helps children to better understand the adult world they must enter. This can include shows about politics and other topics.

9. Children can gain a sense of adventure from TV.

10. Television can help raise the aesthetic level of society by giving children (and adults) a greater appreciation for that which is beautiful and good.

Television *could* do all of these things, Dr. Ziferstein says, but most often it does not. Instead, it tends to harm children.

1. It becomes a constant source of escape from reality.

2. Promising gratification of a child's needs, television, like alcohol and drugs, never quite delivers on that promise. Thus it is in a real sense addictive.

3. It dramatizes and encourages violence, crime, and brutality.

4. Too many shows increase tension and anxiety.

5. It can, under certain circumstances, push children into delinquent acts and criminal behavior.

6. Television may cause "subtle character disturbances."

7. It shows the world in constant conflict, and thus reduces a child's ability or willingness to cooperate.

8. By showing false values it warps the values of children.

9. Because TV encourages conflict and sometimes stresses ignoring or bending the law, it can teach youngsters to be anti-democratic.

10. It makes scientists and other useful people appear to be "mad."

11. TV can damage a child's emotional security by shaking his "confidence in the reliability of his parents, his friends, and the society in which he lives."

12. It encourages youngsters to believe in superhuman skills and to try to act like TV characters.

13. Television provides children (and adults) with a "steady diet of highly hopped-up, condensed, exciting fantasies which bear no relation to reality."

Dr. Ziferstein dwells on the "addictive" aspects of television, noting that when it begins to absorb a major portion of a child's time and energy it also becomes "a substitute for reality gratification."

Another researcher, E. Earl Barcus, a professor of communication research at Boston University, calls the whole process the "seduction" of children.

While reruns and children's shows are damaging enough, according to many observers, millions of elementary school youngsters are still watching TV at 10:00 P.M. and later. And for years many of these shows have been jam-packed with violence.

Professor Barcus talks of shows "saturated" with violence. That is, if violence was left out of the show there would no longer be a story to tell. Not only has this been common fare on late shows, but many violent programs have appeared on local stations in the afternoon and early evenings.

A California citizens group, the National Association for Better Broadcasting, lists 140 such programs, and most of us can remember them from their network days. The list includes:

The Avengers—"Explicit sadism."

Batman—"Violence and morbid suspense."

Daniel Boone—"Excessive violence, historical inaccuracy, and the depiction of youngsters in danger."

Girl from UNCLE—"Explicit horror" and "torture for fun."

Hogan's Heros—"An irresponsible mockery of documented historical tragedy."

Journey to the Center of the Earth—"One of the most repulsive animated series ever made. Terrifying situations with children in constant peril."

Lone Ranger—"Crime and violence in large measure."

Man from UNCLE—"Horror, sadism, and brutality ... a veneer of ersatz comedy which gives ... a cynical approach. One of the most objectional shows for children ever produced."

Mighty Mouse cartoons—"Discredited superman theme ... cruelty."

Mission Impossible—"Murder and other forms of violence for fun ... motivation is greed rather than social reform."

Roy Rogers—"Prime example of violence-for-fun."

The Untouchables—"Vicious and brutal."

Voyage to the Bottom of the Sea—"Produced when networks competed to originate the most nightmarish shows."

Wild, Wild West—"Contains some of the most sadistic and frightening sequences ever produced for television."

Many adults who enjoyed these shows tend to forget that a child is less experienced and less able to separate fiction from fact. If adult foreigners gain lasting impressions of America from films and syndicated television shows (and visitors still stand on Chicago street corners looking for gangsters), youngsters grow up "knowing" about our nation—and their world—in the same way.

To suggest that television is the most effective advertising medium ever devised by man, and in the same breath to add that *only* the commercials have a lasting impact on the viewer, is the height of silliness.

Before television, American children grew up emulating pioneer fliers, boxers, baseball players, movie stars, and others who won wide public recognition. Television has produced new heroes. Even the local anchor man, who may have a deep voice and empty head, is an important figure in his community.

The sale, through the years, of Mickey Mouse hats and toys, of Daniel Boone coonskin caps, Batman T-shirts, and other television-produced fads suggests the impact TV has.

Dr. Liebert, a professor of psychology at the State University of New York at Stony Brook, who taught children to overcome the fear of dogs and dentists with TV films, has concluded that "all of this evidence suggests that what a child sees on television can significantly alter almost any aspect of his behavior."

Dr. Ziferstein suggests that "What [a child] sees on television is *not* meaningless, harmless, useless, or insignificant."

Experts who conducted tests for the U.S. Surgeon General's Scientific Advisory Committee on Television and Social Behavior concluded not only that television can alter behavior but that it also may determine the kind of people we will be. And 82 percent of all American children watch television regularly, the report adds.

There is little question that large numbers of children in reform schools and mental hospitals are TV addicts. No effort has been made to determine whether or not they would have had fewer problems without television. But it is known that the number of children with problems keeps climbing.

Harry J. Skornia, a professor at the University of Illinois and an official delegate, representing the United States, at a five-day conference on television and its impact on the world society held in Perugia, Italy, said:

I fear that never before in human history, including the days of Hitler and Mussolini, have human beings been battered, confused, deceived and conditioned to violence and inhumanity with such frightening power as that of commercial television in general in the U.S. today. This battering is administered not by any government or -ism, but by private economic power: the corporation, which thinks it is only selling "goods" or "the American Way."

In a sense this type of corporation is no longer American. It is multi-national, faceless, anonymous, authoritarian in its inner structure, complete with its own "foreign office" and intelligence service, richer than many nations, and more extensive than any. Its controllers are no longer people but computers, profit statements and boards, beyond the power of any individual to control, self-generating, a new type of power at large in the world.

It is "selling" violence, frustration, confrontation and materialism.

What Professor Skornia did not say is that so many people are so distracted by television entertainment that they have not had time or opportunity to hear his warning or warnings issued by others.

Meanwhile, the advertising agencies, television networks, station owners, and large corporations laugh all the way to the bank. And if they must use armored cars to carry their money, and have locked doors and guards in their apartments and places of work, and if they are afraid to walk the streets of our cities, they do not understand that there may be a connection between how they get their riches and the ills of our society.

18

A New Use for Children

October 4, 1957, ranks as one of the most significant days in American history. And yet it has been nearly forgotten.

It was on that fall day that millions of American were stunned by the news that Russia had launched Sputnik I into earth orbit. For a decade we had been tittering at Russia's claims that it had invented almost everything, from the internal combustion engine to the telephone. Anyone who had studied history in an American school knew it wasn't true. And yet, if we were so technologically superior, why then couldn't we launch our own space vehicle immediately? And why were our rockets—still being developed—inferior in carrying capacity to those built by the Russians?

In August we had, of course, sent a balloonist, Maj. David G. Simons, some 102,000 feet into space as our contribution to the International Geophysical Year. But considering the Russian feat, it was a sorry comparison. Balloons had been around for years. And hadn't Russia announced at about the same time our balloonist was in space that they had developed a guided missile that would change warfare?

Communist-haters and Defense Department boosters in Congress made the most of public doubts and fears. Not only did they demand that the ceiling be lifted on defense spending but they also turned on the American schools—sacrosanct for years. The press and the public joined in the outcry. We are still feeling the impact of decisions made in the months after Sputnik I was launched.

161

Most Americans had, until 1957, opposed federal aid to public education. But now a crisis clearly existed. While we prided ourselves on the local control of schools, considering it a defense against manipulative politicians in Washington, and argued that schools should be individualized and child-centered, it was increasingly clear that Russia used children to meet the needs of their nation. Shouldn't we do the same?

The National Science Foundation announced that America suffered from a serious shortage of engineers and technicians, and that they would help solve the problem by awarding graduate fellowships, and also planned to sponsor a $4 million program to improve the teaching of science. We also learned that we had a critical teacher shortage.

Then, on November 3, 1957, Russia launched Sputnik II with a dog aboard, sending new shock waves through the nation. One week later the U.S. Office of Education issued a report showing that from 1927 to 1957 enrollment in Soviet *technicums* (junior or technical colleges) had climbed from 189,000 to 1,961,000 and that in the same thirty-year period Russian universities increased their enrollments from 169,000 students to 1,867,000. Further, Russia was graduating 80,000 engineers annually, while in 1957 the United States graduated only 34,000.

Responding to the crisis with patriotic zeal, school administrators across the nation began tightening the screws on millions of children. On December 30, 1957, President Eisenhower called for a $1 billion emergency program to beef up school science, mathematics, and foreign language programs.

Congress passed the 1958 National Defense Education Act, and introduced a program to train school counselors to discover talented students and push them into the sciences as quickly as possible.

Soon new math programs were developed, teaching machines designed, and the American Association for the Advancement of Science reported on how textbooks and teaching methods were being improved. By the 1960–61 school year the number of elementary school pupils studying a foreign language soared from under 200,000, before Sputnik, to 1,227,006. States that did not provide kindergarten classes were encouraged to start programs, and by 1963 roughly two-thirds of all five-year-olds were in school, and 99 percent of all children ages six to thirteen were enrolled.

The education push had, of course, begun before Sputnik. World War II veterans had gone to college in record numbers under the G.I. Bill, and while in 1950 the national median education was 9.3 years, by 1962 the median climbed to 11.4 years of schooling, and would have been higher

A New Use for Children 163

had blacks been able to attend school freely, and had their school attendance assured improved employment opportunities.

As more Americans attended school for longer periods, employers raised hiring standards until it became necessary to have a high school diploma to do even fairly menial jobs. The number of students in college continued to set new records each year.

For many students, especially those from striving middle-class homes, where academic achievement was honored, encouraged and rewarded, the screw-tightening of the 1950s and 1960s was beneficial. American children, except for a few of the elite, had never been asked to perform at even a fraction of their full potential. Even the beefed-up programs were easy for many youngsters, and they blossomed and grew from the experience.

The story was quite different for other children. Tougher schools meant frustration and failure. Soon the school dropout and kickout rate became a national issue, and children were seen as unpatriotic or worse when they failed to make it. President Kennedy called the school dropout situation a "serious national problem" and demanded change. A study in the early 1960s by the U.S. Office of Education indicated that 32 percent of the girls and 38 percent of the boys who left school before graduation did so because of "adverse school experience," while 27 percent of the girls quit to marry and 25 percent of the boys left to go to work.

It is worth noting that at about the same time both the national delinquency rate and the number of emotionally disturbed children began climbing. My studies in both fields strongly suggest that school pressure and school failure are directly related to these two problems. School troubles also are a factor in our high runaway rate, in drug abuse, and even in promiscuity. And the use of children to meet national goals in a free society also contributed to the student uprising in the 1960s, although other factors carried a great deal of weight as well.

As I pointed out in a previous chapter, to solve these problems schools must become more child-oriented again. They must give youngsters a sense of individual worth and teach them to care about others.

In a free society, economic and political needs are best met—except in wartime or other crisis periods—through the normal laws of supply and demand. Federal meddling in a society as large as ours—without proper regard for the variety of side effects always produced—creates as many (or more) problems than it solves. The government-created inflation rate, the welfare mess, and the surplus of teachers and other professionals support this point. It may take several more blundering decades to understand the dangers of "Big-Daddyism," even while Russia, which has had poor results and serious failures with rigid state control of the people, seems to be permitting more freedom each year. Nor can we learn, it seems, from England and the Scandinavian countries that socialism is counterproductive.

It may be a chicken-and-the-egg question, but it is unfair to fault the government alone for our problems, at least those involving children. Hedonistic consumerism and the women's liberation movement have encouraged more and more parents to relinquish (or abandon) more and more responsibility for their children to the state. Both day care and the schools have been asked to take on the burden of child rearing.

Even if the dangers our fathers and grandfathers warned about do not materialize—including a kind of national brain-washing—shifting responsibility from parent to state or institution carries with it a great deal of risk. Traditional schools at best reward mediocrity and damage gifted children—those we call creative—and youngsters with mental, emotional, and physical handicaps. And worse results can be found. In California the San Francisco school board was sued in a so-called Peter Doe case because schools—instead of meeting a student's needs—have resorted to social promotions. There an eighteen-year-old was graduated while reading only at a fifty-grade level. One can find students who can not read at all being awarded diplomas.

The question in the Peter Doe case is quite simple: Can schools be held accountable when children do not measure up? Or should the blame continue to rest with the youngsters? One can imagine that if teachers and schools are found to be responsible, then the $52 billion we now spend on education annually will be increased to $500 billion—and even then it probably will not do the job.

Teachers are not trained in such essentials as "touching"; they are themselves largely nice but mediocre individuals, hardly the profound thinkers and brilliant motivators that would be needed; and teaching methods are less effective than those developed centuries ago, when education focused on thinking and problem-solving.

It has often been said the best way to educate a student is to have him sit on a log opposite the a gifted teacher. And the Socratic method of teaching has long been seen as the most effective way of educating a person that has yet been developed. When a person, through his own thought processes and reasoning, finds an answer, it clearly has more meaning than when facts are fed into him through books, teachers, or even teaching machines.

A half-trained teacher, who was a modest scholar in school and who lacks imagination, can hardly expect to produce superior students. And if that teacher, emotionally, is a controlling person rather than one who can give a child freedom and room to grow, then the child will be stifled and damaged.

Why are there so few child prodigies today? Why so few profound thinkers, statesmen, artists, musicians, and writers? We can speculate at length, blaming television, hedonistic consumerism, socialism, and even the poor quality of the "gene pool." But the school must also be considered.

Mozart, the great composer, born in 1756, was educated by his father, an accomplished violinist, and he began lessons on the harpsichord at the age of three, was encouraged to write music at four, and at five performed for the first time in public at a hall at a German university. His father, though very poor, took him and other members of his family on tour the following year. At seven he was singing, playing the harpsichord, organ, and violin, and was composing.

Marie Jean Antoine Nicolas Caritat Condorcet, an eighteenth-century French mathematician, philosopher, and revolutionist, whose writings on the equality of men, classes, and nations are said to have been studied by Thomas Jefferson, gained recognition as a mathematician at the age of sixteen. And Jefferson himself received a classical education that included Latin, Greek, French, and Spanish, and was graduated from William and Mary when he was twenty. He was thirty-three when he wrote the Declaration of Independence.

David Hume, an influential eighteenth-century English philosopher, historian, and political economist, enrolled, despite his father's early death, at the University of Edinburgh when he was twelve, and completed his studies three years later, in 1726. Adam Smith, the eighteenth-century English economist, and close friend of Hume, was sent to the University of Glasgow at fourteen. Both received classical educations.

The highly praised nineteenth-century English philosopher and economist John Stuart Mill, who greatly influenced the American theory of free enterprise, was taught by his father to read Greek at three, and by the age of eight had, among other things, read Xenophon's *Anabasis*, all of Herodotus, Aesop's *Fables*, the six Dialogues of Plato, and the writings of Lucian, Diogenes, and other Greek thinkers. In English he read Robertson's histories, Hume, Gibbon, Hooke's *Roman History*, Watson's *Philip II* and *Philip III*, Rollin's *Ancient History*, Langhorne's *Plutarch*, thirty volumes of the *Annual Register*, Millar's *Historical View of the English Government*, Mosheim's *Ecclesiastical History*, and a great deal more. At the age of eight he also began the study of Latin, geometry, algebra, and continued reading in Greek and English, including Aristotle's logical treatises in the original Greek.

Jeremy Bentham, the early nineteenth-century philosopher and jurist, was also greatly influential in both England and America, especially in the fields of law and legislation. He began the study of Latin at the age of three, and (according to biographers) "eagerly read" adult histories and other scholarly works. By the time he was five he was fluent in French and also could read Greek. At thirteen he enrolled at Queens College at Oxford and was graduated when he was fifteen. He later became known for, among other things, his *Principles of Morals and Legislation,* published in 1789, the same year the U.S. Constitution was ratified.

The list of those who have left their names recorded in history after beginning individualized programs of study at an early age is much longer, as anyone researching the subject knows.

Perhaps a nation of land-clearers, dirt farmers, Indian-fighters, exploiters of natural resources, industrialists, scientists and technicians, purveyors of planned obsolescence and easy credit, and of high-pressure advertising cannot be expected to produce large numbers of artists, classical musicials and dancers, philosophers and moralists. But it seems possible that we *could* produce more talented and thoughtful persons if we wanted to.

Throughout history there have been periods of both great genius and creativity, as well as barbarity and intellectual dullness. Education and affluence play a role in this. Talent blossoms when children are challenged and encouraged at an early age, when education is individualized and truly mind-expanding (in contrast to the effects produced by mind-expanding drugs), and when children are disciplined, rewarded, and admired for early achievement.

Just as America used children to tame the wilderness, to work on farms and in sweatshops, and later as pets, so other societies have used their children in other ways. One has only to look at the fifteenth century and the Italian Renaissance to see that this is true.

The fifteenth century was an age, like this one, of great wealth and international trade. Merchants living in Venice, Milan, Florence, Rome, and other Italian cities competed with one another as patrons of the arts. Unlike American millionaires, who invest in the works created in those days and in subsequent centuries, the Italian merchants searched for talented youngsters, paid for their training under skilled masters, and then kept them busy creating the great works of art that remain unequaled to this day. Who were their discoveries? A short version of the list includes Michelangelo, Leonardo da Vinci, Donatello, Botticelli, Raphael, Bellini, Lippi, Signorelli, and Verrocchio.

If we have a parallel today it is in the competition to develop football, basketball, baseball, hockey, swimming and track stars, and skilled golfers. Or our effort to find and support entertainers. In the past generation our prodigies have largely been film stars, rock musicians, and youngsters who have been models and television actors and actresses. Now youthful sports greats are again gaining more recognition.

Philosophers, historians, and moral leaders are scoffed at and looked down upon. Boys with artistic talent are ridiculed by their peers and even by parents. In Presidential elections in the 1960s and in 1972 large numbers of persons asked why, in a nation of 200 million persons, we could not produce better leaders.

Our schools cannot take all of the blame, for they are, like all of us, responsive to society at large. And yet they can be faulted for failing to provide leadership in their own field. Perhaps it is enough to point out that such writers as John Holt and Piaget are neither profound philosophers nor brilliant students of human nature. And yet these men and others like them are highly regarded at large and small teachers colleges, and by teachers in general. This is a fact that should not be taken lightly.

19

"I was slow."—
Learning Disability

Robert Burton, who runs a private agency for delinquents in Tucson, Arizona, almost always gets a laugh when he talks about his school days.

"Until I was fourteen my teachers thought I was dumb," he says. "Then they found out I could play football. Overnight I progressed from dumb to slow."

An enthusiastic, capable man in his early thirties, Mr. Burton has what some call dyslexia, or a "specific learning disability." Although above average in intelligence, and highly achievement-oriented, he can barely read or write. For reasons hard to explain, his brain scrambles letters and words. Because of this his early school experience was, at times, "living hell." Without strong, supportive parents and above-average talent for football (he still plays semipro ball with a Las Vegas team on weekends) he might have become just another dropout or delinquent with a police record, as thousands do each year. He knows this, and it is one reason he battles for children who are still struggling in the system.

Mr. Burton did not discover his handicap until he was twenty-nine years old. He found out during a routine eye checkup, and until that day he had accepted what he had been told—that he was retarded.

"When I found out I wasn't retarded, that it was dyslexia, it was like being reborn," he says enthusiastically. "The feeling is impossible to describe."

Mr. Burton is hardly alone. Theresa, a pretty girl of six, is a student at the Landmark School in Prides Crossing, Massachusetts. On a standard IQ test she shows up as normal, but on other tests, which take into account her language problem, she ranks in the top 1 percent of the nation in intelligence. She is at Landmark, a nonprofit school for children with learning disabilities, because she has failed to develop verbal skills and finds it difficult to express herself.

Billy, a former Landmark pupil, is eleven. When interviewed by the staff, his parents produced a public school report showing that he had an IQ of 84, was "borderline retarded," with little academic potential. After interviewing Billy, Landmark officials concluded the IQ tests and public school prognosis were wrong. After only four months Billy's IQ soared to 104, officials report. Now he attends a better-than-average private school in New Hampshire, where he is making A's and B's.

A few years ago a medical student taking a second-year-exam produced sentences described by Dr. Richard Maslanz, now a professor of neurology at Columbia, as "nearly incoherent." While the student, who had completed four years of college and two years of medical school, "spoke perfectly well," he could "barely read" or write. He had been able to make it through college because his wife read the textbooks to him, and he memorized what she read.

"If the medical school had insisted that he write his exam he would never have passed," Dr. Maslanz says. "He was tested orally and is now a fine doctor."

There are millions of Americans like Robert Burton, Theresa, Billy, and the doctor. Large numbers of them are the victims of the schools they attend and of their parents, who, lacking an understanding of language disability, label them lazy, stupid, or difficult. And they are also victims of a society that says there is only one way to learn.

Learning or language disability is a strange affliction. First studied in the nineteenth century by the German doctor Rudolf Berlin, but largely ignored until recent years, the subject is widely debated today. Dr. Berlin coined the word dyslexia (*dys*, meaning impaired, and *lexia*, meaning language), but neither he nor others who have considered it since have been able to identify the causes. The symptoms are so varied that many believe that it is not just one problem but many.

Most children who have learning disability, if they are not maltreated because of their handicap, seem otherwise healthy and happy. They have normal or high IQ's but find it difficult to communicate or to assimilate or "process" language—reading, writing, speech, listening, or mathematics.

Dr. Maslanz, who once headed the National Institute of Neurological Disorders and Stroke in Washington, defines learning disability as an affliction of individuals with normal (or higher than normal) IQ, who have specific defects, often hard to identify, that interfere with learning.

Dr. Charles Drake (his doctorate is in education), headmaster at the Landmark School and editor of the *Journal of Learning Disability*, suggests that not only do these language-handicapped children have high IQ's but they also attend good schools and want to learn.

"Most of these children look normal, act normal, and may, in some areas, even be superior," he says. "Teachers and sometimes the parents assume he is faking it [his handicap] because of this, and so they punish him. It can take us almost a year to get the child to the point where he no longer expects to be punished by his teachers and peers in the classroom. These are picked-on children."

Because the phrase "learning disability," compared to "retardation," "mental illness," and "delinquency," is nonstigmatizing and is a multipurpose term that is hard to define, its use has been expanded—especially by parents. As one New York psychiatrist put it, "now that the words 'learning disability' have caught on I haven't had a parent bring me a disturbed child in more than a year." Thus it can be, at least to the public, a catch-all term for children who are spoiled, lazy, retarded, disturbed, and handicapped in other ways.

The Orton Society (named after the late Dr. Samuel Torrey Orton, an American neurologist who pioneered in this and related fields early in this century) is based in Maryland, and is one of the groups that leads the battle for children with language problems.

In the brochure the Orton Society sends out, it notes that while "many man-hours" have been spent on hammering out a definition by "national and international bodies," professionals have not yet been able to agree on what learning disability, specific language disability, dyslexia, or strephosymbolia are. All they know is that large numbers of children suffer from these afflictions, and that they can ruin their lives.

The Society, after excluding learning problems that "result from deprived backgrounds, emotional disturbances, mental retardation, vision and hearing deficiencies and poorly developed motor control" or other identifiable causes, reports that there is "still a host of children whose language difficulties have not been described." Studies suggest that 10 percent or more of American children fall into this group, and many struggle in school, develop emotional problems through school failure, become delinquent, and may never live up to their potential.

Children with dyslexia (that is, with language disability) "show some combination of the following characteristics," the Society reports:

1. Delayed or inadequate spoken language
2. Difficulty in learning and remembering printed words
3. Reversal of orientation of letters, or sequence of letters when written. (Including b and d, and words like was–saw and quite–quiet.)

4. Persistent spelling errors

5. Continued uncertainty as to right- or left-handedness

6. Confusion about directions in space or time (right and left, up and down, yesterday and tomorrow)

8. Difficulty in finding the "right" word when speaking

9. Cramped or illegible handwriting

10. Defective written composition

11. Similar problems among relatives

"Fortunately, very few children exhibit all these patterns; but they have enough in common to distinguish them as a group with unique emotional needs," the Society continues. "Failure to learn can create a variety of puzzling reactions. The child, reacting to his failure, is often forced to find other pathways of emotional expression . . . and he is called naughty, bad or delinquent . . . uncooperative, lazy, or emotionally blocked. If this experience of failure can be exchanged for a sense of competence in learning based on genuine achievement, the child will then be free to master the tools for living. Given appropriate diagnosis and suitable educational procedures, this mastery can almost always be achieved."

Those who want to know more about this handicap can write The Orton Society, Inc., at 8415 Bellona Lane, Towson, Maryland, 21204.

For the purposes of this book, I will leave the subject of dyslexia at this point and broaden the subject to include many handicapped children the experts exclude who also are struggling at school, at home, with their peers and in the community and who fail to reach their potential because of what I prefer to call *culturally imposed learning disability.*

It is my view that not only is dyslexia ignored but so is the damage done to nondsylexic children. And the wider problem includes racial barriers, academic prejudice of other sorts, and the killing off of creativity.

I use the term *culturally imposed learning disability* first to show that I am not limiting this chapter to the area described by the Orton Society (as important as that may be), but also because dyslexia, like the other handicaps, would not be such a serious problem is we did not live in a culture that put so much emphasis on language.

In discussing any form of learning disability, whether caused by inadequate diet, prejudice, dyslexia, retardation, or some other handicap, one must make several basic assumptions. First, if there is a disability, then there must be such a thing as a universal learning *ability;* and, further, that because of its universality this ability is *normal.* (I might also add, desirable.)

Once we assume that learning (of language, subject, or skills) is normal, then we must also assume (at least on the basis of logic) that the inability to learn something that many persons learn without great effort is *ab-*

normal. Next we must assume (based on current scientific thinking) that this abnormality has a cause, although it may be hidden, and that at some point in history (assuming also that mankind will survive) we will not only be able to identify the cause but also will find the method of correcting the disability.

But in all of this, we tend to ignore the fact that there is a cultural factor involved that tips the scale against the person with the so-called disability. The child is handicapped, or labeled as having a disability *only in a culture that stresses that ability.*

Take, for example, a person who cannot carry a tune. That person has, by almost any definition, a specific learning (or language) disability. In a primitive society that communicates through music, that person would clearly be a deviant with a severe handicap. But in the United States, unless you decided to become a choirmaster, opera star (and possibly a cantor or a Lutheran) singing ability is not terribly important (as recent rock stars have proven). The person who is tone-deaf, thus suffering from a specific learning disability, will not be hurt by the handicap because our culture does not consider singing important.

Now consider the child who cannot learn to climb a rope in the school gym, no matter how hard he tries. For whatever reason, youngsters who find rope-climbing impossible may get a low mark for gym, but like singing, this disability does not carry a severe penalty with it because rope-climbing is not an essential skill in our culture.

Finally, what of the child who seems incapable of distinguishing mushrooms that are safe to eat from those that are dangerous—even after studying mushrooms and hearing a lecture on them? The same child, when tested, cannot tell one pine tree from another, nor can he identify many deciduous trees or shrubs in the winter. His knowledge of wild animals and their habits also is limited, and he cannot tell the difference between oats, rye, or wheat growing in a field.

Our great-grandfathers would have clucked and shrugged over such a boy—a handicapped child who could not learn the basics.

My list of abilities (or disabilities) could be much longer: the ability to throw a baseball past a professional batter, or to hit against a professional pitcher; to run the mile in four minutes or less; to understand the controls of and fly a commercial jet airliner; to program a computer; speak Russian fluently; write Chinese; comprehend, compare, and evaluate the works of Spinoza, Kant, Schopenhauer, Spencer, Nietzsche, Bergson, Croce, Russell and Santayana; or to write a modern symphony, for example.

Many of us would find some things on the list difficult to do or learn. Because these are noncritical areas, we would not be punished for our handicaps, however. Nor are we judged on our ability to split rails, shoot a rifle, birth a calf, make noodles and bread, build a cabin or sod hut, spin wool, bank a fire, or shoe a horse.

Instead, our culture has decided that the difference between a bright and dull child (and thus the difference between survival or dependency) lies in the ability to spell, punctuate, read, write, speak, use grammar properly, do arithmetic problems, and learn other subjects mandated by school officials or even those at the state level. Learning ability carries with it the weight of law, and failure to perform adequately has become a quasi-crime. Children who cannot learn and skip school are sent to reform school in many states. Others are subjected to therapy, sometimes without parental permission, and those who are hyperactive are given drugs.

At the very least, learning disability children are failed in most schools, or they are downgraded to the "Redbird" group (and described as "dummies" by classmates with language ability), or are ridiculed, excluded, paddled, or punished in other ways approved by the teacher or principal, superintendent, or school board.

If it is true that schools follow the nineteenth-century Utilitarian philosophy of "the greatest good for the greatest number," educators too often forget that Utilitarianism stressed the happiness and worth of the individual as well.

Two points stand out. First, branding a child a failure because of a language handicap is immoral in every sense of that word. And the decision as to what is critical for a child to learn and what is not is decided upon by persons with language *ability*, not disability. Like those who design school toilets and halls without thought given to children in wheelchairs, so those who design the curriculum give little thought to, and have little empathy for, children with language or learning disabilities.

To understand this, consider what we do to blacks, Chicanos, and other minority groups. Peter Watson, an English psychologist who also has studied and worked in the United States, points out that black children, when given an IQ test by a white person, score lower than when the same test is given by a black person. As early as 1936 this was shown to be true by H. G. Canady in Evanston, Illinois. The point made by Watson and others is that test scores are related to stress and other factors.

Many lawyers, such as Jerrold N. Oppenheim, an American Civil Liberties Union attorney, contend that there are many legal questions involved when IQ tests designed for white, middle-class youngsters are given to black or minority-group children. His views are bolstered by a host of studies, including one by Jane R. Mercer, an associate professor of psychology at the Univerity of California, Riverside.

In a study conducted over a period of several years, Dr. Mercer found that large numbers of minority children are *falsely labeled* retarded because IQ tests do not take into account language differences, or racial and ethnic backgrounds. When persons labeled retarded were tested in another way—on the ability to function normally in society and to adapt to new situations—more than 90 percent of the blacks and 60 percent of the Chicanos (all with IQ scòres of 70 or lower) passed their tests. Few whites with IQ test scores of 70 or less could pass the tests developed by Dr. Mercer, and few functioned well in the community. Yet many black and Chicano adults who scored low on the IQ tests read newspapers, magazines and books, traveled, particpated in sports, held jobs, and had normal social relationships with fellow workers and friends.

And what of children who test low or perform poorly because of inadequate stimulation, hearing problems, visual handicaps, low motivation, lack of sleep, inadequate diets, abuse, and other childhood experiences? Should we write them off because they are neither retarded or able to compete academically? And what of extreme cases of learning disability?

Autistic children, for example, are considered untestable and unteachable. Many do not seem to hear, perceive, or learn; they appear to live mentally in hidden worlds of their own. They seem insensitive to pain, most do not speak, and many refuse to make eye contact with other humans. Yet at Michael Reese Hospital in Chicago researchers have found that some autistic children begin to communicate when they are taught the sign language used by the deaf.

Emotionally disturbed children may, in extreme cases, be totally withdrawn. In one of Ohio's snake-pit mental hospitals a young man did not move from his cot for months. Yet Paul Hahn, a university professor, began to communicate through the sense of touch, and I saw the youth laughing and talking with other inmates, and in time he shook my hand and talked to me.

In one California institution for the retarded I saw great strides being made with children who in most states would have been confined to their beds. And in Texas severely retarded youths were learning to run a truck farm—doing hand-picking jobs with pleasure in an age when some farmers find it difficult to harvest their crops.

Children both deaf and blind were learning in a pilot program in Tucson, Arizona. The effort put into this program makes traditional teaching—even in special-education classes—seem like child's play. How quickly America has forgotten Helen Keller and the contribution she made!

And what of creativity? Since being creative gives one a richer life, and creative persons have made many valuable contributions to the quality of life that we live, should we not encourage it? Is not the lack of creativity a learning disability? Most experts agree that all healthy, normal children are creative when they are young. "Schools squash creativity," says Dr. Pierre Durand, a psychiatrist and head of the Philbrook Children's Center in Concord, New Hampshire. Large numbers of other professionals interviewed agree.

In a rather unscientific survey conducted as I traveled through the nation researching this book, I found that (1) creative students may be less capable than noncreative students in academic subjects; (2) that those who are still creative when they reach college were labeled creative or talented in a creative area at an early age; (3) creative students were encouraged by a parent, relative, teacher, or some other older person they respected; and (4) they did not care what others thought about creative fields such as the dance, music, the fine arts, poetry or writing or what some call "blue-sky thinking."

Creativity is "squashed" for many reasons. First, it requires freedom of thought and the willingness to consider all ideas without feeling that any are "wrong." Yet traditional schools dump large batches of information on children and expect them to feed back, through testing, what they are taught. Those who fail to produce "right" answers fail the subject and are labeled stupid. There is no room for original thought or behavior, and, in fact, creativity is considered deviant behavior by teachers who have no concept of what is "wrong" with the student.

To go a step further, to *become* a teacher one must conform and feed back the information given them by teachers and textbooks, and play the academic game that squashes creativity. It can be assumed that by the time the teacher finishes college whatever creativity may have existed has been throughly drained away. The few innovative or creative teachers I have known are either pushed out or further flattened by noncreative superintendents and principals. Few professionals are more regimented than elementary and high school teachers.

To put it another way (with an apology to Lincoln), teachers are selected "of the system, by the system, and for the system." To become a teacher one must go to college, and to attend college one must do well in the elementary school and high school, and to do well there one must suppress creativity. It is a never-ending circle.

I can speak from experience. Schools nearly destroyed my chances of becoming a writer. Had I not come from a family that rewarded creativity and downgraded the importance of academic performance I might well be working in the child-caring field (or even some other area) rather than writing about it. For throughout school my teachers first graded papers for spelling and punctuation, and then for content. I was always classified as a poor student in English until my junior year in college when I was "discovered" by a professor who also had trouble spelling, but who paid attention to content.

Now I look back with some satisfaction, knowing that few if any of the students getting high marks in writing are today able to earn a living in this field. But also with considerable sadness, knowing that there are large numbers of children who will never have a chance to develop as they should because of a minor learning disability that (like mine) can be corrected with practice and a good dictionary.

As I said at the start, dyslexia is not the only learning disability that should be studied. There is little question that (as Skinner suggests) rewards and punishment by society and those hired to represent society produce the kinds of people that exist in this world. Robert Burton, used as an example in the opening lines of this chapter, was nearly destroyed by the educational system until the school found a talent it was willing to reward—football.

There can be no disagreement that our schools help produce children who are delinquent, disturbed, or otherwise handicapped for life because the schools are not designed to find *some redeeming quality* in *every* child, regardless of his background, handicaps, or behavior. We all must be good at something to survive emotionally!

"It's a pretty dismal world if you think you can't succeed at all," Bowdon Hunt, a juvenile court judge in Florida, explains. "A lot of children I see in court feel that they are absolute failures at fourteen or fifteen years of age. And their school records *show* they've *never succeeded at anything.*

"Can you imagine what your job would be like if you went to work every day knowing that you had been considered a failure the year before and that you were on the borderline again and the boss was about to fire you? School is all that a child has. It is a major part of his life. Did you know that more kids run away the day after report cards are given out than at any other time?"

Someday teachers and other educators will understand this, and when they suddenly comprehend the enormity of what they have done to millions of children and to our society they will feel like wearing sack-cloth and ashes—if they are sensitive at all. It is a gross exaggeration to compare the life-long damage schools do to children with learning disabilities to what the Nazis did to the Jews in the 1930s and 1940s, but, as Jonathan Kozol so eloquently explained in *Death at an Early Age,* there is more than one way to castrate or kill a person.

"Somehow," says Dr. Richard Mazlanz, "we must make the people in the educational system understand that people are different, that each person is an individual with special skills and his own way of learning. We must recognize this and teach each child in the appropriate way. If we realize that each child is different, if we capitalize on each child's strengths, and if we accept the fact that this difference doesn't make one child better or of more value than another, then we will be on the right road.

"We must remember that through history many persons with superior talents were uniquely different, and because of this difference they were uniquely valuable to society."

20

The Cookie-cutter System

A new, local school board member asked me, not long ago, if I thought people were putting too much blame on the schools for the problems of our children. A dental assistant and mother, she still remains somewhat in awe of authoritarian school officials, and so she is inclined to believe the administrator who said public criticism is unfair.

Her question is hard to answer accurately. Many schools do an adequate and sometimes even excellent job of teaching a variety of subjects to mild-mannered, fairly hard-working, academically inclined students. Yet schools still hurt large numbers of youngsters who arrive at the schoolhouse door with serious personal problems. And too many children who are healthy and happy when they enroll in school are damaged by less-than-sensitive teachers and principals, and by crude or cruel fellow pupils.

Perhaps a more important question is this: What do we want our schools to be and do?

Although we spend $52 billion a year on public education, this is a subject few parents, teachers, or school boards think about—just as they tend to ignore technological change, the impact of widespread affluence, television, working mothers, divorce, the influence of large corporations, unions, the state and federal bureaucracy, and an insatiable lust for material things.

Ask the man in the street what schools are for and he will reply incredulously: "To teach children, of course."

"Teach them what?"

"To read. To write. Arithmetic. History. Social studies. Maybe a language or vocational skills. Home economics. Socialization. The normal things kids need."

"Need for what?"

"For life. You know, so they can get into college or a good job. You need a diploma, even a college degree to get a good job today."

It all sounds so sensible. So logical. We forget these are artificial barriers used to screen people *out* in an age of surplus labor. For the same reason we prolong childhood. And we must be sure there are sufficient numbers of people available for menial, degrading jobs. Without an artificial barrier and sense of guilt about foolishness of youth ("I never should have dropped out!") how would we find people to sweep floors, make motel beds, pump gas, work in laundries, haul garbage, or do other menial tasks?

Further, if schools exist to teach basics, why do we hire so many school nurses, counselors, social workers, psychologists, and psychiatrists? Why do we give courses in sex education?

It is, in part, because of parental abdication of responsibility. They prefer to turn child rearing over to strangers, including schools. But it also is tied to the stresses and strains of a world that has drastically changed in the past seventy-five years.

In the simple farming communities of the eighteenth century, when our nation was young, and even in the nineteenth century, when cities began to flourish, one really didn't need to know much to survive. Planting, harvesting, spinning, weaving, hunting, cooking, cleaning, simple bookkeeping, and hand trades were mastered largely by living. Basic reading, penmanship, a little mathematics, and a bit of history were enough for almost any child.

An Abe Lincoln could lie on the hearth and read by firelight, learn the law by working for a lawyer, and about business by failing and trying again. Wrestling, storytelling, and a reputation for honesty could lead to the legislature and the Presidency. But no longer.

We are beseiged daily by economic questions and technological problems that would send a Socrates, Caesar, or Cicero reeling, not to mention a Washington, Adams, Jefferson or Monroe. Even crafty Ben Franklin or Thomas Alva Edison might have had trouble coping with the problems of our age.

There still are persons living (though the number is rapidly dwindling) who were born before there were radios, automobiles, gas stations, paved roads, skyscrapers, airplanes, telephones, electric power lines connecting every home in America. Many of us can remember the first television sets, the arrival of jet planes, helicopters, nuclear weapons, space flights, and so many things children take for granted today.

Technological change comes so rapidly now that knowledge gained in college a mere twenty years ago (and sometimes three or four years ago) is already obsolete. Corporations, unions, and government have become so large and impersonal and so computerized that many individuals feel confused, overwhelmed, helpless, powerless.

Yet our schools muddle along, changing, but most often changing only superficially, even while many administrators believe they are making major strides.

The problem is not just to make learning more fun, or to keep up with expanding technology. It is that we live in such a hopped-up, hectic, overstimulated world that stuffing one's mind with great thoughts of the Western world, mathematics, or spelling and punctuation is not enough. Today's children need more than information.

I remember how, a few years ago, a reform school superintendent working for Los Angeles County drove me from the city government complex up into the mountains. Early in the ride he told me to be aware of the physiological and psychological changes I experienced as we left dense traffic, the pollution, noise, neon flashing lights, and the clutter and clash of stores and buildings and homes behind. The effect was not unlike stepping off a roaring, whirling carnival ride and walking over to the dark and quiet grandstand to sit alone.

What can educators do about this and related problems, including the pace we set for ourselves and children? Can they teach us to cope?

They can and must, for who else is there to do it? Certainly not the family, at least in many cases, until we have trained at least one generation of parents to help their children to survive in a kaleidoscopic world.

But to meet the needs of children in the last quarter of the century the schools must change. Psychologists, psychiatrists, social workers, judges, corrections experts, professionals working with the handicapped and many educators agree on this. But few have a clear view of how schools should operate, or what they should do.

Charles E. Silberman, writing in *Crisis in the Classroom* (Random House, 1970), suggests, in part, that schools cannot reform until educators begin asking themselves the *hard* questions. He cites Wilford M. Aikin, who studied schools and wrote in 1942 that "It is not enough to create better conditions for learning. It is equally necessary to determine what American youth most need to learn."

Some thinkers have considered this question, but Silberman himself, and most other writers, as well as those such as Piaget, Skinner, and Erikson, focus more attention on *how* children learn (or how to help or make them learn) and on teachers and teaching than on *what* children should be taught.

John Holt, in *How Children Learn* (Pitman, 1967) would have us give children more freedom to taste, touch, heft, bend, and break off pieces of the world—strengthening natural curiosity, encouraging risk-taking and close observation, giving youngsters the ability to control their own learning speed and to learn about what interests them. There is value in this, but someone must protect children from themselves and others. Mr. Holt wrote his book before drug abuse swept through America, a time when children already too liberated cried for ever more freedom, when they really needed guidance and firm support.

What children need most is a sense of stability in a complex, ever-changing, unstable, and sometimes dangerous world. This is why the family—with a mother at home and the father involved—is so important. And why schools must change.

The church, family ties, and patriotism were once the glue that helped keep society from falling apart. But today the family home is more a kennel, patriotism is passé, and the church has not kept pace—it does not meet the needs of people.

Neighborhoods die or break up, urban life is impersonal and danger-ous, but the school survives as the one familiar landmark that we can count on.

"What really binds men together is their culture—the ideas and stand-ards they have in common," Ruth Benedict, the noted anthropologist, wrote in *Patterns of Culture* in 1934. If there is a single idea or standard that binds us together, beyond hedonistic consumerism, it is the idea that an education is both valuable and important for all children.

We have few traditions left that have not been overrun by hedonistic consumerism. Christmas has been reduced to a wild spending spree. Easter has lost its meaning. Mother's Day and Father's Day are com-mercial events, as are birthdays and Valentine's Day. The county fair and state fair have become honky-tonk money-making events rather than places to show off the skills of one's hands and mind. And what of Memorial Day or the Fourth of July? They are no longer celebrated in a meaningful way, but rather as escape from work and a time for fun. Shopping centers are open on Sundays, and golf courses do a booming business. And what of baptism, communion, weddings, wakes, special anniversaries, and family reunions? They hardly exist in an era of churchlessness, Forest Lawn cemeteries, living together, easy divorce, abortion, high mobility, and old people's homes. Children have been reduced to a market by merchants, and to the status of pets by parents, and the school remains the one institution, the one place of relative safety and security, free, to some extent, of the influences that have overtaken every other aspect of our lives.

Ruth Benedict could see, forty years ago, what we are only starting to understand today. She wrote: "Our children are not individuals whose rights and tastes are casually respected from infancy, as they are in some primitive societies, but special responsibilities, like our possessions, in which we succumb or in which we glory, as the case may be. They are fundamentally extensions of our own egos and give a special opportunity for the display of authority. The pattern is not inherent in the parent-children situations, as we so glibly assume. It is impressed upon the situation by the major drives of our culture, and it is only one of the occasions in which we follow our traditional obsessions."

Sexual freedom, political corruption, racism, inflation, recession, hedonistic consumerism, change, confusion, and danger roll through our lives like flash floods. We are ripped off by salesmen, repairmen, the Internal Revenue Service, labor leaders, manufacturers, home-builders, drug companies, and almost anyone else who can play on our fears, or dreams, or secret desires.

What if somebody over there (or over here) really does decide to push the nuclear button? What if we cannot eliminate political corruption? What if the crime rate continues to grow? What if we do have an ever-growing number of dishonest policemen and incompetent judges? What if political kidnappings and terrorism grow even more commonplace in our society? What if we cannot control population or produce more food? What if? . . . What if? . . . One hardly dares speculate.

It would seem that the church and other institutions (including the family) are no longer the source of strong moral influence, and that we live in a culture that is run by the morals of the marketplace. If this is true, or at least partly true, then what can we do about it?

Ruth Benedict wrote: " . . . there can be no reasonable doubt that one of the most effective ways in which to deal with the staggering burden of psychopathic tragedies in America at the present time is by means of an education program which fosters tolerance in society and a kind of self-respect and independence that is foreign to Middletown [a symbolic community where the quest for status and material goods is obsessive] and our urban traditions."

Paul Ansel Chadbourne, a long-forgotten nineteenth-century American educator, suggested that "Education does not consist in mastering languages, but is found in that moral training which extends beyond the schoolroom to the playground and the street, and which teaches that a meaner thing can be done than to fail in recitation."

Aristotle told his followers that "All who have meditated on the art of governing mankind have been convinced that the fate of empires depends on the education of youth."

James Russell Lowell, poet and essayist, argued that it is not enough to develop children intellectually, noting that if Napoleon had only had a conscience or heart in proportion to his brain he would have been "one of the greatest men in all history."

Albert Einstein told us that "It is essential that the student acquire an understanding of a lively feeling for values. He must acquire a vivid sense of the beautiful and of the morally good. Otherwise he—with his specialized knowledge—more closely resembles a well-trained dog than a harmoniously developed person."

Aware of the danger of a nuclear holocaust and other serious problems of this era, James E. Allen, former United States Commissioner of Education, called education the key to our survival.

Perhaps never before have we asked so much of education. And clearly our present system fails to measure up.

What should our schools teach to meet the needs of the age? After looking at American schools, including some alternative plans, and after studying the problems of our children, including the need for security, adaptability, and the ability to cope and survive, and after talking to psychologists, psychiatrists, social workers, teachers, corrections officials, and thinkers, I envision a four-part curriculum:

1. Self-realization and self-worth or self-esteem
2. Communicating and caring
3. Problem solving
4. Living and career skills

While this may seem to be a radical departure from the traditional school to some, and a summary of what schools now teach to others, the important difference is emphasis. Such a curriculum would include some of the best aspects of present schools but also would make use of new knowledge and skills developed by those who are studying early childhood development, the training of academically gifted youngsters and those who are creative, persons working in day care, vocational rehabilitation, the job corps, mental health, juvenile corrections, with underprivileged children, the retarded, the deaf, the blind, the deaf-blind, the deaf-blind-retarded, and the physically handicapped.

At present, those who work in these fields specialize, and there is little cross-pollination of ideas, even when newly developed concepts and methods would benefit all children.

My proposal, in part, is to integrate all relevent knowledge and methods into the educational system, and then to make education available to all persons throughout life. Credit would be given for work experience, natural talent, and creativity. The goal would be to turn life into a period of continuous growth and progress, with fewer dead ends. Such a program would encourage flexibility and adaptability, making mental nimbleness and successful living the goal for all students—qualities needed, along with emotional stability, in a chaotic world.

Less time would be spent stuffing dull material into the minds of reluctant students. Early stimulation (at home and in school) would increase the growth potential of all children and adults, as well as improve productivity and the joy of living.

Instead of rewarding the ability to memorize and feed back information through tests, children would be graded on the basis of adaptability, creativity, skill in using problem-solving techniques, sensitivity, and skill in applying academic information to work and living experiences. In early adolescence rewards would be real, for they would work, receive paychecks and learn basic bookkeeping, budgeting, comparative shopping, and the relationship between wages and work.

Because such an educational program would include meaningful work, beginning at the ages of twelve or thirteen, it would ease the transition from childhood to adult status, and remove some of the strain and conflict from adolescence. Since such a program would not stigmatize persons because of age, more would have the opportunity to reach their full potential—without penalty for having been born to poverty or to inadequate parents, or for poor judgment during teen years, or other handicaps that trap many Americans.

Such a system would utilize the best elements of the free-enterprise system, would make education relevant, reward initiative, help end discrimination, provide upward career mobility for all willing to make the effort, eliminate dead-end jobs, reward workers on the basis of merit, and assure survival.

How would it work?

It would begin with parent-training programs as the first step. For it is clear that the first hours, days, months, and years of life are critical. Instead of limiting child-rearing information to those few college students who major in child psychology, it would be available to all prospective young parents.

Service teams would be available in every community to help parents—instead of to penalize them after they have hurt a child. Like plumbers and other skilled workers, the teams would visit the home, observe the problems, and show parents how to deal with them. (Such a program is now available, on a limited scale, through the Dayton, Ohio, child-guidance clinic, and related programs can be found in scattered cities elsewhere for parents of retarded and handicapped children.)

When a child enters school, instead of forcing her/him to conform, the teacher would encourage her/him to discover his/her uniqueness. Courses would be tailored to the child's individual needs. For example, a youngster who struggles with coordination, is immature or slow, would be helped or stimulated in programs modified from those used to train the deaf-blind or the retarded. Balance boards and other equipment used with the handicapped would be available. Teachers would be taught touching techniques used to quiet and support disturbed children.

The school would focus on helping children grow and progress at their own rate. Emphasis would be on helping a child gain a sense of self-worth. Youngsters would have freedom to explore, to test, to try, to overcome fear, to defeat frustration, to enjoy learning. Parents would be shown ways to support these programs in the home. (And some schools *are* doing these things.)

Beyond early stress on self-realization and self-worth—essential to every child—emphasis would be on communicating and caring. Language would not be dull and repetitious, with long lists of spelling words. Instead, emphasis would be on communicating—and caring that the other person gets the message.

One communicates by touching, through body language (kinesics), music, art, photography, dance, sports, sharing, play, the spoken and written word, and perhaps through telepathic communication. No area should be neglected or overlooked.

I include caring as part of the communications course because sharing and giving are important, and obsession with one's self hardly healthy. In art the child should not strive to copy the teacher's Thanksgiving turkey, or to produce a photographic likeness with crayons or paint. Rather, art should be both self-expression and communication. The same is true of writing, speaking, and other communication forms. Just as the deaf child learns to understand the world through his eyes and the vibrations he feels, and the blind through touch, so these skills can be taught to all children with beneficial result.

In the same way communication incorporates traditional subjects such as reading, writing, and spelling, so problem-solving would include mathematics—and much more. With pocket-sized calculators readily available, and computer terminals located in banks and business offices, a child's education no longer needs to be limited to adding, subtracting or even algebra.

Now it is important to understand compound and simple interest, whether or not you can, at sixteen, afford to buy a car. And children need to know how to think through human problems, such as being picked on and what to do when there is marital strife at home. In recent years new problem-solving techniques have been developed at a few universities, and these techniques often are being used by industry. The methods are simple enough to be taught to children, yet profound enough to help them find rational answers. If these problem-solving skills (first shown to me by Professor Donald Gause, of the State University of New York in Binghamton) could be taught in school, and if rational thought became part of our culture, it is possible that children would have the skills to seek alternatives to running away from home, quitting school, bashing a teacher in the mouth, or shoplifting to get something "all the other kids have."

Courses in self-realization and self-worth, communicating and caring, and problem-solving would serve to support the fourth subject—living and career skills. A child might be in better touch with his talents; he would have confidence that he can perform at ever-higher levels; he could discuss his needs with others, overcome handicaps, and put his knowledge into practice. What he learns will be useful on the playground, at school, and at home, and at work when he turns twelve or thirteen.

It is at this point that controversy may arise. What can a child of twelve do? Two or three generations ago the question would not have been asked. Our grandparents, when they were twelve or thirteen or younger, drove teams of horses and later tractors, fixed the hand pump, tended the garden, helped re-roof the house or build a new house, care for the children, bake bread, and cook for hungry thrashers. Apprenticeships also began at this age, and for most Americans an eighth-grade education was enough. Many made their fortune on less education than that.

At the moment we have a half-secret class or caste system that traps men and women in jobs that include making motel beds, cooking, pumping gas, waiting on tables, washing dishes, landscaping, stocking shelves, ticketing merchandise, clerking in dime and discount stores, crating and uncrating goods, low-level tutoring, menial child-care jobs, delivering mail and running errands, and simple assembly tasks in factories.

Ask any man or woman with a small, struggling family business and teen-age children and you will discover that children still do many of these tasks, and do them well. Or visit sheltered workshops in the community and at institutions for the retarded and you will find that a person with a severe handicap, poor coordination, and the intelligence of a five- or six-year-old (and sometimes younger) can, when properly trained and supervised, safely and successfully do many of the simpler tasks now done by normal, healthy adults in factories.

The Job Corps, while underutilized, provides relevant academic training while teaching work skills. Some Job Corps groups clean up cities and do other work otherwise left undone. While the chronological age of Job Corps recruits may be higher, many job corps workers are mentally and emotionally twelve-year-olds (or younger).

What I propose, in effect, is a kind of Job Corps experience of one or two years for *all* children. Those too giddy or immature to work in the community would first enter a sheltered workshop program. Community work would pay more, and would be clearly established as a progressive step for advanced students. Those with special skills and talents would work in related fields, as apprentices did a few generations ago. Youngsters would, of course, continue to receive high-quality academic training, but they would learn what it is like to work, how to be responsible, and how to budget and handle money.

I have seen young retardates in Tucson stripping down junk cars and taking parts of air force planes apart for salvage. Delinquent children in Kalamazoo work in a sheltered workshop successfully. In Gary, Indiana, the Job Corps once cleaned slum alleys. In other cities young people have cleaned stream beds and helped recycle metal and other materials.

But wouldn't some adults be displaced? Of course. But some would train and supervise the young people. And others would utilize the schools vacated part or all of the day and enter programs that would help them move up the employment ladder. Among other things, they would learn traditional service skills—and new ones that will be proposed later in this book.

Adults, like adolescents, would move up both academically and financially when they mastered new skills. They also would have more job mobility and a greater opportunity to explore career opportunities. Most working people hold their present jobs not by choice but rather by accident. They needed work and they found an employer who would hire them, and they seldom have had the opportunity to reach their full potential. Millions of Americans lead desperate lives, struggling to keep food on the table. Children of middle- and upper-class parents have—not because of talent or intelligence but rather because of experience and opportunity—a clear-cut advantage over youngsters who are black, brown, red, or born to poor whites. Millions of men and women find themselves locked into menial roles because in their teens they engaged in foolish or delinquent acts, became pregnant, disliked a teacher or school, or behaved immaturely. And we must change that.

If overpopulation is really a problem, and if we want to preserve our economic system and avoid stagnation, we must find ways to help people grow.

Charles Silberman has called our high schools "repressive," with an "almost prison-like atmosphere." He is hardly alone in this belief. Alternative schools have been springing up across the country, but these often are little better, and sometimes are far worse. Elementary schools are improving, but not fast enough and not in really meaningful ways. Many psychologists and psychiatrists insist that our schools are designed to produce automatons—not truly free, intelligent individuals capable of self-realization. In short, at best we have a cookie-cutter educational system.

If we could only teach children to explore and think, to be creative, to communicate with and care about others of all ages, to work and grow as individuals, to handle money and to solve problems in skillful ways, then the purpose of universal education, as envisioned by our founding fathers and outstanding thinkers through the centuries, would be realized.

But bringing about change will be difficult. Persons in positions of power, as well as the electorate, have been brainwashed by advertising and by the present educational system. Most have forgotten the things their grandfathers knew about life and about America.

21

America the Beautiful

Early June is gently brushed with shades of green and gold in the central hills of New Hampshire. On this June day the sun was unusually warm, so much so that the girl who pumped gasoline into my car complained of the early heat. Even with the warmth the air was light, making it the kind of day poets write about when they want to tell of rebirth, promise, a bright tomorrow.

But on this June day I felt only discomfort, for, after several months at my typewriter, I was re-entering the hidden, dreary, sometimes brutal, forever-November world of unloved and unwanted children. Writing a book on children requires more than reading professional papers and reports and pondering in an impersonal way the problems that exist. One must visit warehouse-like institutions, among other things, exploring the back wards as well as the showcase units. And it is essential to look at the children, damaged, grotesque, in pain, and sometimes dying slowly.

Returning to the world of the deviant after several months away produces a shock on one's system if he is sensitive at all. It is not so bad after several weeks on the road, for, like the professional staff and the attendants, you get used to it and grow hardened, no longer seeing or feeling, even becoming confortable with it all.

But I find the first days out painful, although the shock is not the kind you get from plunging into an icy stream on a hot day. That provides an instantaneous jolt that is over quickly.

Instead, it is more like being at a concert and slowly realizing you are going to be sick after a big dinner. Your seat is up front in the center of a long row, and the orchestra has just begun to play. Your head is growing hot and moist, your hands and feet feel cold, and you sit there, fighting it off as long as you can, then suddenly you stand and begin pushing past knees because it is nearly too late, choking back the moist fertilizer taste in your throat, and someone, perhaps angry, refuses to let you by, and then foul-smelling and wet and noisy it all comes gushing out on you and your clothing and everyone around you.

That is a shocking experience in the way visiting institutions for unwanted, useless children can be shocking, if you care at all, and if you understand what you are seeing. And it is easy, even normal *not* to understand, for there is little in everyday life that can help you comprehend.

The November world I enter from time to time is not the America shown in travel brochures and posters and the airline commercials, nor the nation we see in the pages of *Holiday* or *National Geographic*. Nor is it the America we know from watching the *Brady Bunch*, always laughing and smiling, or the *Partridge Family*, singing and kidding their troubles away on TV.

I have walked on the dark side of America, where truth is shrouded in the shadows from people who do not want to know. Once you have been there it is easier to understand why America still has slums; why we seem to care so little about the highway death toll; why we ignore alcoholism; and why (and it seems like ancient history now, but was making headlines when I began thinking about this book) we could shoot children in cold blood at Kent State in 1970 without anguish, or kill women and children in Vietnam, telling ourselves it was in the "national interest."

But I have learned more. One might conclude, after at last comprehending what we do to children, that Americans are cruel or monstrous, but this is not so. Rather, we are merely mortals, experiencing a small part of the mental evolution that has been taking place for centuries. Sometimes we move ahead, and often we fall back. But when considered in historical perspective, progress is being made. This in spite of the fact that we are a people both gentle and violent, generous and insensitive to suffering, wasteful and conservative, intelligent but unthinking.

America is not unique in this. If we suffer from excesses, it is, in part, because from the beginning life here has been projected larger-than-life on a panoramic screen in vivid colors. If we do not see the whole truth and nothing but the truth it is because we live in the age of public relations. It is the public-relations man who is the exaggerated American, for with talent and ingenuity he has learned, truly, to make a silk purse from a sow's ear.

There is a bit of the public-relations man in all of us. We groom our hair, polish our shoes, smear our bodies with cosmetics, cover up natural body odors with chemicals, dress in a way we know will be acceptable, drive the right kind of cars, throw the right parties for the right people, and, at least in the suburbs, we maintain well-groomed and beautifully landscaped lawns surrounding freshly painted houses. And at the same time many of us worry about the debts we owe because of the cars, clothes, parties, lawn, and house. What if the stock market slides? What is we lose our jobs? What is we are found out? What would be left of us if this shell of glitter and glamour is gone?

William Sherer, administrator of the Dayton Children's Psychiatric Hospital and Child Guidance Center, tells of children who live in new, four- or five-bedroom homes, complete with family room, formal dining room, fireplace, and a three-car garage, who are ashamed to bring friends into the house "because there is no furniture." Because of this, he adds, social life in the suburbs often is centered around "the club."

I too have opened the doors to expensive but empty houses, and am surprised by it, but not completely surprised because I too am a product of America and can see the public relations training in myself as well as others.

In the same way, some who run institutions and programs for children prefer to keep me (and others) out. They know how bad things are, and how empty and meaningless their therapeutic treatment programs can be, and they are ashamed, like the children who live in the big, empty houses. When I stand firm and insist on seeing it all, I am almost always escorted by a personable staff member, and sometimes by the top administrator himself, and there is much explaining and justifying and reassuring, and talk of "plans" for the future, strung together with many "ifs," mostly concerning money.

And who can blame them? They have families to support and children to send to college and mortgages to pay off like the rest of us. This is their bread and butter and anyone with the public ear—writers, broadcasters, reporters, platform speakers—put administrators in jeopardy.

I remember the well-meaning public-relations man in Pueblo, Colorado, who gulped and did not know what to say about a facility for the retarded. It was not really under the control of his boss, and because he was more candid, more honest than most in the field, and aware that he could not con me with words even if he had wanted to, he could only say that he had not visited it before, that he was surprised to find such conditions, and that the facility was about like the mental hospital, where he worked, before reform.

Ohio, which has one of the worst systems in the nation, has hired bright, young, high-powered public-relations men who put out propaganda in many ways, and won national publicity for their governor when he spent an hour or two massaging the back and legs of one of the children. Sadly, it is to a large degree puffery—a cover-up of the truth about the Ohio institutions.

I have been flattered, taken to dinner, asked to address staff members, and threatened by public officials hoping to help me overlook conditions in institutions. And I have heard every excuse imaginable and some original beyond imagination to keep me out of institutions. This is understandable, but depressing.

Public relations is not the whole problem, however. Some who run these programs honestly believe they are doing their best. They have no experience elsewhere, and thus no basis for understanding or comparing. And many who work in an institution simply are used to it. This is why many howl with pain or anger when I point out serious flaws.

The professionals, at least the more sensitive ones, have gone through a toughening process that impairs insight. Like the surgeon who cannot be squeamish at the sight of blood, pus, or an infected organ, so those who work with children either leave the field quickly or steel themselves against pain.

I remember as a young reporter, covering fires and accidents, how this worked for me. In one crash, involving a car and train, the state troopers were gathering up the parts of a woman's body in a basket. The head had been severed from the rest of the body and the skull crushed, and a trooper used a shovel to pick it up. After that experience I was hardly bothered when, near St. Johns, Michigan, I watched attendants stack the bodies of several small children like cordwood on stretchers already bearing their parents' bodies, after a crash that took eight lives.

Each time I return to the road now to visit an institution or to look at handicapped children it is a bit easier. When I have been out two or three months at a stretch, visiting facilities every day, I begin to stop seeing and smelling and hearing and feeling. Like those who work in these places, I become used to it, insensitive, almost indifferent. Surely the worker who enters the same room month after month, year after year, no longer has the capacity to understand. Through familiarity the senses have been numbed.

The administrators and workers are not the real villains. Instead the blame rests with the legislators, judges, lawyers, and governors—and with psychiatrists, psychologists, social workers, pediatricians, and others who should know better and shout loudly and demand more than carefully guided tours.

Those charged with public trust, constitutional responsibility, and codes of professional ethics let us—and children—down. Where are the pulpit-pounding ministers, the ethical philosophers, and the muckraking press? It is hard to say. Perhaps children do not rank high on their list of priorities. Or it is possible that they simple do not care.

Insensitivity and even indifference are understandable. But they are hardly excusable. Until the plight of our children becomes a national cause, the changes that take place will be insignificant. And a cause needs leadership—something the field is sadly lacking.

Perhaps television has played a part in this. After watching the evening news for several years, or detective programs, what is there that can stir Americans to action? Mayhem is so common, so natural, that anything less seems hardly significant. But that is not all we see on television. There is another, equally exaggerated side to life constantly depicted.

George Melly, writing in *The London Times History of Our Times* (Norton, 1971), says: "Basically, American television offers an image of the American family both homely and acquisitive, undisturbed by doubts, the moving equivalent of those *Saturday Evening Post* covers which performed the same reassuring function between and after the wars."

If television can disturb children and provoke crimes, it also can produce detachment and ambiguity. A few years ago I prepared a series of films for the White House Conference on Children, and one film included young people getting ready to use and using heroin. It was the real thing, taken by cameramen familiar with the drug scene, but those assigned to edit it later had a great deal of difficulty. Since I am no lover of drugs and needles, I resisted getting involved until it was clear that section of the film could not be finished in time for the conference without my help. Then, for eight hours without a break I sat at an editing table, playing the scene over and over again, and at the end I found myself passive and indifferent. It was still a shocking sequence to those viewing it for the first time, but I had become conditioned to it and no longer felt anything.

We all are conditioned to things that are dangerous for children. We have lived so long with crowded urban streets that we cannot see that they are not designed for children's safety. Nor do we really understand, when designing subdivisions in the suburbs, that we could, if we wanted to, more carefully consider the safety of children.

I remember visiting a nursery filled with abandoned infants in the

District of Columbia General Hospital and feeling that they looked and acted like all other babies I had seen through the years. It took conscious effort on my part to feel concerned—they seemed so healthy and well cared for. But the words of Dr. Thomas Reichelderfer, chief of pediatrics at D.C. General, helped me change my mind. He told of finding them in doorways, sewers, one in the jaws of a dog. And reminded me that "infants require constant love and care from a mother [or mothering person] to develop into emotionally healthy individuals." He pointed out that hundreds of babies are abandoned each year in America, and that many lack love and care.

Rationalization plays a significant part in what we do to our children. Books and articles on the working mother are often like that. I remember reading in a magazine not long ago how one woman justified leaving her children after her husband announced that he had been raised by a nurse and concluded that "I'm all right. I wasn't hurt by it."

What the husband, a professional man, said may well be true. But to generalize from the specific in this way, and to fail to understand that one person's experience cannot be duplicated, reflects the rationalizing that takes place. Further, to advocate that others should follow suit—persons lacking the mothering skill, professional training, or money available for care—is irresponsible. One also could argue that since people survive auto accidents every day reckless driving is not really a serious problem. Too many people are maimed and killed in auto crashes, and too many children are hurt because of working mothers, divorce, and related problems.

It is easy to rationalize about institutions as well, or the welfare practice of shuffling children from one foster home to another, ignoring child abuse, or acts committed by policemen, juvenile court judges, and others dealing with children.

How many judges have told me that they shipped a child to reform school "because we didn't have any place else to send him"? Killing young people at Kent State was okay because "They asked for it—those kids shouldn't have been there." Locking a retarded child in a cell or tying him to a bench for months or years is considered reasonable because "We just don't have enough staff." Crushing a child's ego with wit or put-down in school can be justified because "He was disturbing the whole class." Showing violence on TV is so often shrugged off with "That's what people want."

We are a nation that seems incapable of understanding these things, in part because we are taught to "watch out for number one." Unfortunately, children are dependent and cannot watch out for themselves. We build cities for cars and commerce, houses to satisfy adult egos, and schools and institutions to meet staff needs or to keep children off the streets.

If we lived in a culture that really cared about children, then our schools would change, teachers and child-care workers would be more important than professional football players or golfers; we would replace the Miss America pageant and the Academy Award ceremonies with accolades for those who cared most about youngsters; social workers would work nights; and parents would stop treating their offspring like objects or pets.

It is true that large numbers of American children live in a June world, filled with fresh air, green grass, and sunshine. But millions—through no fault of their own—see only November. They live in the shadows on the dark side of America, hidden from public view.

22

Children Who Irritate

I found Anna locked behind a steel door in a thick-walled solitary confinement cell in the large children's jail across the street from Atlanta's $18 million sports complex.

The probation officer assigned to visit Anna complained that she is neither trained nor qualified to deal with a retarded girl. Further, her caseload is so large that she seldom has time to visit Anna.

Anna was locked up by her parents. They signed a paper stating she was an "ungovernable" child. Most states still permit parents to turn children they can't handle over to the juvenile court—to be supported by the taxpayers. Many courts place these children in jail or reform school, since more appropriate placement is seldom available in the United States.

Anna's parents were exhausted. Their retarded daughter couldn't go to school. It was impossible to find a baby-sitter for more than a day or two. So they left Anna home alone while they worked. Neighbors complained that sometimes Anna would stand naked at the window of her parent's second floor apartment and shout obscenities. This offended the neighbors. An angry child who would fight at the least provocation, Anna also tried to injure a child who taunted her from below by throwing bricks down on him.

Doubly damned because she is both retarded and delinquent, Anna will probably spend the rest of her life as a guest of the taxpayers in an institution. Because she is both vulnerable and aggressive, those who run the Atlanta's children's jail decided that solitary was the place to keep her.

On that same visit to the Atlanta facility I saw a severely disturbed boy of fifteen in a cell in another wing of the jail. He spent the day screaming, moaning for his mother, throwing himself around, spitting through the small barred opening in the door, and crying on his cot.

In most short-staffed children's jails, as well as institutions designed for longer stays, solitary confinement is used to "Provide for the safety of the child and for the safety of others." It also is widely used as a form of punishment for minor rule infractions. Heavy doses of tranquilizers also are used in institutions for the retarded, mental hospitals, reform schools, and sometimes in county jails and children's jails. Some call it a "chemical straitjacket."

When I first toured the reform schools in the late 1960s I was shocked to find so many retarded, disturbed, dependent, and handicapped children locked up with delinquents. Now it does not seem so strange—in part because I have seen so many of these children behind bars, and because I have found that mental hospitals and institutions for the retarded are often very much like jails and prisons. In some states children in reform schools are now better treated than those in more specialized institutions. And reform school children have a greater chance of getting out.

State institutions like to specialize. Those who take retarded children may reject aggressive or "disturbed" children. Many mental hospitals are selective, although in some states judges have the right to commit a youngster to a mental hospital instead of a reform school. But the reform schools are the dumping grounds for unwanted children—and too often for unemployed men and women who can't find work elsewhere.

While wise and compassionate people may run reform schools, brutal treatment is all too common. I have found children beaten with fists, leather straps, wooden paddles, and in one state with broken hoe handles, broom handles, pieces of hose, and chain. Children who run away may be beaten, then locked in cells for weeks and months, handcuffed to beds, and subjected to extreme forms of verbal abuse. ("Hey, John, a nigger I know told me he's your mother's new pimp. Says she's pretty good. Maybe I'll try her this weekend.")

While in theory children are taught to work, a number of reform schools teach children to dislike work by using it as a form of punishment. Children also are forced to stand for long periods with their toes on a line, or with their noses pressed against a locker or the wall. And larger, stronger inmates often control smaller ones. Many youngsters are forced to commit oral and anal sexual acts, and gang oral rape sometimes occurs.

Conditions have improved in scattered states in the past decade, but remain brutal and intolerable in others. Even before a child goes to reform school the brutalizing process begins, as youngsters are locked in adult jails or special children's jails awaiting their day in court or court placement in a foster home or institution.

Maltreatment of delinquent children is generally accepted by the people of America, who have concluded that these children deserve it, or that they should be able to control their behavior.

As a society we shrug off the married businessman who sleeps with his secretary, though he knows better. We say he is an ambitious man, and men like that can't help themselves when it comes to sex. A housewife who has become an alcoholic is usually considered "sick." The husband who walks out on his nagging wife, or who is over his head in debt, is excused. Few condemn the car salesman who will discount the price whenever pushed, but takes every cent he can get from a widow who thinks buying a car is like purchasing a dress, and so pays the sticker price. But these are, in the main, useful, productive people.

The child who is failing every day in school, or is ridiculed by a teacher for his stupidity and eventually skips school, is not useful. More than that, his behavior irritates adults. The youngster who cannot resist the temptation to run away, or to use drugs, or has a compulsive urge to joy ride in a car he does not own, or takes a candy bar or pocket radio from a store, or participates in similar activities is not excused. He is delinquent—useless and bad.

In the past eight years I have interviewed several thousand of these children. Some may justify their behavior with faulty reasoning, but I have yet to meet a child who *really* wanted to be bad. A child may be able to choose between chocolate and strawberry ice cream. But like the executive who sleeps with his secretary, or the salesman who slickers a widow, other factors enter in when it comes to delinquent behavior. Some operate on impulse. Others see the unacceptable behavior as the only alternative open to them. Many act without thinking of the consequences to themselves or others.

Consider the case of sixteen-year-old Linda. On a rainy day in the fall of 1970 I interviewed her in a halfway house in Maine. Linda's father is an alcoholic. Her mother, a member of a fundamentalist religious group, threw Linda's father out of the house when Linda was ten, giving little thought to what impact that might have on the family. About a year later she told Linda that her behavior was bad, and that she could no longer care for her. At the age of eleven Linda was thrown out of the house.

She wandered the streets for hours that day, and late in the evening an eighteen-year-old girl living in a commune with several other young people took her in. Linda lived there for several months, but then the police raided the house and found drugs. Linda went to jail with the others, but eventually went to a children's home in the southern part of the state. Discipline was rigid, Linda was not the kind of child who easily won affection, and soon she ran away. After several runs and after irritating staff members in a variety of ways, she was committed to the reform school.

When I asked this quiet, retiring little girl about how she felt about other people, she said that she didn't trust anyone. When asked about love, she said softly: "Love? I don't know what love is. I've never loved anyone, and nobody has ever loved me."

In time Linda was transferred to a halfway house, but then was caught with drugs. When she turned eighteen she was released by the Maine Bureau of Correction. She had acquired a high school diploma and a college scholarship—but was still starved for love. A few months after entering college she became pregnant and decided to keep her baby. Unless some unusual event occurs, Linda's baby may well spend many years as a drain on the tax rolls, for Linda is no better prepared for motherhood than her own mother was.

Linda is not retarded mentally. But her emotional retardation is great, although few people understand the implications of this.

There are many differences and similarities between those we label retarded and those we call delinquent. One difference is that retarded children in institutions come from both rich and poor families, while delinquent children usually come from lower economic levels. Delinquent children from middle- and upper-class families tend to go to psychiatrists, mental hospitals, or to private schools and institutions.

A financially comfortable, highly educated couple often send a retarded child to an institution more quickly than a slum parent will. Slum mothers tend to protect vulnerable children, while those in higher economic brackets, who enjoy extensive social lives, weigh the impact a retarded child will have on the other, normal children as well as upon their income and their own freedom as parents. Many believe the parents who send a child to an institution are right, and that if there is something wrong with this it is that the institutions are not as good as they should be.

The way a child gets to an institution also varies widely. Most retarded children are locked up without a hearing. If an institution for the retarded will take a child, the parents simply show up at the door with the child and its clothing. At least in theory a delinquent child is entitled to a fair hearing, and in some communities he gets one.

In a few states there are "diagnostic centers"—places where a judge can send a child for observation, testing, and a recommendation for placement. While some retarded children and the more severely disturbed youngsters may be weeded out in these centers, so little is known about the causes of delinquency that the testing is really meaningless. Further, even when the diagnosis is appropriate and accurate, most states have not provided the facilities for appropriate treatment. Whatever the diagnosis, the children are all treated in the same way.

To draw a parallel, for those who best understand the medical model, it is as if a doctor decided one child had measles, another child a cold, a third cancer, and a fourth syphilis. Then all four were given the same prescription.

In a similar way we ignore the causes of delinquency. A child drinking from a contaminated well may get ill. If a doctor is called he may prescribe medicine, but if the child keeps drinking from the contaminated well then there is little chance of cure.

To understand the delinquent child, two things should be known: the nature of the child's behavior, and the cause of that behavior. While some may find my list incomplete, it includes fifteen categories:

1. *The incorrigibles.* Or, as Massachusetts prefers, the stubborn child. In the eyes of adults this child is running out of control. His parents cannot curb him. Or they do not want the child. He is too much bother.

2. *The runaway.* Some federal officials have estimated that in the 1970s as many as a million children run away each year. These children almost always are running either to something or away from something. For example, some girls who run are victims of incest—although no one bothers to find this out. Others are enticed by the excitement they see in the streets.

3. *Truants.* Most of these children are failing in school. It is impossible to stay and fight, so leaving seems to be the only alternative. At least 90 percent of all children in reform schools in America are one to five years behind their peers in school. Reading is a major problem.

4. *Dependent and neglected children.* Just as most reform school children are in trouble at school, so they also have serious problems at home. Sometimes they react to neglect in delinquent ways. In other instances a state has nowhere else to send them.

5. *Drug users.* In 1967 and 1968 I found very few of these children locked up, for drug use then was quite limited. However, in the 1970s millions of American children use drugs, and many are found to be delinquent.

6. *Promiscuous girls.* While it takes two to be promiscuous, boys are seldom accused of this offense, even when they are much older than the

girls. Rich men's daughters usually are given contraceptives, while poor girls who copulate may well be locked up.

7. *Aggressive children.* These are children who use their hands or other weapons to solve their problems. Some are intolerable bullies, and many who are locked up have swung on a teacher or other adult in authority. Seldom does anyone ask if the teacher has taunted the child or provoked the assault in some way.

8. *Petty thieves.* Millions of American children shoplift, steal from other children, from teachers and parents. In most areas a child is not locked up until several offenses are discovered.

9. *The vandals.* Some children break antennas off cars, topple tombstones, throw rocks through school building windows, and commit other malicious acts.

10. *Burglars.* These youngsters break into stores, slip into vacant homes, and steal money, alcohol, and things to sell.

11. *Auto thieves.* While the term auto thief is common, it is considered inaccurate by some officials. Most children do not take cars to sell. Rather, they engage in "joy riding." Because cars often are wrecked by these children the act remains costly to insurance companies and the owner, whatever the reason.

12. *Purse snatchers.* Grabbing a woman's purse is all too common in our large cities. In the summer of 1973, while researching this book in New York City, a woman across from me on a subway train began screaming. A boy had been waiting for the moment before the doors closed, and at this moment grabbed her purse and dashed out to the platform. He was lost in the crowd before I could stand up, and the train was already moving down the tracks. Sometimes, as when a youngster knocks an elderly woman down in the act, the consequences are even more serious.

13. *Arsonists.* Children who are emotionally disturbed, extremely angry, or who simply seek vengeance or thrills sometimes set fires.

14. *Robbers and muggers.* These youngsters use weapons, force, and sometimes the strength of numbers to threaten people and take away property. Sometimes the victim is killed.

15. *Killers.* Sometimes children overreact in a robbery and kill their victims. Children also kill parents, friends and strangers out of anger, hatred, vengeance, and because of emotional problems. Some simply do not have consciences.

It is traditional to look only at the act, and to punish the culprit for his sins. Our criminal law is moral law, and it is largely based on religious beliefs—especially those of old England and of our Puritanical forefathers, who believed in a real and personal devil.

Today fewer persons control their behavior because they fear eternal punishment. Our views of the human mind have been altered by psychologists and other professionals. Yet little has been done to change our methods of dealing with deviant and intolerable behavior. Only in murder cases does the law seriously consider the motivation and mental state of the person who commits the act. And yet when considering children, if rehabilitation is really the goal, understanding motivation and mental state is essential.

Lengthy interviews with several thousand children in trouble—as well as interviews with professionals working with these children—suggests a long list of things that bring about behavior adults find intolerable.

1. *The frightened child.* These children are victims of abuse, anger, hatred, and other forms of maltreatment. Many run away, while others swallow their feelings until in time they explode.

2. *The loser.* This child feels that he can do little that is right at home, at school, or with his peers. He may withdraw into drugs, act up in class to gain recognition, or find other—sometimes criminal—means of proving himself or striking back at those who make him feel inadequate. This child does not like himself, and so can hardly care about others.

3. *The homeless child.* Rejected by parents and other adults, feeling no one cares whether he lives or dies, this child may hurt himself or others.

4. *The love-starved child.* While this child may have a home, may be an adequate student or athlete, and may even have friends, she does not get the attention and love she craves from her family. A girl like this may offer her body to the first man who promises her love. Many of these children do not know how to form lasting relationships.

5. *The immature child.* While some persons grow up physically and intellectually, they do not mature emotionally. This person remains self-centered, while others grow aware of the needs and the interests of others. Just as the two-year-old doesn't care if his screaming will wake the baby, and only wants mother's attention *now,* so the sixteen-year-old may not care whether or not his actions hurt others, for he wants what he wants, and he wants it now.

6. *The overstimulated child.* Living in crowded, noisy, exciting urban areas may create a nervous tension in children that leads to unacceptable behavior. This is especially true when there are no parks or green spaces in which to unwind and grow calm.

7. *The "I want to hurt mother" child.* Many children have a strong sense of revenge. When released through normal play, it is tolerated unless other children get hurt. Vandalism often is revenge against a school, merchants, or society itself. Some children want to get even with poor parents, and more than one girl talked of getting pregnant because it would be the worst thing she could do to mother.

8. *The angry child.* Just as animals that are teased or maltreated may become vicious, so children develop angry temperaments. Some strike out without thinking, and are hard to reach, hard to change.

9. *The manipulators.* These are children best suited to sell used cars in Chicago, deal cards in Las Vegas, or handle the patent medicine accounts at an advertising agency. They may not be aware of what they do, but they believe other people are to be used to achieve their own ends. This is not illogical in Americans in the last quarter of this century. But it can get a child in trouble.

10. *The retarded.* Easily lead, not always grasping the difference between right and wrong, wanting to be accepted by the gang, and vulnerable to manipulation, this child often is depicted as the fall guy in movies—doing the dirty work and getting caught.

11. *The bad seed.* Our ancestors believed that children were born bad and needed to be beaten until they were good. Some children believe that they are bad and act bad for this reason, just as a child who is told he is a born athlete may well succeed in sports. Self-concept is an important key to behavior.

12. *The odd child.* A child with crossed eyes, who is rejected by the "in group," or is ridiculed by his peers sometimes reacts in ways that are not acceptable in our society.

13. *The child overwhelmed by injustice.* This youngster sees the world as so unfair that his misdeeds are justifiable. Some black children, for example, see white maltreatment in a way that makes them believe that striking back is right. It is not just revenge, but rather a moral or holy cause. Poor children also can feel this way, regardless of color.

14. *The adolescent in crisis.* Some children react rather violently to physiological and emotional changes that take place during adolescence. (While sexual maturation takes place in retarded children, there is no evidence that they experience the emotional crisis normal children sometimes feel.) This can lead to behavior that is considered intolerable.

15. *The spoiled child.* Like the immature child, this youngster sees the world revolving around himself. This is taught to the child by over-indulgent parents. Such a child may throw a tantrum or strike out when he does not get his own way. A few of these children find their way into reform schools. The number is small.

16. *The emotionally disturbed child.* While this child might be best suited for a mental health clinic or hospital, when he is discovered by the police, and his acts are serious, he is often regarded as delinquent rather than disturbed.

17. *The brain-damaged child.* This youngster has suffered brain trauma, and, according to psychologists, there is little that can be done when the behavior is antisocial.

18. *The conscienceless child*. This child may have fallen into one of the other categories at an earlier age but has reached a state where he gives no thought to what he does or how he does it. This child is the most dangerous, and probably the most difficult to help—although he may seem pleasant and normal as long as he gets his way.

Not all children in America who fall into these categories get into trouble, nor are large numbers of them caught. And some are fortunate enough to be discovered by those outside the juvenile justice system. Mental health officials, social workers, and those working with the retarded are more inclined to examine the child's mental state than are policemen and judges. In the past, school officials tended to take simplistic views, and many children having trouble in school were sent to reform school following an act provoked by a teacher or principal. Today schools employ more social workers, psychiatrists, and psychologists and so fewer children with school problems are found to be delinquent without some effort being made to help them.

There is no national approach to the problems of these children, although during the Nixon years a stern approach was often considered best.

While many kinds of children get in trouble, most children in trouble have three things in common: they are behind in school; they have problems, real or imagined, at home; and they do not get positive recognition from their peers.

When these three factors coincide in the life of a child, it is highly likely the child will ultimately be locked up.

But when a child who has a bad home, and does poorly in school, can throw a football, he is not as likely to get into trouble. Good homes are a major factor, and so is success in the classroom. But nothing is more important to a youngster than acceptance by his peers.

23

Warehouses for
Retarded Children

There is, on a gray day in 1972, after the leaves have fallen and blown, something eerie about Polk, Pennsylvania. Not really Polk itself. Polk is the kind of place that brings out the cliché in the best of us: Blink twice when you drive through Polk and you'll miss it.

It isn't that Polk is eerie. Rather, it is the institution—the Polk State School and Hospital—looming above the town that gives one the uncomfortable feeling.

In an exaggerated sense the Polk State School and Hospital is a symbol of what is wrong with our institutions for the retarded, or feeble-minded, as the inmates were called in 1897 when the doors first opened. The Polk School is, like so many institutions for unwanted children, large, remote, inadequate, improperly staffed, promising promises that have not and cannot be kept to parents long without hope.

For many years the major industry in town, run in 1972 by a friendly but weary man who said he wished he had had more courage when he was younger and less tired, staffed by people doing their best—a best, when compared to what is happening in a few excellent institutions, that is not nearly good enough—the Polk State School and Hospital is filled to overflowing with society's useless children and adults. It is a place largely forgotten (except at Christmas) by the people of Pennsylvania, who apparently feel relieved that they do not have to look at or even think about the sometimes grotesque, occasionally nearly normal, too often inhuman humans that spend their lives there.

Polk is eighty miles north of Pittsburgh, well off the traveled path. You can't reach Polk by Interstate. You get there after you leave I-79, which runs from Pittsburgh north, at Jackson Center and following Road 965, which winds northeast through hills and woods and farmland toward Oil City and Franklin. When you reach US-62 you drop steeply down the east side of a hill that a man, say, from Lincoln, Nebraska, might call a mountain. Just before the valley spreads out into farmers' fields the highway slips by a handful of homes and buildings very much like those you have passed earlier, and you are in Polk.

On the flattened hill above the town the institution juts up against a steel-coated sky. An imaginative child might think he was looking up at a haunted medieval castle, complete with turrets, a bell tower, and cone-shaped roofs.

As you approach the institution, following the long driveway, you find the grounds silent and lifeless. Only the cars in the parking lot suggest that this is the twentieth century. The reception area has a high, beamed ceiling and massive varnished woodwork; in a front office, on the first floor of a turret, near a fireplace, stands the desk of the superintendent, Dr. James H. McClelland, Jr. It is cluttered but not messy. The doctor, you find, is a tall, slender man who appears either to dislike tight-fitting clothing, or is wearing a suit purchased at a plumper time in his life. He rises to greet you.

When you meet Dr. McClelland you feel he is a nice man, in the best sense of the word. You feel sympathy when you learn that his wife has passed on in the year past. His smile is warm and honest, although at times he seems a bit cautious. One has the instant impression that this gentle, bespectacled man is simply a well-meaning, if ineffective, civil servant, waiting out his years, doing his best in the time left. He speaks in a low, soft voice:

"I've worked in this field a long time. We do the best we can with what we have. By my nature I like to see things worked out thoughtfully and slowly, rather than by crash programs. Everything that happens must be absorbed by the institution. Because of a court ruling on educating the retarded we haven't been able to have school here through October. We've had to devote hundreds of hours to filling out both sides of a fourteen-page report on each school-age child."

Dr. McClelland reflects on what he has said.

"Now, more than anything else, I'd like to be left alone."

His tone is not one of bitterness. He is a practical man, a psychiatrist who might have made more money in private practice but who has enjoyed certain benefits as superintendent at Polk, including a southern colonial-style house in an apple orchard on a rise overlooking the grounds. Now, reaching the end of his career, he wonders aloud about what might have been had he fought harder for his inmates.

"When I took over perhaps things would have been different if I had had the guts to tell them we needed more buildings," he says. "I'm not crazy over this renovation business. We should walk away from these buildings and start over."

If you do not dig deeply, it is hard to find fault with Dr. McClelland for what he has done—or has not done—during his career here. Fighting for the rights of retarded children has not, until recently, been a popular stand. Even today, most Americans prefer to avoid the sights, sounds, and odors of the retarded.

One would not suspect at first glance in the fall of 1972 that in roughly a year Dr. McClelland would be fired for permitting "cruel, degrading, and inhumane conditions" to exist at the Polk State School and Hospital. Yet in October of 1973 such charges, first made by Mrs. Helene Wohlgemuth, Secretary of Public Welfare in Pennsylvania, were repeated and upheld by the State Civil Service Commission of the Commonwealth of Pennsylvania.

Dr. McClelland seemed to be a nice, if lonely, man. But you do not see the attendants or even the superintendent of state institutions, unless some extraordinary event catches your attention. Other things grab for your attention.

In most institutions for the retarded it is the smell that hits you first. Television has blunted the impact of unpleasant things seen with our eyes, what with war dead, accidents, and TV detectives and thrillers. But how can the typical American, doused with perfume or shaving lotion, sprayed with deodorants, wearing freshly laundered clothing, after having scrubbed with scented soaps in a shower, face the odor in a ward for the profoundly retarded?

Those who are not toilet-trained, even grown men and women, usually wear diapers. While their minds are limited, their organs and bodily functions are normal. Often inmates are heavily drugged, for in this way a smaller staff can watch over a larger number of inmates. Some inmates, known in the trade as "strippers," pull off their clothing no matter how hard attendants try to keep them dressed. Others may wear jump suits, farmers' overalls, or sports clothing.

Many inmates are open-mouthed, and saliva may drip down their faces. Tooth-brushing in a poorly staffed institution may be limited.

Menus, while usually balanced, are based on cost-cutting demanded by legislators, and so run heavy on starches. To ease feeding problems food may be strained, chopped, or pureed.

Rocking, head-banging, head-rubbing, picking, biting, and other forms of self-mutilation are common. Inmates in most state institutions are bored. They sleep on the floor, sit on benches or in chairs, or wander about their room, holding a doll or staring blankly. Feces smearing is an institutional problem. So is playing in pools of urine. Often the rooms are empty except for the benches. More often than not I was overwhelmed by the thick, putrid smell of these wards—especially on hot summer days. Most buildings I visited, even in hot climates, are not air-conditioned.

Back wards are very much the same across the nation, whether Parsons, Kansas; American Fork, Utah; Brandon, Washington; Laconia, New Hampshire; Pineland, Maine; Sonoma, California; Orient State, Ohio; Dixon, Illionois; Fort Wayne, Indiana; Pueblo, Colorado; Whitten Village, South Carolina; Rosewood, Maryland; or points between.

Depending upon the state and the honesty of the officials, the stench is blamed on staff shortages, lazy employees, poor administrators, overcrowding, insufficient funding by lawmakers, the presence of PKU (phenylketonuria) victims, and the wrong kind of floor wax. Also noteworthy, better institutions such as Grand Junction, Colorado, and Pauls Valley, Oklahoma, do not have this foul odor.

Most institutions for the retarded are subdivided, with inmates separated by sex, mental age, chronological age, and ability level. Those with a variety of handicaps, unable to crawl or walk, or who are seriously ill, are housed in the hospital section—sometimes a building complete with surgical staff, but more often similar to a nursing home.

Young preschoolers are kept in what is called the nursery. As they grow older they are moved from cottage to cottage—which often means from one look-alike room or wing to another. Usually when an inmate reaches his teens he is not expected to progress further, and so is mixed with older inmates stalled at a similar mental level.

Beyond the foul-smelling back wards for the mobile profoundly retarded, it is the hospital sections (normally clean and with far less odor) that most disturbs visitors.

The first time I saw a teen-age hydrocephalic, a boy with a head that seemed to be the size of a two-drawer filing cabinet, with a fairly normal mouth, nose and eyes, it was hard for me to deal with it emotionally. Nothing in my experience had prepared me for this. I was told that this was a human, but I felt as though I were looking at a large fish on the white sheets, a fish with human arms and legs, quite small in size. My guide explained to me that certain body fluids were trapped in this huge head, and the head kept stretching to contain the fluids.

Almost as difficult to accept for those who have never seen them are the spastics. Knees may be pulled up in fetal position, or splayed oddly, while others have limbs that remind one of a child's swing rope that has been twisted. So lacking in flesh are some limbs, and with muscles taut, one feels they are living mummies. I saw inmates who have been in these beds for fifty years and more. Some must be force-fed, or fed through a tube connected by surgery. These grotesque bodies must be turned frequently to avoid bedsores.

My first exposure to such a ward was in Laconia, New Hampshire. Despite years of training, my notes are brief, the result of the emotional impact of what I saw. As I walked through a ward I wrote:

"Grotesque girl, age 21.

"Girl of 35 with a diaper, front teeth knocked out, big smile.

"Woman—age 36—can talk. Water on brain. All beds metal sides to keep them from falling.

"Girl in red-checkered suit and diaper. Rhythmic movements.

"Woman in green nightgown. Age 55. Fetal position, sucking thumb, slow motions. Teddy bears. Mental age, infant.

"Woman in wheelchair has chest restrainer (she was tied in an upright position with a cloth around her chest). Head hangs.

"Eleven-year-old girl has giant-size crib. Pink.

"Some can't get up at all . . . move them with stretchers. Only one can walk. Woman 68 in wheelchair. Can sit up all day. One talks, wants to 'go school.' Slurred.

"Some cry, make animal noises. Life span is long.

"Next room. Girl 21 in crib bites finger of nurse who teases her. Giggles and makes baby noises. Wears blue denim jump suit. Fed ground food. We missed feeding.

"Another girl grotesque. Tied to bed—legs doubled up in strange position. Nurse talks baby talk. Another says she bites.

"Girl 16—baby shape.

"Fat girl 26 screams.

"Girl 25 going blind. She scratches face, digs until it bleeds, just had measles.

"Woman, 52, in fetal position.

"Fat girl cries, moans, puts fingers in mouth.

"Girl, 17, head banger. Arms restrained. She can't open eyes. Semi-closed.

"Woman 45. Sits on knees. [Attendant] must wipe her nose. They have dolls and toys hanging.

"Girl age 12. Pretty face. Tiny, grotesque legs. Spine curves in.

"Another girl, age 16, has front teeth out. She bites. Scrawny legs. Puts fingers down throat, throws up.

"Girl 19 in metal crib. White crib. Cannot walk.

"Some soiled diapers, coming out.

"Girl 16 has arthritis through limbs, in diaper and T-shirt.

"All on medication.

"Girl, age 30, about size of 7-year-old, throws up, scratches self until bleeds.

"Girl makes gasping sounds and shakes head.

"Girl rips blouse. Holds rubber doll.

"Girl 19 losing hair, sucks thumb. On floor, crawling. She's like old lady. Took five of us to hold her to get blood sample. Rolls on floor.

"Another girl. 15, has [rubbed] hair off back of head. Doesn't like to have diaper changed.

"Girl on floor rolls head back and forth, curls around foot of bed.

"Two epileptics. Both bed-ridden. Can't sit up. One is 10, the other 7. Seven-year-old has bright eyes. She likes to be hugged. Smiles. Parents took 10-year-old out, let her get sunburned. Girl 7 smiles a lot.

"Sound like babies, although from 7 to 60 years old. Ceramic tile walls. Linoleum on floor.

"Next room, boy 15 has radio over bed, hands restrained, feet in tennis shoes, restrained. Wears padded helmet. He 'wants it on.' Beats himself. Hands tied to keep out of pants all time.

"Girl 12. Her boney legs are rigid. Stiff. Terribly tense. Her face is scarred from scratching self. Spastic.

"Another girl, 10. Cross-eyed. Spastic. Cries when fed. Turns over. Arms and legs same position, twisted.

"Girl 18 throwing up for week. Thin. I can see outlines of bones. Bent backwards so back of hands nearly touch back of wrist. She is here for life.

"Boy watching TV, has sox on hands.

"18-year-old claps feet together. Terribly thin legs and grotesque shape. TV is on. Some have books. Baby animal book. They kick side of bed but feel no pain!

"Boy all tied in knots sits up with legs at side. Ear is bleeding, arms restrained. Some people wait five years to get kids in here!

"Boy 14 is blind. Can't open eyes. His upper limbs normal. Legs twisted. How could one person have so many problems?

"29-year-old, but size of 7-year-old and looks like one. Hair not developed, legs grotesque. Acts like 2 months old.

"Man, age 40, legs, arms all twisted up.

"Tiny 24-year-old smiles a lot. About size of 9-year-old.

"Age 23. Tied to bed. Tears it up.

"Boy 24, mouth open, eyes closed—has on strait jacket.

"Boy 26 sits and rocks. He is tied up in knots. Rocks. Rocks. He has bed with chrome sides too.

"A head-banger, age 25, arms tied. Normal legs. Tied to bed.

"Boy, 24, arms tied, tied to bed, slipped crosswise. Deformed boy next to him stares at us. Scoots like crab across floor. Sunken eyes crossed. Pink T-shirt.

"Smell of feces.

" 'They enjoy music,' attendant tells me. 'They sit and rock to it.'

"Sun porch: boy stands in pen, looks out window. Another boy with arms strapped in blue denim, rocks. Two more in chairs.

"Staff sick a lot. These are least desirable jobs. Why are people who work with children paid less than others? They work shifts, nights, Sundays, holidays.

"Strange roaring noises. Movements spastic. Boy, hand in mouth, 'massaging gums.' Grunts. Groans, like zoo. Boy in play-pen so twisted you can't tell back from front. Very thin head. Another small boy waves head around, groans, hoots. Small boy—hair gone from back of head, apparently rubs it off. Another boy in wheelchair sounds like crow. Has little book he waves in short, spastic motions.

"Boy in pen rolls around large plastic ball. He is on stomach. Looks up at me by folding self backwards. Clothing on backwards so they can get him out of it.

"Man, 36, can talk. Quite large. Paralyzed. Has been here 34 years. Intelligent. Rheumatism and arthritis. He's folding clothes, watching TV. Could have records. Says his family visits sometimes."

Children in hospital wards may be largely ignored in some institutions but at least they are not maltreated in the ways those who are classified as ambulatory and aggressive are. Solitary cells are often used to punish the children. Staff members also may slap them, tie them to benches for months or years, lock them in cages, or simply turn their backs as they bite, scratch, or pound on other inmates. A few institutions engage in what some behavoir modification advocates call "aversive therapy." At least some versions are not pleasant to watch.

In the summer of 1972 I visited the Utah State Training School in American Fork. My guide, a pleasant woman, led me accidentally into a room where aversive therapy was being used, and even she seemed surprised by the events that took place.

As we entered the door a man in a yellow sport shirt was standing near a window, arms crossed, a cattle prod (electric shocker) in his hand. At that moment a younger man shouted to him and the man in the yellow shirt charged an inmate who had stuffed a crayon in his mouth. When the boy dodged and ran, the bulky therapist jumped over a bench and pinned the boy on the floor under a table. He shocked the youth repeatedly, trying to get him to spit the crayon out. Incapable of speaking, the retarded boy whined and cried, cowering, throwing his hands in front of his face, trying to pull away from his attacker.

Eventually the frightened, whining, mindless youth spat out the crayon, and the man in the yellow shirt returned to his position by the window. My guide assured me that he was trained by experts in behavior modification techniques and had not hurt the boy. But I felt that she was a bit shaken by the experience.

Many sins are committed in the name of therapy in our nation's institutions. While employees often are attracted to such places for humanitarian reasons, others seek work just for the money, while a few are unstable or sadistic persons hired because a shortage of qualified workers hinders screening practices.

Finding the right kinds of employees in the small towns where these institutions often are located becomes difficult for other reasons. Jobs are scarce, and in some communities whole families have worked in the institution for two, three, or more generations. It is difficult to change old habits and traditions, or replace incompetent employees without community anger.

In most institutions for the retarded, staff members are little more than baby-sitters except at feeding time, or when one inmate begins to injure another. Sometimes an extreme incident occurs, as in a California institution for the retarded when a staff member held an inmate's head under water and almost drowned the child before another staff member stepped in. But usually the maltreatment is less extreme, yet severely damaging to the children.

In most institutions in America, whether for retarded, delinquent, or disturbed children, boredom is a major problem. In reform schools children get into fights or other forms of trouble. This also happens in mental hospitals and schools for the retarded, but retarded children tend to be more passive in many instances. Large numbers are self-abusive. Rather than having staff work with them, meeting their needs, helping them, too many institutions solve the problem by putting the children in strait jackets, tying them to beds, putting cloth or plastic mitts on their hands, or by keeping them in cages. As I have mentioned, drugs and solitary cells also are used to control children.

In Maine's notorious Pineland Hospital and Training Center young staff members in one cottage controlled children by shouting at them and slapping them. The youngsters were six and seven years old and varied in the severity of their retardation. They had surprising table manners and were quite advanced in their ability to feed themselves—but at the expense of their emotional health, for several were quite disturbed from the constant pressure and punishment. While many retarded children are gentle and warm, like friendly puppies, these were angry and aggressive—pinching, punching, and gouging me in their playroom. It seemed clear that their aggression was the result of their treatment by their keepers.

In several institutions I visited, the inmates had their front teeth pulled. Some officials explain it is the result of poor brushing, or the wrong kind of medication. But a few staff members said it was done to protect staff and inmates from biters, and was done before drugs were widely used to control the behavior of aggressive inmates.

At the Polk school, inmates who were deemed in need of punishment were locked in solitary confinement cells, sometimes for weeks. They were penned up in little wooden cages on the cement floor for days, months, and apparently even for years. Large numbers were bound up in strait jackets and tied to benches. The Civil Service Commission that held a hearing also found many staff members lacked training, and that "by his own admission, Dr. McClelland shows he lacks breadth of imagination required by the superintendent of a facility for the mentally retarded."

If Dr. McClelland, Polk's superintendent, deserved to be fired, so do two or three dozen other superintendents in institutions scattered across the country. The number I use is deliberately conservative.

Our society always seeks to blame some individual. We find it is less painful to do that than to accept the blame ourselves. What member of the legislature, what newspaper reporter, what lawyer, judge or representative of a citizens group, or what individual citizen cared enough to speak out before Mrs. Wohlgemuth finally acted in the Pennsylvania case? And who would have been listening?

It is interesting to note that in a minority opinion, Civil Service Commissioner Herschel Jones points out that "Dr. McClelland's performance was rated 'excellent' for 1969, 1970, and 1971, and 'very good' for 1972 by his superiors." Had his superiors become used to seeing inmates locked up, or sitting on the cement in the cages, or tied to the benches? Or were they negligent in their inspection of the institution, and rating of his performance?

I spent many weeks touring institutions for the retarded. Now, months later, as I write this chapter, the sights, sounds and smells come flooding back. It is all less painful now. Like a funeral director who has learned to deal with corpses and death, I am now emotionally numbed, nearly indifferent to the sight of America's living dead. To sustain the shock one first feels would be unbearable.

24

Not a Pretty Sight

David. Against the soiled green walls, in the dim light that filters through dusty, barred windows, David's pale, naked body seems almost luminescent.

Tall, blonde, and athletic, he lopes sideways in a long-legged crab scoot, grabs the metal window rungs, shakes them with force, then throws back his head and howls. In a room without curtains of furniture, except for wooden benches, the noise rebounds off the cement walls and tiled floor, but does not disturb the diapered and half-clothed child-men who stand dumbly with their mouths open, sit and rock, or sprawl on the cool spots on the floor. To the inmates, David's behavior is normal. They have lived with him hour after hour, day by day, week upon month upon year.

David. Loping crablike, disturbing no one, drops to all fours, then pushes off, sliding on his pale belly across the tile. Reaching out he swishes his hand through somebody's stale pool of urine, then lifts his head to howl again. Scrambling up he lopes to the window, shakes the bars, skids to the urine, moving like an erratic machine, not noticing the stench of full diapers, warm unwashed bodies, saliva, smeared feces, and pools of urine.

David. Without a memory; without a past; without a future; perhaps even without a present. Scooting, sliding, howling, rattling bars despite the high drug dosage he has been given by his keepers in Pueblo, Colorado.

David is someone's son.

Rose. A smiling, outgoing child-woman with an almost normal face, spending her days in a similar room in Laconia, New Hampshire.

Spotting me, a stranger, Rose runs with little geisha steps. Plump. Twentyish. Smiling, saliva running down one cheek, Rose nearly knocks me down as she lunges at me, trying to give me a hug. Laughing, wanting to press her dirty, slobbering mouth against mine, she believes I am her father.

"Daddy. Daddy. Daddy. Daddy. Daddy."

Rose wears a cotton print dress that hangs down past her thickened calves. Her fingers are stubby, the nails broken and dirty. Her dark hair, roughly cut in what might be called a pageboy, smells sour as she tucks her head against my shoulder and cries "Daddy" over and over.

Now other girls, half-alert in their drugged state, crowd around. Some are shy. Coy. A tall, thin child of over thirty-five who has been here since infancy reaches out and pinches my arm, trying to get my attention. An older, toothless woman, also crying "Daddy," punches Rose hard, breaks her grip, making her cry. Another woman standing aside, waiting her turn, waves a filthy rag with a plastic head.

"See my dolly? See dolly? My dolly!"

Grinning, circling, dancing, a moon-faced Mongoloid joins the ring around me. The woman who pinched my arm begins hitting. Hard. Slamming me back. The attendant notices and tries to pull her away, but she grabs me and hugs, then slides down my body, out of the attendant's reach, and hugs my shoes.

The stench is the same as in Colorado. So strong that I want to hurry away and vomit. From down the hallway a series of deep moans blend with the sounds of other inmates—grunts, bird calls, simple words, bleating, groans, senseless laughter. And from some rooms, only silence.

In a dark corner a diapered woman sprawls beneath a bench like a toddler exhausted from being dragged from store to store by an unthinking mother. Nearby a naked woman in her fifties sits cross-legged on the floor, moaning and rocking. Her hair is stringy and turning gray, her breasts sag like a fat man's jowls. She sits, rocking and moaning, never looking up, naked.

I am glad these are not my daughters.

This is the nether world of the institutionalized retarded. Like our nursing homes, a graveyard for the living dead. Unlike nursing homes, many of the inmates are toddlers and young children. While worse than the best, and not as bad as some, such as those in Ohio—which tends to have some of the worst institutions of all kinds in America—what I saw in Colorado and New Hampshire was all too typical of how we care for the retarded in America. And yet a handful of institutions are proving that it need not be this way.

As in all areas involving the unwanted children of America, there are no accurate figures on the number of retarded persons in the United States. The U. S. Department of Health, Education and Welfare estimates 126,000 retarded babies are born each year, while the National Association for Retarded Children reports that annually between 100,000 and 200,000 babies are born that eventually will be identified as retarded. Most authorities agree that roughly 3 percent of our total population is retarded—some 6½ million persons. Of these, 2½ million are under twenty years of age, and some 200,000 of all ages are institutionalized.

One reason statistics are hazy is that milder forms of retardation are not always noticed until the child is in grammar school or in junior high. (It also should be noted that these same children are not counted as retarded later, if they leave school and work in factories or at menial tasks. *Useful* people are not tagged with demeaning labels.)

The longstanding practice of hiding retarded children continues, although to a lesser degree than in the past, since the political sons of Joseph and Rose Kennedy announced to the world that they had a retarded sister. Still, how many are kept in backrooms, attics, or in rural areas is unknown. Many retarded children die at birth, or those born with many handicaps do not live to school age, when they can be counted.

Further, retardation is relative. As I have already noted, a child struggling in school may be labeled retarded, but later, if he is able to work in a laundry, wash dishes, work on a production line, or dry cars in a carwash, the label is removed.

Earlier in this country's history many youngsters labeled as retarded or delinquent and retarded would have worked on farms and ranches, in the cotton fields of the South, or even in factories. It was not so important to be able to read and write or understand arithmetic and physics in the early years of our country.

Even today there is less than total agreement on what constitutes retardation, since cultural differences, language barriers, and the late-blooming of a child may result in low IQ test scores. Sometimes children with hearing problems or with difficulty with their eyes also are labeled retarded. Yet with help, understanding, and proper stimulation these children can catch up with their peers.

While many children are severely retarded, labeling a child as such can do lasting damage. In Los Lunas, New Mexico, I met a girl of twenty-one of Spanish and Indian background. Living at the institution for the retarded, she was working in the canteen, frying hamburgers, dishing ice cream, ringing up the cash register, making change, and keeping records on supplies to reorder.

When she was younger she was found living in a hovel in the desert with her sister, who also was pronounced retarded. The two girls had been abandoned at an early age and grew up with almost no outside contact until they were found and taken to the institution.

The older sister was out, working in a laundry. But the girl I met was unable to leave. Although shy, she carried on a normal conversation, and I asked why she was still institutionalized. It was, I learned, because she had nowhere to go, and having grown up in an institution for the retarded, was very vulnerable.

In many states efforts are being made to find alternatives to institutionalization. But many state officials are blunt and critical.

"Special education is neither special nor educational," says one state official in Maine. "Most programs are a waste of taxpayers' money."

"Institutions are horrible," adds Dr. Samuel L. Ornstein at the opposite end of the nation, in Olympia, Washington. Dr. Ornstein is that state's chief of the Office of Developmental Disabilities in the Department of Social and Health Services. "Institutions serve the professionals that work there and they serve the needs of parents," he continues. "A child comes into one of our institutions as a voluntary patient, but it is the parent, not the patient, who has volunteered. Then, forty years later, somebody writes a newspaper story about this deaf, normal person, and wonders how he got into an institution for the retarded."

While there are many abuses, it is not all guesswork. More states have now established standards for admissions to institutions, and even if testing is an imperfect science, efforts are being made to properly place children when appropriate programs exist either in the community or in institutions.

Testing is under attack. Based on standardized tests, about two-thirds of the people in the United States have IQ's (intelligence quotient) of between 84 and 116, with a mean of 100. This is the so-called normal range. But most experts now agree that tests are only valid when given to white, middle-class children from "normal" homes. And even then tests are limited in what they show. And yet these tests provide the best guide available for those dealing with the retarded.

A 1961 chart developed by Rick Heber, a professor of education and child psychology at the University of Wisconsin, lists the *profoundly* retarded as those having an IQ of 0 to 24. Those in the *severe* range test at

218   PART II · THE SYSTEM UNMASKED

between 25 and 39; while the *moderates* test between 40 and 54. The *mildly* retarded score between 55 and 69 on standardized IQ tests. Those who fall between 70 and 84, and slightly higher than 84 are thought of as *borderline* or *dull-normal* people.

Usually, children with an IQ of 35 and over are considered "trainable," while those scoring in the 40s and 50s are known as "educable." Trainable retardates can learn to use the toilet, to feed themselves, button their clothing, and do simple tasks on an assembly line. The educable can deal with low-level abstractions like counting or adding, and they can use written words as symbols for people and objects.

Because of growing opposition to IQ tests as a method of measuring intelligence, those working with the retarded sometimes prefer to study a child's growth patterns. For example, a retarded child may be, as an infant, extremely fretful, he may have no interest in his surroundings or in other people, and will make no attempt to sit up or grasp objects, according to Dr. Walter Jacob, director of the American Institute for Mental Studies in Vineland, New Jersey. Seizures may be common, he adds.

"If by the time a child is three years old he is obviously backward in a number of growth stages by as much as a year, mental retardation should be suspected. . . . Such factors as poor environment or ill health should be corrected, if feasible, to eliminate them as further contributors to the lack of development," he explains.

To ease the minds of parents of a slow child, he also notes that while "children may be slow in several areas, a normal child is not slow in as many areas as a retarded child."

A governmental pamphlet from HEW says it more simply. If a child is slow to "sit up, crawl, walk, and talk, it could be that the child is retarded—but not always."

Measuring retardation is not easy. At least three groups with different views exist. One group contends that intelligence is reflected in the ability to think rationally; in the ability to learn and retain knowledge; and the skill needed to make decisions and see relationships based on reasoning—along with the ability to care for oneself and to communicate and compete more or less successfully with other intelligent people.

A second group talks in terms only of academic achievement, relating intelligence to the ability to do school work, pass tests, and read at grade level.

The third group contends that intelligence is whatever an intelligence test measures. A child tested in flying could be tested in this area and would be found to be highly intelligent. Yet ask him to discuss Shakespeare and he would be found to be lacking. Although able to explain airflow and jet engines, he might well struggle with a math test.

While the first approach appears reasonable, it does not seem to consider mental illness, lack of interest, or physiological events such as strokes. The second category reflects the thinking of many Americans who are steeped in our educational tradition. They see academic ability as the end-all of intelligence, and to counteract their beliefs we have now established vocational schools and the use of life experiences for school credit to assist those who are intelligent but do poorly in school. It should be added that there are many "A" students who have the ability to feed back what teachers give them, but have neither original thoughts nor practical uses for their knowledge. Many of our brightest students cannot rebuild a carburetor or repair a door that sticks. If testing were based on hand-skills they would be classified as retarded.

The retarded are lacking in many areas, but most have useful talents. Being able to stick to a boring job for long periods should be recognized and rewarded.

Profoundly retarded persons, even when they are old, appear to be at the same mental stage as infants of a year or less. The most profoundly retarded cannot even recognize the presence of another human. Others smile and react to their names, are amused by toys, and may even speak a word or two. Many are able to crawl or walk.

Those classified as severely retarded appear to be somewhere between the ages of one and two—whatever their chronological age may be. Unless physically handicapped or emotionally disturbed, they may have some speech. Even short sentences are possible. Many are able to walk, run, and can feed themselves and are toilet-trained. Some perform simple work tasks, although often slowly and with poor motor control. Most respond to others, want to communicate, and may be very playful.

I find it more difficult to differentiate between the moderately and mildly retarded, except the less retarded the child is, the more normal his face may look—although this is not always the best guide. The higher the level of intelligence the more logically a child is able to express himself. The moderately retarded child may react like the preschooler, jumping up and down when not too heavily drugged, perhaps counting and talking, but tending to repeat what others say.

Many classified as mildly retarded seem little different from people one meets in the streets of a large city, working in menial jobs, or taking "general" rather than college preparatory work in school. Some seem to be more innocent; less able to grasp complex ideas, but many can pass as normal in our society if they are not labeled by school officials and parents.

HEW suggests that "the tendency today is to speak of a person's retardation as 'mild' if he has the ability for self-support with some supervision; 'moderate' if some earning power, but needing more supervision; 'severe' when unable to learn reading and writing, but capable of some useful work; and 'profound' when requiring complete care for all body needs."

The New York-based National Association for Retarded Children (NARC) explains that retardation is "a condition where the brain is prevented from reaching full development, limiting the victim's ability to learn and put learning to use, retarding social adjustment." NARC's literature adds that retardation is found in "every race, religion and nationality, and every educational, social and economic background. Mental retardation crosses every line to impair the minds of thirty out of every thousand Americans."

Walter Jacobs puts it another way: "Mentally retarded persons are quite different. Theirs is a case of incomplete mental development, which limits their ability to learn. Since learning is cumulative from one set of items to the next, theirs is a progressively worsening problem in a society geared to achievement."

Perhaps that is why what we do to retarded children is so depressing. Even the most thoughtless members of our society can recognize that a retarded child is retarded through no fault of his own. But if the child is not considered useful—that is, if he is neither a producer nor a consumer—then he is a drag on our society and as dispensable as an empty milk carton.

25

Life and Death
in Polk, Pennsylvania

This is the story of Raymond Helman. I use his real name because everyone should receive some recognition in his lifetime, beyond a brief birth announcement in the local paper. And if one does not receive that recognition, at least some mention should be made of his achievements after he has died. And now Raymond Helman is dead.

Newspaper reporters like to use facts when writing an obituary. The deceased person's age, address, place of birth, the name of his parents, the schools he attended, his occupation, and the names of his survivors, are usually included.

I know that Raymond Helman was thirty-two years old when he died. And that he spent his last twenty-two years at the Polk State School and Hospital in Polk, Pennsylvania. But there is very little additional information about him.

If I were asked to fill out a newspaper obituary form, under "occupation" I might be tempted to note that he spent much of his life in a kind of strait jacket, tied to a bench in Cottage One. State records are fairly confidential, and while I have had the full cooperation of state officials in learning about Raymond's life and his death, I did not ask to see if a file somewhere still lists his parents and brothers and sisters. Perhaps it is better that they remain unknown.

Raymond didn't keep a diary. Those who give IQ tests would say he didn't have enough intelligence for that. But others, those faceless at-

221

tendants who apply for work in institutions after they finish high school because it is the local factory, those decent, well-meaning people who methodically follow the orders of higher-ups like Superintendent James McClelland, kept what might be called a diary.

The books are bound in leather, and the jottings are in bright colors—red and green and blue, a strange contrast to the gray life Raymond Helman lived.

The last few days of Raymond Helman are recorded, along with notes on his fellow inmates—call them his "brothers and sisters" if you will, for they were closer than blood relatives to him. Pennsylvania officials have given me permission to publish these cryptic notes kept during his last days. It is included, as furnished by the officials, in this chapter to give readers a better understanding of how he lived and died.

It is worth noting that, with a few exceptions, one day was very much like another. To get the full impact, you must picture him starting it out on a hard wooden bench, a stained cloth strait jacket pinning his folded arms across his chest, the jacket tied by a strong piece of cloth rope to the bench. Sometimes he was placed in solitary confinement—a windowless room. Raymond was described as "mean, loud, uncooperative"—but how should one act after years of having his arms bound and tied to a bench? Jovial? Cheery? Joyful?

Entries from Log Book of Cottage One

8-25-72—6:00 a.m.
—Medications omitted. Raymond Helman in a.m., refused to go to breakfast.
—Resident's behavior, Raymond Helman mean, loud, uncooperative, would not go to breakfast.

8-25-72—2:30 p.m.
—Restraints. Raymond Helman sleeveless jacket tied to bench and to bed in locked sideroom.
—Resident's behavior, Raymond Helman very unruly and loud.

8-26-72—12 midnight to 6:30 a.m.
—Restrained, Raymond Helman in a sleeveless jacket, tied to bed and locked in sideroom.
—Raymond Helman, upset tray at breakfast, boy shaved and frisked, silverware checked.

8-26-72—2:30 p.m.
—Restraints, Raymond Helman sleeveless jacket tied to bench and bed in locked sideroom at bedtime.

8-27-72—12 midnight to 6:30 a.m.

—Restrained, Raymond Helman in sleeveless jacket tied to bed and locked in sideroom.
—Medications omitted, Raymond Helman would not go to breakfast.
—Restraints, Raymond Helman in sleeveless jacket and tied to bench.
—Resident's behavior, Raymond Helman loud, uncooperative, would not go to breakfast.

8-27-72—2:30 p.m.

—Restraints, Raymond Helman sleeveless jacket tied to bench and to bed in locked sideroom at 9:00 p.m.

8-28-72—12 midnight to 6:30 a.m.

—Restrained, Raymond Helman, sleeveless jacket, tied to bed and in locked sideroom.
—Restraints, Raymond Helman in sleeveless jacket and tied to bed 6:00 a.m.
—Medication omitted, Raymond Helman refused to go to breakfast and lunch.
—Resident's behavior, Raymond Helman loud, mean and uncooperative, refused to eat breakfast or lunch.

8-28-72—2:00 p.m.

—Restrained, Raymond Helman tied to bench in sleeveless jacket and locked in sideroom at bedtime tied to bed.

8-28-72—2:00 p.m.

—Resident's behavior. Raymond Helman loud, misbehavior, didn't eat any supper.
—*Note:* Helman to ego outing at 5:30 and returned at 9:15.

8-29-72—12 midnight to 6:30 a.m.

—Restrained, Raymond Helman in sleeveless jacket and tied to bed in locked sideroom.
—Restraints, Raymond Helman in sleeveless jacket and tied to bed 6:00 a.m.
—Medications omitted, Raymond Helman at 6:45 a.m., didn't go to breakfast or lunch.
—Resident's behavior, Raymond Helman would not get dressed, didn't go to breakfast.

8-29-72—2:30 p.m.

—Restraints, Raymond Helman in sleeveless jacket and tied to bench.

8-30-72—12 midnight to 6:30 a.m.

—Raymond Helman, sleeveless jacket and tied in bed, locked in sideroom.
—Medication omitted, Raymond Helman refused morning medications and noon.

—Resident's behavior, Raymond Helman refused to go to breakfast, lunch, no medication.

8-30-72—2:00 p.m.
—Restrained, Raymond Helman in sleeveless jacket tied to the bench, locked in sideroom and tied to bed at bedtime.

8-31-72—12 midnight to 6:30 a.m.
—Restraints, Raymond Helman sleeveless jacket tied to bed and locked in sideroom.

8-31-72—6:30 a.m.
—Restraints, Raymond Helman sleeveless jacket tied to bench.
—Medication omitted, Raymond Helman refused medication at 7:00 a.m.
—Resident's behavior, Raymond Helman refused to get out of bed this a.m., he also refused to go to breakfast, and his morning medication, noon also.
—Unusual happenings, Raymond Helman belligerent all day.
—Raymond Helman to hospital for x-ray, spoon lodged in stomach. Escorted by Mr. ——— and Mr. ———, had to call security to bring him back. (Sent back to cottage by Dr. ———.)

8-31-72—2:30 p.m.
—Restrained, Raymond Helman locked in sideroom and tied to bed at bedtime.
—Inoculation, Raymond Helman received 50 mg/Vistral given by Mr. ———.
Note: When Raymond Helman is bad and hyperactive he is to be locked in front hall and when the rest of the cottage goes to meals, attendant is to stay in the cottage with Helman. Orders from Mr. ———, witnessed by Mr. ———.
—*Note:* Send Raymond Helman to dispensary on 9/1/72 to have his upper left leg and back checked, has two bad sores.
—*Note:* Raymond Helman refused to go to supper.
—*Note:* Raymond Helman was real good after he was put in the hall.

9-1-72—12 midnight to 6:30 a.m.
—Raymond Helman, restrained in sleeveless jacket and tied to bed in locked sideroom.

9-1-72—6:30 a.m.
—Restrained, Raymond Helman in sleeveless jacket and tied to bench.
—Resident's behavior, Raymond Helman refused to get out of bed, complained of stomach hurting. Ate no breakfast.
—Raymond Helman, T-99 o/r P-92 at 6:15 a.m.
Raymond Helman, T-99 6/r P-112 R-20 at 9:15 a.m.
—Mrs. ———, R.N. and Mr. ——— came down at 9:45 a.m. to see Raymond Helman. Mrs. ——— to reapproach Dr. ———.
Census change: Raymond Helman to hospital.

9-22-72—6:00 a.m.

—Raymond Helman, restraints sleeveless jacket, tied to bench.

Note: Raymond Helman from hospital—Raymond under no circumstances is to have plastic sliverware. He will eat with a tablespoon and the attendant will cut anything needed cut. If Raymond refuses to go to the dining room, no meal will be brought back to him without the doctor's permission. (Per Dr. ———.)

—Raymond is also to sleep in dorm unless he becomes belligerent, then he is to be locked in sideroom and ——— put in dorm. The spoon that he uses is to be checked, and if it comes up missing is to be reported, time, day, etc. Both bundles made up by Mr. ———. Mr. ——— and ——— to hospital for Raymond Helman.

9-22-72—2:30 p.m.

—Raymond Helman in sleeveless jacket tied to chair and tied to bed at bedtime.

9-23-72—12 midnight to 6:30 a.m.

—Restraints, Raymond Helman sleeveless jacket tied to bed.

9-23-72—6:00 a.m.

—Restrained, Raymond Helman sleeveless jacket tied to bench.

9-23-72—2:30 p.m.

—Restrained, Raymond Helman in sleeveless jacket tied to bench and bed at bedtime.

Special Note: Raymond Helman was raising ——— in the dorm. He had to be taken out of his bed; was taken out of the sideroom at 9:15 and let sleep in the dorm. Raymond Helman was put in the sideroom. Restrained in bed because he was very violent, per Mrs. ———, Supervisor.

9-24-72—12 midnight to 6:30 a.m.

—Restrained, Raymond Helman in locked sideroom, and in sleeveless jacket tied to bed.

Note: Raymond Helman wet the bed tonight.

—Restrained, Raymond Helman in quiet room, per Dr. ———.

—Resident's behavior, Raymond Helman very violent, knocked clock off wall, broke glass, upset benches.

9-24-72—2:30 p.m.

—Restrained, Raymond Helman in the quiet room.

—Raymond Helman fed in the quiet room per Mrs. ———. Raymond Helman's tray and spoon returned to the dining room.

Note: Raymond Helman didn't want to come back to the cottage, so he is not to have a blanket, per Dr. ———.

9-25-72—12 midnight to 6:30 a.m.

—Restrained, Raymond Helman locked in quiet room.

9-25-72—6:00 a.m.
—Raymond Helman in quiet room, fed in quiet room.

9-25-72—2:30 p.m.
—Restrained, Raymond Helman in the quiet room.
—Quiet check—3,4,5 fed (6 given a drink) 7,8,9.
—Fed in cottage, Raymond Helman fed in cottage, food and tray returned by Dr. McClelland. *Note:* Dr. McClelland—Raymond Helman tried to put the spoon he had down his throat.

9-26-72—12 midnight to 6:30 a.m.
—Restrained, Raymond Helman in quiet room.

9-26-72—6:00 a.m.
—Raymond Helman in quiet room.
—Quiet check 6-7 fed-med–8-9-10-11-12 dinner-med 1 & 2

9-26-72—2:00 p.m.
—Restrained, Raymond Helman in quiet room.
—Fed in quiet room.

9-26-72—2:30 p.m.
—Unusual happenings. Raymond Helman tried to swallow large spoon.
—Raymond Helman in quiet room.
—Quiet check: 3-4-5-6-7-8-9,10.

9-27-72—12 midnight to 6:30 a.m.
—Restrained, Raymond Helman in quiet room.

9-27-72—6:00 a.m.
—Restraints, Raymond Helman out of quiet at 8:15 a.m. to Cottage #1.
—Disciplinary Measures—Raymond Helman to quiet room 8:20 a.m.

9-27-72—2:30 p.m.
—Restraints, Raymond Helman locked in quiet room, fed also.
—Helman fed and bathed, quiet room checked 3-4-5-6-7-8-9-10.

9-28-72—12 midnight to 6:30 a.m.
—Raymond Helman in quiet room.

9-28-72—6:00 a.m.
—Raymond Helman in quiet room.
Quiet check—7 fed, 8 med, water, 9 cleaned 10, 11, 12 fed, 1 & 2.

9-28-72—2:30 p.m.
—Restraints, Raymond Helman locked in quiet room, also fed in quiet.

—Disciplinary measures, Raymond Helman in quiet room.
—Raymond Helman received another night shirt, as he had torn the one he had to pieces.

9-29-72—12 midnight to 6:30 a.m.
—Raymond Helman in the quiet room.

9-29-72—6:00 a.m.
—Raymond Helman in the quiet room, also fed and medication in the quiet room.
—Inoculation. Raymond Helman given a shot in the quiet room, because he refused his medication from Mrs. ———.
—Quiet check 6, 7, fed 8:35, given shot at 9, 10, 11, 12, fed 1 & 2.
—Raymond Helman's spoon returned from breakfast and dinner.

9-29-72—2:00 p.m.
—Restraints, Raymond Helman in quiet room.
—Disciplinary measures, Raymond Helman in quiet room.
—Quiet room checked 3, 4, 5 fed, 6, 7, 8, 9, 10.

9-30-72—12 midnight to 6:30 a.m.
—Restrained, Raymond Helman in quiet room.

9-30-72—6:00 a.m.
—Raymond Helman in quiet—Helman out of quiet room.
—Raymond Helman to be tied to bench in corridor at foot of stairs.

9-30-72—2:00 p.m.
—Raymond Helman tied to bench in sleeveless jacket, tied to bed at bedtime.
—Resident's behavior, Raymond Helman would not go to dining room, not fed.

10-1-72—12 midnight to 6:30 a.m.
—Restraints, Raymond Helman sleeveless jacket and tied to bed.

10-1-72—6:00 a.m.
—Raymond Helman in sleeveless jacket tied to bench in hall.
Special Note: If Helman refuses to go to breakfast, is to be left in the cottage and someone is to stay with him, confirmed with Mrs. ———.
Note: Raymond Helman started to raise cain just as soon as he got up this morning; refused to go to both breakfast and dinner. Supervisor Mrs. ——— notified.

10-1-72—2:00 p.m.
—Raymond Helman in sleeveless jacket and tied to bench in hall, tied to bed at bedtime.

10-2-72—12 midnight to 6:30 a.m.
—Restrained, Raymond Helman sleeveless jacket and tied to bed.

10-2-72—6:00 a.m.
—Raymond Helman in sleeveless jacket and tied to bench.
—Raymond Helman taken to x-ray in a wheelchair.

10-2-72—2:00 p.m.
—Raymond Helman in sleeveless jacket and tied to bench and bed at bedtime.

10-3-72—12 midnight to 6:30 a.m.
—Raymond Helman, strait jacket, tied to bed.
—Residents' behavior, very good except for Raymond Helman.
—Raymond Helman in sleeveless jacket tied to bench in stairway per Mrs. ———.
Note: Raymond Helman refused to eat breakfast and lunch.

10-3-72—2:30 p.m.
—Raymond Helman tied to bench and in bed at 9:00 p.m.
—Inoculations: Raymond Helman given 7½ grs. Sodium Amytal at 2:05 p.m. by Mrs. ———, R.N.
Note: Raymond Helman has lump on side of head and scratches around incision, noticed at approximately 2:00 p.m.

10-4-72—10:00 p.m. to 12 midnight
—Raymond Helman, sleeveless jacket tied to bed.
—Raymond Helman tied to bench.

10-4-72—2:30 p.m.
—Raymond Helman in sleeveless jacket tied to bench and bed at 9:00 p.m.

10-5-72—12 midnight to 6:30 a.m.
—Raymond Helman sleeveless jacket and tied to bed.

10-5-72—6:00 a.m.
—Raymond Helman in sleeveless jacket and tied to bench in hallway.
—Disciplinary measures, Raymond Helman tied to bench.
—Residents' behavior, good except Raymond Helman didn't go to breakfast.

10-5-72—2:30 p.m.
—Raymond Helman sleeveless jacket tied to bench and tied to bed at 9:00 p.m.

10-6-72—12 midnight to 6:30 a.m.
—Raymond Helman in sleeveless jacket tied to bed.

10-6-72—6:00 a.m.
—Raymond Helman in sleeveless jacket tied to bench.
—Residents' behavior, Raymond Helman refused to go to breakfast or lunch.
—Unusual happenings, Raymond Helman refused to eat breakfast or lunch.

10-6-72—2:30 p.m.
—Raymond Helman sleeveless jacket tied to bench and to bed at 9:00 p.m.

10-7-72—12 midnight to 6:30 a.m.
—Raymond Helman sleeveless jacket tied to bed.

10-7-72—6:00 a.m.
—Raymond Helman in sleeveless jacket and tied to bench.
—Residents' behavior, very good except for Raymond Helman.
—Unusual happenings. Raymond Helman did not go to breakfast.

10-7-72—2:30 p.m.
—Raymond Helman sleeveless jacket tied to bench and bed 9:00 p.m.

10-8-72—12 midnight to 6:30 a.m.
—Raymond Helman sleeveless jacket tied to bed.

10-8-72—6:00 a.m.
—Raymond Helman in sleeveless jacket, tied to bench.
—Residents' behavior, very good except for Raymond Helman acting up, would not go to breakfast or dinner.

10-8-72—2:30 p.m.
—Raymond Helman sleeveless jacket tied to bench and bed at 9:00 p.m.
—Inoculations. Raymond Helman at 3:30 p.m. shot given by Mrs. ———.
—Residents' behavior. Raymond Helman acting up this evening, broke out of his sleeveless jacket twice, Supervisor notified, he also cut inside of upper lip, nurse said it would be OK.
Note: Raymond Helman seemed to have an excessive amount of dried blood on his clothing at 2:30 p.m. Mr. ——— was notified at this time. It was stated that one of the residents hit him at the request of an attendant.

10-9-72—12 midnight to 6:30 a.m.
—Raymond Helman in sleeveless jacket, tied to bench.
—Residents' behavior, very good except for Raymond Helman—mean, unruly, would not go to breakfast or lunch.
Please Note: All blood on Raymond Helman's clothes was put there by himself.

10-9-72—2:30 p.m.
—Residents' behavior, Raymond Helman and all others, good this evening.
—Raymond Helman did not go to supper.

10-10-72—12 midnight to 6:30 a.m.
—Raymond Helman in sleeveless jacket, tied to bed.
Notice, Supervisor's Office notified 6:50 a.m. of Raymond Helman complaining of

stomach hurting in area of incision by Mr. ——— 6:00 a.m. vomited. Medication given by Mrs. ——— at 6:45 a.m. and 11:45 a.m.
—7:27 a.m., Raymond Helman moaning and crying, vomited 7:29.
—Raymond Helman 8:30 a.m.—Temp. 97.6—Pulse 84—Res. 14   12:00 noon Temp. 99.2.
—Residents' behavior, Raymond Helman sick in a.m. okay in p.m.
—Unusual happenings, Raymond Helman did not eat breakfast.

10-10-72
—Dispensary, Raymond Helman.
—Raymond Helman in sleeveless jacket and tied to bench.
—*Please note*, check Raymond Helman's temperature every 4 hours and report to R. N. or Supervisor's Office if it is elevated. Raymond Helman vomiting quite a lot.
—Temp. 99.2—Pulse 84—Res. 19, 4:00 p.m. Temp. 99.0 Pulse 86, Res. 18   8:00 p.m.

10-11-72—12 midnight to 6:30 a.m.
—Raymond Helman—Temp. 98, Pulse 86, Resp. 18 at 12:00.
—Raymond Helman in sleeveless jacket and tied to bed.
—Raymond Helman—Temp. 98, Pulse 84, Resp. 16 at 4:00.
—Medication omitted, Raymond Helman refused morning medication (took it later).
—Residents' behavior, good except for Raymond Helman, refused medication.
—Raymond Helman; sleeveless vest, tied to bench.

10-11-72—10:00 p.m. to 12 midnight
—Raymond Helman, sleeveless jacket and tied to bed.

10-12-72—12 midnight to 6:30 a.m.
—Raymond Helman, sleeveless jacket and tied to bed.
—Restrained, Raymond Helman in sleeveless jacket and tied to bench.

10-12-72—2:30 p.m.
—Raymond Helman in sleeveless jacket and tied to bench.

10-13-72—12 midnight to 6:30 a.m.
—Raymond Helman, sleeveless jacket tied to bed.

10-13-72—6:00 a.m.
—Raymond Helman in sleeveless jacket and tied to bench.
—Residents' behavior, good except Raymond Helman.

10-13-72—2:30 p.m.
—Raymond Helman sleeveless jacket and tied to bench, tied to bed at 9:00 p.m.

10-14-72—midnight to 6:30 a.m.
—Raymond Helman, jacket and tied to bed.

10-14-72—6:00 a.m.
—Raymond Helman jacket and tied to bench.
—Residents' behavior, good except for Raymond Helman.

10-14-72
—Accident, Raymond Helman put his hand through annex window and would not let anyone treat cuts on his hand.

10-14-72—2:30 p.m.
—Raymond Helman, sleeveless jacket tied to bench and tied to bed.
Note: Raymond Helman should be taken to dispensary to get fluid out of left elbow.
—Painted Raymond Helman's hand with Merthiolate.

10-15-72—12 midnight to 6:30 a.m.
—Raymond Helman in sleeveless jacket and tied to bed.

10-15-72—6:00 a.m.
—Raymond Helman in sleeveless jacket and tied to bench.

10-15-72—2:30 p.m.
—Raymond Helman in sleeveless jacket, tied to bench and tied to bed.

10-16-72—12 midnight to 6:30 a.m.
—Raymond Helman in sleeveless jacket and tied to bed.

10-16-72—6:00 a.m.
—Unusual happenings—At 5:45 a.m. Mr. ——— went upstairs to awake the boys, and found Raymond Helman on the floor with a tie down rope wrapped around his neck. Dr. ——— was notified and checked him at approximately 6:20 a.m. At 6:30 a.m. Raymond Helman was taken to the hospital for a possible strangulation. Mr. ——— filled out an accident report. Dr. ——— the coroner, and an investigator came in at 9:30 a.m. to talk to Mr. ———. Clothing and personal belongings of Raymond Helman turned in at Northside Clothesroom.

—Sprayed for ants this morning.

26

The Nut House Cure

Our ancestors believed that demons and witches caused insanity and other forms of deviant behavior. Exorcism and miracles at holy wells and shrines were thought to be the only cure. Certain saints were said to possess the power to drive away evil spirits. For all clerics, exorcism was an early and normal part of the training, and it could be practiced before reaching the priesthood.

Through the centuries so-called idiots and those only mildly mad wandered through the countryside. Others were locked in backrooms by their families. When patients were taken to monasteries and convents to be cured, the forerunner to the mental hospital was established. Near shrines families rented room, and colonies were formed. But in the worst of times the insane were banned, beaten, burned, crucified, guillotined, hanged, or imprisoned and tortured. Crowded into airless cells, dressed only in rags, and with foul straw to sleep on in summer and to keep them warm in winter, the more fortunate died.

Today, not even the most neglected back wards in the nation's worst institutions are as bad as those of the past. While many remnants of the snake pits of the 1930s and '40s remain, progress is being made in most states. But that is not to say that all is well. The basic question remains: Are mental hospitals, or even the children's psychiatric units, the best places to help American boys and girls? Or to put it another way: Just how good is the nut house cure?

Even the superintendents of the best-run institutions are often skeptical. Many are openly opposed to institutions for children. While mental health officials suggest that millions of children need help, they add that, like reform schools and facilities for the retarded, mental hospitals too often serve as dumping grounds for unwanted children.

And yet these youngsters must have somewhere to go. For many families, poor and disorganized, the job of caring for these children is too great. Nor can we let them roam the streets, picking through dumps and garbage cans, stealing or begging, as in other parts of the world.

So the question remains: Is the mental hospital the best place for these children? Should we build hundreds of institutions to accommodate the millions of children reported to be in need of help? Or are there other, better solutions?

I could find few experts with answers, partly because so little is known about mental illness. And largely because psychiatrists, psychologists, and the others have no panaceas. The cost of mental hospital care is high. In most states the range is from $10,000 to $30,000 per child per year. If the average taxpayer knew how few children are cured at this price, he would be outraged. And yet those who run the institutions say sentencing a child to a lifetime of custodial care or welfare payments costs even more.

Many present practices are intolerable. I have found far too many disturbed children in jails, detention centers, and reform schools. While some institutions still use straight jackets and other restraints, many rely on heavy doses of drugs—"chemical strait jackets."

As states build more children's units, younger children are institutionalized. It is not unusual to find six- or seven-year-olds locked up, and in some states the children are even younger. Most often the younger the child, the longer he stays. Six-year-olds may grow up in a children's ward and graduate to an adolescent or adult unit. Others are placed directly in adult wards while very young.

While a few children in mental hospitals are deeply disturbed, more are diagnosed as "behavior problems" or as having a difficult time adjusting to adolescence. One finds these children in both mental hospitals and reform schools. The courts label them "incorrigibles" or "in need of supervision." Many are runaways. Others are truant from school, or use drugs or alcohol. Some steal. Girls may be promiscuous.

Most often those sent to mental hospitals are children of the poor. Middle-class youngsters find private help, or are permitted to grow out of bad behavior. When a middle-class child is sent to a mental hospital, the problem is usually severe or the parents also have problems. Commitments often depend upon who first labels the child—the police, welfare, mental health, the schools, or fed-up parents. Many children reach mental hospitals after a series of foster homes, probation, and reform school. Most have had little professional help.

Judges buy time and seek help by sending a child in trouble to a mental hospital for "observation." But there also is strong evidence that mental hospital commitments are increasing because Supreme Court rulings and the arrival of lawyers in juvenile courts have made it more difficult to ship children off to reform schools. The corrections system has been under attack, and mental hospitals can serve as a convenient alternative.

But there are other reasons. Some experts insist that children presently in trouble are more deeply disturbed than in years past. Because of faulty funding, poor staffing, and politics, many local mental health clinics fail to help children. Too often youngsters get worse while being treated. And as schools hire more psychiatrists, psychologists, and social workers, youngsters who once were ignored, tolerated, punished, or kicked out of school now are labeled "sick" or "disturbed." Once labeled, the path may lead to a mental hospital.

Unfortunately, those who run these institutions seldom have magic potions (beyond controlling drugs) or secret systems of bringing about "cures." While most are more humane than reform schools, since the children are sick, rather than bad, mental hospitals can be damaging. If a child's self-confidence and self-concept are important, it hardly helps to confirm that he is crazy and deserves to be locked up in the nut house—a charge that his parents may well have made more than once. And what of the child who must, for all time, write on all military, government, school, and private personnel forms that he has been held in a mental hospital for treatment?

The depth of the injustice becomes more evident when one sees the *kinds* of children committed. Or understands the *causes* of deviant behavior. If you have children of your own, you might ask yourself whether or not you would want one of them to go to such a place, and then ask if *any* child should go.

Dr. Erica M. Loutsch, director of the Manhattan Children's Center, a small, fairly new facility, told me that when she "opened the doors in 1971 all of the children were black or Puerto Rican."

"Ninety-nine percent of our kids are what you would call behavior disorder children," she continues. "They are not psychotic. But most are aggressive, overactive, and cannot be handled at school or at home. Many have learning disabilities. They don't need twenty-four-hour institutional care, and most wouldn't be here except that they have problems, like mothers who drink heavily. They haven't had services in school or the community. We found that fifty percent of our inpatients needed glasses, but no one bothered to find that out until the kids came here. I'm talking about nine and ten-year-olds. If the schools or the community provided basic health services we wouldn't have as many children here."

Across town, at the Queens Children's Hospital, the largest mental hospital for youngsters in the nation, Dr. Gloria Faretra, the director, says that many of her inmates are "severely disturbed." But she quickly adds that her hospital is twenty years old, and so it has "accumulated a chronic population."

"I hope to take a hard look at all of our kids and at our attitudes," she says. "We must find answers as to why these children are here, and which children we tend to keep."

The parents of most of the children she deals with are either on welfare or from the lower economic levels of society. When a researcher with a doctorate in social work attempted to study the mothers and fathers of the patients, she couldn't find enough fathers to make the study. Many had disappeared. Some of the children had been born out of wedlock. Others were on skid row, using too much alcohol, or on drugs. Many were in jail or prison.

"Between twenty and twenty-five percent of our children have no family at all," she says.

At the Philbrook Children's Center in Concord, New Hampshire, I found no minority-group children among the sixty-five who were hospitalized. But almost all were from low-income, welfare, and disorganized families.

"Most of the children here are not *disturbed,* but they are *disturbing,*" Dr. Kenneth Rulx explains. "They don't do what the schools want them to do; they don't do what their parents want them to do. They may get out of their seats and walk around at the school when the teacher wants them to sit quietly and read a book. School plays a big part in their coming here. We don't get as many during the summer months, and the number coming in drops off during the Christmas holiday season."

That is the normal pattern nationally for reform schools, children's jails, and mental hospitals. When teachers go out on strike, for example, the schools close, the delinquency rate drops, and fewer children are identified as "disturbed." After a summer lull, most institutions begin to fill up a few weeks after school opens in the fall.

The children in the Philbrook Center are largely preadolescent, and more than three-quarters are from low-economic-level families, or have "no families at all."

"The mother can't be found, and if there is a father, he's in jail in New York or Georgia," Dr. Rulx says.

Unlike Vermont, which prides itself in a high level of services to children, New Hampshire has a shortage of foster homes, specialized group homes, and other facilities for unwanted children.

"There are only two places for a problem child to go: here or to the industrial school," Dr. Rulx says. "We get many who are considered 'at risk.'"

An "at risk" child, he explains, may come from a family where one or both parents are emotionally disturbed, or the children may live so far back in the woods that they are "victims of social isolation." They are also the offspring of drug users, alcoholics, prison inmates, or even a divorced person who authorities believe cannot give the children proper care. A child suspended from school or who has dropped out of school also may be found to be "at risk," along with those who are physically and neurologically impaired, or one who is a member of a "multi-problem" family.

If the state would provide good group homes or even adequate foster homes, Dr. Rulx believes that "seventy-five percent of these children could leave tomorrow." He sees the mental hospital as the dumping ground for many unwanted houngsters, especially adolescents, for the children have no rights and so parents drop them off as "voluntary commitments."

"Some parents just say 'the hell with it, I've put up with this kid for fourteen years, and that's enough,'" he continues. "And welfare puts children here when they can't find anyplace else for them."

Other New Hampshire children go through a court process, or are sent to the state hospital after being examined by a physician, while in neighboring Vermont the trend is toward small group homes for these youngsters, usually in an old farmhouse on the edge of a town. But some children, especially adolescents, are mixed in with the adult population in the state hospital, as in most states. These are far more disturbed children than many who are committed elsewhere. And Vermont has a special hospital wing designated as the "Youth Treatment Unit," a facility that specializes in the hard-to-reach autistic child, largely because this is the area of expertise of Dr. Claire O'Shea, who heads the unit.

The autistic are among the most neglected children in many states. When I visited the grim facility for emotionally disturbed children at the Pineland Hospital and Training Center in Pownal, Maine, I found autistic children separated from the others and locked in cells, getting no therapy at all because no one knew how to work with autistic children.

Yet in Wisconsin, as in Vermont, these children were getting special help in the summer of 1972, and many of the children who had been withdrawn, without speech, and living in a dream world, were now playing happily, speaking, and relating to others for the first time. Unfortunately, the man responsible for the program soon took a post in another state.

Unlike reform schools, which must take all kinds of children, the mental hospitals tend to be selective. While Vermont believes it can help autistic and other severely disturbed children, officials will screen out the more "sadistic, acting-out adolescents" because they find it difficult to work with them. Perhaps this is the most honest approach for institutions. It is difficult to help a child you dislike or find unpleasant. And yet someone, somewhere, must help them before they become dependent or dangerous adults.

Carol Pressman, the Cincinnati area coordinator of children's programs for the Ohio Department of Mental Health, says her job is to deal with this problem.

"One of my jobs is to find resources, to out-shout, and, if necessary, to humiliate other professionals into serving these children," she says. "In Cincinnati alone there are thousands of children who need help but never get it. I know of nearly two hundred who have never been to school, not even kindergarten, although they're of school age. The parents took them to school and the schools told them 'no way.' A lot of these are autistic-like children. And there are thousands of others we never reach."

She sees the Department of Mental Health as "the only agency in Ohio willing to work with many of these kids." But she concedes that so far she has hardly been able to make a dent in the problem.

Some hundred and fifty children are committed to the Children's Unit at the Longview State Hospital in Cincinnati. Sixty percent are sent there from the juvenile court, as an alternative to reform school or to an institution for the retarded. About half of the children have IQs that fall into the retardation range.

Because Ohio's institutions are generally bad, and some rank with the worst in the nation, parents tend to shop around for a diagnosis, hoping to get them into Longview. Some parents sign papers declaring the child to be "unruly" in order to get him in.

The strength of the Children's Unit at Longview is Nicholas A. Seta, a reformed professional gambler and now Ohio's leading advocate for children. Each year he single-handedly supplements his budget by making public appearances and speeches. The money he gets goes to help the youngsters. Mr. Seta takes a personal interest in every child, has the courage to speak his mind while others hide, and has the support of his staff. Education and personal warmth are used, rather than high-powered psychiatric programs. Children considered "too violent," and those who run away, are excluded from the Children's Unit. Some end up in adult wards in a hospital that has the reputation of being "the last of the old-time snake pits."

Ms. Pressman sees two kinds of children being accepted in the Children's Unit: those who have problems coping with the stresses of adolescence, and so "do poorly in school, run around at night, and get into trouble, but have no problems with dealing with reality," and children who are "small, cute, often with little language, who, at the age of six or seven, set fires and do other things that cause parents to throw up their hands."

A few miles to the north, in Dayton, Ohio, William Sherer, administrator at the Children's Psychiatric Hospital and Child Guidance Center, explains that "mental health hasn't been a vote-getter in Ohio." That is why the eighty-four-bed facility must serve twenty-five counties, and why officials are pushing the hospital to serve eleven more.

"We can't serve twenty-five counties adequately, and our budget has been frozen by the state, so it would be impossible to try to serve eleven more counties," he says.

The institution, which is known as a "medical model," since it provides traditional psychiatric and nursing services, tries to keep its count to seventy or below, because when the number goes higher "children tend to become just statistics." The population ranges in age from six to sixteen, and at the age of sixteen they must go to a group home, boarding school, foster home, or to the state hospital, located nearby. No children with an IQ of less than 50 are accepted. And patients range from the severely psychotic to homosexuals and the victims of child abuse, including incest. The Dayton hospital also screens out children.

"We just got rid of a cute little con artist," Mr. Sherer says. "His family didn't want him and we weren't getting anywhere with him. Right now he's in a children's home, but he'll eventually end up in jail."

Even in Ohio, where there seems to be little concern for children, the cost of care is high. The Dayton facility costs out at roughly $60 per child per day, or nearly $22,000 a year. It is a high price to pay when some children are held nine or ten years before being sent on to a boarding school or the adult hospital at sixteen. But the cost would be even higher if the quality of care was raised, or if psychiatrists and other professionals were paid on a par with Indiana, Michigan, and other states. Mental health facilities, whether they are good or bad, require high salaries for qualified professionals.

Because of these high costs and low success rates, some states have moved away from institutions, toward community-based programs. It is less expensive to help a child during the day, while he is housed, fed, and clothed by his own family. But the quality of the staff in local programs often is low, and some children simply cannot remain in their own homes.

California is one of the states where efforts have been made to lower high institutional costs both through budget cuts and by closing the institutions down. I found one state institution for the retarded there working with children only three days a week—warehousing them on Friday, Saturday, Sunday, and Monday.

At the mental hospital in Napa, California, Dr. Clifford Brackenridge, a psychologist, said that like many others, when he entered the field his goal was to "work myself out of a job" and to help close institutions for children.

"I've changed my mind," he says. "The community sees us as a place to send the aggressive child. Children with behavior disorders, with destructive behavior, who are untrained, unsocialized, and who are aggressive, can only be redirected in a place like this. Here we can deal with some pretty wild acting out—we can work with children who would not be tolerated in the community."

It is hard to argue with this point of view, inasmuch as aggressive unwanted children must go somewhere. Yet most professionals believe the institution is not that place.

"Institutions are very destructive to children," says another Californian, Dr. Norbert I. Rieger, who enjoys a national reputation for his work with children at the state hospital in Camarillo, where he is medical program director of children's services. "We need a professional staff and satellite homes that take four children."

Dr. Rieger is opposed to the traditional foster home because foster parents are untrained, and they are not backstopped by a professional team. He believes his satellite homes would solve that problem, and provide a method of both treatment and "normalization."

One can readily see why he does not like institutions. On the summer day I visited Camarillo I found children engaged in highly sophisticated therapeutic and educational programs. But I also found children spending long periods clinging to a chain-link fence near their living unit. Several seemed lonely and called out to me as I walked by. It was at that point that it struck me as being very much like an obedience school for dogs, with the animals in kennels and runs between classes.

As I have noted, many states are building separate children's units near state hospitals. I visited one near Mid-Missouri State Hospital, and like many fairly open institutions it is "plagued with runaways."

When I was there, in 1973, many of the children were being held roughly two months for diagnosis, while large numbers were there for longer periods because they had run from home, were caught drinking, using marijuana or other drugs, were considered promiscuous by their parents or others, or for being "beyond parental control." Referrals are from the courts, parents, school counselors, "or even a friend," while some over sixteen "sign themselves in," according to Dr. Elmer Jackson, who runs the facility.

"Many of our patients carry the label of retardation or of borderline retardation," he adds. "But often the child has only been in school thirty or forty days during the year, so how could he be up to grade level?" He finds it difficult to know how many children are helped and how many are hurt by the institution.

"We do know that many are sent here just to get them off the streets," he says. "When we are told they are being sent for 'long-term treatment,' I ask: 'What do you mean by that?' For some young people six months is long term. Treatment of the adolescent is a fairly new field. There are a lot of questions that need to be asked. I don't have all the answers, and I don't believe anyone else does. At best we can review the patient's progress and ask: Is his problem worse? Is he better? The same? Or does the problem no longer exist?"

In Missouri, as in other states, I found little difference between the child in reform school and the youngster in the mental hospital. In fact, if you look at both institutions, it would be fair to say that those sent to the reform school are more "disturbed" than children at the mental hospital.

Most children's units transfer hard-to-handle children into adult wards or to reform schools. Often they return them to the court with a report indicating that the mental hospital is an "inappropriate" setting. Reform school superintendents often complain that they cannot send their psychotic children to mental hospitals, for it is a one-way street, with corrections getting the *most unwanted* children of all. It is not a long route for a child from a welfare foster home to jail to a mental hospital and on to a reform school. The next step may be an adult prison. Often some of the meeker children reach prison as runaways—children who run from homosexual attacks and other forms of violence in institutions.

Thousands of children are held in adult mental hospitals. In Massachusetts, for example, once considered a progressive state, there are some two hundred teen-agers in adult hospitals, although there are two children's units in the state.

I visited the seventy-bed children's facility attached to Metropolitan State Hospital in Waltham, just west of Boston, in the spring of 1973, and received a cool reception, especially when I asked to tour the facility. The superintendent, who had refused to be interviewed because she was "much too busy," listed several excuses why I could not go through. When I noted that it was the only mental hospital in the nation to turn me down, she told me I was an "unpleasant person," she did not want me to go through, but, if I was willing to make an appointment "in a few weeks" I could return for a tour. Although I was enroute to New York City, and then to the West Coast, I agreed to return, the date was set, and I left. The day before my second visit the superintendent called my home to report that "something has come up," and so I would not be able to visit after all. Nor would she set a new date by phone. I felt I knew why. When the superintendent announced that she was too busy to see me, she arranged for an interview with Dr. Paul Schneller, a psychiatrist. Among other things, he told me that he felt they had a "good program in a poor physical plant."

"This is a typical Massachusetts public building," he said. "It's run-down because of lack of maintenance. They've cut it back even more this year. It's rundown, but within limits the physical plant can be overcome by staff. A few years ago there were more than two hundred children here, but now it has been cut back to well under one hundred. Our staff is largely untrained. But it's young, and they make up for their inexperience with enthusiasm, idealism, and inventiveness.

"But this job is exhausting. I'm just a consultant. I can hide in my office. I had my time on the wards when I was in my twenties. After two years even these young people get tired. A year and they're at the peak of their effectiveness. At the end of two years they're worn out. If we could give them a leave after two years, even three months without pay, perhaps we could keep them."

In all institutions the line staff poses major problems. Many institutions take advantage of idealistic young people. They pay them starvation wages and burn them out. Or they hire old-line staff, and they serve like keepers in a zoo.

If staff members burn out in the average institution, at least in those who do not zonk youngsters with heavy doses of drugs, consider the young people working in New Mexico's Children's Psychiatric Unit. Housed in shabby buildings in the school for the retarded in the dusty little town of Los Lunas, the facility was moved there to keep the children out of the state's horrible adult hospital.

To open the doors the employees (all, including the director, in their twenties) scrounged furniture from basements, attics, and even the dump. The facility is run by twenty-four-year-old Garry Cole, who has a master's degree in counseling. Cole is paid $660 a month, while a young woman, also with an M.S., earns $460. Another staff member has her master's in special education. All handle a variety of jobs, and Mr. Cole doesn't even have a secretary. There are twelve people in all on the staff to watch over and work with the children twenty-four hours a day, seven days a week, fifty-two weeks a year. Vacations, illness, or other problems mean that people must double up.

The patients range from those who are extremely aggressive to a fifteen-year-old autistic boy and a ten-year-old who hallucinates. The youngest when I visited the facility was six, a boy "caught in the middle of a messy divorce." To keep classes small they attend school from forty-five to ninety minutes a day. Some work on the farm with the retarded children or in the institutional laundry. Others have too much time on their hands and tear the unit apart.

No girls were in the institution during the summer I visited. Two part-time local men, hired to fill in for regular staff members, became involved sexually with some of the girls. Since the newspapers missed the story there was no scandal. Most staff members feel that had the story leaked out, the facility would have been closed.

Why do staff members work so hard for so little money?

"We're still young and excited about what we're doing," says Ms. Dana Cavallero, the special education teacher. "I've been here two years, and sometimes I know we've tripped over our own feet, we're so inexperienced. But when you see a child make progress then everything is worthwhile.

"We can make and spend money for the rest of our lives. We feel we are pioneering because so few people in New Mexico are doing anything for these kids. But there are times when we talk about taking our kids to Santa Fe to let them loose in the House of Representatives. . . ."

The interview with Ms. Cavallero ended when a small boy dropped by for hugs and to be mothered. A few minutes later a fourteen-year-old dropped in to discuss the steer skull he had found on a field trip. It was nearly dinner time, and most teachers in traditional schools had been home for more than an hour. But to Ms. Cavallero, a pretty young woman, the children were more important than her social life.

The vitality found in the New Mexico facility was in marked contrast to what I found in Rhode Island, where children were being warehoused. The youngsters were heavily drugged; staff members were much older, seemed tired, and spent much of the day sitting and chatting; there was no school program; and very little therapy. The walls were painted a drab green, but were so dirty they nearly matched the gray tile floor. Some effort had been made to brighten the sleeping quarters. The girls' area was painted in peach, the boys' blue—a rather clear hint at the level of imagination used there.

In fairness, I must add that Dr. Hugo H. Halo, who is from the Philippines, had only taken charge three weeks before I arrived. But others, not working in the mental health department, said that because of strong institutional unions, it could take years before the facility begins to measure up.

The "union problem" is a frequent complaint in the East, as well as in other corners of the country. Because they hold so much power, and could close all institutions in an entire state, creating chaos or worse, union leaders are feared by officials. The leaders sometimes take a "let the inmates be damned, we'll get ours" attitude.

Whether or not this is true, wages at state hospitals and other institutions have long been low—often far below wages paid at factories or for hand labor in the area. Further, the problem is not limited to unionized institutions. In many states civil service regulations make it nearly impossible to fire a brutal staff member or to make those who want to sit with arms folded to get involved with patients, most administrators say.

But often as not this is the result of long tradition, when warehousing was an accepted practice, or when administrators were unskilled or didn't care. In more states than one the motto has been "keep the budget low; don't make waves." Those who try to move too swiftly are defeated by the staff or are fired. Those most successful often are administrators who open new facilities and have a free hand in picking employees. This was the case in the adolescent unit attached to the state hospital in Austin, Texas.

"Staff morale picked up when we came into this new building," Pat Sullivan, a registered nurse, told me. "We've only been open a year. But it doesn't feel like an institution. You feel good."

While the unit can hold sixty, there were only forty-six inpatients in the summer of 1972. The facility is "school-oriented," and credits earned count toward graduation. Those not in school are involved in "occupational therapy," physical education, arts and crafts, and work assignments on the hospital grounds.

Those who behave, do their work well, and show progress can use free passes on Mondays and Thursdays provided by a neighborhood theater. They play basketball, take part in drama classes, and make craft items—candles, paper flowers, and other objects—to raise money for more equipment. Volunteers work with the youngsters. And some earn the right to shop in town or to go on dates with young people in the community.

As I mentioned, that was in the summer of 1972. By the time you read this, much may have changed. Institutions yoyo between being good and bad, depending upon the state political climate, budget cuts, the administrator and his philosophy, and whether or not staff members are enthusiastic or burned out. A single incident, if it raises eyebrows in the community, can tighten the screws on inmates and end theater trips, dating, and other privileges.

I feel uneasy when I praise or criticize an institution, because change is so rapid. And yet, nationally, there is little change. As one state begins to improve its institutions, another, with a change of governors, or because the legislature refuses to meet rising costs, slips downhill. A new administrator may be fascinated with behavior-modification techniques, and for a few months or even for a year or more the token economy system will work. But as the staff grows weary, or when a superintendent moves up, the program begins to fail. Like corrections, the mental health field is filled with faddists. Group therapy was the magic answer for nearly a decade, after individual therapy, shock treatment, and brain surgery failed to provide answers. Now behavior modification or operant conditioning has been in vogue for a few years. But it too has begun to lose luster. There is a great deal of talk about "normalization"—which usually means returning the children to the community for treatment, or simulating community conditions on or near institutional grounds.

"Humanization" also is a popular term, but most often it is the work of public relations men who see that an institution gets a little fresh paint and a few chairs and a carpet or two—enough to call in the press for stories and pictures. Ohio mastered the technique under Governor John Gilligan, even when budget cuts and political manuevering began to hurt children. It is the old shell game with a new twist, or perhaps further proof that you can fool a lot of the people (and the press) most of the time.

The institutions that tend to make real progress are those that worry least about fads, or hiring expensive psychologists and psychiatrists who sit in their offices and pontificate. Those that were helping children did not hire public relations men and paint a few walls to draw attention from the awful things happening to children.

The Children's Treatment Center at Colorado State Hospital in Pueblo made headway (but was less than perfect) under Kailash N. Jaitly because he "turned things upside down" and involved line staff in the decision-making process. Although many workers were in their middle years, I found them enthusiastic and intensely proud of what they were doing. Drug use, in the summer of 1972, seemed quite low, and the children seemed happy and relaxed—far more so than in the secure facility I visited in Wisconsin, the grim institution in Maine, the facilities in New York and California, and those I visited in a dozen other states.

But perhaps no facility compared with another Colorado institution for disturbed children, the René Spits Children's Division at Fort Logan Hospital near Denver.

Working on the theory that schools and families produce many disturbed children, and that the juvenile court and other authoritarian agencies tend to compound rather than cure the problems that schools and families create, they developed a variety of programs designed to meet the individual needs of the children. But emphasis was placed not only professional skills but on warmth and caring as well. Volunteers were encouraged to work with children, and staff members with impressive degrees were quick to point out that the volunteers often produced the most striking results.

"Take the boy who, for psychological reasons, couldn't use one of his arms," says Carl Bates, the assistant administrator. "We knew he couldn't use his arm. It was in all of the records, reports, and it showed up in the testing that was done. And then one day one of the staff members walked in and found the youngster pounding nails—using the arm for the first time. The boy was working with a very warm, intelligent volunteer. When we asked him how he got the boy to pound nails with a hammer he just said, 'Oh, I didn't know that was Tim's problem. I didn't know he couldn't use the arm.' He accomplished something that a team of professionals couldn't do just by being there and caring."

The facility's school program was one of the best I have seen, and the key to its success was a close interaction between the child and the teacher—or in simpler words, a great deal of touching.

"One of my teachers will say, 'Boy, I was pulled apart today,' and he really means it," says Richard Hawkins, the young principal. "Disturbed kids need to be in contact with you. Teachers colleges make it clear that you shouldn't touch children because you'll get sued or something.

"It's difficult to get close to battered children, and to a few others, but most children need it. My theory is, 'Teacher, shut your mouth and get involved.' Our children are immature, and they get a lot of oral satisfaction. Candy goes down like crazy. They get a great deal of satisfaction out of touching. It has to be spontaneous, of course. I don't want teachers who are uncomfortable with touching."

As is the case with reform school children nationally, Mr. Hawkins sees his patients as victims of schools that cannot tolerate losers and deviants, or are so crowded that overworked teachers ask themselves: "What kids can I push out of here so I can get a little relief?" One responsibility of the mental hospital is to help the teachers back in the community learn how to work with these children.

An effort also is made to meet physical needs. One child who needed a liver transplant got it. Another, who was scalded by a family member when he was small, arrived at the institution with bleeding ulcers and the inability to walk because he had lost parts of both feet. Before coming to the institution he had had many skin grafts, and had become depressed and suicidal. Now, with the help of special shoes, he has returned to the community and is able to walk to school every day. Under the institutional tutoring program, and with other help for his emotional problems, his reading level increased by five school years in less than two months.

"We're not that good," Mr. Hawkins says, modestly. "But we did help him solve some very serious physical problems, and we gave him the setting for success and opportunity."

Another staff member, James VanderWeele, who was the chief psychologist for the juvenile court and now serves as a team leader at the hospital (each team has a psychologist, psychiatrist, speech therapist, an arts and crafts specialist, a physical education specialist, a researcher-psychologist, two special education teachers, as well as others), is convinced that the children are "victims of the pathology of their families" as well as of the schools.

"I go into a school and ask a teacher what motivates a child, and they look dumb," he says. "Schools focus on materials, not on kids. They don't understand that success, recognition, and pride in their work motivates children. Self-pride is the greatest motivator."

Mr. VanderWeele is "pessimistic" about changing family pathology, noting that studies show that "children run away from home as an alternative to going crazy.

"I've got a seven-year-old girl in my cottage who was sexually assaulted by her mother's boyfriend. He sexually assaulted both of the woman's daughters and the mother still think's he's a great guy. So how do you expect the little girl to act?

"Some have been dumped by their families. Literally dumped. They have alcoholic fathers. One of my kids has a father who really believes he's a werewolf. I'm not kidding. The father gets down on all fours or his haunches and then his wife grabs him by the neck. That's supposed to cut the blood off to the brain, and then he becomes normal again. How could a kid grow up in a home like that and not have problems?"

I felt good about what I was seeing. A small institution. A strong, intelligent staff. Excellent teaching methods. Children who *really were seriously disturbed getting help*. A great deal of warmth. Community orientation—with follow-up, after the child was returned home or placed in a group home. An individualized therapy program. An excellent art program. Good gym and outdoor recreation. A proven success record. If we have to have institutions, they should be like this, I said to myself. Minutes later my euphoria splattered on the sidewalk.

"The legislature has cut our budget," Mr. Bates, the assistant administrator, told me as we left the building together. "They told us we were serving too few children and spending too much money."

27

"I thought he was stubborn . . ."

Jean is of average intelligence; has a nicely shaped head and a pretty face; a strong, growing body; and good health. Since she is not deformed, no one stares at Jean when she walks down the street. So how can she be a little victim?

Because Jean suffers from one of our most misunderstood hidden handicaps—deafness.

Americans do not like deviants, and so they do not really like deaf persons. In fact, being deaf is a little like being a chronic drunk. If you stay away from people, then nobody bothers you. But if you wander about in public, some people find you offensive. In fact it's not unusual to hear someone shout angrily at a normal child or adult: "What's the matter with you? Can't you hear me? Are you deaf?" The tone of voice is the same as that used when we shout: "Are you drunk?"

Millions of people who should know better combine the words "deaf and dumb." And it is true that a person who has never heard the sound of a human voice (or any other sound) finds it difficult to talk. Language is learned through repetition, and we forgive the fumblings of the infant and even find his lisp and lapses "cute." Since speaking is as easy as sneezing for most of us, and because we cannot remember the time when we could not talk, too many of us assume that older children and adults who cannot talk really are "dumb."

Being deaf is bad enough. But the way deaf people are treated makes it far worse. Even the hard-of-hearing child has problems. His parents know that he responds part of the time, so when he fails to answer, they conclude that he is difficult or stubborn. Teachers also grow impatient with these children. People believe they are unfriendly when they do not answer on the street, failing to understand the child has not heard the greeting and, until he is seven or eight or older, does not even understand—if he is totally deaf—that there is such a thing as language.

A friend of mine with normal hearing once experienced the unfair treatment we so often give the deaf. A brilliant young man with a degree from Harvard and an outstanding vocabulary, he also was a Japanese-American and looked very oriental. He did so well for the American firm he worked for that the company transferred him to Tokyo—giving no thought to the fact that he knew little Japanese. And that's when his troubles began.

Japan has a very high literacy rate, and the people he worked with in Tokyo had grown up in Japan, had attended Japanese schools, and of course lived in all-Japanese neighborhoods. When they looked at my friend's Japanese face and found him struggling with the Japanese language, they concluded that he was exceedingly stupid, never guessing that he was highly intelligent and highly regarded in America.

That's roughly how it is to be deaf in America. You look normal. You have normal intelligence. But you can't speak the language because you don't know it. And so people, sometimes even your parents, treat you as if you were stupid, a process that is very destructive to one's self-concept. If people always look angry when they look at you, if they punish you and you do not understand why, and if you have no earthly concept of language, what chance to you have?

Take the case of Sally G., a little girl of three and a half who lives in a small Vermont town. When I met her, and interviewed her mother, she had been talking for three months.

"We were pretty worried about Sally," her mother says. "I'm a teacher and my husband is a college graduate. Other kids her age talked so well, and sometimes we got pretty upset. Friends would say, 'Oh, she'll talk—don't worry.' One told me that Einstein didn't talk until he was four, and I found myself repeating that to other people when they asked what was wrong with Sally."

The G's were afraid their daughter was retarded. Months after being told it was "just deafness" they still wondered, the mother said, if the problem was "more serious than that." Nor could they understand why Sally, supposedly deaf, could be so sensitive to very loud sounds and high tones. A train passing nearby, a noisy car muffler, or snowmobile would send Sally screaming into the house.

"The doctor told us that certain sounds may be as much as four times louder for her than the rest of us," her mother explains. "Because she acted this way when she heard loud noises, and because we could tell she was listening when her sister played the flute, it was hard for us to accept the fact she actually has a hearing problem. Why, at the age of one she could hear and match the tone of A when it was played on the flute. She even did it at a concert."

Sally also responded to her mother's shouts and that caused more problems.

"I was yelling a lot at her because that was the only way I could make her pay attention," Mrs. G. says. "I was pretty uptight. As a teacher I believe in a great deal of discipline, and I thought that's what Sally needed. But when I hollered too much Sally became hyperactive."

Her parents' impatience and inability to understand were only part of the difficulty. When Sally was small she enjoyed playing with other children. But as they began to talk, they rejected her because she did not respond. This resulted in Sally's withdrawing into what her mother called "periods of great concentration." She sat alone, paying little attention to the world.

Sally, who felt rejection both from her parents and other children, now wears two hearing aids, is starting to talk, and—now that her parents are more relaxed and accepting—tends to cling to her mother.

Although Mrs. G. still wonders if it is "just deafness," and is, it seems, unwilling to accept her daughter's handicap, she has mellowed a bit in her attitude toward children who have trouble learning in school.

"I used to believe these children just weren't applying themselves," she told me. "Now I can understand there may be many different reasons why they can't seem to learn."

Many deaf and hard-of-hearing adults tell similar stories about childhood experiences, and some believe they were emotionally damaged by parents who did not understand.

Mrs. Connie Tullos is a beautiful, dark-haired (and totally deaf) wife and mother who works with the deaf at the Mississippi School for the Deaf in Jackson, and whose husband is principal of the school. When we talked about her experience her husband, Olouse, served as interpreter. She told me of misunderstandings, frustration and pain, of the sense of rejection a child feels when the youngster is unable to communicate with her parents. And even when the parents learn sign language, deaf children are left out.

"Your family has company, and everyone is sitting around laughing," she says. "You wait, expecting someone to explain, but no one pays attention to you. So you ask, in sign language, what everyone is laughing about and somebody will answer, 'The cat,' and then go right on talking to the hearing people. You look at the cat and you don't see anything to laugh about, and so you have to break in again and ask, 'What about the cat?'"

Deaf children must depend upon their eyes for answers to many questions. Body language, facial expressions, and physical activities become extremely important to them. But what one sees alone can cause questions and fears.

Jim Keller, the dynamic principal at the Arizona School for the Deaf, reminds one of a tall, mod Captain Kangaroo. When working with deaf children he plays games, prompts laughter, and reacts in an animated, theatrical style. But he tries to be sensitive to the silent signals he is sending out, and issues warnings to parents.

"One of our children watches his mother pack several suitcases," Mr. Keller says. "Then he sees his father putting the suitcases into the car. But no one explains to the child what is happening. The child wonders whether they are moving, going to visit grandma, or if his parents are taking him somewhere like this school. He feels a sense of anxiety until they pull into a state park and start putting up a tent, and discovers they are going camping. The deaf child misses out on so much."

Deaf persons say they had, as children, a great deal of difficulty understanding normal family relationships. No one bothers to explain that "this is grandmother," or Uncle Jim or Cousin Betty. Strangers fade in and out of a deaf child's life like phantoms, without explanation.

Like other youngsters, a deaf child sometimes must be disciplined. Yet he has no idea why his parents are hurting him if the parents fail to learn sign language, and large numbers do not bother. While some children are punished without explanation, others turn into little tyrants because parents are overprotective, or feel they must let the youngster have his own way.

Harry Anderson, who works for the Florida State Vocational Rehabilitation Service at the Florida School for the Deaf and the Blind, is hard of hearing, has a deaf wife, and two deaf children. He also attended a school for the deaf, and is now losing his vision. He is concerned because, among other things, deaf children know so little about the world they live in because of their handicap.

"I work with all of the students," he says. "And when I sit down with them I ask them what they want to do when they graduate from the school. Most of them don't have any idea. They can't even tell you what their father does for a living, or, if their mothers work, what they do.

"I'll ask, 'Does your Dad work out of doors or indoors,' and the child doesn't know. He can't tell you if his father works with people or machines. The deaf child sits at the dinner table every day with his mother and father and brothers and sisters and they talk about school and work and sports, or explain how Joe got a black eye, or how mad Dad got at his supervisor, and the deaf child just sits there all by himself, hearing nothing, and learning nothing about his family or his world.

"Not many deaf. children are close to their fathers," he adds. "And some aren't even close to their mothers. Their brothers and sisters may learn sign language, and so they become the go-between for the deaf child and his parents."

Being deaf also means being excluded from many normal family activities—even shopping at the store. Parents are embarrassed because of the noises a deaf child may make. Unable to hear even his own voice, he may amuse himself by experimenting with the vibrations he feels in his throat or mouth, never knowing that others are hearing grunts, groans, buzzing sounds, or shrieks coming from his mouth.

His deafness also may cause insensitive and curious people to ask his parents embarrassing questions, and it becomes easier to leave the child at home or locked in the car. Because he cannot hear cars, and may forget to look both ways before crossing the street, and for many other reasons, the deaf child is left out or left behind while his brothers and sisters romp in the park, go to a movie, bowl, attend Dad's office picnic, or play baseball or football. Not only does this severely limit the child's world, it can cause emotional problems.

"When all of the other children go with the parents and the deaf child is left behind, he says to himself, 'I'm being punished. I'm bad,' " Mr. Anderson points out. "He has no way to find out if he really has done something wrong, or why he is being rejected, and that can hurt deeply."

Because deaf children are sometimes ridiculed, and often are the target of finger-pointing by hearing people who ask questions, some deaf children grow up believeing that *all* verbal conversation in their presence is about them, and no one tells them their fears are unfounded.

Being deaf can also get a child into serious trouble. In one case not long ago a Chicago policeman saw a youngster running, and thought he was a suspect in a delinquency case. When the officer cornered the child against a fence the policeman demanded answers, and when the youngster did not comply the officer beat the child to the ground with his club—convinced that the boy was simply giving him a hard time.

Being deaf in a large city has additional dangers, beyond the threat of traffic. He may be attacked, mugged, robbed or raped, and has no way of calling for help or telling police what happened. It is, in our society, almost impossible for a deaf child to report a fire or some other kind of emergency. A child left home alone with an elderly baby-sitter or relative has been forced to run for blocks seeking help when that person has fallen or had a heart attack.

It is possible, for a modest sum, to install Western Union equipment that transmits a typed message on normal telephone lines to a teletype at a police station or fire hall, solving this problem. But for reasons hard to explain police and fire stations are reluctant to install the equipment, although the cost is quite low.

Experts agree that the most difficult problem for deaf children, beyond the emotional pain they experience at the hands of insensitive adults and children—who would never be cruel to a crippled or blind child—is learning the English language. (Or any language, for that matter.)

"If you are born without hearing then you are born without language," says Edward W. Tillinghast, the veteran superintendent of the Arizona State School for the Deaf and the Blind. "Hearing persons acquire language through hearing it spoken, whether it is French, Arabic, Chinese, or English. Babies must hear words thousands of times before they can communicate. We learn language through repetition and without effort. For the hearing person, language is simply absorbed."

Those who teach language to the deaf cannot repeat words thousands of times in the classroom, as parents and others do in the normal routine of living in a hearing world. A deaf child, without even the basic concept of language, may find English as difficult as the hearing child of six would find algebra without the concept of numbers, and the ability to add or subtract or divide. Yet deaf children must communicate with the hearing world by writing their thoughts on paper, and even older children may make grammatical mistakes.

"People who see these errors often conclude that the deaf are stupid," Mr. Tillinghast says sadly.

Even when deaf children learn language through signs and lip reading, they cannot hear inflection, emphasis, voice tone, or other coloration that we take for granted. Such a simple (but subtle) colloquialism as "What's up?" will prompt a deaf child to turn to the sky, because he takes words at face value, Jim Keller explains. This too leads unthinking hearing persons to draw wrong conclusions.

Much of the humor of children requires an understanding of language that the deaf child does not acquire for many years. The old joke, "What's black and white and red (read) all over" loses something in translation, at least into sign language, which is a kind of shorthand (no pun intended). Even adults who are deaf may have as many problems with puns as Americans have understanding dry English humor.

All children need love and care. And tender touching is the best way to communicate with a child, deaf or hearing, during the first months and years of life. But parents of a deaf child also should begin to use sign language when he is a few weeks old. Just as the hearing child learns to speak by hearing words over and over again, so the deaf child will learn to "say" bottle, mama, daddy, and other words as soon or sooner than the hearing child.

It is interesting that hearing children with a deaf parent or parents also excel in school because at the age of two or three they learned to spell words with their fingers, and consider spelling a normal part of communication. One also finds that deaf children who receive sufficient love and care (but are not overprotected) seem happier than the typical hearing child. My impression, verified through conversations with persons working with the deaf, is that deaf children smile and laugh easily, and are less cruel, demanding, and resentful than youngsters growing up today with full use of their senses. I do not have the same feeling about blind children.

One can speculate at length on why this is so. Perhaps it is because deaf children are isolated from television, films, and from the word and sounds of the word—and often from books as well. It is probably true that tantrum-throwing, whining, demanding, and cruel teasing are learned and not "natural."

I can best contrast properly reared deaf children with the youngsters I have seen in a Hutterite Colony in South Dakota. These religious and farming communities isolate their children from the world in a way not too different from the isolation the deaf child experiences, and the Hutterite children—loved, cared for, and properly disciplined—are happy, giggly, open, and filled with joy.

I found a similar innocence and spontaneous joy among children on the Greek Island of Crete, in the Indian children living in the villages of Peru, in slum children in Brazil, black children in some sections of the United States, and children I have observed elsewhere. But I am not yet prepared to say with scientific certainty (in a way that would meet the approval of psychologists or sociologists) that it is this isolation that frees deaf children from unpleasant behavior patterns, for other factors may well be involved.

Whatever the facts, it is clear that deaf children *are* different from hearing children, yet have the same needs. As in the case of other handicaps, experts agree that early identification is essential, and parental guidance important. Even today deaf children are sometimes "hidden away" by parents who are emotionally incapable of admitting they have a handicapped child.

Mr. and Mrs. Tullos, of the deaf school in Mississippi, told me of one boy who did not receive help until he was eighteen. And while he is intelligent and can learn many things quickly, certain abstract concepts seem impossible to grasp.

"He understands how to use money, but putting money in a bank or the stock market is beyond him," Mr. Tullos says. "And our political system is a concept he cannot understand. The words 'senator' and 'president' mean nothing to him."

Deaf children often learn to lip-read with or without help. But some experts say only 30 percent of what is said can be read from lips, and deaf persons tell me that regional accents can be as difficult as a foreign language even for those skilled in lip-reading.

Deaf children also can be taught to talk, and well-meaning but (apparently) misguided parents and teachers who push children may do far more harm than good. Mrs. Tullos refused to speak in my presence, although she knew I was sympathetic and would not ridicule her. She has been, she said through sign language, hurt so deeply and so often by unthinking adults that she cannot bring herself to use her voice.

Jerry E. Prokes, director of the Child Study Center at the Florida School for the Deaf and Blind, tells of an incident he observed not long ago in a St. Augustine store that makes the point clearly.

"I was in the store, about to buy something, when I saw one of our high school students come in to make a purchase. The woman standing at the cash register has worked in that store for years, and our students go there often. She is a fine, friendly person, and when the boy approached her she was smiling. But when he opened his mouth the whole expression on the woman's face changed. She wouldn't give the student a chance. She looked pained and stuck this pad of paper and pencil in his face. Now he had pretty good deaf speech. Even a person not experienced with the deaf could have understood him with a little effort, and this woman has been waiting on deaf children for years. The boy had been practicing speech, and getting along in the hearing world in our school, because he will graduate soon and have to life in the hearing world. And when the woman treated him in this way he was crushed."

In one thoughtless minute we undo months and even years of work by dedicated teachers, and damage children in the process, until they are, like Mrs. Tullo (as I have said, a beautiful and kind woman), emotionally incapable of even trying.

The batttle between those who advocate the use of hand signs and those who believe in teaching deaf children to read lips and to use the speaking voice, sometimes reaches angry heights among the professionals. The media, entranced by the idea of the "dumb" speaking, have been promoting it—unaware of the consequences, according to those who, like Mrs. Tullos and the boy in St. Augustine, have been constantly hurt.

Howard Palmer, who teaches math and drama at the Mississippi school, and who has toured the country with a deaf actors' group (and is deaf himself), calls forcing the deaf child to communicate through speech alone "pure torture—worse than trying to make a left-handed child write with his right hand." The key, he says, along with many other deaf teachers and teachers of the deaf, is what is called "total communication." This involves the simultaneous use of hand signs, the speaking voice, lip-reading, and, when they will help, hearing aides.

"If the oral method was really successful, then we could close all of the deaf schools," he says. "But if we teach total communication to the child's family, then no member of the family is left out."

Mr. Palmer speaks from experience. His parents never learned sign language, so when he visits them he must go to the home of a relative, who can communicate with him, to "find out what's going on." Other deaf adults report hardly seeing their parents, explaining there is little use going home to feel excluded as they did when children.

Schools for the deaf have just begun to use new techniques and equipment to help children function better in the world. At the school in Tucson each classroom is equipped with a small radio transmitter that broadcasts the teacher's voice to hard-of-hearing children, even those who are very close to being totally deaf. The teacher wears a microphone and the children have miniature receivers and wear earphones. The cost per classroom: $5,000.

The Tucson classrooms are equipped with small ovens, hot plates, and sinks and tables so that children can bake cookies and make other treats. Snacks are part of the learning process. Children learn to read directions and names of things like flour, dough, and popcorn. And they may read the story of the gingerbread man before baking it or while eating one.

When a class made popcorn they learned simple directions: 1. Pour oil in a pan. 2. Add 5 spoons of corn. 3. Plug in the pan. 4. When popped, pour popcorn in a bowl. 5. Eat it.

Little tots must set the table, pour the milk, and help with the dishes during snack time, because these are skills they need to survive in the world on their own, and overprotective parents may do these things for them at home.

Socialization is important for children who have been isolated, so they sit around a table in a tight circle, and while one child blows soap bubbles, the others have a contest to see who can catch or pop the most bubbles. Touching, laughing, and having fun together, they learn to live with one another without hurting.

Teachers also sit in the cafeteria during lunch because the Arizona officials have found that a great deal of learning can take place during a meal—just as it does at the dinner table in a happy home.

The Arizona children learn to use typewriters, teaching machines, and games as well. Playing cards are used to teach youngsters to add, subtract, or just to learn numbers. I watched one group of youngsters stack paper cups in patterns designed by a teacher, the first step in learning to follow directions. Another teacher gave a girl of seven small squares of cloth and a bottle of perfume. The game was to see if the children could learn which squares were dabbed with perfume and which were not, so that the children could understand the concept of odor and where it comes from, something hearing children learn just by living.

Deaf children also must be taught such simple abstract ideas as "top, middle, and bottom." The hearing child learns this when his mother says, "Your book is under the bed," or "I've put your toy car on top of the refrigerator until you can behave."

"We're told that language is acquired between the ages of zero and four," Mr. Keller, principal of the school, says. "When a child arrives here we can predict fairly accurately how far he will go. It all depends upon how much was done for him at home."

In an effort to do more, the Arizona school now has two persons on the road, one working with the parents of the deaf, the other with those who have blind children. The state is large, and both travel many miles each year. But they find the rewards great.

If institutions damage retarded, disturbed, delinquent, and orphaned children, do they also hurt the deaf? Several factors are involved in an answer to this question. First, like other institutions for children, they suffer from funding problems and underpaid house parents can be as cruel to deaf children as they are to other youngsters. The quality of the teaching staff, methods used, and equipment available is important. But so is what happened (or happens) at home.

If there is a sound educational program for the deaf in the community; if the deaf child has parents who are warm, understanding, and accepting; if they are not ashamed of their child and treat her normally, taking her to stores, parks, playgrounds, museums and to other places; and if the parents have learned sign language and use a system of total communication both in the home and on the street, then the child is best off at home. Otherwise, if there is a high quality school for the deaf, with warm, capable staff members and proper equipment, the deaf child is probably best off there. But the schools are hardly substitutes for the right home and community program.

There seems to be no satisfactory answer for deaf children who want to experience a full social life. Most are encouraged to date and marry other deaf youngsters because of communication problems and other challenges of a "mixed" marriage. The child in the community may find it difficult to date, while the institutionalized youth may be expected to live a Victorian life, and is sometimes punished for holding hands, hugging or kissing. And sadly, homosexual problems may be the result—although the subject is hushed up in most states in the best Watergate manner.

Even when they become adults, and try to participate fully in the community (which is difficult because hearing persons are so often crude and cruel), deaf persons who attend a party find themselves isolated—or spending the evening with other deaf persons, if some are present, while everyone else moves freely around the room.

They are isolated in other ways as well. For example, deaf children are less likely to find summer jobs, and lacking work experience they have trouble competing for and holding jobs. Employers also worry about insurance problems, although few exist according to vocational rehabilitation experts.

While Florida leads the nation in vocational counseling of the deaf, according to one study, Stephan F. Greene, supervising counselor for vocational rehabilitation at the school in St. Augustine said there are many problems. Graduates not only lack work experience but their training is little better than the typical high school vocational program, and they must compete with children who can hear and learn easily because they hear.

Further, Mr. Greene feels that all deaf children must be carefully schooled in money management, shopping skills, the law, government (beyond social studies), banking, how to rent an apartment, how to deal with neighbors—"all aspects of life"—that are more or less absorbed through living by at least some hearing children.

"Last summer we held a workshop here just to teach deaf children about governmental agencies and services—who provides what," he says. "Even the brightest students do not know what services are available to them."

To provide work experience, they place older students with the national guard and other state agencies but often must fund the jobs through vocational rehabilitation. Even after graduation they try to support the children because the deaf have problems with the police, doctors, dentists, welfare workers, and in hospitals and hospital emergency rooms. Society just doesn't seem to care, and even the so-called helping agencies are poorly prepared to help in most states.

Like those who insist that the deaf learn to lip-read and to speak (ignoring the fact that even a skilled lip-reader may not be able to differentiate between pear, pair, pier, peer, par, part, or park, to list a few words), so all of us insist that the deaf compete on *our terms*, or fail. Living in isolation in a hostile nation, there is little doubt that deaf children are little victims.

28

More Than Darkness

David Meyers, a slender boy with dark, wavy hair, runs the 100-yard dash in 12.6 seconds. While this is a respectable time for any high school sophomore, it takes on more meaning when you understand that David is totally blind.

The day I visited his home in South Portland, Maine, in the spring of 1974, David was to take part in a play put on by his church youth group to raise funds for a camping trip. While David didn't have the lead, he had seventy-one lines to memorize, and was required to walk on and off the set several times.

The only blind student at South Portland High School, he rides the school bus, attends regular classes with sighted students, and is studying German, English, geometry, and biology. Not only is David an honor student, but he is vice-president of his class, attends dances, sporting events, and participates fully in other school activities.

David was not blind from birth. When he was a few weeks old doctors found cancer in one of his eyes and removed it, hoping to stop the disease from spreading. He was able to use the other eye, and underwent treatment at a Boston hospital for his first seven years. Then doctors told his parents that his remaining eye would have to be removed. Otherwise, David faced death.

Long aware of this possibility, David's parents had enrolled him in a

Portland parochial school doing pioneering work with the blind and visually impaired.

"When David was three they taught him to move around with a blindfold on," says Carl Meyers, David's father, a South Portland police sergeant. "By the time he was five or six he could type and read Braille."

"We hoped for the best but prepared for the worst," adds David's mother, Barbara, who by coincidence now works for an eye specialist.

David's father says breaking the news to his seven-year-old son was the "toughest thing I've ever done." While both Carl and Barbara believed the Boston specialists were correct in their verdict, they decided to take David to a New York specialist for a second opinion. There they received the same dreaded answer. They immediately launched out on a whirlwind tour of the city, visiting the Empire State Building, Statue of Liberty, Times Square at night, Radio City Music Hall, and museums and other tourist attractions—hoping that they could give David enough memories to last a lifetime.

When the tour ended three days later they told their small son what the doctors had said, including the fact that by losing his eye his life would be saved. David took it in good spirit and even reassured his mother, saying: "Mommy, the only thing I won't be able to do is see." They took him immediately to Boston, the operation was performed, and when he awoke he was totally blind.

The Meyerses had been warned by various experts that sometime after the operation David would fall into a deep depression—in reaction to the loss of his sight. But it never happened. His parents give much of the credit to his teacher, Sister Maguil, who had taught him not to fear blindness. (She has since left the school.)

David attends sporting events and listens to the play-by-play on radio; he sometimes plays a little basketball or football with his older brother; has normal clean-up chores at home; is able, when it is his turn, to read the Scriptures at church from a Braille Bible on Sunday morning; moves freely about the school he attends; and has many friends.

Sgt. Meyers, a Methodist, ranks Sister Maguil as the outstanding woman in America for the help she gave David and the family. But one feels certain that the parents also deserve recognition for the way they have worked with David, refusing either to pity him or to overprotect him, and helping him lead a normal life.

David has a nicely honed sense of humor. When the power went off one night, plunging the family into darkness, he teased them a little about their fumbling around in the darkness, then went to the basement for a lantern because he was concerned that the sighted members of his family might fall and be injured. A friend tells how he confessed one day at school that carrots were not his favorite food when he found them on his plate in the cafeteria. At first he offered them to the friend, but then joked that perhaps he should eat them because he had read that "carrots are good for your eyes."

Not all blind children, or youngsters suffering from other handicaps, cope as well as David. This raises a key question: Why do some youngsters succeed, while others fail? It is a difficult question to answer because each child is an individual with a unique background and individual needs. Yet without some kind of answer we cannot begin to find ways to help no-hope youngsters.

David's case and other success stories suggest:

1. While many handicapped children are stigmatized, blindness is usually more tolerated than other forms of deviance. Blind children are less likely to be teased and tormented by other children, and less often face criticism from teachers and other adults. At least some blind children have a better self-concept than other handicapped youngsters.

2. Handicapped children with strong, intelligent, supportive parents are more likely to succeed than youngsters who have either overprotective parents or parents who reject them. Poor parenting can cause problems more crippling than the physical handicap.

3. Even the best parents need help from trained specialists. If these specialists are available when the child is young, it is quite possible the handicapped child will be able to remain at home and in the community school.

4. Most experts now agree that the child who can remain at home, and who receives the help of trained specialists along with equipment and special materials, is probably better off than institutionalized children. But institutions vary, and some provide services that will never be available to handicapped children in small communities.

5. If the American people are willing to spend only limited amounts of money on handicapped children, then it is important to invest in early childhood training and in programs that assist parents. Waiting until a child is school-age may well be too late.

6. Mental and language handicaps, and those that produce behavior unacceptable in our society, are more disabliing than either blindness or accidents and diseases that leave the mind healthy but cripple the body.

7. While in some states there is a trend to do more for handicapped children, far too little is being done for youngsters who are about to leave school and enter the world. Many Americans want to help "cute" little children, but large numbers of teen-agers walk dead-end roads.

8. Of all groups representing handicapped persons, none is more

skilled in making the American political system work for it than that for the blind.

9. Persons concerned with the plight of other handicapped youngsters must learn from the blind groups how to influence lawmakers and win community support. This is more difficult than it sounds because people pity the blind and fear or dislike other groups of handicapped children.

Because of their lobbying ability, and the skill of those who run direct appeal for funds from the public, the blind have won many special benefits, including welfare payments, travel concessions, franking privileges (mailing letters without stamps) and income tax exemptions. While few really begrudge what the blind have achieved, some believe that other handicapped persons deserve the same level of support. Yet many are afraid to speak out. One who is not is Dr. Samuel L. Ornstein, chief of the Office of Developmental Disabilities in the State of Washington.

"I'm not suggesting that we steal from the blind," he says. "But it seems unfair to single out one group for special treatment. When a blind man shows up at a legislative hearing and bumps into a table the legislature votes for whatever he wants.

"We have these vending stands for the blind to run, and some make a profit of $20,000 a year. It costs the state $100,000 a year to set up a few new vending stands. I'd like to know why we can't get an extra $100,000 a year to provide programs for the deaf, or for those with other disabilities.

"We are willing to send one hundred twenty-eight blind kids to college to get a B.S. or M.A. or Ph.D., and you can guess what that costs. But we can't get enough money even to provide humane care for other children. The injustice seems even greater when you understand that we don't even have meaningful standards for the blind. The criteria are very vague, and some who get help can see very well.

"We don't have much for the deaf or multihandicapped kids, or even for the deaf-blind or blind-retarded. But if you are visually handicapped and have an IQ of one hundred and thirty then you can have everything that you need."

The quarrel is not really with the blind. Rather, it is with lawmakers who are willing to help one group but ignore so many others. In Maine, lawmakers have been willing to help a wide variety of visually impaired persons who are not even close to blind, yet have been quite reluctant to help many other children, including the retarded and the disturbed. In 1974 some 340 Maine children were, according to state officials, receiving special care because of visual impairment. But of the 340, only 140 were "legally blind." The rest have a visual handicap of at least 20/70 in the best eye, says David Dorr, the state consultant in charge of the program.

To be *legally blind* in the United States a person must not have better than 20/200 vision in the best eye after correction, or narrow vision (tunnel vision). In a booklet often handed out at blind schools, entitled *"What Can We Do About Limited Vision?"* and published by the Public Affairs Committee, a New York-based, nonprofit educational group, readers are told that while legally blind persons may be totally blind, "others have considerable useful vision.

"A 'legally blind' person, then, is one who, while wearing glasses, can see less at 20 feet than a person with normal vision can see at 200 feet; or whose field of vision is limited to a narrow angle," the booklet explains, adding that "tunnel vision" is like looking through a soda straw.

I was surprised that a legally blind teacher, who attended a school for the blind, could remove his glasses and still see distant power poles, trees, and mountains.

One federal study suggests that there are 12.5 million children in the United States with "eye conditions needing specialist care." And the trend is to provide this care to these children.

The trend today is to move away from institutionalization of visually impaired children. In Maine, for example, only 11 of the 340 children receiving state assistance (books, equipment, special classes, training) for visual handicaps are in institutions.

"We found that we can do as much for the child at home and in the public schools as in institutions, if we provide the child, the parents and the schools adequate help," says Mr. Dorr. "Our philosophy is that the blind child is more normal than he is different."

At this writing, Maine has five regional consultants who act as advocates for visually impaired children, and eight "itinerant teachers" who travel through several states providing help to children in their homes and at school.

There are critics who say the program falls short of the ideal, and others use stronger language than that, pointing out that some of the itinerant teachers are more skilled and better trained than others, and that the level of dedication also varies. Others add that school officials tend, in some instances, to resent having to think about handicapped children, believing their jobs are hard enough meeting the needs of those without physical handicaps. Family settings also vary, and critics contend that visually handicapped children would be better off away from their parents.

But even if the program falls short of the ideal, the concept is hard to fault. Children with adequate parents lead normal lives, are less isolated, do not risk becoming "institutionalized," and—with the right support—blossom as David Meyers has.

Even from an economic standpoint the program makes sense. Maine officials say they must pay roughly $7,500 a year to send a child to the Perkins School for the Blind in Watertown, Massachusetts, one of the best-known, best-endowed facilities in the country. And for $7,500, Maine can assist several children in their homes.

In-home services for the blind increase each year. In Arizona, the school for the blind, which is on the same campus as the school for the deaf, sends out a staff person to work with parents of preschool children with vision problems. A fairly new program, it is designed to help parents avoid pitfalls that will only make their child's handicap more of a disability.

"When a family does not get guidance and assistance, most parents tend to overprotect the blind child," says Ed Anderson, principal of the school in Tucson, who is legally blind and a graduate of the institution. "They tend to do things *for* the child, rather than letting him explore the world freely."

But other parents reject their handicapped children. Herbert Angus, the assistant principal at the blind school in Florida, feels that too many children arrive at the institution with emotional problems. Some experts suggest that it would be better for some youngsters to arrive at the institution at an earlier age, unless we provide the parents a great deal of support "as soon as the child is born." Sending a child to an institution is a poor second choice in the eyes of most experts, however, and even a third choice if an excellent foster home can be found.

"If everything at home was as it should be, our school could not possibly serve as a substitute," Mr. Angus says. "When it is impossible for a child to remain at home, then we do our best to help the child in an institutional setting."

Only in the 1970s has such honesty been so widespread among those who work in institutions. In the past such a statement could be classified as heresy or worse. But increasingly those who work with children are more concerned with the welfare of the youngsters than they are with job security.

Whatever one's view of institutions or community programs may be, all agree that blindness is more than living in darkness. While some contend that the blind can do almost anything a sighted person does, except drive a car or fly a plane, this is not fully accurate. We live in a nation that seems to care little about handicapped persons, and in most traffic-clogged cities just crossing the street can be a dangerous experience.

High curbs, unrepaired sidewalks, silent traffic lights, dogs running loose, the lack of public transportation, suburban sprawl, and public buildings designed only for sighted persons are all hazards. One cannot overestimate the seriousness of the handicap in modern America.

Experts agree that, like other children with handicaps, those with vision problems need special care at home, but all stress that overprotection is nearly as damaging as neglect.

The sighted infant begins lifting his head at an early age to look at the world, and is motivated to crawl across the bed to reach a toy. He can be stimulated with bright colors and movement, and may watch the family cat as it walks silently across the floor.

Mr. Anderson suggests that "even chewing solid food may be learned through visual experience." And some blind youngsters reject solid food until they are past school age.

Just as sighted children must learn at an early age to use their eyes, so blind children must learn to use their hands, Mr. Anderson adds. But untrained and overprotective parents may be afraid to put the blind child on the floor, to let him play in a sandbox, to crawl on the grass, or to explore his home.

"The first six years are critical," he says. "The blind child who sits in a playpen, who is idle, may be so traumatized that he will never fully recover."

Mobility—the ability to move around freely—is a major problem for the visually impaired. And so is understanding the world, since we tend to describe it in ways best understood by sighted persons. When children at the Arizona school visited a nearby air force base a little girl standing beside a jet bomber was incredulous.

"How big is an airplane?" she asked. "I'm standing on my tiptoes and I can't even reach the top of the wheel."

Even an automobile can be an enigma to a totally blind child, officials add. By touch and by reason she must come to understand the use of headlights, the windshield, steering wheel, and the motor under the hood.

Mr. Anderson recalls walking with one student in a mobility training class on the campus. When they passed under a tree he asked the youngster to reach up and touch the leaves.

"He was totally blind—a senior in high school—and he still had no concept of a tree and how it branches out," Mr. Anderson says.

How does one explain a three-story building (not to mention a sky-scraper) to a blind child who has never seen a three-dimensional object and only understands height, distance, and spacial concepts from walking or stretching out his arms? One partial solution, used at some schools, is to have the blind child stand at an upper floor window with a ball of twine. Holding one end of the string he throws the ball down to another child. Then the youngster goes back downstairs and tries to comprehend the height of the building by walking along the string from one end to the other.

The ability of blind children to grasp complex or abstract ideas varies greatly. Like all children, they have a wide variety of skills and aptitudes. While some are academically inclined, others have mechanical ability. Some easily learn to use drills, saws, lathes, and joiners, just as sighted children do in a vocational high school. Blind children in the better schools, like Perkins School for the Blind in Watertown, Massachusetts, learn to use a ham radio, to swim, scuba dive, engage in gymnastics, dance, shop in a grocery store, cook, go to Boy Scout camp, sing in a chorus or play an instrument, and to live fully.

While the trend is toward community programs for the visually impaired, including those who are totally blind, many who work with the blind ask if communities can do all of these things for youngsters. For many schools fail to meet needs of nonhandicapped children—especially minority groups.

"Some public school teachers with twenty-five other children in the classroom feel they are incapable of taking on the added responsibility of a blind child," Mr. Anderson says. "Here our teachers have master's degrees and are trained to work with the visually handicapped, we have specialists in mobility and orientation, we teach wood-working, metal-working, upholstery, small-engine repair, auto mechanics, business machines, art and physical education. These are subjects that our children do not always get in the public schools."

He also points to the institutional library, with Braille novels, textbooks, and reference material, and such magazines as *Popular Mechanics, National Geographic, Ladies Home Journal, Seventeen,* and *Boys Life* also in Braille. There are tapes and recorders and other special equipment; and a physical education program that includes wrestling, football, kickball, basketball and volleyball. So that time does not drag for the children after school there is a recreation room with a snack bar, juke box, pool table, and other games.

How important these programs are when compared to living in one's own home with loving parents, brothers and sisters is a matter still being debated. It is doubtful that institutions for the blind can ever be closed, but quite possible that they will begin to take in more children with multiple handicaps.

But however that problem is resolved, one point stands out. The blind have shown that even with a severe handicap children can learn to make it in the world if given help and half a chance.

We use a rather disparaging phrase about the "blind leading the blind." But anyone who looks at the problems of deviant children understands that it is possible that the blind will lead the way for all handicapped persons. That may be the most meaningful achievement of all.

29

When a Child Can't Walk

Dr. Thomas Benson is frustrated.

As head of the medical team at the highly regarded, privately run Crotched Mountain Center in southern New Hampshire, he works to rehabilitiate more than two hundred children with multiple physical handicaps and related emotional and educational problems.

Students at Crotched Mountain include those suffering from cerebral palsy, deafness, severe speech difficulties, spina bifida, muscular dystrophy, neurological impairment through accidents or from other causes, and other handicaps.

Dr. Benson and his staff care deeply about these children. Within the limits of their budget, every effort is made to meet their needs, and many make marked progress. But when it is done, after the staff has helped the severely disabled child to function at his highest level, society takes over. And as a nation we have provided very little for these children.

"We spend $8,000 or $9,000 or more a year for several years to educate and rehabilitate a handicapped child, and then what?" he asks. "After all this effort and expense the child ends up at home in a back bedroom watching TV all day, or in a nursing home with elderly people, or in some state institution. Sometimes I feel so frustrated that I ask myself why we go to this expense and effort when society doesn't seem to care."

Fortunately for the handicapped children of New England, Dr. Benson and his colleagues do their best despite this nagging concern. Sometimes it is enough to know that the handicapped child will be less dependent and more capable of being happy than if nothing were done. And they feel rewarded when they see a no-hope child respond, progress, and even go on to college or find a steady job and live in an apartment and require only minimal care.

The staff takes a child as far as he can go, but many are so severely handicapped that they can only make it in a sheltered workshop.

"And how many sheltered workshops are there in America that include living facilities and the medical and physical care some of our students need?" he asks.

This is a serious problem worthy of the attention of all who are concerned with the plight of our little victims. But it is not the only thing that worries Dr. Benson and others in his field. Among other things, they talk of the need for early identification of handicapped children so that a long-term plan can be worked out; the need for more family doctors who are better informed about handicapped children; the need to help parents who are not emotionally able to face the fact that they have given birth to an imperfect child; the lack of facilities for children with multiple handicaps; the fact that some parents search the nation for years seeking help; and that Crotched Mountain must sometimes turn away children, and when that happens parents leave with a feeling of desperation.

It is the shock of giving birth to a multiply handicapped child that is most difficult for many parents. Mrs. Jennie Fish, chief of social services at the Center, explains the reactions many parents experience.

"At first they don't believe it," she says. "Then they mourn the child they expected, but who never came. This may last for some time, but then they begin going from doctor to doctor, trying to get some other answer. Then they turn to religion. We have a child who just came back from Lourdes. When religion fails they talk to friends and neighbors and get a lot of misinformation. Eventually they get advice from a psychiatric social worker, who helps them sort things out, and then they find help."

Information also may come from a newspaper story, magazine article, radio or television programs, public service commercials, a public health nurse, or special education teacher. Sometimes parents are referred by a medical specialist who has heard of the Center. But most parents report that finding help is extremely difficult.

Dr. Samuel L. Ornstein, whose assignment in the State of Washington is to help disabled persons, suggests that one can almost always find services for those with *mild* handicaps, but too little is available for the rest.

"We provide services for one hundred percent of those who have sprained eyelashes," he says. "But try to find a program for a child who really needs help. Most often we really serve the professionals. They select the handicaps they want to work with and reject the children they don't like."

There are many reasons for this. First, professionals tend to specialize. And many prefer to work with children they can most readily help. There are more than enough moderately handicapped children to keep the professionals busy and to assure them success. Foundations and private agencies also prefer to specialize, and many dislike the hard-to-handle children as well as the multiply handicapped. Even state agencies can be selective, turning away chidlren who do not fit "the program."

Even Crotched Mountain Center, which takes children with multiple handicaps, draws the line. William W. Roots, director of public affairs, explains that it does not accept children who are blind; it turns down those with severe organic retardation; and does not accept children who are extremely hyperactive.

Few facilities in the country accept the wide variety of handicapped children who go to Crotched Mountain, although there are many specialized programs for physically handicapped children across the nation. Mr. Roots believes there are "about ten" residential facilities for children with multiple handicaps that provide the complete range of services offeed at Crotched Mountain. But Mrs. Fish rejects several on his list and insists there are "only three."

Whatever the number, there are too few. Further, getting money to pay for the care of a child is a major problem. At Crotched Mountain it can cost up to $10,000 a year to care for a seriously handicapped child, according to Mr. Roots. Parents are asked to pay as much as they can; the Center can provide some help from contributions, but much of the cost must be paid either by governmental agencies or by groups that solicit funds for handicapped children on a state or national basis. But this can lead to arguments over who pays what share of the cost for a child with multiple handicaps. Or which state should pay.

One Crotched Mountain official recalls the classic case of a New Jersey child who was refused help by the Easter Seal group in that state because he was living in New Hampshire, while New Hampshire Easter Seals argued that the child's home was in New Jersey.

Some who work with these children would like to see a board established that could evaluate a child's needs—medical, physical, emotional, and vocational—and bill the appropriate agencies for their fair share.

The problem clearly will not go away. More handicapped children survive than at any time in history, and large numbers live normal life spans. In the broadest sense of the word, all of the little victims described in this book are handicapped. As Dr. James W. Moss suggests in a background paper prepared for the 1970 White House Conference on Children, "a person may be considered handicapped if he is prevented from taking full advantage of the opportunities which society provides for him and is constantly unable to achieve his expected place as a contributing member of society." He narrows this a bit by adding that the handicapped child "cannot lead a normal life at home, in the school, or on the playground. He is a child who needs special services in order to obtain an education and take his place in the community as a successful adult."

He also believes there are more than 8 million children in America who "will not progress normally through schools without special attention of a continuing nature." And he adds that "four times that number [32,000,000] will need some type of special services before completing high school." This number includes a wide range of handicaps, including language disability, emotional disturbance, and forms of retardation.

For generations we provided little help or care for handicapped children, except for the blind and a few other groups. But now more remain at home because local hospitals and clinics provide specialized medical care and physical therapy as well as treatment for emotional problems.

Until special education became an important independent field of study in the past two decades schools accepted only children who were physically and academically able to compete with other students. But that is rapidly changing. One large reason is that federal courts have ruled that all children, including those who are severely handicapped, are entitled to both therapeutic treatment and an education. States are rapidly changing their laws, and several now require local school districts to serve all children.

But as always has been the case, issuing a court ruling or passing a state law does not assure a child that his needs will be met. This has been most evident in the problems that still face black children and other minority groups.

If schools are incapable of helping children with such minor handicaps as language disability, mild emotional disturbance, petty delinquency, or some retardation, how can they deal with children with really serious problems? And yet they are being ordered to do so.

In Massachusetts, for example, state officials estimated early in 1974 that some 200,000 children between the ages of three and twenty-one would qualify for special services under the special education law (called Chapter 766) passed by the legislature. Each community is required to establish evaluation teams that include a doctor, psychologist, teacher, registered nurse, and sometimes a parent. These teams must consider the needs of the children, discuss programs that should be provided, and find ways to include as many handicapped children as possible in regular classroom programs. But implementation has been difficult.

Those opposed to this change include some parents of the handicapped. They complain that school districts do not have qualified teachers; that schools are not equipped with wheelchair ramps and elevators; that they do not have toilets and other facilities designed for the handicapped; that they lack physical education and therapy programs; that they cannot provide costly special equipment that often is needed; and that they do not have safety features needed to protect the handicapped.

(It is often pointed out that our communities and public buildings are designed for physically healthy persons between the ages of fifteen and forty-five, and not for the young, the old, or the handicapped.)

Perhaps the most difficult problem will be accountability. It is nearly impossible to keep tabs on the institutions that care for handicapped children. As I have pointed out, many abuses exist. By scattering handicapped children through thousands of school districts across the nation that problem can be serious compounded.

And yet the concept is right. If schools can be made to accept the responsibility for these youngsters, long-term gains could be great. For if schools begin to meet the needs of severely handicapped children, they will be more sensitive to the needs of those who are mildly deviant. Parents will feel less stigma than in the past. And students who attend school with youngsters who are confined to wheelchairs and who are retarded, blind, deaf, or suffering from multiple handicaps should be less inclined to tease and torment their less fortunate peers.

(Dr. Benson contends, as do others, that children are not naturally cruel, but rather learn to hate the handicapped at home or from teachers or other students who learned at home.)

One can expect some of the same problems that have plagued the community mental health clinic to exist. And as more schools demand the services of special teachers, it is possible that the colleges will crank out those that are incompetent, as has happened in the field of psychology.

If it is difficult now for a handful of institutions to exchange information about programs that work, and if existing programs tend to follow fads seen as panaceas for everything from hang-nails to suicide prevention (as in the case with behavior modification, for example) then handicapped children are in for trouble.

But there is another problem with community-based programs. Many parents cannot face the burden of caring for a handicapped child. It can be so physically taxing and produce such emotional pain that some parents will go to any length to place their child in an institution.

"Some parents want their deviant child safely out of sight," says Mrs. Fish. "Your children are a projection of yourself. Some parents find it very hard to accept a child that is severely disabled."

This does not always change with time. In fact many people can feel great sympathy for a very young child, but when he reaches his teens a handicapped child "is no longer lovable," Mrs. Fish contends. So even those who received adequate care when they were small may face rejection later in life.

While the community school concept is an important step, if certain checks and balances can be built into the system as in other fields, the real answer seems to lie in prevention.

Many experts argue that premarriage testing and counseling can make an important difference. Certain forms of retardation as well as other handicaps are believed to be genetic. That is, the handicap is inherited in the same way red hair, blue eyes, and body shape are handed down from one generation to another. I have been asked, in recent years, to look through microscopes and at slides and pictures, and to read reports that experts say prove this beyond a doubt. These same experts say that with more research money, and with genetic testing and counseling teams in every community, would-be parents can be warned if they are apt to produce a handicapped child—and what it may mean if they take the risk.

Some, like Dr. Benson, also would like to see improved methods of testing the fetus for handicaps. If a test could be made early enough, then some experts would urge a therapeutic abortion.

Other experts also call for tough regulations governing prenatal care, pointing out that an inadequate diet, or drug abuse, alcohol, and tobacco—and perhaps other chemicals—can damage the unborn infant. Prevention of measles during early pregnancy also is seen as a method of avoiding handicaps.

Less is said about serious problems caused through careless, incompetent or ignorant doctors both at the time of birth and later. Too much oxygen used in cribs designed for premature babies has been a major cause of blindness, for example. Forceps deliveries also are blamed for brain damage and other handicaps, although at the time of their invention forceps were considered a life-saving device.

Inaccurate prognosis also leads to problems. A doctor may decide that an infant will only live for a few days, and yet somehow it grows up to be a handicapped teen-ager. Corrective surgery or therapy shortly after birth could make a great deal of difference, according to some experts.

Mrs. Fish points to children suffering from spina bifida, or more simply, an open spine. Some reached Crotched Moutain as teen-agers still in diapers, when a simple operation would have solved the problem.

"Can you imagine the emotional impact of wearing diapers until you are fourteen or fifteen, and always wet?" she asks.

All experts call for early identification and evaluation of handicapped children. Dr. Benson explains that it is important to develop a long-range plan for the child when it is small. The more help a family gets when the child is small, the better chance the youngster has of making rapid progress in a special school or therapy program later, he says.

In his report to the White House Conference Dr. Moss stresses the importance of prevention and early intervention, noting that among other things the "lifetime care and earnings loss of a seriously retarded child," for example, could total $750,000.

"It is well known in health, education, and rehabilitation fields that treatment and rehabilitation are generally most successful and effective if provided as soon as possible after the injury or handicapping condition arises," he continues.

When children are so severely impaired or injured that they "cannot be restored to social effectiveness and ultimate self-sufficiency," then society must offer open-ended programs that truly meet their needs, he adds.

One need that is not only left unmet but that is seldom talked about centers on the handicapped person's sex life. Like the rest of us, most handicapped persons are constantly bombarded by erotic material on television soap operas, commercials, in magazines, books, and even newspapers.

Most handicapped persons, nor matter how grotesque their bodies may be, have normal sexual feelings. Those who will talk about it admit that the lack of love, human contact, and sexual release drives them "crazy." One cerebral palsy victim, when discussing the sex life of the handicapped person at a convention on the problems of the handicapped, said that he appreciated the liberal views being expressed by those who work in the field, but wondered if they were willing to "undress us and put us in position?" Many wheelchair-bound Americans cannot even go to the bathroom without the help of an attendant.

While handicapped persons may have normal sexual feelings, professionals agree that even in a nation obsessed with sex, the typical American finds the idea of a handicapped person having a sex life repulsive. This is because sex in our society is tied to physical attraction, "lovableness" and similar concepts, and many persons consider a physically handicapped person "revolting." When one European nation tried to solve the problem by providing handicapped persons with specially trained prostitutes the plan was a "disaster" because the handicapped persons were looking for love and acceptance, not just sexual release.

Large numbers of Americans look upon highly intelligent handicapped persons as subhuman. This attitude is hard to change, but if it ever is changed the lives of millions of Americans will improve.

In Dr. Moss's view it really is a "question of relative priority."

He asks: Can the nation afford to allow large numbers of children to be born with or incur mental and physical handicapping conditions? And if they arise, what priorities does the country place on the remediation, rehabilitation, and care of afflicted children?

His questions are only beginning to be answered.

30

The Burned-out Syndrome

Lauretta DeHaney pulled back the white curtains on the third floor of her Brooklyn brownstone and looked down at the street. She didn't like what she saw. It wasn't the tightly parked double row of cars that bothered her. Nor was she overly disturbed by the deterioration of some of the buildings. In the nineteen years she and her husband had lived in the brownstone on the edge of Bedford-Stuyvesant the change had come gradually enough to live with. Mrs. DeHaney was concerned about the children she saw. Some of them were mere toddlers. Unsupervised. Playing in the dirt in the gutter. Running between the parked cars. And it was growing dark.

Then Mrs. DeHaney looked almost straight down and saw Andy, a boy from somewhere down the street, about three years of age, jumping off her weathered stone steps. When she saw that she hurried downstairs and opened the door. Andy grinned up at her.

"You'd better start on home now," she said. "Your mother's looking for you."

"No, she isn't," he said brightly. "Mama's not home."

And Andy was right. He had been left with a baby-sitter who was lord-knows-where, and was left to roam the streets until well after dark. In a way three-year-old Andy personified Mrs. DeHaney's concern. For as a consultant to New York City's Bureau of Public Health Nursing (and a nurse for thirty years), she is concerned, to a large extent, with preventive health care, and that includes all aspects of the environment and family life. There was little she could do about Andy, not to mention the thousands of other children out on the streets on that spring evening.

The Public Health nurse has taken on a heavy burden in recent years. For if the social worker has become a crisis-handler and form-filler, and if the policeman spends his working hours in the impersonal steel shell of his car, and if the family doctor refuses to make house calls, and if clergymen no longer drop in on parishioners, the Public Health nurse stands almost alone as the front-line soldier dealing directly with the people in their kitchens and living rooms.

It is not enough to give shots or massage someone's back or look at a newborn baby. Now she is counselor, confessor, problem-solver, help-finder, and friend to families and children in need.

In a city the size of New York, with people constantly shifting from one overcrowded tenement to another, living desperate lives, malnourished, alone and lonely, frustrated at being unable to climb out of the deep pit they were born into, and struggling to cope in hostile ghettos, the Public Health nurse—out there on the front lines day after day—can feel "overwhelmed, almost helpless," Mrs. DeHaney adds.

Nor are the nurses alone in this. Dr. Albert Pisani, a Chicago pediatrician, who worked in a slum area clinic there, talks of the "burned-out syndrome" that many physicians experience after a year or two in the ghetto. The doctors work long hours, dealing with difficult problems, caused by what seem to be incurable social ills, and with too few success stories.

"We put a child with severe pneumonia in the hospital and she gets excellent care," he says. "She is released in a few weeks and the hospital bill totals $2,000. Then she returns to the same environment, with the broken windows, inadequate heat, filth, and a sixteen-year-old unwed mother who is still a child herself. In two weeks we have the child back in the hospital."

Dr. Pisani began as a pediatrician in a private, white, middle-class neighborhood on the city's far south side, and then, after ten years, moved to the Mile Square Health Center, a program funded by the Office of Economic Opportunity (OEO). Now he has moved on to the comfortable western suburb of Hinsdale, where he has a private practice.

The health care of these inner-city children is marked with what he considers to be "insoluble" problems. The delivery of medical services is possible, but the efforts are negated by the wretched social ills that prevent normal solutions. For what can a physician do about housing, rats, lead paint, malnutrition, poor parenting, the schools, job opportunities, or the lives the people lead?

Even the welfare system works against the poor. Dr. Pisani, who was dedicated to helping them, found that he could not make an adequate living for his family in the slum. He charges $10 for an office call. Welfare will only pay him $6, and then a doctor must "handle the paper work and wait a year for payment." And the slum doctor has a "no-show" rate (persons who do not show up for their appointments) of "forty to fifty percent," he adds. This because the slum mother has so many other problems to wrestle with that "medical care apparently isn't high on her list of priorities."

Dr. Stanley L. Harrison, who has just retired as associate director of the American Academy of Pediatrics, based in Evanston, Illionis, adds that the entire health care system is designed to exclude the poor. He talks of "overutilization" of the health care system by middle- and upper-class mothers who live in near isolation in the suburbs, without relatives to call on for advice. At the same time, the urban and rural poor have little meaningful access to what is being called "comprehensive health care."

He points out that even free or low-cost clinics are not utilized by the poor, and even when the clinic is used, it "doesn't change a lot." This is because environmental problems negate a doctor's efforts.

"Getting people *into* system is just as hard, and just as expensive as giving them adequate medical care," he says. "It can cost $25 or $30 a visit because you need social workers, a public health nurse, nutritionist, and a large office staff. The pediatrician in private practice charges only $8 or $10 because he does not need the staff."

Doctors who have worked in the free clinics say that they must be overstaffed in part because the clinic funded by the government has required administrators to hire from the local neighborhood. One does not find competent workers living in slums. Persons with talent, education, and initiative have fought their way out of the ghetto and do not want to return. Thus training is difficult and costly, absentee rates are sometimes high, and it can take two workers to do the job of one elsewhere.

Dr. Harrison also points out that it is difficult to get either white *or* black physicians and nurses to enter the slum because they may be mugged, their cars are damaged and broken into, their tires may be slashed, or their lives threatened. Wives refuse to move into inner-city neighborhoods, the doctor's children would not be safe there, and their white, middle-class friends would not visit them.

Dr. Pisani points out that persons living in the immediate area of the clinic protect the doctors and nurses who come in, but persons wandering into the neighborhood from other communities do endanger those trying to serve the poor.

The 1970 White House Conference on Children, in the report to the President, tells of these "appalling deficits of our current health system." It notes that "study after study has reiterated that services are too often fragmented, discontinuous, far from the ideal in terms of availability and accessibility, hobbled by health manpower problems, and frequently delivered with little concern for the consumer's preferences, his understanding, his convenience, or even his personal dignity." Then in stronger language the report adds that "for children whose future well-being and even survival are at stake, the implications are catastrophic."

Infant mortality rates in America are often cited as proof of how little we care about children in America. America ranks below at least twelve other nations in this statistic, as we have already pointed out. And children born to the poor have far less chance of surviving than do those born in middle- and upper-class homes.

In a report, Dr. Richard W. Dodds, of the Department of Health, Education and Welfare in Washington suggests that we might save 40,000 children's lives a year with better care and improved environment. Some 470,000 poverty-stricken mothers (many unwed teen-agers) do not get proper maternity care; 3.5 million "poor or near-poor women" of child-bearing age do not have access to family planning services; 35 to 40 percent of the children who lie in poverty are inadequately immunized; 70 percent of the children living in poverty have never seen a dentist; 4.2 million fifteen-year-olds have an average of eleven decayed, filled, or missing teeth; and more than 13 million American children under the age of sixteen have one or more chronic health problems.

If the Public Health nurses are the front-line troops in the health care field, there are too few of them. While there are nurses working for private agencies and public programs such as Head Start and day care, it is the Public Health nurse who works in New York's 22 clinics, 77 well baby clinics, and 1,500 elementary and 350 secondary schools. Miss Margaret O'Brien, who heads the program, reports that she has 500 full-time nurses, 190 who work part time (up to twenty hours a week), some 400 persons who have had some training and handle clerical jobs and may weigh and measure children, and some 380 "health aides," many of them former welfare mothers, who assist in the schools, patching skinned knees and handling other routine jobs.

Public Health nurses are hardly policemen. They cannot force expectant mothers to eat properly, to avoid drugs, alcoholic beverages or tobacco, or to seek prenatal care. Nor can they require parents of infants to provide adequately for them, although this is the most vulnerable and important period of a child's life, according to the child care experts. Rather, they must be low-key, slowly winning the confidence of the mothers, and then, after many visits, encouraging them to do what is needed.

Miss O'Brien recalls how, twenty or thirty years ago, a Public Health nurse would be known by everyone in the neighborhood, and would attend the "weddings, wakes and christenings" of the families they worked with—often going on their own time on Saturdays, Sundays, and in the evenings. Now, with the high rate of mobility of slum dwellers, and new health department policies, it is far more difficult to build up these intimate relationships that permit a nurse to be highly influential in the family's life.

Mrs. DeHaney tells of knocking on doors, only to find an empty flat, of having to scrape and soak caked feces from the sore bottom of a neglected baby; the problems of unwed teen-agers who have no comprehension of the needs of their babies; the related problems of drug abuse, alcoholism, and malnutrition; and school officials who consider black and other minority children to be "things," not small human beings. She has met parents who have little interest in their children. A father who refused to provide his children with glasses recently called it "foolish" and a waste of money. Large numbers of young mothers who let their children "grow like weeds," and are too immature and self-centered to care also frustrate nurses. And how there is some satisfaction when a nurse is able to get some other agency to provide help.

A nurse recently found a young mother overwhelmed with ten children, including four sets of twins. She was able to get an agency to provide a homemaker, she collected clothing from her friends, and worked with the mother and the oldest daughter, who was ten. Now the little girl visits the nurse whenever the nurse is in the school and shows off her clothing and talks of the changes that have been made at home. These small successes keep the nurses going, Mrs. DeHaney says. Most try not to think about the tens of thousands of others who need help but cannot be reached.

While hospital emergency rooms provide medical care, along with the clinics, a few doctors, and Public Health nurses, it is hit-and-miss, and does not approach the comprehensive health care that considers the whole child and his environment. Millions of American children living in poverty are suffering from health-care-related handicaps, including retardation, mental illness, and delinquency. The present system does not work, and will not work—unless drastic changes are made.

The story is somewhat different in the suburbs. There, lonely women live in self-imposed isolation, reading articles on being "fulfilled" in their women's magazines. They fear they have been trapped by their environments, husbands, children. It is a feeling of being useless and unnecessary in a complex, high-speed world.

Linda Wade is a Public Health nurse in wealthy, suburban Westchester County north of New York City. She tells of the poor tucked away on the side streets and in flats above stores—hidden from the public view. Of how she sat at the bedside of a ninety-seven-year-old man and simply held his hand and talked to him in a reassuring way. Of the sixteen-year-old unwed mother who does not yet even know the right questions to ask about child care, and how she spends much of her time building a relationship with the girl. Of the mother of a fourteen-year-old boy with cystic fibrosis who must go to the hospital and needs someone to provide her son with the necessary therapy twice a day while she is gone. The nurse's life involves shots and TB tests, referrals and counseling. But another role has emerged in recent years, as the extended family has dwindled and died. The Public Health nurse is the patient listener, the reassuring friend, the reliever of deep-rooted anxiety.

Take the former school teacher who, after several years of being childless, quit her job and moved with her husband to the suburbs to begin a family. She had lived a full, rewarding life as teacher, wife, and lover. Now, suddenly, she was home alone with a helpless and totally dependent infant. She was desperate for reassurance, professional counseling, help with her anxious feelings of inadequacy.

Or consider the small woman with the large, forceful, authoritarian husband. This mother seems unable to please him, especially in the way she is rearing their toddler. When he is away from home and the child is obnoxious, her actions sometimes border on child abuse. While she knows this is wrong, and is deeply worried about it, she feels she must have help to understand herself, her child, her struggle to cope.

It is to this kind of problem that Linda Wade devotes more and more of her time. It is not the old bandage-changing, shot-giving kind of nursing one so often thinks about. But it is meeting health needs as the needs change. And who else (beyond the Avon Lady) takes the time to sit down in the kitchen, sip on a cup of coffee, and listen to women in pain pour out their troubles? Who else is there to comfort them, to reassure, and help them see their strengths and good points when they are depressed, confused, lost?

This too is the growing role of the pediatrician. Dr. Harrison points out that in an earlier day doctors had to deal with life-and-death children's diseases. Today, with inoculations and good diets, suburban children are larger, stronger, and healthier than at any time in history. Now the pediatrician is called upon to deal with behavior problems, drug abuse, drinking, mental instability, delinquency, and learning disability. It is a new role, and Dr. Harrison says that many old-time pediatricians are finding it difficult to change their ways of dealing with patients. This, he believes, will result in a continuing upsurge of the Marcus Welby-styled physician—the family practitioner who brings care and comfort to the home.

Like welfare, health care is in a period of change. More concern for one's entire environment is emerging. Slowly, those working in the field are growing more concerned with the emotional needs of the patients. Shots and surgery are not enough, even in the suburbs.

Perhaps the day will come when doctors will have the authority to prescribe better housing, a less crowded neighborhood, cleaner air, fewer pressures, and better diets for the poor, just as he tells his wealthy patients to spend a few says in Bermuda or Tucson soaking up the sun. Green grass and quiet can do wonders for some patients.

Until that day comes there seems to be little that professionals can do to meet the health needs of inner-city children. And even then—considering the problems of suburban families—that may not be enough.

31

The U-Haul Children

Pity the children of the poor. Not only are they dirty, ragged and hungry, they also are hated. If you listened to the typical suburban taxpayer, you would believe that every child born to poverty had petitioned God for parents who would provide him with the opportunity to live off welfare in slum housing so that he could beat off the rats and roaches and nibble on paint chips laced with lead.

For at least a decade welfare recipients have been on the national hate list. Even today few topics stir more anger. I have, while sitting in comfortable homes, or eating in stylish restaurants, heard my fellow Americans lash out at the poor with words once reserved for anarchists, Nazis, communists, or hippies. Nor is the concern (or disdain) for the poor new. One finds a wide range of references (for and against) to the poor in the Bible and other literature dating back through the centuries. How could we celebrate Christmas without Tiny Tim and Ebenezer Scrooge?

The Talmud suggests that "The noblest charity is to prevent a man from accepting charity; and the best alms are to show and to enable a man to dispense with alms."

In *Fog*, the American playwright Eugene O'Neill wrote: "The child was diseased at birth, stricken with a hereditary ill that only the most vital men are able to shake off. I mean poverty—the most deadly and prevalent of all diseases."

In March of 1971 California Governor Ronald Reagan put it in slightly different words in a message to the legislature: "Today, some 2.4 million

Californians are receiving welfare and Medi-Cal benefits. Recipients fall into four major categories: Aid to Families with Dependent Children (AFDC), Aid to Totally Disabled (ATD), Aid to Blind (AB), and Old Age Security (OAS). If present laws and regulations are not changed, California's welfare rolls could swell by as much as another 600,000 by July, 1972, raising the total welfare population to roughly 3,000,000 persons. . . . This would mean that one in every seven Californians would then be on public assistance. . . . The numbers are especially staggering when you consider that only ten years ago the total welfare caseload in California amounted to only 620,000."

I have been looking at the problems of the poor for years. In 1957, while a young television reporter in Grand Rapids, Michigan, I visited elderly persons living in slum housing. Later, I slept in Negro shanties in Mississippi and Alabama, and visited welfare families in cities across America. In 1965 I lived, for eighteen weeks, in Gary, Indiana's midtown slum, trying to understand the life of welfare children. And I have interviewed hundreds of children from welfare families in jails, reform schools, prisons, mental hospitals, group homes, foster homes, and other institutions.

If there is one thing that I learned it is that as with other segments of our society, it is difficult to generalize about the poor. I have seen both clean and filthy homes in such distant places as Portland, Oregon, and Portland, Maine, in Los Angeles, Chicago, New York, Florida, Georgia, South Carolina, Wyoming, St. Louis, Kansas City, Detroit, Minnesota, Arizona, Colorado, and Montana.

I met the working poor—near starvation, but too proud to take a hand-out; middle-class housewives deserted by their husbands; women who were promiscuous; others who were chaste and God-fearing; some with boyfriends living in the home, using the welfare check to supplement his meager income; out-of-wedlock mothers in their early teens; small children with sores and boils and festered places on their faces; retarded women with large broods, each with a different father; college students and college graduates taking advantage of loopholes in the law; commune-dwellers getting doles; out-of-work fathers with little hope of finding work because of little education, poor skills, and worse health; women determined to fight their way up and out; others without drive and with personalities as empty as yesterday's wine bottle; chronic drunks and tee-totalers; a toothless woman who took in children as others collect stray cats; some women who admitted getting a divorce because welfare provided more money than her husband could; and a woman living in an $80,000 house, abandoned by her husband, waiting for the bank to foreclose and throw her out.

There is no question that welfare is big business. In 1973 AFDC (Aid to Families with Dependent Children) alone paid out more than $7.3 billion to 7.9 million children and 2.9 million parents—and that figure does not include such things as administrative costs, staff training, postage, or services rendered by social workers, or doctors. Nor does it include food subsidies and other benefits.

In that same period United States Steel had sales of $6.9 billion; J. C. Penney's totaled $6.2 billion; Westinghouse grossed $5.7 billion; Goodyear's sales were $4.6 billion; RCA did $4.2 billion in business; and Coca-Cola $2.1 billion.

In light of this, and other knowledge, there are at least three things that I can say about our child welfare system: (1) the cost is quite high, considering the return taxpayers get on the money they invest in it; (2) while some basic needs (food, shelter, clothing, education, and health care) are sometimes (but not always) met, the program often does more to harm the recipients than help them; and (3) since welfare does not "cure" poverty, and may even cause more problems than it solves, it might well be wise to review and rethink the welfare system.

To reform the system one must understand it—a task that is almost beyond the capacity of mere mortals. For example, it is impossible to learn how much money we spend on children of the poor. For beyond direct AFDC payments there are expenditures (local, state, national and private) for medical care, public education (welfare mothers do not pay taxes), Head Start, day care, foster care, low-income housing, school milk, school lunches, food stamps, services to the handicapped, mental health services, vocational rehabilitation, the Job Corps, Vista, family planning, Public Health nurses, visiting nurses, free legal aid, institutional care, "purchased services," money spent by the Law Enforcement Assistance Administration (LEAA) for delinquency prevention, the police, juvenile courts, detention, shelter care, probation and parole, emergency service in hospitals, and services rendered by a wide variety of volunteers. (I am certain I have forgotten many programs and services as well.)

By checking with various agencies in Washington one finds that some figures are available. For example, in 1973 a total of $400.7 million was spent on Head Start, and 379,000 children were enrolled in 1,545 programs, including those that run "full year," and others in the summer, or in rural homes. But ask the same agency about the cost of day care and you draw a blank.

I feel safe in saying that we may spend $40 million a day on these children ($14.4 billion a year) and the figure could easily be much higher than that. Nor is the question really money. We are a rich nation and we can afford $40 million a day and more—if it really makes a difference.

There are those who say that, in a sense, poverty is a state of mind. In a small book, *Growing Up Poor*, published by the U.S. Department of Health, Education, and Welfare (HEW), Dr. Catherine S. Chilman writes of how the "lifelong patterns of behavior, values, goals and attitudes of chidlren are strongly associated with the characteristics of their parents, especially as these are expressed in child-rearing and family life styles." Then she adds that these are "crucial" both to the individual and to society, "since children of very poor families are apt to contribute, in time, a disproportionate share of their numbers to the mentally ill, the delinquent, the broken family, and the socially rejected, as well as to the undereducated and unemployed. . . ."

It seems axiomatic that to lift children out of poverty and into the middle class—which seems to be at least one goal of our society—we must begin to deal with the child in the home. Teachers, social workers, mental health workers, and other professionals complain that all of their work is undone by the child's parents and peers, and others in the community in which he lives.

It is hardly necessary to point out that our present welfare system breeds dependency. That is one reason why social workers and sociologists talk of the "cycle of poverty"—one generation following in the footsteps of the last. Further, the more money we pour into welfare payments and services to the poor the more attractive the programs seem. In a way welfare is addictive, if not hereditary. With a little effort one can find third- and even fourth-generation welfare recipients.

As strange as it may seem, social workers, persons employed in corrections and mental health, and in many other fields, consciously or unconsciously increase the ranks of the poor. If we wiped out poverty and lower-case life-styles these people would be out of work. In a somewhat cynical article in the July-August 1971 issue of *Social Policy*, Herbert J. Gans, a sociologist at MIT, points out that those who fight poverty actually benefit from it, and he includes on his list penologists, criminologists, social workers, Public Health nurses, and even newspaper muckrakers.

But the list is longer. Liberal political candidates draw votes from the poor, he says, while the conservatives win votes by railing at them. And who else would do dirty jobs for low wages, or "prolong the economic usefulness" of used cars, rundown buildings, cast-off clothing, or day-old bread? Mr. Gans also sees the poor providing a group for laborers to look down on, and offering "vicarious participation to the rest of the population in the uninhibited sexual, alcoholic and narcotic behavior in which they are alleged to participate."

Whether or not he is right, it seems as if many states want to make sure the poor remain poor. The amounts paid sometimes change rapidly because of inflation or for other reasons, but in the latest report available as this is being written, the average AFDC child in Alabama received $21.07 per month. The same report, issued by the State Department of Pensions and Securities, shows that the average *family* on AFDC in Alabama received $73.10 a month. (Data is based on September 1973, when 157,154 persons, including 117,855 children, received "benefits.")

In Kansas City children are not much better off, according to Miss Mabel Bridwell, Child Welfare supervisor for Jackson County. In 1973 the typical mother and child received "about $80 a month," she said.

"I don't know how a mother with nothing but AFDC can make it," she adds. "Our workers beat themselves on the head, trying to get churches, civic groups—anyone with a little money—to help out."

In Connecticut a welfare mother with three children was getting $310.64 a month in 1973, officials told me. In California the typical AFDC child received $87.99 a month, while the average family (the figure is *not* comparable with Connecticut) received $196.50. In New York City the average AFDC child got $80.26, while in upstate New York the monthly payment averaged $72.99 a month. But such figures can be grossly misleading, considering the other benefits and services available in some states.

I do not suggest that AFDC children wallow in wealth. But most would be better off in every way if they took advantage of the free and low-cost services available to them. It is silly to suggest that if only they had been born to aggressive parents who doggedly fought for services in the way middle-class Americans struggle to reduce their income taxes or to achieve in their jobs, the needs of the poor would be met in most states. In this age such parents would be in the middle class, and their children would be ineligible for services.

Write the parents of the poor off. Not as human beings, but as effective shakers and movers. Beat down, sometimes angry but incapable of focusing their frustration and making it work for them, emotionally stalled in the dependency stage, unable to mount political pressure on government without outside help, AFDC parents are losers. Ergo, the social worker.

The social worker has been around for more than a half-century now. The profession has its own colleges, graduate schools, student-screening processes, and degrees. Full-fledged professionals have ethical standards they are to follow and tack "M.S.W." after their names just as doctors use

M.D. One sees their framed certificates on office walls across the country, and it is all very impressive. They talk of therapy and practice it, borrowing from psychologists, psychiatrists, and quacks.

If psychology is, as some say, "the new religion," social workers are the priests and nuns. They can be found in mental health clinics, hospitals, reform schools, mental hospitals, prisons, and public schools. They have learned to "diagnose" social ills and human quirks; most love to listen to "confessions," and to sit in grand and grave judgment, nodding wisely or looking sympathetic, encouraging, counseling, reassuring their "clients."

Richard S. Laymon, the child guardian for the Illinois Department of Children and Family Services, defends his colleagues (he is not a social worker) by pointing out that the field is new, and that "before the 1920s we had little ladies with their baskets.

"We still have more nontrained social workers than trained," he adds. "They start out as warm, compassionate people with empathy and a sense of mission, but they get so busy rushing around from one bonfire to the next they don't have time to catch their breath. The bureaucracy burns them out."

It is true that most so-called social workers are untrained. Some complain that, like those in probation and corrections, many social workers are middle-class losers who drifted into the field because they couldn't find work elsewhere. Many have degrees in music or art history, in English literature or political science. Yet they usually are well-meaning persons who take temporary jobs, and like the man who came to dinner, end up staying—often getting their M.S.W. (Master of Social Work) at taxpayers' expense.

I met Don Pearson, a pleasant, twenty-two-year-old black social worker in Kansas City. A graduate of Northwest Missouri State in 1972, he applied for work at the welfare office because he remembered a college friend was hired under similar circumstances. Don's degree is in "biology and psychology," he says.

"I don't see this as a lifetime career," he told me. "But it's a job. A lot of graduates weren't able to find work, and we were living off our parents. I'll stay here awhile, and if nothing better comes along I'll probably go back to graduate school."

Don had been struggling for days trying to find a foster home for a girl rejected by her own family. He was learning by doing, a common practice in all fields, but a bit more bothersome when one realizes that his actions have an important impact on human lives.

I have met hundreds of social workers through the years, and I cannot remember disliking any of them—although I have not often been impressed with their brilliance or ability to lead or get a job done. Most tend to grab at pop therapy—convinced beyond doubt that they have the "real cure." I remember talking with a long-time friend in Michigan, a M.S.W. with a great deal of warmth and concern. Knowing him well, I unburdened myself about his profession, and he admitted that many social workers are less than effective.

"But now we've got TA," he told me. "It's fantastic! I've got two groups going now."

TA, or transactional analysis, group therapy, behavior modification, Gestalt therapy—all are being used by social workers both trained and untrained, and often as panaceas. It is difficult to measure how much good (or harm) they do. But studies that have been made show the impact of the social worker is seldom great.

In 1965 the Russell Sage Foundation published a study called *Girls at Vocational High School.* The research project involved two groups of girls, two hundred to a group, both groups containing many youngsters who were possible candidates for delinquency. After four years of intensive counseling and therapy, the two hundred girls under the care of professional social workers were neither significantly better or worse than the two hundred who grew up free of social-work influence.

Bruce Borgie, assistant program deputy for the Los Angeles County Department of Social Services, points to another study "back in the 1960s when we cut caseloads of workers hoping to get people off" the welfare rolls. But the effort failed.

Another book, published by Scarecrow Press, entitled *The Multi-Problem Dilemma: A Social Research Demonstration with Multi-Problem Families,* makes a similar point. Edited by Gorden E. Brown, executive director of the State Communities Aid Association of New York, it opens with this statement:

"The objective of this study was to assess the effects of intensive social casework on a group of fifty multi-problem families, in contrast with the effects of normal public assistance services given a control group of fifty similar families. The intensive service was given by caseworkers who had earned the Master of Social Work degree, and who had previous field experience. Caseloads in the demonstration group were limited to less than half the usual number carried by public assistance workers, and greater emphasis was put on using other available community services. . . . The essential finding was that while the demonstration group attained a slightly better degree of family functioning, its margin of progress over the control group was not significant in the statistical sense. That is, the demonstration group's greater advances could be attributed to chance alone."

Edward W. Maher, deputy commissioner of the Department of Social

Services in the State of New York, and admittedly not a social worker, calls for "more hard data, more research" into what works and what does not work in the field. Meanwhile, direct services in many states have been cut because of "a high degree of skepticism on the part of a lot of people, including a substantial number of legislators," Mr. Maher says.

Miss Mabel Bridwell, child welfare supervisor for Kansas City and Jackson County, Missouri, summed up the view of the career professional in the social work field when she said that "there are a certain number of children and a certain number of parents that seem beyond help. We just don't know how to rehabilitate them, how to make them well enough to function. As a result, some children grow up under welfare care more disturbed than if we had left them alone."

But if the social workers have failed, so have we all. At the moment many states are retrenching, trying to hold the line against even larger welfare rolls. They are in conflict with the social workers, who, if they have failed to rehabilitate their clients, and to push through guaranteed annual income legislation, have done their darndest to search for poor Americans who qualify for welfare benefits, and to get them enrolled.

One can speculate at length on their motivation (compassion, frustration, anger, reaction to the Nixon administration's decisions, or confrontation politics born on the college campuses), but the impact of the swelling welfare rolls was to cause swift action on the part of men like Ronald Reagan in California and Nelson Rockefeller in New York.

"The thurst in the last four or five years has been to introduce better management to the welfare field," says Mr. Maher, whose background is that of an administrator at the medical and dental schools at the University of Connecticut. His assignment has been largely to reduce the "intolerable levels of ineligibility and errors" from the welfare rolls, and to "try to restore public confidence" in the welfare system—an almost impossible task.

In his legislative report, Governor Reagan of California warned of an unending burden to taxpayers if welfare growth was not stopped, and suggested the answer was to create "changes in eligibility determination and by a work-training program to move people into private sector jobs," and to "close all possible legal loopholes that lead to abuse." And in both New York and California, toughness has stemmed the tide—at least for the moment. But it is hardly the whole answer.

Seymour Katz, M.S.W., director of eligibility reviews for the New York Department of Social Services, points out that a key problem is the fact "the goals of welfare have never been clear.

"And I'm not sure social workers should be defining goals," he adds. "What does the community want? What does the community want to do about a woman with little knowledge of birth control, who keeps having illegitimate children? What do the people want to do about neglect or abuse? How about children with mothers who have emotional problems? What does the community want to do about hunger and housing? Are the people for or against foster homes?

"The welfare system gets blamed for society's problems. That's unfair. Social workers didn't create the problems. There are a lot of good, dedicated people in the field doing the best they can. I don't quarrel with those who want to ferret out welfare frauds. But when you talk about services to families, to children, the elderly, and to others the public has never been clear on what we should be doing."

In his view, social workers are in what psychologists call a "double bind."

"The better job we do the worse off we are. If we develop a good program to take care of the poor, then we end up taking care of all of the poor and the caseload and costs go up. That makes people mad. Anybody who finds a solution to the welfare problem will be a national hero."

How do you measure a social worker's success rate? What should be the goal for a nation of over 200 million persons with more than 20 million of them poor; a country where the mating system produces shaky marriages and unwanted children; where millions of children are abused sexually, physically, or emotionally; where the infant mortality rate, illegitimacy, and venereal disease rate are high; where tens of thousands of men abandon their wives and children; where children still die from eating lead-based paint chips; where slum landlords can still make a handsome profit by milking the poor; where millions of persons suffer from emotional problems of varying intensity; where tradition and television contribute to a high level of violence; where private ownership of guns can be more important to millions than any other cause; where schools still ignore language and learning disabilities; where, after we rehabilitate the physically handicapped, we sentence them to life in a nursing home; where more than 90 percent of all children commit one or more acts that would, if they were caught, result in their going to a reform school; where the number of muggings, murders, robberies, rapes, burglaries, thefts, and other crimes is astronomical; where we do not know how to cure the emotionally ill or the delinquent or criminal; and where we pump children full of drugs to keep them calm, or send them off to warehouse-like institutions, or both?

What is the social worker's role in a nation where the President's highest aides approve of burglaries, wiretap innocent citizens as well as criminals, and discuss vengeful methods of using a variety of federal agencies to punish enemies of the President? What should the social worker do in a nation that spends more on alcohol, tobacco, and entertainment than on helpless children in institutions? What can they do to assure all expectant mothers of proper prenatal care; to protect the newborn from clumsy doctors, inadequate diets, lack of early childhood stimulation, or to help children of the poor gain the kind of self-concept that will permit them to make it in society?

Perhaps it is not that America is more evil or damaging than other, earlier societies—for any student of history knows that it is not—rather, it is because of an awakening to the ills and evils of society and a growing sense of compassion, that more and more of us feel the pain of those who are handicapped, poor, black, or are otherwise mistreated through no fault of their own.

It is a higher sense of justice that makes many Americans see the injustices of prejudice, wealth, and poverty, and abuse of power. But justice is, at least in theory, the work of the courts—not social workers or social reformers. Nor can trained (or half-trained) psychologists, psychiatrists, teachers, ministers, Boy Scout leaders, penologists, or guidance counselors solve the problems of our society. Answers do not lie in better genetic counseling, new math, more leisure time, free love and trial marriages, women's liberation, strong labor unions, giant corporations, improved productivity, more trade with Russia, gay liberation, better television, open classrooms, behavior modification, skilled surgeons, alcohol, drugs (legal or illegal), a higher minimum wage, better unemployment benefits, free dental care, or a guaranteed annual income.

The answers are far more difficult than that. One must return to real basics. What is the value of human life—not just our own, but others? What is one man's responsibility to another man? To himself? Can we learn to accept all men for what they are, whether poor or rich, white, black, brown, tan, or some other color, athletic or crippled, brilliant or dull, articulate or tongue-tied? Or must we set out to reshape them? Can we give those who are physically, mentally, or emotionally deviant full value—or should we mark them down as inferior or defective merchandise? Are we to remain a nation that worships at the advertising agency's altar—practicing a state religion called sensual consumerism? Should our lives be governed by economists or moralists? Is pregnancy really an inalienable right, or should parents be required to support and properly care for their offspring? If we license people to drive cars, or as beauty-shop operators, should we license parents—making them take a test before they have children? Is it a higher crime to make a profit off the poor (and thus cause crime) as a slumlord or credit-gouger than to steal bread to feed your babies? If so, why does a bread-stealing mother go to jail, while the slumlord pays a small fine, if that?

Facing other pressing problems that have ranged from the cold war to inflation and energy shortages, the President and Congress have not been able to turn to questions such as these—even if they have thought of them. In recent decades politicians have been more concerned with public opinion polls and the skill of public relations men to manipulate the press and public than with the teachings of moral and ethical philosophers.

In this century we have been transfixed by technological progress, industrial productivity, and self-gratification. Except for brief periods, including the Great Depression of the thirties and the more recent black revolution, social agencies have been left to drift, instructed to make as few waves as possible.

The welfare worker's bag of tricks has been limited to salvaging families through direct financial aid, and when that fails, to turning unwanted waifs into U-Haul children—moving them off to institutions, foster homes, or group homes. Most social workers spend little time with troubled families. They use the telephone, the courtroom, money, or therapy programs in someone's office. They call in the police when they need muscle, and turn to judges and lawyers to take children from parents who refuse to obey their orders.

Like it or not, social workers are master manipulators. They know how to threaten, how to soft-soap, to stir people by helping them see themselves as others see them, by making them dependent, and even by forming welfare rights groups to picket and challenge. But they are not really effective in changing either people or the political system. They do not know how to make the political system work.

The social workers and welfare workers have impossible jobs. They do not have the authority or power of a school principal or of the policeman. Yet they are called when a mother crushes her child's skull, or when a father dumps boiling water on his son in a fit of rage. Sometimes they are asked to help the police or prosecutor to investigate an abuse case, and sometimes they do it alone—gathering the evidence in hopes it will satisfy a judge who will make a decision. Methods vary from state to state and even from city to city.

Some courts, at the request of a social worker, will remove a child from his home. In Kansas City all cases are handled by the court. "If a mother says she is going to kill her child, we can't intervene," until there is court approval, according to Mrs. Donna McPherson, a family service supervisor.

"Under the Missouri law, something has to happen to the child before we can act, and all of our complaints must come through the courts unless a public assistance worker sees the child and refers it directly to us," she adds. "It is easier for us to prove neglect than abuse because in the case of neglect we can show that the child is malnourished, or that there is a poor housekeeping problem. We may be able to prove that a child was injured in the case of abuse, but it is pretty hard to prove that the injury was the result of abuse, and not an accident, or to prove who did the abusing."

While Mrs. McPherson or one of her workers may urge the court to remove the child from its home, the judge may not agree. Further, "we are not permitted to keep the case open, we cannot stay in the picture to see if the child, or other children in the family, will be abused," unless the judge orders it.

Jack Benson was in charge of protective services for Albany County, New York, when I visited the community in 1973. There, and in the rest of the state, abuse and neglect are reported directly to the welfare department. While the more serious cases are taken to court, minor abuse (severe, but not medically damaging paddlings, for example) is often dealt with informally—especially when a parent is actively seeking help.

Mr. Benson, M.S.W., publishes his home phone in the local newspaper so that he can get abuse referrals twenty-four hours a day. The welfare department does not provide round-the-clock staffing, or even an answering service, but Mr. Benson knows that abuse does not always take place between nine and five, five days a week.

"I have a gnawing knowledge that five or six kids are going to be hurt tonight, and there is little I can do about it. This is a terrible burden that is felt by my staff and social workers all over the state, and a lot of them are looking for other jobs. Whenever we hear that a child has been killed somewhere we pray that it won't happen tonight in our county."

To help lighten the load, Mr. Benson often tries to get other agencies, especially those supported by Red Feather campaigns, to help. But many have their own budget problems, or have been spoiled by the "purchased services" plan where state agencies pay for the care of children they send.

The Albany Child Guidance Center *does* work with families that abuse children, and Dr. Lenore Sportsman, a child psychiatrist, notes that income from the United Fund decreases each year.

"We haven't been able to enlarge our staff for fifteen years," she says. "Yet there is no other child outpatient psychiatric program in Albany County."

Like Mr. Benson and others, she is disturbed by the lack of services available to families. It is hard to blame the parents, who may not have wanted the child in the first place, couldn't find help, and have reached the end of their emotional ropes—and in this tormented state of mind abused the child, she says.

In some states the welfare department sees defusing these bombs as the role of the welfare department. Ms. Estelle Griffen, a program specialist in child care for the welfare department in Minnesota, sees welfare "providing alternatives to parents." She admits that prevention of abuse is only a goal, and has not yet been fully realized. But it is an important goal because "we know that what happens to a child when it is small is very relevant to its later behavior." Thus punishing the parents and patching of the wounds does not heal the emotional scars that cause emotional illness, crime, and delinquency.

In St. Paul, Minnesota, a Ramsay County Child Abuse Team has been established. According to Shirley Pierce, a social worker, the team includes representatives from welfare, the police department, the juvenile court, two hospitals, the county nursing service, the mental health center, and a representative from a private foundation that finds homes for children. The team has been at work for five years, and is as concerned with prevention as with uncovering abuse cases.

"The law requires physicians and others to report all suspected abuse cases," she says. "We may get a call from a nurse in a doctor's office who reports that a four-year-old child has just been brought in for treatment by his aunt. The child has severe strapping marks on his buttocks, back, and legs. The nurse feels there is no way the child could have been injured by falling. She reports the name of the child, the parents' names, and the name of the person who brought the youngster in for treatment.

"As soon as she hangs up I communicate with the welfare contact on the team and the police. They check their records to see if this case is active with any of the social agencies. In this instance we find there is no active case. So an intake worker is immediately assigned, and the police investigate to see how the injury happened. The welfare worker contacts the aunt and gets a statement, then talks to the father, who is home, and assesses the family environment. When the child's mother arrives home from work the social worker talks to her. She decides that the injury is not accidental, and that it is a case of abuse. We learn that a county Public Health nurse has worked with the family, but not for a year and a half. We talk to the nurse and she helps us understand what the family is like, what the child is like, and what we can expect to happen. The team then determines whether or not the child should remain in the home or be removed; whether or not the parents can be worked with voluntarily; what agencies should take responsibility. The welfare worker is assigned, along with a mental health therapist. They work with the family and the team keeps reviewing the case.

"When it is possible, we prefer to let the child remain in the home. We do not want to punish the parents. We know that they may be guarded, hostile, frightened—and we take that into consideration. We want to help them, but the safety of the child is our first priority. When we must remove the child from its home, our goal is to return the child as soon as possible. But the burden for that decision doesn't rest with one person. It is a team decision."

Ms. Winifred Scott, a child psychologist working with the team points out that often battering parents "tend to be alienated, isolated. They tend to have a lot of problems. Some were juvenile delinquents, or they may have acted out sexually when they were younger, or they may have been in foster homes, or were chronically depressed. A lot of them are mentally ill."

It is asking a lot of the most skilled social worker to cope with these problems. Often undertrained, overworked, underpaid, tired, and worried, they carry this burden with them—working at a thankless job.

"Too many doctors, lawyers, teachers, clergymen—too many people—just don't give a damn about child abuse," Mr. Benson says. "I know of one case where somebody beat up a little nine-year-old girl and then held her head under water. She was taken to a hospital half dead, but she pulled out of it. I didn't get there until it was too late to do anything. The police had already arranged for the child and her mother to stay with a minister because supposedly her boyfriend beat the little girl up while the mother was at work. The mother was terribly frightened, and she took off from the minister's home at two-thirty in the morning for Pennsylvania with the child. I didn't get called until the next morning, and then it was too late. I did find out that the mother is crazy over tough guys, and is always getting beaten up. I don't know what's going to happen to the child."

He also tells of a three-year-old girl who was systematically burned with an electric iron as punishment by her psychotic mother. She kept burning the child in the same spot, until after several weeks the bone was exposed. The little girl lived only a few miles away from the statehouse and the office building, where politicians, who have never seen an abused child, make decisions that affect their lives.

Child abuse is not the only problem welfare workers must deal with. What does one do if he must take a child away from the parents because of abuse or neglect, or when a mother tells them she can't care for her children, or doesn't want them? Too often the social worker has only two choices—find a foster home or send the child to an institution.

While institutions still are being used, they have fallen out of favor. Many experts believe they do irreparable harm. Children in institutions often are isolated from society, and while they may learn to conform to institutional life, they do not know how to cope with the world when they are released. The younger the child, the more damaging the institution can be.

As institutions lost favor, more social welfare agencies turned to foster homes and group foster homes for answers. (A foster home is simply a family willing to take in one or more children for a small fee and treat them more or less as if they were their own.) But studies show that foster homes can be as damaging as institutions. Too often children are shufled from one foster home to another, either at the request of the foster parent or because the child has asked for a change. The use of foster homes varies from state to state, and even within a large city, depending upon the agency involved. Some are short-term, while others serve as a home for a child until he becomes an adult and is on his own—and then he visits the foster parents as if they were his real family. There also are specialized foster homes that care for the deaf, blind, retarded, crippled, disturbed, and delinquent children. Philosophy varies.

Mrs. Dorothy Filson, of Phoenix, who heads the state office that provides foster care in Arizona, believes that foster care should be short-term, and "ideally the child should be returned to his own family or to a relative," but that's not always possible. When I talked to Mrs. Filson in 1973, foster parents were paid $75 a month for room and board, and the child was given clothing, medical and dental care, psychiatric help when needed, plus pocket money. For "hard to place" children, the state pays $100 a month. In 1973 there were 1,100 foster homes in Arizona.

Mr. Borgie, in Los Angeles, told me that the top rate for foster care in his county was $204 a month—or $600 for institutional care. That seemed strange, since most agree that if one had to choose between an institution and a foster home, foster care is preferable.

Mr. Borgie did not quarrel with this, and added that while foster care was once seen as a panacea, it now is considered damaging.

"The child is disconnected from his family; he is sometimes maltreated; while he is away other members of the family may use and break his toys or throw them away; if he is a difficult child, the foster parents can't cope; the younger child can't understand why he can't be with his own parents; he feels kicked out and keeps asking himself, 'Why don't Mom and Dad want me?'; he feels he may be defective because he can't go home; there is the trauma of being in a strange home with different standards and rules from those he is used to; and he looks at the other children in the foster family and feels he is different—he is a stranger, a foster child.

"Almost every child who goes into foster care sustains some damage. We must weigh this against his *not* going into foster care. Are there any alternatives? Can we put the child into day care while the mother, if she is psychotic, receives outpatient care? Would it help if the child was able to do the laundry or the dishes or help care for the house?

"A social worker can only go one of two directions. We are either taking a family apart or putting it back together. Not enough people have understood this, and there has been too much 'wait and see' in this field: 'Let's try it, let's put the child in foster care for a while, and wait and see what happens at home.' Before you know it, the child has been out of the home for five years, and then it's too late to do anything."

In Kansas City in 1973, foster parents were paid on a sliding scale from $66 a month for an infant to $96 for a child seventeen and over. For a retarded child, or one with multiple handicaps, the fee can go up to $150, adds Miss Bridwell. Nor is there a foster parent training program, although Miss Bridwell would like to change that—but doesn't have the staff. She believes that one reason foster children are moved so often (in some states five, six, on up to eight or nine times in a period of six or seven years) is that foster parents do not know how to handle these children who have been so damaged in their own homes. If they were trained, if they received a little more money, more social work support, and if the selection process was better, then foster care could be a helpful program, she says.

"It's terrible what we do to children," she told me. "But I don't know what to do to change it."

Foster children may go for months without contact with a social worker in some states. Sometimes years go by. I learned that a few get lost because they only exist as a file number in some cabinet, or in someone's desk, and social workers come and go, files get lost, and so do the children.

What happens when the foster parent is moved by his company from Binghamton to Los Angeles? In many instances the child is returned to welfare for a new placement, either because of state laws or for other reasons. Too often the child, feeling abandoned and rejected, turns to delinquency, has school problems, or becomes disturbed.

Experts agree that each month a child is in foster care, the more difficult it becomes to make a permanent arrangement for the youngster—either returning him home or putting him up for adoption. Connecticut is one state where officials are trying to monitor each child's experience during the first two years, because they believe after that it is probably too late.

"We've got to knock ourselves out trying to get the child back into its own home," says John Ely, acting director of social services for the state. "That means we have to help the mother find an adequate apartment,

perhaps get her to mental health or on a drug maintenance program—
whatever it takes. If, at the end of a year or a year and a half, it is clear
that this parent isn't going to be able to make it, then we must do what
we can to keep the child from limbo—from the never-never land. We
know that if the child just drifts along in a foster home, after two years
between eighty and ninety percent will *never* return to their own homes.
Right now we have eleven hundred kids in limbo in Connecticut, and
we've got to change that."

The picture is "bleak" for "limbo" children, who drift along year after
year, waiting and hoping, wondering, trying to forget. Mr. Ely talks of
many children in this category, like the "one who came to us when he
was six months old. He would have been easy to place in a good adoptive
home then," he adds. "Now he is five, and it may already be too late."

Adoption may provide a child with permanency, a sense of being
wanted, of belonging, but like foster parents, few adoptive parents are
helped or trained. More and more states are turning to subsidized adoptions for hard-to-place children—helping adoptive parents foot the bills.
But few have answers for the children in their own homes, foster homes,
or adoptive homes who start out as sweet little "swans" and grow into
pimply faced, chain-smoking, smart-mouthed, adolescent ugly ducklings.
These are children that only a dedicated mother can love.

I could write a great deal more about AFDC, foster care, neglect and
abuse, social workers, adoptions, and related subjects. Welfare is such a
broad and important subject it deserves a book by itself. I feel that I
should deal at length with Head Start, day care, the school lunch programs, homemaker services, the Job Corps, Vista, and public housing
(and I probably will when this book is completed). But for now it is
enough to say that welfare is a terribly complex and difficult field, that it
too often damages children when it should be helping them, that social
workers are ill-equipped to deal with society's overwhelming problems,
and that America must—if it is to cut crime and delinquency, mental
illness, child abuse, and other ills—think more and do better about these
little victims, the U-Haul children.

32

The Missing Mandate

Item: A Connecticut radio station reported, in May of 1973, that the state legislature had been balking at funding certain programs for the retarded. At the last minute, just as the measure seemed doomed, a member of the legislature with a retarded son took the microphone and made an eloquent speech in behalf of his son and the retarded. The lawmakers, visibly moved by the appeal, quickly passed the measure.

Item: In June, 1973, editors of *The Maine Times* published a long article on a boy with a specific language disability. It told how he "flunked" first grade, was "diagnosed" by social officials as either "lazy or crazy," because he could not keep up, and at last got help in a special summer program at a private school. The youngster's mother raised the money for her son ($1,000) by appealing to civic clubs and other groups. Several parents filed suits in Maine courts, hoping to force local schools to provide programs for learning (or language) disability children.

Item: Throughout 1973 and 1974 (and for several years before that) scattered newspapers across the country reported on neighborhood groups formed to fight against opening small group homes for mentally and physically handicapped, emotionally disturbed, and delinquent children.

Item: In November of 1973 a number of Ohio newspapers reported on the firing of Dr. Dean Coddington, a child psychiatrist, who was fired by the state as head of an innovative program for disturbed children at

Nelsonville, Ohio. Dr. Coddington was fired after he promoted, then demoted, a Mrs. Charlotte Pancake, a clerk-typist who had asked to work with children. Dr. Coddington said he demoted Mrs. Pancake when she failed to support the program and to cooperate with other staff members. It was noted that Mrs. Pancake's husband, Charlie, held a regional office in the AFL-CIO. Reportedly, he used his office to put pressure on state officials, including Governor John J. Gilligan, in behalf of his wife. Mr. Pancake's lawyer, James F. Shumaker, told me in an interview that the Pancakes had the leverage to get the doctor fired because Governor Gilligan needed labor support for re-election.

Item: On February 4, 1974, *Time* magazine reported that Ohio Governor Gilligan had made a "special effort to improve conditions of the hospitals in which the state's mentally ill and retarded live." It also said the Governor "donned a white coat and walked the wards for a couple of hours as a psychiatric-aide trainee" at Orient State Institute, a dismal facility for the retarded near Columbus. The magazine did not report that several high-ranking officials in the state mental health field complained that the *Time* item was a masterful coup on the part of the young, high-powered public relations team working for the Ohio Department of Mental Health and Mental Retardation, and that the "improvements" have been cosmetic, and have not helped patients.

Item: In February of 1974 the *NEA Reporter*, published by the teacher's organization the National Education Association (NEA), announced that a national fund-raising campaign was underway to raise large sums to help elect candidates to Congress. The article said the candidates the NEA planned to bankroll "will give education top billing among the nation's priorities and support NEA's goals of one-third federal financing and guaranteed collective bargaining rights for teachers."

Item: The New York Times, on May 22, 1974, had three page-one stories on education. One article reported that, "A tradition in the city's public schools having separate classes for 'bright' students and for 'slow' students is resulting in repeated situations in which pupils walk through doors of schools that are outwardly desegregrated only to find themselves in racially imbalanced classrooms."

The second story, with a Washington dateline, began: "The Department of Health, Education and Welfare is studying data collected from the 20 largest cities, including New York and Newark, in an investigation of the disproportionate number of children from minority groups expelled or suspended from public schools."

The third article stated: "Two junior high school deans who have been accused of using a thick wooden paddle, leather belts, and their fists to beat students who misbehaved were removed from their posts yesterday by the district superintendent." A few days later the *Times* reported that because of public pressure the two men were reinstated.

Item: In the March/April 1974 issue of the *Magazine of Westchester,* published in the wealthy county just north of New York City, Ingrid S. Braslow, a lawyer, wrote in an article: "Exactly one year ago I wrote an article for this magazine called 'Confessions of a Juvenile Court Lawyer.' The responses to the problems I posed were positive and sympathetic. Yet, one year after my article [appeared], and four years after the . . . law [requiring all counties to provide non-secure detention for delinquents and for dependent children was passed], not one non-secure detention facility for boys and girls exists in Westchester." She also noted that delinquent and dependent children were mixed together.

Item: In Tucson, Arizona, the juvenile court judge John Collins was suspended then reinstated, apparently after some of his colleagues on the bench felt he was getting too much publicity in an election year. Judge Collins had made more than five hundred speeches in a twelve-month period on behalf of children who appeared in the juvenile court. After his suspension, and while he was being "investigated," a radio station circulated petitions in his behalf and thousands of signatures were collected. After the investigation was completed and he was returned to the juvenile court, a testimonial dinner was held for the judge.

Item: In an editorial on May 25, 1974, *The New York Times* pointed out that the United States Government, apparently piqued at the North Vietnamese for failing to live up to promises made in the peace agreement, told the United Nations Children's Fund (UNICEF) not to spend American money on programs that would help children there. The editorial added that "The United States Government, on the contrary, has a shameful history of neglect for child welfare in Vietnam, even in the South. It was only after the most intensive prodding from Congress and private citizens that the Administration agreed recently to step up its contributions to the South's war-destitute children—including thousands of illegitimate offspring of United States servicemen—to a meager $7.2 million."

I use these random news items to show that unwanted children are getting attention from the press, and also to show that children, sadly, also are victims of the political system.

The Connecticut legislature was swayed not by reason or deep-rooted compassion but by the emotional appeal of one man from within their ranks with a retarded son. He did what outsiders could not do. In Maine, parents of children with specific language disabilities found their children being hurt and were forced to turn to the courts for leverage. I mention the neighborhood groups fighting against group homes for deviant children because they are using power politics on the local level *against* children, and most often no counterbalancing groups were formed to fight in behalf of the youngsters.

The Ohio items show that (1) a professional who does not understand politics can easily be wiped out by crossing even a clerk-typist, when that clerk-typist has power behind her, and (2) to show how a skilled public relations team can fool large numbers of people by getting a well-meaning governor to don a white coat for reporters and photographers. Such a move makes political hay, but hurts children.

I report on the NEA fund-raising campaign because one who thinks carefully about it, and reads between the lines or asks questions, finds that well-meaning, dedicated, and deserving groups can unthinkingly exploit children for personal gain. Anyone who has watched the NEA in recent years can only conclude that beneath the rhetoric about helping children there lies one core issue: teachers' wages.

The three *New York Times* stories on page one show that major newspapers do believe the plight of children is newsworthy. They also show how little real progress has been made in stemming racial problems, and that apparently both professionals and the public continue to believe that children with learning handicaps can be helped through beatings.

I included the Westchester item because it shows how government seems little concerned about children or the laws of a state, and to point out that one of the richest counties in the nation is little better than poorer areas.

The plight of Judge Collins in Tucson (I visited him during the period he was in legal limbo) suggests that when your power base is with the people, political opponents find it more difficult to topple you—but some will try. He is hardly the first judge who has fought for children to come under attack. Such judges have been ousted in Phoenix, Denver, Milwaukee, and other cities, when their only offense was caring about youngsters.

And finally, *The New York Times* editorial on children in Vietnam hints at the current thinking of politicians in high places. To use children —even enemy children—as political pawns in either a cold or hot war is unthinkable in a truly civilized society. And balking at supporting street children sired by American GIs during the Vietnamese conflict only echoes our indifference to all children—at home and abroad.

It is with this last point that I am most uncomfortable. The *Times* editorial had a chilling effect on me. I had been confident, as I researched and wrote this book, that if I could only tell the story of our unwanted children to the American people, then our nation would understand and respond. I am less sure of that now.

There is something to be said about the public numbness caused by Watergate and other events of the past two decades. It was an urgent sense of moral outrage that moved the nation to demand that civil rights be extended to American blacks and other minority groups. And similar anger spurred on consumerism, the ecology groups, the women's rights battle, and the gay liberation movement.

Perhaps part of the reason these groups have made gains is that they are carried on the momentum of self-interest. The children's movement must depend upon adults to speak out for them, and it is possible the adults do not care enough to make the necessary sacrifices.

There will be opposition from strongly entrenched professionals who now earn their living off children and children's problems. Like others, I have had to face and fight this in my earlier battles for children. In some states I am still hated by persons who treated children brutally or supported maltreatment of delinquents. Some were fired, but others have changed their views and still work in the field, now helping instead of hurting youngsters.

Most important of all, the child-caring field is fragmented. The people and politicians throw the various groups and agencies chicken feed and one finds those who run them pushing and clucking and pecking one another to make sure they get their share. This is too often true of private welfare agencies, local mental health organizations, the YMCA, Boys Clubs, the Easter Seal drive, the campaign for muscular dystrophy, the March of Dimes, state agencies and institutions, and others who depend upon public doles for survival. They fail to understand that they must unite and make the American political system work for children as well as for bankers, oil companies, and gun enthusiasts.

Those who speak for the blind have a strong lobby—but they fight only for the visually impaired. Parents of retarded children have, since the Kennedy family introduced the late President's retarded sister to the world, been able to organize and fight for change. A few small groups now battle for the deaf. A decade ago social workers helped organize welfare mothers to fight for their rights. Slowly foster parents are organizing—hoping to get more money and better treatment. Through the efforts of a few dedicated men, child abuse has at last become a national issue, and parents groups patterned after Alcoholics Anonomyous have been formed in scattered cities. Various groups concerned with the quality of children's television have been pushing for change in that area. While teachers groups do battle for children, some have been taken over by those only interested in more benefits and higher wages. Institutional superintendents complain of civil service regulations and unions that prevent them from helping children. Local judges crusade for delinquents—frustrated because their court lacks alternatives. And local newspapers, large and small, publish reports of inhumane treatment of children.

If these groups, divided, scattered, and often small, could join together—as the national gun lobby has—to speak in a single, concerned voice, it is possible, just possible, that the politicians will listen. And if that happens, America's little victims will, for the first time, have real hope.

PART
III
Seeking Solutions

33

Making the System Work

Question: If infants and children cannot make the American political system work for them, is it because the children fail or because the political system is not designed to respond to children?

Answer: Clearly the fault lies with the system, not the child. In our form of government the systems must be responsive to the people who use them, not to those who are in political power, or the professionals assigned by the politicians to serve the citizens.

Anyone who has had to deal with government—local, state or national—knows the frustrating feeling of being an insignificant number on a card. But adults have at least some measure of control over their lives, and the ability to resist or appeal, perhaps with the help of a lawyer, when decisions by those who work in the systems are oppressive or intolerable. Children are powerless.

What control does the unborn (or unconceived) child have over the American mating system? Can the fetus decide to live or die? If an infant is not properly cared for, if its basic needs are not met, should we blame the child? If the child lacks food, shelter, health care, special help because of a handicap, or love, is it because the child is inept or irresponsible? Who should be held accountable in the field of education, the highly trained professional teacher or the child?

While we continue to debate the question of whether a child is shaped by "nature or nurture," few would deny that the adults who surround a child—the parents, relatives, teachers, baby-sitters, neighbors, and television performers (if the child is a constant viewer) have *some* impact upon the child and its growth, behavior, and future.

Even those who believe a child's every thought and action is genetically programmed must ask whether or not a child's genetic makeup is the fault of the child. Does the deviant youngster—different because of either training or hereditary factors (or both)—deserve to suffer pain and punishment because of those differences? Should the child who is a loser by birth, at school, with his peers, and society be required to pay the full price when he violates society's codes and standards? Or does some responsibility lie with the adults who produced and shaped him?

Logic and justice suggest that the child, at least the child who is small, should not shoulder the blame. And yet teachers, the police, juvenile court judges, parents, and others in our society tend to turn on the child when things go wrong.

This is the *terribly* tragic flaw of the average juvenile court. Most often the innocent are punished, while the guilty—the parents and teachers and others who damaged the child—go free. This happens not only in the justice system but also the mental health system, and in those assigned to handicapped children. Many are sentenced to fifty or sixty years of earthly purgatory, at taxpayers' expense.

One who ponders the problem only briefly must find it incredible that parents, school officials, or neighbors can have a child picked up like a stray dog and hauled off to a children's jail and to court, and that the child has little protection and almost no recourse. Adults also can subject children to so-called therapeutic treatment, put the child in an institution or foster home, or administer painful punishment (within limits) and the child can do little about it. If he runs away, he is returned, and if he refuses to return, he is further punished. The child must endure all, short of extreme physical abuse or neglect, and without protest.

What can a child do when he is poorly taught, scapegoated, ridiculed, ignored, or flunked by an incompetent, unstable, or vengeful teacher? What can he do when thrown out of his own home, and placed with foster parents he hates, or in an institution where few of his needs are met, or where he is brutally treated by sadistic adults? In the name of therapeutic treatment he may be manipulated by behaviorists, worked over in group therapy, studied and tested by psychiatrists and psychologists, subjected to electric shocks, locked in solitary confinement, or have drugs injected into his body. I have seen all of these things and more. Adult society—and our justice system—assumes that adults have the rights to do these things simply because he is a child.

Instead of protecting the innocent, our society subjects the innocent to treatment that would not be tolerated for an adult prisoner of war under the Geneva Convention rules. That is because in the eyes of the law an American child is property—not a person.

It would be grossly presumptuous to assume that I—or even the hundreds of persons I have interviewed—could redesign either society or its systems in a way that would be satisfactory to all Americans, or that would truly meet the needs of our children. Yet, it is not enough to raise questions and describe problems without several chapters discussing changes that could be considered.

As I said at the outset, I am not a radical, ready to tear down America and begin again. Rather, I see myself—along with many others—on the cutting edge of a reform movement that will take existing institutions and make them work. I do not call for vast new funding programs. Rather, I am convinced that reallocation of existing funds—putting our money where it counts—is the key to resolving what seem to some to be insurmountable problems. While we have, through technological progress, entered the era of space exploration, atomic force, and computerized learning, our social or human systems have, in some instances, changed little since the days of feudal monarchs and ox carts. And even those systems that have evolved in more recent years, including social work, health and mental health care, and penology have not been planned systems. Rather they sprouted like wild trees in the forest, and have grown without cultivation or adequate thought. What I call for is review, the broad overview, and the merger of those systems that clearly overlap, or that are in conflict with one another.

I know that schoolteachers complaining about dull children could profit by learning techniques used in the best programs for the retarded. Those with hard-to-reach students might well gain insight by watching teachers of children who are both deaf and blind. I found, surprisingly, mental health making the same mistakes that better reform schools made a decade ago—but those in mental health and juvenile corrections seldom talk to one another.

But perhaps it is logical, when thinking about systems that have a bearing on children, to begin with the American mating system. While experience shows that sexual attraction is a poor basis for choosing a mate, it remains a primary reason for mating and contributes to the failure of marriages, common law or sanctioned.

The question of when society has the right or obligation to intervene in the life of a child or actions of a family needs further study. We know that physically handicapped and mentally retarded children are most likely to succeed when they receive professional help in their homes at an early age. We also know that in many instances parents contribute to the production of disturbed and delinquent children. Some professionals believe that trained observers may well be able to spot behavior patterns that may produce problems later when the child is very young. We must ask whether or not, as a society, we should wait until the child becomes grossly delinquent or disturbed before we intervene—or provide help to families seeking it. Further, we must review the impact present methods of intervention have on the child. Many professionals believe youngsters get worse in their care.

Should there be certain minimum standards of child rearing required of all parents? We inspect automobiles, electric wiring, building foundations, septic tanks, and drinking water in many areas, all without public complaint.

What of the rights of children when their parents are being divorced? Milwaukee has long appointed an attorney to represent the children in contested cases, and a few scattered courts recognize the need for legal council for children in divorce proceedings. No-fault divorce may be convenient for the husband or wife who is unhappy, but it hardly meets the need of children, who become pawns.

In preceding chapters we have discussed the various systems designed to provide therapeutic treatment to children with problems. And how selecting children for one or another system is so often haphazard, and the diagnosis faulty. Perhaps the logical step is to provide a diagnostic clinic for every community and make it as visible and accessible as the traditional neighborhood school. It is quite possible, in fact, that a day-care center, school, and diagnostic center could be part of the same educational complex—with the educational program designed to meet each individual child's needs.

The diagnosticians should be specialists in diagnosis in all fields—trained to understand the needs of the total child. This would result in a new profession, with a university curriculum that would include psychology, medicine, education, social work, dentistry and related fields. Let those who specialize take over when the trained diagnostician has doubts, or when remedial skills are needed. Further, assign every child without strong parental support an advocate to see that the child's needs are actually met.

In addition to regular teachers, the school would have skilled therapists for crippled children, those with speech problems and visual, hearing, or mental handicaps. Instead of forcing each child to fit the school's mold, schools would be required to fit the program to the child. This would eliminate the failure factor that contributes both to delinquency and emotional disturbance. It also could build on the talents and strengths of the child, aiding gifted children and producing graduates with greater skill and more potential than at present.

Teachers, like musicians or painters, should be allowed to teach only when they have a special gift or talent for teaching. Like the second-rate artist who cannot make a living in his field, so should the teachers with modest talents look for work elsewhere.

Social workers, psychologists, psychiatrists, physicians, nurses, policemen, lawyers, judges, probation officers and child care workers also should be more carefully screened. Training, frequent retesting and licensing should be considered to protect the child from inept practitioners.

Family dynamics and problems might also be diagnosed, either upon request, or in public welfare cases, and when parents produce one or more children who are damaged, delinquent or disturbed, and require public care. It is extremely important in all of this to provide safeguards to protect the rights of children and parents—but it is not right that society should be burdened with criminals and disturbed persons or chronic welfare cases without trying to provide remedial services.

There is another school of thought that also deserves our attention. A few people are beginning to argue that government should not be in the child-caring business. If it is true that private hospitals, institutions, and schools and universities are often better than facilities that are publicly run, and if it is true that the free enterprise system is superior either to socialism or communism, then this may be the route to go. Even now parents with the financial ability often send their children to private schools and institutions, including those that care for the retarded, disturbed, and physically handicapped—and with positive results in many instances.

Further, if the state-run reform schools, mental hospitals, and institutions for the retarded that I have seen cannot be upgraded (and I must stress that a very small handful in America are already excellent) and are the best state governments can provide, then they deserve to be closed. Too many of them damage children.

Let the government set high standards and then embark on a tough program of evaluation and licensing—with a built-in appeal system so that second-rate bureaucratic grunts could not kill innovative programs. Hold these institutions accountable for what they do to children. Those with a high success rate should prosper, while those with poor records should fail. This would eliminate a key problem for those facilities that are state-run. They are accountable to no one, and operate under the philosophy that "the king can do no wrong." When a child is maltreated in a state institution, he has nowhere to turn for help.

Accountability is the key. While I have applauded the closing of large, impersonal institutions, and have supported small group homes in the community, my concern has grown because as we scatter children hither and yon no one is checking on what happens to them. In Boston in May of 1974 officials were seeking a clergyman who had been running a group home for delinquent boys. The man apparently fled the country—and was charged with sexual abuse of the youngsters. We can expect to see more problems of this sort appear as we disperse children without proper supervision.

Perhaps the problem can be solved by training skilled child advocates, assigning them small caseloads, and building a method for the advocate to hold the system accountable. Such an advocate also might be used for children in certain one-parent homes, or when both parents are present but are not aggressive in fighting for the rights of their children.

Oliver J. Keller, who has a cabinet-level post in the field of human services in the State of Florida, talks about professionals in the system "messing over" children, and warns that in time these children return as adults who strike back at society.

The time has come to review these systems, to look at what the professionals do, and to bring about change. Anything less than massive and total reform should be unacceptable to those who care about children.

34

The Honor Roll

A professor from a Georgia university once told me that he had been in trouble as a child, but was rescued by his high school band director, who gave him the encouragement that he needed. So it is with most little victims who make it. In almost every instance someone has reached out to help in a way that worked.

Through the years I have met many concerned, dedicated, giving persons helping children. Most get very little recognition. Some of their names have already appeared in this and my other books. Yet even briefly documenting the works and deeds of all of them, scattered through fifty states, would fill a book this size or larger. At best I can only select a representative handful, knowing that the others will understand.

Sister Kathleen

There is something about Sister Kathleen that immediately commands respect. She is, in her warm, gentle way, a clear-eyed, no-nonsense person, strong- but soft-spoken, trained as a nurse, dedicated to children, trying to serve God and man.

I met Sister Kathleen in Tucson, in the Casa de los Niños, a remodeled house on one of the city's busier streets. The home serves as a round-the-clock nursery where parents can drop off children in jeopardy without questions being asked, and without argument or judgment being

313

passed. Many are battered, abused, or neglected, and receive loving care and, when required, medical treatment, in a warm, home-like setting.

Sister Kathleen served, for many years, in the obstetrics ward at St. Mary's Hospital, not far away. Through the years many persons, including mothers, children grown up, and lawyers handling adoptions, called on her to discuss the growing problem of child abuse. They came more often as more young mothers began using drugs, endangering or damaging their children. Sister Kathleen listened and pondered what to do. It was when she learned of the death of an infant, a child who died while his mother was spaced out on drugs and was buried without a marker in the desert, that Sister Kathleen felt she must act. Her first step was to talk to Judge John Collins of the juvenile court. When she found that he too was concerned, and hoped she would do something for the little victims, she began talking to others, including the county attorney and prominent businessmen. Within a week she had twenty letters of endorsement from prominent citizens. As a nun, she was obligated to send her plans to her superiors in Los Angeles. Then she settled back, expecting to wait several months for a reply. But it didn't take the usual time.

"I received approval in three days," she recalls. "They told me to start immediately. There was nothing else to do, then, but to try."

Sister Kathleen then returned to the twenty persons who had given her letters of endorsement and asked if they would serve as a board. They agreed. This was in late February of 1973. It was not long before she found a suitable home—rent-free. It had to be renovated, and when the work was finished a contractor told her that she received at least $60,000 in free labor from craftsmen—plumbers, painters, carpenters, and others. But she still faced what seemed to be an insurmountable barrier. The city fire code required a sprinkler system, and the lowest bid was $12,000. She did not have the money but began to make the rounds of suppliers, and within one day received 2,000 feet of copper tubing free. Then the company with the low bid installed the system, and "forgot" to send her a bill.

Even before Casa de los Niños opened a mother abandoned a baby on the front porch with a note to Sister Kathleen. Then on November 26, 1973—just nine months later—the home was officially opened. In the first thirty-six days she took in thirty-seven children.

The day I visited Casa de los Niños, early in 1974, there were eight children in her care. I found the home large and pleasant, air-conditioned to keep the children comfortable, and carpeted so that they could crawl about freely and take tumbles without injury. Only six staff members are paid, although the home is open round-the-clock seven days a week. More than 250 persons, including housewives, college and high school students, are on the list of volunteers, along with forty-five registered nurses. Most volunteers work three-hour shifts.

The children range in age from a few days to three. One child arrived to permit the mother to enter a drug rehabilitation center. Others reach the home via institutions for alcoholics. The drug-using mother dropped off a "very high-strung, frightened little girl who wouldn't sleep and had terrible temper tantrums," Sister Kathleen says. The volunteers gave her a great deal of love, good food, and—apparently for the first time in her life—a steady routine. When the mother picked her up, the daughter was calm and much happier, and she said she would try to be more accommodating to her daughter.

Unwed mothers have knocked on the door. One, from the Midwest, said her father, an unforgiving man, was a wealthy doctor. The young mother sought help and got it without charge.

Many of the children have lacked attention and stimulation. One toddler sat almost motionless for forty-eight hours, paying little attention to the nurses and volunteers. Many felt like cheering when he reached out to touch a toy, and then began playing. The mother explained that she cannot tolerate a mess and so had kept him isolated in his crib. When she took him home Sister Kathleen told her to bring him back for another visit if she felt she could not meet his needs.

A two-year-old boy weighed only twelve pounds. The mother explained that she was so poor she could give him little food, and kept her son alive by nursing him. The staff provided the boy with his first solid food. Another two-year-old arrived with cigarette burns on much of his body, and was so weak he couldn't walk. When placed in a highchair he could not hold himself upright, and slumped over on the tray. In a few weeks he was sitting up, then walking and eating with little help.

Sister Kathleen is meeting a very important problem head-on in a and neglected children in Tucson. She believes that dozens of children die and their bodies disappear in the desert. She bases this on conversations with young mothers who use drugs and alcohol. The purpose of Casa de los Niños is to save these and other children before they are hurt—and she reaches out to people who have never had help before because their life styles conflicted with the law. Some down-and-out mothers also drop their children off while they seek work or a place to live. That means some children stay only a few hours, while others have been there several weeks. More than one mother has admitted leaving the child untended for long periods, sometimes knocking it out with oven gas or plastic bags filled with glue fumes.

Sister Kathleen is meeting a very important problem head on in a unique way. Homes such as hers should be available in every city in

America. If they were, it is possible that we would have fewer little victims in America.

Joseph Deacon

I met Joe Deacon on a hot Saturday morning in July of 1972 at the institution for the retarded in Pauls Valley, Oklahoma. The first thing I noticed was that his office is very old, it does not have central air-conditioning, and the state-made desks have been around for years. In many institutions for children I found the superintendent in a modern, air-conditioned building, seated at an executive desk, with pictures on the wall and carpet on the floor, and most of the comforts of the General Motors executive suite. But Joe Deacon has a curious idea. He believes the needs of children come first, and that administrators should wait until the children's needs are met.

I was surprised that Joe—he is much too personable to call "Mr. Deacon"—was so willing to spend a Saturday with me, and Sunday, if my work required it. Most superintendents objected to my visiting on weekends, and some leave for the weekend early Friday afternoon. A number were "too busy" to see me, no matter what day of the week I came, although I found that to be more of an eastern trait than one that is national. (The men with the largest numbers of junior executives were often the most "busy.") But Joe Deacon had time, and later I found that he makes the rounds every Saturday and Sunday, just as he has for the past thirty-five years.

There were other surprises. It was Saturday, but the children were active—no long, dull weekends here. And no foul odors! Even buildings half a century old were clean and fresh, with as much homelike atmosphere as possible in an institution once used for male delinquents, epileptics, psychotics, and other unwanted adults. In a school and recreation complex, newly built, I found an indoor wading pool, swimming pool with diving board, and a third pool for children in wheelchairs. (They ride down a sloping ramp and float out of the chairs with the help of an attendant.) Joe has five water-safety instructors on his staff. In addition to the pool and modern school, where children with varying degrees of retardation are taught, there is an excellent gym, theater, art and music rooms (the school has a chorus of retarded children), and a sheltered workshop.

While the campus, compared to some, like Ohio or even California, is impressive, it is Joe Deacon that makes the difference—again proving my theory that the superintendent *is* the institution. For just as Pauls Valley reflected the personality of Joe, so other institutions reflect superintendents who are pompous or emotionally pinched-up, who are lazy or insensitive, or who do not trust people.

Joe Deacon is warm, decent, conscientious, and strong but sensitive. Not only did he know every staff member (full and part-time) by name (many superintendents only know a handful of employees), but he knew the children, their family backgrounds, and their hometowns. And more important, he was personally involved with the children, and most knew him. In so many, many institutions staff members stand around the wards, their arms folded, waiting, waiting for their tour of duty to end. Not so, even on Saturday, at Pauls Valley. Staff members were playing games, reading, and involved in other ways. They held the smaller youngsters on their laps, let them touch and hug, and communicated "I care about you" to almost every child.

It was that way because of Joe Deacon. He did not order his staff to get involved. Instead, he taught by example. He played games with the children, sometimes sitting on the floor, and he let them touch and hug him. He took time to talk. To listen. To be impressed with the decorations for a party, or to admire a scribbled crayon drawing. Even after thirty-five years he still draws his strength from the children. And Joe Deacon wasn't faking it. He wasn't putting on a show for my benefit. He really cares. Joe Deacon doesn't often make the headlines. But he's the kind of man I'd like watching over my child.

Judge Duncan McNabb

Judge Duncan McNabb no longer sits on the juvenile court bench in Schenectady, New York. And that's a pity. A wiry, white-haired man, he left the post after his wife of many years died.

I met Judge McNabb several years ago while lecturing in upstate New York. He sat quietly in the audience, the only other man present, and waited until the others gathered around me after the speech had left. He asked a few questions, then, speaking softly, almost timidly, he said that if I was interested he would tell me about some of the things his staff was doing. They were, I soon found, doing many of the things I had talked about—and more. I was younger then, and more impressed than I should have been with my own knowledge, and it took a few minutes to sink in. He talked of his nonsecure detention home—pointing out that instead of locking children behind bars he put them in an old farmhouse on the edge of town when they could not return to their own homes. I learned, after asking him questions, that in some eight years on the juvenile court bench he had put no more than half a dozen children behind bars. Cities smaller than Schenectady often put several hundred children in secure detention each year. He also talked about creative forms of probation, working with families, the child's sense of self-worth. His goal really was rehabilitation—not just in words, but in deeds. I understood then that he was far more qualified to have given the speech, but he had listened quietly and with real interest.

Later, I returned with a film crew to feature the open detention home where both boys and girls stay unguarded, except for a house mother, and without incident.

There are many juvenile court judges who attend conferences, lecture, write, or put on a show. Judge McNabb was not one of them. He was too busy helping his community's little victims for that.

Karl Menninger, M.D.

Some may wonder why I include Dr. Karl Menninger, the world-famous psychiatrist, on this list of relatively unheralded persons who help children. It is because, while I do not know him well, I have seen a side that may not be familiar to the public who know him only through the Menninger Clinic and Foundation in Topeka, Kansas, or his writings, or reputation in the mental health field.

When my book *Children in Trouble* was first published, he not only wrote to congratulate me but also sent me a signed copy of his own book *The Crime of Punishment*. And then, without ever telling me, he purchased copies of my book and mailed them to people he felt would benefit from it (something he also has done for other authors). Then, more than a year later, I was startled to find him in an audience where I was lecturing. Afterward he came up to shake my hand, to tell me he was following my work, and to invite me in person to visit the Menninger Clinic and Foundation in Topeka.

I did not get there until 1973, a few days before his eightieth birthday. (He spends much of his time in Chicago, and I was fortunate to find him there.) He was deeply interested in *The Little Victims*, and we talked at length. Thus I feel it would be a mistake not to mention him, his concern for children and for all humanity, and his willingness to take the time to be kind and attentive to someone without the background that would permit him to be Dr. Karl's equal.

Harry Anderson

I have already mentioned Harry Anderson in an earlier chapter. A vocational rehabilitation counselor, he works with the deaf and hard of hearing at the state institution for the deaf in St. Augustine, Florida.

Harry Anderson would insist that he is just an ordinary guy doing an ordinary job, but I disagree. For he brings a cheerfulness and enthusiasm to his work that are hard to find in any field—although those who work with the deaf and the blind tend to be highly motivated and dedicated. Not only is Harry a graduate of a school for the deaf but his wife and two children also are deaf. And Harry also suffers from retinitis pigmentoso. That means he is slowly losing his eyesight, and in time will be blind.

For years he was so sensitive about this handicap that he could not talk about it. Often his wife would speak out, explaining why her husband sometimes acted strangely. For example, when he passed staff members on the sidewalk and they would nod and say hello he would not respond, because his vision problem requires him to keep careful watch on his path. Some thought him snobbish.

When Harry was told that he was slowly losing his sight he became depressed. How, he wondered, will I communicate with my wife and children if I cannot use sign language with them? But now he has worked through the trauma and fear, and spends part of his time talking to others about his handicap, and the handicaps of other people.

"Nobody will ask a handicapped person how it feels or what it's like," he says. "So it's up to us to speak out, to help people understand, to open the door to communication. When people begin to understand I think they will be more responsive, more willing to help these children."

I hope Harry Anderson is right. And I admire him because he works hard every day without self-pity and with good humor, doing his best for unwanted children.

Robert E. Carrel, M.D.

The medical director of the Tri-County Regional Center, a facility designed to provide community treatment programs for the mentally impaired in Santa Barbara, California, and the surrounding areas, Dr. Carrel is phyically handicapped. He has "two punk hips" that "make it hard for me to get around." Perhaps this, as much as his training as a neurologist, leads him to spend as much time as possible convincing parents, school officials, and others that children with varying degrees of retardation, or with other handicaps, are not only salvageable but in many instances are far more capable than most believe.

He does not raise false hopes with parents. But in private he suggests that many children diagnosed retarded simply have lacked proper attention and stimulation. Of those brought to him for diagnosis, 15 to 20 percent labeled retarded elsewhere are not retarded. And, sadly, through the years too many of these children have found their way into institutions. He can cite specific cases. Like the four-year-old, living in a foster home, the victim of a divorce. Authorities believe the youngster was battered by both of his parents, and at the age of nineteen months he began having convulsions. At the age of four years ten months, he flunked his required preschool tests, and officials said they thought him to be retarded.

Dr. Carrel was asked to re-diagnose the case, and he quickly discovered that because of an error the little boy was getting four times the dosage of medication needed to control his convulsions. Further, while receiving love at the foster home, he was not being properly stimulated. He spent much of his time sitting in front of a television set. No one read to him, or told him stories, or sat on the floor and played with him, Dr. Carrel says.

It was recommended that the medication be changed, that the little fellow be enrolled in a language-stimulation program, that the welfare department send out a social worker to teach the foster mother how to provide proper stimulation, and that the school assign a speech therapist to the case.

"The boy improved dramatically in just two weeks," Dr. Carrel says. "We've enrolled him in a private nursery school because he has so much ground to make up because of his deprivation. But we feel he has the potential of becoming a bright child now."

Many children—like all of us—never reach their full potential, he adds. This includes the retarded, especially those labeled "borderline." We still know too little about the human mind, and while a therapist can do little to *change* a child's *potential*, given an early enough start—perhaps in the first weeks of life—we are more likely to find the potential, and to reach it, whatever it may be.

Dr. Carrel is the only professional I have met who is truly enthusiastic about the retarded delinquent. Most give them up as hopeless cases, to be locked away for life.

"I find it exciting to work out a program for a boy brought in by probation as a retarded delinquent," he told me, "because I feel that in many instances we can help that boy. We can work out a program to change his behavior. I get a great deal of pleasure out of saving a child like that."

And often he does succeed. But considering that there are 1,200 children already on the rolls in this three-county area, and large numbers of others in need of help, he worries about them. For he feels that he and his staff would be "immobilized" if even greater numbers sought help (800,000 people live in his district).

I include Dr. Carrel on the list for many reasons, but not the least of them is his apparently unshakable confidence that mentally impaired children, if helped early enough and in the right way, can do better than vegetate in an institution. He does not get widespread publicity, as do those who experiment with heart transplants or seek cancer cures. But for the retarded and brain-damaged, Dr. Carrel is a true friend and a pioneer. For he is working to salvage children that many others write off.

Sue and Allen Soule

The Soules live in a large, old Vermont farmhouse near the little town of Plainfield. For ten years Allen was the Vermont State Historian, but then he wanted to do something with his life that had more meaning. Now he and his wife operate a small group home for unwanted and disturbed children. All ten of them have been with the Soules for two years or more.

Some have had experience with the mental hospital, and most have been thrown out of school—some in the primary grades—as unmanageable. Of the ten (six others have already left them, and three of the six are "doing fine," while the others still struggle) children presently living with the Soules, three are now back in the public schools, one attends a nursery school, and six attend a private school the Soules run on the farm.

The ten children, both boys and girls, range in age from five to eighteen. To care for that number, and to give six an adequate education, the Soules have help, young people who work for as little as $200 a month plus room and board. Edd Balagot is the certified teacher, and he works with the children individually, teaching them reading, writing, arithmetic, science, history, anthropology, geology, and other subjects using traditional school texts. On Tuesday and Thursday they spend the afternoons fishing, hiking, making maple syrup, bread, or gardening. They also are involved in candlemaking, pottery, and other craft projects, and on the day I visited they were making things to sell to raise funds.

The eighteen-year-old was about to graduate from high school, and I seldom have seen a boy so grateful as he was for the help he has had from the Soules. His father had died when Dean was still an infant, and his mother had placed him in a foster home. He had been shuffled through seventeen foster homes before reaching the Soules.

Another child, a fourteen-year-old girl, had lived the life of a little animal, and the Soules had to contend with biting, fighting and scratching at first. The other children came to them with a variety of depressing labels. All were no-hope children. Yet I found them happy, cooperative, acting very much like normal children.

While flourishing at the Soules, it is still uncertain that they will make it when they must face the adult world. Much depends upon the damage done before they reached the Soules, and how willing society is to accept them when they leave. But there can be little question that they are more likely to make it now than if they had remained in their own destructive homes, or lived for years in institutions.

As co-directors, Allen and Sue each earn only $275 a month. The remaining money, paid them by the state, is used to improve the home and the school and to meet the needs of the children. Sometimes when I drive through a comfortable suburban neighborhood and see the cars and landscaping and fathers leaving with their golf clubs, while the children watch, I think of the Soules. They may not have much money, but in a way they have much more. And give much more.

And Many More

I could write at length about Nicholas A. Seta, in Cincinnati, a one-time professional gambler, who works with disturbed children and makes speeches throughout the state to raise funds for children in a state institution.

Judge Frank Johnson, who sits on the federal bench in Alabama, has taken many unpopular stands but has upheld the Constitutional rights of the retarded and other unwanted members of our society. Instead of praise he often has faced severe abuse. Perhaps someone else will write an appropriate tribute.

In an earlier book I mentioned Dr. Earl Patterson, a psychiatrist in Meriden, Connecticut. He was fired from the reform school when he stood against brutality, and his name was smeared and ground into the dirt by crude and unthinking people. But he has stuck it out and runs a nonprofit clinic for children, often paying the costs out of his own pocket because funding is hard to find.

As I said at the outset, I could write a book of some length on the men and women who give so much and get so little. I must ask to be pardoned for adding just one more name to the list—that of a person who had a profound influence on this book and my interest in this field: my father.

Howard A. James, Sr.

This advocate for children died more than ten years ago. And on the last day he spent in this world he gave of himself to a child. A high school art teacher in Elkhart, Indiana, he was always popular among minority groups, and often defended the losers in the school. When I was young I was encouraged to bring home unwanted children to share Thanksgiving or Christmas, or just dinner. And they were treated with respect.

I was in Michigan on that last day, but school officials told me how it ended for him. He had arrived in the classroom feeling ill, but did not return home. On the way to the school cafeteria that noon he learned that a struggling student—a youngster not even in one of his classes—was truant.

The boy had been warned that if he missed another day of school he would be sent to the horrible reform school in Plainfield, Indiana. And so my father skipped lunch and walked to the boy's home and talked him into returning to school. Then, only an hour later, my father suffered a massive heart attack and died.

For those who have wondered, it is this, as much as anything else, that has spurred me on in my effort for America's unwanted children. He taught me that there is no limit to what one should give in defense of the helpless.

35

Some Need Help

Perhaps rabbits and robins perform their parental duties without training. But in this complex world many human mothers and fathers need help. So say most professionals I have interviewed, including psychologists, psychiatrists, physicians, social workers, sociologists, and those who work with the blind, deaf, and delinquent.

Most of us learn to parent as children at home. As adults we either copy the methods of our parents, albeit unconsciously, or, remembering the pain of childhood, we do what we believe to be the opposite. At the same time, many observers bemoan the fact that high quality parenting has, for a grocery list of reasons, been diluted to the point that it is a rare find. Assuming that this is so, and recognizing the importance of good child rearing to our society, one must ask: Can good parenting be taught?

More and more Americans are saying it can, but I do not find the question so easy to answer. My experience shows that really good parenting, like swimming, is hard to fake, and difficult to teach to older students.

Parenting is tied to the kind of person one is. Those who are warm, open, relaxed, steady, dependable, giving, patient, firm, but understanding—and with the time to give to their offspring—will usually do well, and with a little guidance may do even better. But would-be parents who are excitable, easily angered, tense, self-centered, lack empathy or understanding of the young, and ride an emotional pendulum, will learn little until these characteristics are wiped away. And heaven help the child whose parent is a sociopath, psychotic, or otherwise truly antisocial.

If we have only recently discovered that there is something called a "learning disability," think of the trouble we will have admitting that because of deprivation we have personal needs so great that we have a *loving disability!* And yet those who work with children today say that this is why we have so many little victims. Those of us with *loving disability* may intellectually be able to grasp what is being taught about parenting, but find it very hard to put the knowledge into practice.

A growing number of persons suggest that parenting can be taught in the public schools. It is tempting to believe this is true. Begin in junior high. Tie in with a day care center. Teach children, boys and girls, the basics of child care. It sounds sensible and simple, until you consider the track record of the schools.

Inner-city schools struggle to teach children to read, write, or speak clearly, and sensibly. They also require students to study history, literature, government, and geography, but few graduate with a clear concept of these subjects. We also have courses in vocational training, but many are so Mickey Mouse that high school graduates have trouble making minor repairs in their own homes and must take additional training to find a job. Schools also teach home economics, but one who visits the homes of former students, or eats at their tables, must conclude that what they learned (or didn't learn) at home about housekeeping and cooking has a great deal more to do with their adult experience than anything they picked up during their teen years at school.

Or consider sex education. I attended a very progressive school in the 1940s and early '50s, and our course in sex education clearly equaled almost anything being taught today. And yet I feel that what I was told has little to do with my adult experience or youthful behavior. Again, what my parents taught me about love and relationships has been far more important.

Our schools and colleges provide a smorgasbord of courses to sample, but few teach real skills. Nor, with their grade-oriented, competitive setting are they especially character-building. In fact the very qualities that make a good parent tend to be downgraded in the typical school. It is the passive child, who feeds back exactly what the teacher has said, who excels. Parents who try to please their offspring as they pleased teacher tend to turn out tantrum-throwing little monsters.

One further point. If parenting could be learned as an academic subject, then surely America's teachers, social workers, psychologists, psychiatrists, and pediatricians would always produce excellent children.

Sadly, some do not. Whether their children tend to be better or worse than the national average is a matter of speculation.

If it is true that large numbers of Americans fail as parents, especially when they give birth to a handicapped child, and if what one learns through living at home overshadows anything a child will get in the classroom, then is the problem of parenting impossible to solve? Hopefully not. The first step may lie in making parenting more important in America.

In an article in *The National Observer,* written with a light touch, in May of 1974, motherhood is called a vanishing art. The article also pointed out what some consider to be the anachronistic aspects of the contest that selects the American mother of the year.

If, as a nation, we have learned to scoff at motherhood or fatherhood, and casually form and dismantle families like so many Tinker Toys, even while taking gourmet food, wine, sex, automobiles, or leisure-time activities seriously, then perhaps we have inverted our priorities. If we do not care who has children or how children are treated, short of starvation, mayhem, or murder, then parenting and child rearing really do have little importance in this nation. At least not until the child grows up to become a criminal, alcoholic, heroin addict, con-man, or receiver of public welfare.

For reasons hard to explain, Americans do not connect the deviant adult with his childhood experiences. We seem to believe that unfortunate adult behavior just "happened" and is a mystery, never to be explained. Perhaps this is because we cannot face our own failures as parents, or still believe that such behavior is the work of a real and personal devil, as was taught for so many centuries. The devil theory may even make it possible for us to live with ourselves, a small fiction that prevents one from being overwhelmed with guilt.

Whatever the reason, far more parents are more concerned with the quality of a child's *formal* education—even while ignoring the far more significant *informal* learning that truly shapes the child. At every turn I find evidence that what happens *before* the child enters school and in the home after school is a hundred times more important than what takes place in the best of classrooms. The most promising child, when placed in the hands of gross parents, shrivels like a spring flower caught in a frost.

Are there, then, no answers? In the past decade we have begun searching for solutions beyond foster homes and institutionalization. And those working with children have noticed that it is possible, with professional coaching, to improve one's golf swing, or to teach a fellow with two left feet to ski, dance or play tennis. Now some experts believe that with professional coaching it also is possible to improve parenting skills.

One does not learn just by watching. If that were the case then large numbers of Americans could run a four-minute mile, or play professional football or baseball. But weekend television viewers can neither throw, kick, or run because of the hours spent in front of the tube. It takes dedication and practice to make it on the field, along with careful coaching.

Coaching and on-the-field practice have been used with marked success when dealing with parents who abuse their children. Dr. Ray Helfer, now of Michigan State University, and others have found that the best answer may be to assign a strong, warm, experienced woman who has successfully reared her own family to work in the home, rather than to remove the child. This because a mother (or father) who batters a child often was battered as a youngster, and when properly mothered—even as an adult—can outgrow this tendancy.

I visited a program based on this concept in the South Bronx in New York City in June of 1973. There I found mothers accused of abusing their children, and those who work with them, in a pilot project headed by Mrs. Aurealise Martinez. Mrs. Martinez is a warm, grandmotherly type, a psychiatric social worker, who makes all who meet her feel good, important, worthy. And her experience had convinced her that parenting has nothing to do with academic experience and everything to do with one's own childhood.

"You can't go by credentials," she told me emphatically. "Schooling has nothing to do with it. The ability to parent depends upon the way you were brought up. My mother is ninety, and her house still is full of children from all over the neighborhood. Sometimes there are fifteen or twenty of them in her home at the same time. She bakes cookies for them, and buys two-cent lollipops and sells them to the children for a penny. She is a loving, happy person. That is the key to being a good mother— being happy."

The battering mothers Mrs. Martinez works with are quite different from her ninety-year-old mother. I found them to be uptight, frightened, angry, unhappy, defeated and even disoriented persons. Like others who work in the field, Mrs. Martinez talks of their "role-reversal." The parents act like children and demand that their children act like parents. Many are "infantile, childish," she adds.

I met several such women in the Bronx. Doris, a frizzle-haired, nervous white woman of—I would guess forty, although she could have been younger—was assigned a black "homemaker" a few years her senior to work in her home. Doris only called the homemaker "Mama" and treated her as a parent. The homemaker is a friend and confidante, and helps care for the children and the home, teaching the mother, in this case Doris, the mothering role.

Doris has three children and a live-in boyfriend (one of a series) who does not work and assumes no authority, but helps himself to the food she buys with the children's welfare checks. A social worker assigned to the case says this "husband" is as immature as Doris, and makes the same demands on her as the children. The oldest child, Robby, who is most often the victim of physical abuse, is, at four years of age, "the man of the house, expected to care for the two younger children." On the day I was there the staff discussed what to do about Robby, a dark-haired, bright-eyed lad who is starved for love and attention.

Doris was waiting to meet with the staff when I arrived at the program center, and we shared a small waiting room for nearly an hour. I watched her with the children, and found her constantly picking at them, ordering them to be silent when they laughed or talked, threatening them with violence if they did not behave. I watched Doris ridicule her three-year-old daughter for coloring a rabbit in a coloring book purple. Then Doris demanded that the child hand over the book, so that she could "show her how." For more than a half hour Doris used crayons, coloring neatly, nicely, perfectly within the lines—sharing her finished pages with me, hoping, I felt, that I would praise her work. And she chattered, from time to time, about the program and how much help "Mama" was giving her, and how she enjoyed the program. In addition to the homemaker, Doris was in individual psychotherapy, took part in group therapy with other battering mothers, and spent her days at the project center learning to sew, bake, and care for her children.

If putting a warm, supportive homemaker into the home of an abusing mother can, at least in some cases, reduce child abuse and its long-term effects on society, so other kinds of in-home services also help, often while saving taxpayers money.

For a number of years the Flint, Michigan, public schools, with the help of the Mott Foundation, have provided homemaker services when children arrived at school ragged, dirty, or improperly nourished. The trained matrons meet the immediate needs of the children at the school, then visit the parents to see if they can provide additional help at home.

In-home services is hardly a new concept. In pioneer days neighbors would care for the children of a mother who was ill, and help in many other ways. The old country doctor visited his patients in their homes, and when things were amiss would speak his mind. And clergymen called on families and some felt free to comment when things were not right.

Scattered welfare department offices have used homemakers for many years, usually when a mother was hospitalized, so that their children could remain at home and in school. And visiting and public health nurses have also provided some services, depending upon the need.

I found several states now using circuit-riding therapists to work with parents of the deaf and blind, as I pointed out in earlier chapters. For in this area, as in others, the professionals have become aware of the fact that early care and stimulation make a major difference in what can be done with the handicapped later in life.

In Santa Barbara, California, where Dr. Robert E. Carrel has been hired to develop community programs for the mentally handicapped in a three-county area with a population of more than 800,000, I found in-home services being used. There trained therapists—usually college students or recent graduates—visit the homes of retarded children and teach mothers behavior modification techniques that are used in institutions to teach children to feed and dress themselves and to use the toilet.

Mrs. Bonnie VanAnglen, a social worker on Dr. Carrel's staff, says that most of the parent-trainers spend up to fifteen hours a week in a home until parents fully understand the techniques. She also gives them reading material and provides charts so that they can record the progress of their children.

In Dayton, Ohio, four young college graduates divide into two teams to provide in-home services to parents with child-rearing problems. They work under the supervision of Dr. Rita Muller, a psychologist at the child guidance center there. The program involves sending a team to the home when parents call, asking for help with behavior problems. Most of the children are very young and throw tantrums, kicking, stomping, or screaming, or they exhibit other forms of deviant behavior, but are not disturbed enough to require care in a mental hospital. Often they are referred to as "normal, but exhibiting obnoxious behavior."

The team operates from an ordinary house in an ordinary neighborhood. The initial interviews with the parents are held there, before a decision is made to provide the family with services. If an understanding is reached—and both parents must, in most cases, be willing to cooperate—then a team comprised of a young man and woman visits the home and observes the family in action.

"At first we may work with a family three or four times a week," Dr. Muller says. "It is important that Dad is involved, for he can undo our work in the evening after we have worked with the mother during the day. But we find quite a few fathers working eighty hours a week.

"Most of the parents we work with assumed that they knew how to be parents simply because they were adults. But that's not true. Even when they say, 'I won't raise my children the way I was raised' they do because that it is all that they know.

"Children want structure, limits, and support. Many may fight parents in these areas, but they need and want these things just the same. They need consistency. If mother says 'from now on' and then forgets or changes her mind, the child feels very unsafe. A normal child will push at the limits, but if those limits move, then the child feels unsafe. Many parents create problems because they give in. A mother will say, 'Tonight you'll go to bed at seven o'clock,' and then the child fusses to see 'just one more TV show.' If the mother says yes, then the limits move, and she has a problem in putting the child to bed at seven from that day on.

"Of course some parents are so rigid that the child has to rebel to break through. But most often the problem is caused by a parent's inability to be consistent. A child caught up in pushing at limits can spend all of his energy trying to find where the final limits are."

Dr. Muller also stresses the importance of giving the child a great deal of emotional support—especially to reward positive behavior and not negative. She suggests that because we live in a society that stresses the negative instead of the positive, children learn to misbehave just to get the attention they crave.

"At the initial interview we get a litany of negatives from the parents," she says. "They tell us all of the things the child does to upset them. Then we begin to teach parents to change their way of thinking, to begin looking for positives."

To help parents understand what behavior is rewarded or reinforced, the team shows films to a small group of parents, and they stop the film when a parent and child interact to ask whether good or bad behavior is being reinforced. They may ask, "What is that mother encouraging when she gives a lollipop to her daughter when she cries? Is she reinforcing positive or negative behavior?"

"We are geared to the negative in our society," Dr. Muller stresses. "Positive behavior is expected. The child plays quietly for a couple of hours and we ignore her. But as soon as she starts screaming and banging things around we rush in. Children pick up on that quickly. They realize that the way to get mother's attention is to be obnoxious."

The teams—Bill Francavilla, and Mary Schommer, and Diane Drummer, and Fred Duff—report back to Dr. Muller their findings about the family life, and she helps them work out a program. No single or pat method is used.

Both teams said, when I interviewed them, that the majority of the families they work with either have marital problems or the home is already split. But the teams deliberately avoid getting involved in the family conflict and focus their attention on working with the behavior of the child that is considered unacceptable, leaving marital counseling to others. The teams also work closely with the schools and with other agencies, if other agencies are serving the family.

Follow-up is one secret of the program. The teams visit the homes for weeks or months, watching the mother use the techniques that have been given her. Because the parents ask for help, and it is not forced on them, most are cooperative, and even enthusiastic about trying the program—especially after they see it work.

In a case handled by Bill and Mary, the mother, whose husband had disappeared, leaving her to care for four children on a small welfare check, complained that her four-year-old was extremely destructive and often refused to eat. When Bill and Mary visited the home they found the mother to be extremely inconsistent. When the children climbed on the furniture she would scream at them on one occasion, but ten minutes later would ignore the same behavior.

"I was skeptical when I began with this program," Bill says. "But I've changed my mind. In this case we were working with a pretty perceptive mother. We worked out a program involving consistency, setting limits, and sticking to limits. We explained how children learn behavior, and helped her with the plan for a few days. Now, after two months, she has things pretty much under control. The whole family is a lot happier."

Not all cases go as smoothly as that. Yet at other times they see overnight results. Mary told me of a four-year-old who was wetting the bed after the family split up, sometimes twice a night. The child's mother was exhausted from being awakened to change the sheets and blankets.

"We found out that the boy liked little toy cars and trucks. So his mother bought several of them, and told him that he would get one every night that he was dry. The next morning he was dry, and then was dry the second night as well—the first time he had been dry two nights in a row since his father left."

I asked what they did when a welfare mother, without the money to buy toys, had a problem. And they told of how two children were rewarded for good behavior. The mother kept a chart in the kitchen where they earned stars. For a certain number of stars they were permitted to watch a half hour of television, or to go to the park, or to play in the house with friends, or a weekend visit to a cousin's house.

Dr. Muller and her associates stress that this is not the only answer. Others involved in in-home services do not push it as the final solution to problems involving parents. But it is an important start when families are isolated from relatives, when they badly need help—sometimes just someone who cares to talk to, or when parents need to learn special skills when dealing with a handicapped child.

In-home services are a new-old tool that need to be further developed—especially now, when many feel that parenting is getting worse instead of better. It solves many problems created by foster homes and institutional care. And, when effective, can save the taxpayers a great deal of money over the long haul.

36

Making Them Useful

An August sun beat down on the rich farm land near Lubbock, Texas. Dr. John Gladden pulled the car into a shaded spot beside a small farm house and grinned broadly when ten robust, sun-tanned youths came whooping and laughing over a small hill.

"Hey, what are you fellas so excited about?" he asked.

One of the boys waved several dollars. "Sold beans," he said. "See. Money. Sold beans. Sold beans."

Dr. Gladden gave him a solid thump on the shoulder, the kind a football coach gives a player when he is pleased with him.

"Good work," he said. "How much money did you get?"

The youth handed over his treasured fistful of money to Dr. Gladden and the other nine gathered in close, watching him count it, sharing the glory. All were participating in an experiment at the Lubbock State School, an institution for the retarded. Dr. Gladden, the superintendent, believes that given the right support the retarded can make it in a world that usually excludes them.

The experiment involves growing vegetables in partnership with a local farmer. He provides the land, seed and fertilizer, and the once-institutionalized youngsters the labor. They split the income 60-40.

Because the boys are too retarded to live on their own and fully care for themselves, the institution has hired a young air force couple to act as house parents. The wife does the cooking and sees that they make their beds, sweeps up, and take baths when they need them. And the husband settles the living-together squabbles that boys may have and backstops his wife.

The problem is not getting the boys to work, Dr. Gladden says. Most have lived too many years in institutions, and they welcome the chance to get out into the fresh air and sunshine and to stretch their muscles. Even though they are retarded, the youths have a feeling of achievement when they see their vegetables growing in a neat, weed-free field. The farming project has given new meaning to otherwise wasted lives.

The secret of the success of the project is in training the youths to survive outside of an institution, in having a responsible adult around to see that all goes well, and in selecting a crop that requires hand labor and will bring in a profit. Considering the price of vegetables and the shortage of persons willing to do farm labor, Dr. Gladden believes they will do very well, and soon may come close to supporting themselves financially. And on the farm they are tanned, robust, and full of enthusiasm. It is an atmosphere far different from the hospital-like settings of so many institutions for the retarded.

Several hundred miles away, in Tucson, Arizona, I watched a dozen retarded youths of about the same age, and also laughing, tanned, and healthy, flip over a junked car on a covered patio outside a sheltered workshop on the grounds of the Arizona Training Program, an institution both for day students and for those who live on the grounds. When the car was resting on its top the boys—their IQs in the 40s—took wrenches and with a great deal of enthusiasm began to dismantle the car.

Inside the workshop, young men and women were seated at tables and on benches or working on the floor, disassembling aircraft parts from the adjacent air force base. Not far away other retarded youngsters were running saws and other power equipment and making things out of wood. Projects included beehives for Arizona's beekeepers, pollen catchers for an entomologist, stakes to be used around building sites, and markers for the city cemeteries. Others were weaving, knitting, sewing throw pillows and quilts, making chess sets, and other things to sell.

Dr. Ridgely W. Chambers, who has a retarded son, and who worked on the Apollo space project as an enginering psychologist specializing in communications before deciding to devote his life to the retarded, believes there is "no justification for just warehousing bodies" in an institution. He also feels that the retarded can, with help, do many useful things in society.

Dr. Gladden and Dr. Chambers are hardly alone in this. In fact, since 1970, a quiet revolution has been under way. Those who work with handicapped children realize that in our present society deviant youngsters must no longer be a drain. They must become useful.

One does not read about this revolution in the newspapers. Ask the typical man on the street about it, or even the average judge, social worker, or member of the state legislature, and he will only shrug. Nevertheless it is growing in size. Institutions (as I will point out in the next chapter) slowly are being phased out. Inmates are being returned to the community, there to perform useful, needed tasks.

Already they manufacture candles in more than a dozen states. I have watched them assemble packing boxes, make birdfeeders, package clothespins, hairnets, hair curlers, and two hundred other items. In New Hampshire they were sorting out broken golf tees for a manufacturer. In Nebraska I watched the retarded assemble plastic items, drop them down a slot, and trigger a device that rewarded the successful worker with a piece of candy. They were shipping 150,000 hair curlers and 1,000-dozen shower caps a week when I visited Beatrice, Nebraska. In Connecticut the retarded were making industrial cleaning rags, among other things, at the institution in Mansfield. The retarded were doing final assembly on hair driers and hand mixers as well. Even the blind retarded had work to do—preparing the wicks for the candle-making industry.

Making an unwanted child (or adult) useful is not an easy job. It requires time, patience, and the talents of trained psychologists who are skilled at behavior shaping. Most often the deviant work in sheltered workshops not unlike those run by Goodwill Industries for many years. Allowances must be made for disabilities. New tools sometimes must be designed. But with this, and other help, the handicapped can be useful, productive workers. Many, after years of sitting on benches, perform dull, repetitive tasks with joy—feeling for the first time a sense of self-worth.

More and more they are moving out of the sheltered workshops. In Tucson, Dr. Chambers also has an "outside crew" that builds fences, does cleanup work, and has even dismantled a cooling tower. And across the country the retarded are beginning to work at car washes, to pump gas, wash dishes, work as janitors and on lawn maintenance, and other low-skill jobs.

But there are still barriers. Our society emphasizes competition, and has a low level of tolerance for the slow producer. Dr. Chambers suggests that Darwin's theory of the "survival of the fittest" has permitted us to reject the deviant, to turn our back on those who do not fit into a "normal" pattern or mold. Part of the problem lies with professionals in the medical field, he adds. Unthinkingly they announce, with great authority, to a parent that "this child will grow up to be a vegetable," and few parents know enough to prove the doctor wrong.

Today more people are challenging this verdict. Efforts are being made to show society that the deaf are not "dumb"; that the blind can see with their hands and can compensate with their minds; that delinquent children may be more creative than many of us; that wheelchair victims can do many things; and that even severely retarded children can be taught to be productive in a society that considers those who are unproductive "bad."

Doctors told Dr. Chambers that his son would be a vegetable. But the youth, now in his early twenties, is able to work, live in his own apartment, and travel around town on a motorcycle. It is not easy for him. Rejected "fifty times a day" by unthinking people, the first to be fired when something goes wrong, he also has little to do in the evening. We may have provided recreation for many Americans, but there is too little for the handicapped to do.

In Texas, Dr. Gladden would solve this problem by establishing self-sufficient communities or colonies of handicapped persons, with farms, sheltered workshops, and work crews. Already his young men hire out to chop cotton for area farmers, and can help with the harvest. Girls, he believes, can run chicken farms, pick strawberries and other crops that are best harvested by hand.

For years institutions have run farms, using inmates as slave laborers. This still goes on in many states, although workers may make a few dollars a week. Many work in institutional laundries, as grounds-keepers, diaper-changers, wheelchair pushers, and in a variety of other ways.

We use delinquent and youthful prisoners in forest camps, state parks, and even cleanup campaigns. Welfare departments are pushing able-bodied mothers to learn work skills. In Europe both the retarded and emotionally disturbed are often expected to hold down jobs.

The use of another group of unwanted and deviant Americans, the elderly, in institutions for children has been paying off. It is called the Foster Grandparent Program, and in most institutions where it has been given a fair test officials tell remarkable success stories. I have watched men and women in their sixties, seventies, and even eighties push children on swings, play checkers and other games with them, work on craft projects, read to them, or just hold them on their laps—giving them the attention and affection they need. More than once I have heard of a Foster Grandparent teaching a child to walk or talk, to dress himself or use the toilet after the professional staff had given up. New Mexico's school for the retarded in Los Lunas had a large program using these senior citizens. After interviewing the Foster Grandparents I went away believing that they gained as much as the children. Being needed gave these elderly Americans a reason for living, new dignity, physical activity, and a little money to help supplement meager pensions. Many said they were growing healthier and happier each working day.

If there is a quiet, underground revolution under way, the American people should learn about it and give it a strong forward thrust. They will save tax dollars—and lives—by doing this.

If the retarded can find happiness by growing and picking strawberries, building beehives, assembling hair curlers, or dismantling old cars; if delinquents can help themselves mature while cleaning campgrounds and building mountain trails; if many emotionally disturbed Americans are capable of working; if the elderly can profit from helping handicapped children; if those on welfare can be taught to support themselves, while their children receive stimulation and proper care and encouragement in day care centers, then it is time for the people of America to take down the remaining barriers, and make it possible for unwanted children to become useful and accepted.

Why not train welfare mothers to work with the handicapped, and provide them with a career ladder that—with schooling—can lead to careers in recreation, therapy, or nursing? Why not use the experience and intelligence of senior citizens to run more sheltered workshops? Let those who are good listeners serve as therapists for persons with emotional problems. College students who need scholarships could be asked to serve as in-home trainers; help group-home parents in the evening and on weekends; teach sign language to the parents of deaf children; tutor youngsters with learning disabilities and other handicaps; and serve unwanted Americans in other ways. If we required all schoolteachers to intern for one year in a program for the handicapped before entering the public schools we would have a revolution in education. For any teacher that has helped teach a student who is both deaf and blind, or has worked with the severely or profoundly retarded, or an autistic child, will have more patience and understanding than is presently displayed. No longer will they be outraged at deviant behavior in the classroom or feel put upon when asked to work with children who struggle to learn.

If we could only require all young Americans to spend one year helping the handicapped—just as we have, in the past, required young men to undergo military training—we would soon have a different kind of nation. For if it is true that in this world of future shock, of sensual consumerism, and the threat of nuclear annihilation, many young people are confused, alienated, or lost, spending a year helping a slum mother as a homemaker, or teaching a crippled child to walk, or a retarded youngster to feed himself would help them plant both feet firmly on the ground and give life more meaning. Helping handicapped Americans is a settling, maturing experience.

When this nation was being built, and Americans lived in log cabins and sod huts and crossed the prairie in covered wagons, we shared and supported one another. It would not hurt America to return to this.

37

Recycling Institutions

It was in 1925 that Robert H. Link, a Rochester, New York, scoutmaster, coined the word "boondoggle." Through the years it has come to mean, according to Merriam-Webster, "any wasteful or unnecessary project." Now, a half century later, state officials have constructed a fitting memorial to Mr. Link's word in his hometown—an unnecessary multimillion-dollar institution for the retarded, run by the Department of Mental Hygiene. Similar structures also have been erected in Brooklyn and Schenectady.

The three new institutions for handicapped children weren't meant to be boondoggles. Born of compassion, they were built to meet the retarded child's every need—at least as the needs were known ten years ago. Even now staff members are working overtime, using old-fashioned American ingenuity, trying to turn the new facilities into assets. Despite widespread criticism from many quarters, including experienced professionals, it is just possible that they will pull it off.

The story of the boondoggle dates back to 1964, when the late Senator Robert Kennedy blew the whistle on Willowbrook, often described as the biggest and worst snakepit in the state. The Department of Mental Hygiene was clearly distressed by the criticism, and about a year later announced plans for the three deluxe, medium-sized (by New York standards) facilities for the retarded. Now, a decade later, the Brooklyn institution is in use and the Rochester and Schenectady projects are nearly finished, much to the chagrin of state officials. And not just because the cost overrun would do justice to a Defense Department contract. For since the buildings were started the national philosophy for dealing with the retarded has changed. So even before the Rochester and Schenectady buildings are finished and fully operative they are obsolete.

The problem doesn't lie in poor design. As residential institutions for the retarded, they are unsurpassed. Rather, they are obsolete because the national trend is toward community programs and away from putting children on institutional shelves. Handicapped persons are encouraged to live as normally as possible. Those who cannot be on their own or live with their parents are being placed in foster care, group homes, and small private facilities.

From Maine to California, the construction boom in the institutional field—which peaked in the 1950s and '60s—has faded. Public schools are being asked to hire special education teachers. The elderly and mildly handicapped in institutions are being culled out. When this shift to community-based treatment hit the country in the 1960s, most states scuttled their construction plans. Unfortuantely, New York's Department of Mental Hygiene couldn't find the stop-button. And so construction has been dragging on for years.

The Schenectady facility started out as a 1,000-bed facility, according to officials. It was then scaled down to 744, and later to 500 beds. The budget called for a $21 million institution. By the summer of 1974 the price tag was up to $28 million, and workmen were still on the job. Yet some sections of the Schenectady complex have been open for more than a year. At the moment it serves as a kind of 30-bed hotel (officials call it a hostel) for retarded persons until other accommodations can be found. (The horrendous old state schools for the retarded have long housed between 3,000 and 5,000 inmates.)

It was Dr. Hugh LaFave, a free-wheeling psychiatrist, who was assigned the job of doing something with the Schenectady white elephant. Dr. LaFave heads the Eleanor Roosevelt Developmental Services Agency and his staff serves some 2,000 to 5,000 handicapped persons (no one is sure of the number) in a six-county area with a total population of 750,000. Dr. LaFave admits that his job would be easier without the $28 million albatross. (In Santa Barbara, California, a three-county district with a total population of 800,000 operates its programs from an old house on a tree-lined street, and must have cost $27,950,000 less than the Schenectady facility.)

But Dr. LaFave and New Yorkers have their center, and it is too valuable to use as an old legislators' home, so much of his energy goes into finding creative ways of making use of the unwanted institution. Because he is a diplomat as well as a psychiatrist, he credits his superiors in the Department of Mental Hygiene, the governor and legislators, with being far-sighted in permitting him to use much of his budget outside of the institution, and to find new uses for the buildings.

Because the institution backs up the Mohawk Shopping Mall, Dr. LaFave has been inspired to call his facility a "shopping mall for human services," meeting the needs of not only the retarded, but children who are disturbed, blind, deaf, autistic; suffering from cerebral palsy, learning disabilities, and delinquents. At other times he calls it a "human services cafeteria," where parents and their children can pick out the services they want and need. And instead of the institution becoming the keystone of the Eleanor Roosevelt Developmental Services, it is just another building block.

Some taxpayers are critical of pouring $28 million into a building complex that is really a resource center, but Dr. LaFave believes that to sentence 500 persons to life in the center would be a greater crime. The cost of staffing residential institutions runs high, he points out, and even with that it would be necessary for a sizable field staff, since there are more than 500 handicapped children in the area.

Dr. LaFave has been permitted to invest the $10 million budgeted for staff in professionals and skilled workers in the field—using only a fifth of his budget on the institutional staff. As could be expected, given the kind of challenge he has faced, Dr. LaFave has not yet solved all the problems in his program. For this he has taken his share of lumps from laymen and professionals alike. But he believes that if he has time to work out the remaining kinks, and he does not underestimate their magnitude, he will have a program that will meet the needs of children and make good use of the complex as well.

If he pulls it off he may well have a plan that can be picked up by other states. Many find it hard to turn the key in the door of an institution and walk away. And yet more people are starting to understand how inhumane it is to sentence a handicapped person to life in a prison-like setting. And parts of his plan should be of interest to public schools. Most programs for children, including the schools, operate at the convenience of staff members. Not so at the Eleanor Roosevelt Developmental Services, where Dr. LaFave is trying to tailor hours and services to fit the needs of children and their families.

The Schenectady complex is open from 7 a.m. until 10:30 p.m. In addition to a contract with a school bus operator, Dr. LaFave has a small fleet of mini-buses. As this is being written, the Department of Transportation is developing an experimental program. And when no other solution has been found, state judges have ruled that agencies provide transportation for children.

But field workers are not assigned to funnel children into the center, as one might suspect, although growing numbers are using it. Instead, the staff acts as advocates for children—kicking open schoolhouse doors when necessary, urging and pleading with agencies to serve handicapped individuals when appropriate. The YWCA in Troy and Albany and the Jewish Community Center in Troy now have swimming programs for the youngsters. The Troy YWCA has also opened a hostel for handicapped children who have nowhere else to live. Several bowling alleys have opened their doors without charge. And civic groups, schools, and churches are beginning to do their share.

The goal of the Eleanor Roosevelt Developmental Services Agency is to evaluate the needs and provide services for every child in need in the six-county region in the Capitol district. This can be complex when the programs are tailored to the family's needs as well.

Take the mother of a handicapped child who would be on welfare without help. If she goes to work at 7 a.m. and the child's special education program doesn't begin until 9, then Dr. LaFave's staff seeks a group willing to work with the child for two hours, and with other children with the same problem. If the same child's class adjourns at 3:00 and mother doesn't get home until 5:30, then the staff looks for an after-school recreational program, a therapist, a homemaker to help out—whatever the child needs.

As for that $28 million complex, there are now both day and evening programs. Children may attend one or both, depending upon what is available elsewhere in the community, his parents' work schedule, and again, their individual needs. Activities include training in self-help skills (toileting, self-feeding, and self-dressing), a variety of educational programs, physical therapy, arts and crafts, swimming, bowling, movies and athletic programs in the gym.

Mr. Jefferson, the assistant director, sees the facility providing large numbers of parents with what in the field is called "respite care." Rooms that were designed for long-term residents provide short-term care for children (and adult retardates) while parents or substitute parents go on vacation, or a mother goes to the hospital, or when the family simply is getting uptight and needs a break. (This is being done in a number of states already, and with marked success. Many officials say that if parents were required to care for a retarded child 365 days a year, 24 hours a day, many could not stand it, for the burden would be too great. But with the handicapped person leaving the home for schooling, recreation, and for a few weeks of institutional living while the parents take a trip, many are able to live at home instead of in an institution.)

Staff members also talk of bringing entire families into the center to live and undergo training, so that they may better work with their handicapped family member. They have also planned a "drop-off" program since parents of the handicapped often find it difficult to find a baby-sitter when they go to the dentist, visit a friend, go shopping, or simply enjoy a meal and movie alone.

Already sixteen community groups use the complex, and some have moved their entire programs there. They serve children who have a variety of handicaps, as well as "normal" youngsters, like members of 4-H clubs and scouting groups, as long as they are willing to include handicapped children in their activities.

The complex also serves as a staging area for retarded adults who have spent years in the institutional grind in the state schools, and need to be trained for re-entry into the community. Those who have moved into community housing and cannot cope with the free world also return to the institution for more tutoring in the ways of the world.

It is a noble experiment, and one can see traditional high schools being reorganized in similar ways so that they better meet the needs of children. Already the phasing out of institutions has created problems, because too few alternative plans exist.

In Maine the state legislature has eliminated so-called status crimes —offenses that were designed only for children, including school truancy, curfew violations, promiscuity, and running away. In doing this they have nearly closed their institution for delinquent girls, and the number of boys held in the reform school in South Portland has been cut drastically. Yet Ms. Ward Murphy, who heads the Maine Bureau of Corrections, reports that many communities are going "crazy" because there are few programs or activities for once-institutionalized children.

And the lack of activities before and after school for the nation's physically handicapped, not to mention just ordinary youngsters, is appalling. The day of farm chores and working youths has long been ended, but communities have done little to solve the problem of too much free time. If phasing out institutional care for all but the severely handicapped and hard-core criminals adds to the problem, perhaps it will create the kind of crisis that prompts people to act.

Closing down institutions may be done, in part, for altruistic reasons. But in some states officials have other things on their minds. Class-action lawsuits won in federal courts in Pennsylvania, Alabama, Indiana, and in other states have forced institutions to stop merely warehousing children. Now they must provide them with therapeutic treatment with provable results. But skilled professionals are hard to find, their skills remain primitive, and they run budgets sky high. Add to this the fact that unions have, in recent years, organized many institutions, and administrators have a new set of problems. Again budgets have been pushed up, it has been increasingly difficult to fire an incompetent and even brutal worker, and some employees now stand around, acting more like jailers than child-care workers.

For many years institutions could house an unwanted person in an institution for $2,000 or $3,000 a year. Now the cost has soared to $10,000 or $20,000 and even higher, and still with few positive results.

Monstrous institutions are like dinosaurs, and should die off. But communities cannot ignore handicapped children, as so many do. If the program developed in Schenectady is less than perfect, it is better than what I found in most sections of the country. If communities would open their schools at night, providing services for all children, handicapped or not, and if there were paid advocates for children, searching for persons who will help, we would be on our way to a solution.

38

Who Speaks for
the Children?

In October of 1971 the Justice Department and other federal agencies summoned several persons interested in children to Washington to discuss delinquency. The session lasted four days, and I left convinced that those who had called the meeting had hoped to uncover a multibillion-dollar panacea that could be packaged and shipped to cities across the country. Of course no such easily packaged panacea exists.

At that session I tried to tell government officials about what I call the Lafayette Plan, a model program developed in Lafayette, Indiana, in the spring of 1971. I even asked two leaders of the Lafayette Plan to join me in Washington, but because the program does not involve massive spending, or a complex bureaucratic structure, many officials found it hard to comprehend.

The Lafayette Plan is based on several premises that have been discussed in detail in this book. (1) Because children are dependent, they are subject to the whims and decisions of adults. Since they are too often hurt by adults, children need protection and support. (2) While federal and state programs may affect children, the crucial decisions are made in the communities where they live. Thus reform must begin there. (3) In the community, services are fragmented, selective, or nonexistent. Unlike the free-enterprise system, where entrepreneurs aggressively seek opportunities, needs of children may go unnoticed and unmet for years. (4) Even when services exist, parents must not only recognize the special needs of their children, they must be motivated to seek out help. (5) Too often the local community looks only to the symptoms of a child's problems, and so fails to see or meet their most basic needs. (6) Because agencies and people working with children and families find it difficult to get funds, they compete with one another instead of working together. (7) Only a carefully concerted effort will meet the needs of all (or most) children in the community. (8) While there are always capable people willing to work in behalf of children, they must have access to the right information; they require encouragement, must see some small victories in a reasonably short period of time, and must have successful methods of achieving their goals.

The Lafayette Plan addresses itself to these points, and is designed to make the American political system work for children at the grass-roots level. Not only has the Lafayette Plan taken root, it has branched out into a statewide organization which could, if enough people care, grow into a national coalition.

While the Lafayette Plan was developed in that community by the people there, I played a small role in encouraging the seeds to be planted, and I watched it grow with relief and pleasure.

For several years I had been touring the country, lecturing to a wide variety of groups. While this was profitable, and helped me meet the financial needs of my family, and while I felt my lectures were well received, I felt far too little was being done for children. For in most communities people did not know where to begin in turning things around.

The Lafayette Plan officially came into being on May 1, 1971, although I had been thinking about a community coalition of the sort that emerged for some time before that. In fact, for several months I had been looking for a community that would meet the challenge of its children with minimal involvement on my part—a city of manageable size, with normal (but not impossible) problems, with conservative leanings (I felt, perhaps erroneously, that a liberal community would not have been a fair test of the concept), in need of "turning around," and with persons capable of serving as leaders. Lafayette met the test in almost every way.

Lafayette has a population of roughly 45,000 persons, while some 20,000 live in adjoining West Lafayette. Another 40,000 persons are scattered through the small towns and rural areas of Tippicanoe County.

While in a rich farming area, West Lafayette is the home of Purdue University, and Lafayette has several medium-sized factories. While the number of minority persons there is quite low, the community does not differ greatly from several hundred others scattered across America.

When I first visited Lafayette there was one juvenile court judge, a large bullpen in the county jail where several hundred children were held for varying reasons and periods each year, a thirty-two-bed children's home, provided by a prominent family several years earlier, and the normal range of health and welfare services, including a YWCA that remained in the downtown area and a YMCA that had followed the middle class to the outskirts of town. Each year the more obnoxious children were shipped off to Indiana's two awful reform schools near Indianapolis, and to other institutions.

In looking for a community that would develop a comprehensive advocacy program for children, I had considered my role, and had concluded that I could not impose my views or personality on the people. As a writer, I had watched Martin Luther King move the nation largely on the strength of his personality. Earlier I had spent a week covering the huge Billy Graham rally in Chicago for the *Chicago Tribune*, and saw his personal forcefulness. I also was familiar with the techniques used by Sol Alinski, a highly successful community organizer, and, as a political writer for the *Christian Science Monitor*, had covered campaigns over a period of several years in a dozen states. But these methods did not fit my personal philosophy or my conviction that to be lasting it would have to be the community's own program.

The story begins with a letter I received from Mrs. Patricia Truitt, a pert, persuasive, highly intelligent housewife with a master's degree in political science and excellent leadership qualities. She had heard that I was holding a seminar in the Lafayette area for social workers and wondered if, while I was in town, I also would hold a public lecture to be sponsored by the auxiliary groups that assist the Carey Home for Children.

I called Mrs. Truitt and told her that I was weary of giving speeches that produced few results, but offered to meet with a group of community leaders to discuss developing a community advocacy program. I explained that while I would serve as a resource person, my role would be limited. She agreed to the meeting and it was held, a few weeks later, at the Lafayette YMCA.

Not only was I impressed with Mrs. Truitt's enthusiasm and ability to get things done, but also found other leaders there, including Betty Revington, a vivacious and optimistic person who also wanted to help children. A representative of the Chamber of Commerce also voiced his encouragement.

After many months of thought, I had hoped to find a community that could launch a full-scale advocacy program with less than $1,000 in start-up money that would work within the existing political system, would involve me in no more than a one-day session, would have staying power long after I left, and that could serve as a model for other communities. Lafayette did all that and more. It also "seeded" other areas in the Midwest without my involvement, and in time became the basis of a statewide advocacy group for children.

I was pleased that I would have the opportunity to work with a community in Indiana—the state that fought hardest against my efforts to bring about changes in the juvenile justice system. For when I first wrote about the plight of children in trouble for the *Christian Science Monitor*, mentioning the deplorable conditions in Indiana, Governor Edgar Whitcomb and others launched an attack that, in retrospect, had a bit of the flavor of Watergate in Washington. With that kind of opposition, I felt that Lafayette would serve as a true test for my theory that a community, with minimal outside support, could turn itself around. I only agreed to make one or two talks, and to serve as a consultant, available by long-distance telephone.

In mid-April I visited Lafayette again and gave an hour-long lecture. Meanwhile, Mrs. Truitt and Mrs. Revington and others were preparing for a community conference, scheduled for May 1. They hoped to bring together a hundred persons, including business leaders, professionals in the child-caring field, educators, policemen, parents, politicians, and children.

The day-long Community Conference was held in a 4-H Club camp not far from town. The weather was good, and while we wondered if we would lose some of the people to the golf links and other springtime activities, more than 110 persons turned out—more than we had expected. The mayor was there, along with his chief political rival (who won in the next election), and agency heads, educators, police officials, housewives, lawyers, and influential businessmen took part. I spoke briefly, introduced Judge John Steketee, of Grand Rapids, Michigan—who had come to the meeting at his own expense as a resource person—presented research material gathered by community people, and showed a few minutes of my film *Children in Trouble*. But the real purpose of the meeting was to involve those present in serious dialogue about the problems of the children in the community, and to see if they could find ways to meet the needs of those children. To that end, those present were carefully divided into groups of eight, and each group was asked to produce, before the morning ended, a list of the fifteen most serious problems affecting local youngsters.

Each participant brought his own long-standing feelings about children to the meeting, along with some measure of expertise. Groups were small enough to permit everyone to voice his views, and the leaders were asked to encourage all to present their opinions fully, and to prevent anyone from dominating the group.

In many instances it was the first time that policemen, teachers, social workers, ministers, parents, young people, and businessmen had ever met, face to face, to listen to one another, although many had discussed the problems freely with friends and colleagues. As I made the rounds of the small groups I found deep interest in the subject and strong views being expressed—exactly what we had hoped would happen.

During lunch, which was served to the conferees cafeteria-style, Mrs. Truitt's husband, Bob, and another businessman tallied the lists of problems, and when the afternoon session began we were able to announce the consensus of the conference, and to rank the problems in priority order. Following lunch, meeting in the same groups, the second goal of the conference was announced. Each group was asked to prepare a new list, this one of suggestions for solutions to the problems listed during the morning session. These "solutions" were to be practical steps that could be taken within a year. When the afternoon small group meeting ended, and we reassembled after taking a break, the new lists were tallied. We closed the conference by reading the list, suggesting that these could become priorities for the community. In the enthusiasm that followed it was agreed that an ad hoc committee would be formed to discuss long-range plans, and Mrs. Truitt was named chairman. Because of the diverse representation, we felt we could honestly report that the results of the conference reflected the thinking of the community. Mary Elizabeth Weil, wife of the publisher of the *Lafayette Journal and Courier*, was an active participant, and the paper gave the program excellent support.

A few days later I left for nearly five months in Europe, Mrs. Truitt called the first in a series of meetings, and the Lafayette Plan was underway. It was decided that, because it involved a coalition of local groups and agencies, it should be called United Stand for Children and Youth. The first priority: to encourage county officials to convert Carey Home, which served dependent children, into a facility for children who were on the edge of delinquency, with the goal of keeping them out of reform school. To achieve this, and to get the needed funding, representatives of United Stand called county officials and later appeared before sessions of the County Council and the County Commission. Made up of conservative Republicans, they rejected a plan to use federal funds, then agreed to scale down the project and fund it with local money.

Meanwhile, several task force groups, each with a chairman, began working on other items on the list produced at the Community Conference. The Youth Service Bureau Task Force began planning to form a highly visible umbrella organization, where both parents and children could seek help from local agencies, and get it. And the Juvenile Justice Task Force began studying the need for a short-term shelter-care program for children who might otherwise be locked in jail, and then to open a shelter home.

While a tutoring program existed in a community center in the older section of town, the center had deteriorated and had been condemned. The School Task Force set out to pry open the doors of the schools themselves—hoping to tutor there, despite much opposition from administrators. That was achieved when school opened in the fall, and the program has continued to expand with broad community support.

The Juvenile Justice Task Force began meeting with local probation officers to develop a program, used in other cities, utilizing volunteers working directly with children. A Homemaker Service Task Force also began work a few months later, exploring the need for homemaker services (described elsewhere in this book) for persons in need of help.

While these groups were at work, others were carefully researching additional problem areas, including plans to build a wing on the jail to house hard-core delinquents who did not fit into the shelter program. Seminars on minority groups were held for teachers, and books in the library on minority groups were identified and organized so that they could better be used for minority-group study. Still others considered the problem of special education programs in the schools, the need for vocation education, and developed a summer youth employment program, financed a year later with donations from local industries totaling $20,000. Another group considered ways to provide diagnostic services to evaluate a child's needs and to find help, while a second shelter home, for teen-age boys, was studied and developed.

The leaders of United Stand also recruited business leaders, a state legislator, a bank president, Arthur Hansen, the President of Purdue, and others to serve on committees, and to meet with or call city and county officials, state legislators, and members of Congress to request funds, legislation, or to provide support to various programs for children in the Lafayette area. With these higly respected community leaders speaking out for children, the politicians listened—often for the first time.

In the first three years almost all of the priorities were achieved. To continue community interest, United Stand has, among other things, focused attention on the problems of children and those who work in the field by sponsoring an annual Juvenile Justice Day. The group has also helped provide foster homes and has been involved in foster-parent training programs. Efforts have been made to improve all community programs for children. A directory of mental health and remedial services for children was published and distributed. It includes information on the staff, fees charged, and the methods of obtaining services.

During this same period United Stand encouraged (successfully) the establishment of a Boys Club in Lafayette, and greater involvement of civic groups, development of day care, better, more varied, and coordinated services from child and family-serving agencies. Judge Warren Thompson is now assisted by a juvenile court referee, Judge Michael Riley. Discussion of the activities of United Stand prompted a variety of organizations to think of the needs of the children, and helped produce support for those interested in a crisis center.

In June of 1973 the Lafayette Plan went statewide when more than 300 leaders in the field from across Indiana met at the University of Indiana Law School in Indianapolis to form the Indiana Juvenile Justice Task Force, Inc. A second meeting, with 270 persons participating in a statewide conference, was held on June 8, 1974, in Kokomo. Board members included Willis Zagrovich, state president of the AFL-CIO, Robert DeBard, superintendent of the Indiana State Police, and Senator Daniel Huff, chairman of the Senate Judiciary Committee, along with judges, lawyers, businessmen, and other prominent Indiana citizens.

After three years there is little question that the Lafayette Plan works. Since the May 1 meeting there in 1971, Community Conferences have been held in other cities, with Lafayette's United Stand providing the kind of encouragement and advice that I offered Lafayette in 1971. A few days before this chapter was written, in 1974, I received two long reports from Rockford, Illinois, a city of 150,000 (the second largest city in Illinois) located in a county of nearly 250,000 persons. We held a one-day conference at the Unitarian Church there in November of 1973, and at that session ACT—Action for Children in Trouble—was born. Judge John Layng serves as Moderator (or chairman), and already the group is reporting progress in another conservative, Republican community.

Similar sessions were held without my involvement in scattered other cities, turning to Lafayette for advice and help. Hopefully these community groups will continue to multiply and will broaden their area of interest to include all of the children I write about in this book. It is possible, just possible, that by the end of the 1970s, and perhaps sooner, a national coalition of community groups will exist—using its strength to provide services and meet the needs of America's children. It is only a dream now, as the Lafayette Plan was once a dream. But if a national coalition could be established, with branches in every state, there would be far fewer little victims in America.

39

What You Can Do

If you are interested enough in children to have read this far, then you may be asking what you can do to help bring about change. There are many things that you can do, whoever you are, wherever you live, whatever your talents.

At the outset, you can search your own heart and mind to see if you are, as they say, "part of the problem or part of the solution." Do you find retarded children ugly, repulsive, even frightening? Do you still refer to the deaf as "deaf and *dumb*"? Does anger well up inside you when you hear of delinquent acts? Do you demand retribution instead of rehabilitation? Do you go along with drugging hyperactive and otherwise challenging children? Do you see crippled children as a burden on society? Do you resent children on welfare? Are you repelled by children with rotten teeth, filthy bodies, crossed eyes, misshapen heads, suffering from malnutrition, who have skin coloring different from yours, who attend the "wrong" church or synagogue, or live in the wrong part of town? Do you cover your eyes to neglect and abuse, convinced that it is none of your business? Do you shrug off the way we *use* children—without regard for the impact it has on them? Can you sleep soundly at night, knowing what is happening to children in institutions throughout the country?

If you must answer yes to some of these questions, then it is possible, just possible, that you *are* contributing to the problem. If you want to help, rather than hurt, these children, then begin with your own mind

351

and your own heart, and when you have convinced yourself, convince your friends.

All children need love, attention, and care. They also need the opportunity to reach their highest potential—whatever that may be. That is not possible when you are locked in a bedroom at home, or held captive in a custodial institution. In the last quarter of the twentieth century it becomes increasingly clear that we must begin to meet the needs of these children in the community.

The word *community* includes the word *unity*. In this era we find unity in diversity. It would be hard to survive today if all who live in a community were butchers, bakers, or saxophone players. To belabor the obvious, a community, if it is to function as it should, must be made up of mechanics, teachers, farmers, grocers, janitors, judges, shoe salesmen, social workers, manufacturers, entertainers, and many others. Each of these persons could, if they would, make life more interesting—more bearable—for the children I have been writing about. And by helping unwanted children, the adult members of the community would profit as well.

It is hard to be whole and happy in isolation. We profit most from sharing and giving. Reaching out to a child can give purpose and meaning to life.

Here then, in rather random order, are a few of the things that you can do to help:

1. Join an advocacy group. In cities scattered across America groups are being formed to fight for the rights of children. While the concept of children's rights is relatively new, and advocacy groups are looked upon as radical, most are made up of concerned, responsible citizens.

2. If an advocacy group does not exist in your community, start one.

3. As an individual, or with a group of friends, start a baby-sitting service for handicapped children. But seek guidance from a local child-care agency first. (If one agency refuses to cooperate, call another.) Too often parents of these children are unable to find a skilled, trustworthy person—even for an evening out.

4. Encourage your club, church, or friends to open a day-care center for handicapped, neglected, unwanted, or abused children. There are many centers for normal, healthy children; too few for those who need special care and attention.

5. Become the friend of a mother with a handicapped child. Often tied down at home, shy about the fact that she has a deviant child, she may need someone to help her shop, or just a friend to talk to.

6. Teach your children to understand the special needs of special

children. Much pain could be avoided if children were more sensitive and compassionate. Concern for others is learned at home.

7. Get your club, church, or neighborhood group to sponsor a conference on children. (See Chapter 38.)

8. Encourage your school board to sponsor seminars for teachers, so that they may better understand the children discussed in this book. Great progress can be made when teachers care.

9. Offer your services as a volunteer at an institution. Read to children; play games with them; take them on walks; bring a small tape recorder and play music or record their voices; teach them to play simple musical instruments; show slides; teach a child to knit; or just be a good listener.

10. Become a pen pal—and exchange letters with children in institutions.

11. Encourage your local court to establish a child-guardian program. When a parent is unable to meet a child's needs, but can keep the child at home, able citizens can serve as guardians—calling on school officials, helping a child manage money, shopping for the child, tutoring, and in many other ways. While the guardianship is established by court order, it is helpful to have parental support in the plan to avoid conflict. Many women without husbands welcome outside help.

12. Press local child-caring agencies to provide in-home services to parents with problems or problem children.

13. Start a volunteer agency that provides in-home services to parents of blind, deaf, retarded, and other handicapped children. Train workers to train parents to be more effective in helping their children overcome their handicaps.

14. Help start a child drop-off center for parents who are on drugs, who are alcoholics, disturbed, or abuse their children. (See Chapter 34.)

15. Encourage local judges to require lawyers to represent the interests of children in *all* divorce cases.

16. Become a foster parent. But sign up for the long haul. Dumping a child that has already failed in his own home (or whose home has failed him) may only compound his problems. Insist on training and adequate agency backup!

17. Help establish small-group homes in the community for delinquents, disturbed children, the retarded, abused and neglected youngsters, and others who need support.

18. Start a letter-writing campaign in support of programs or legislation for children. Write newspapers in your area; call radio talk shows; write lawmakers and city officials; and get your friends to do the same.

19. Start a fact-finding group and gather information on children in

need of help; resources available; community needs; and community problems. Then lecture at service clubs, churches, and before other groups.

20. Form a hiking, camping, or sports club for special children. Most handicapped youngsters are excluded from groups that normally engage in these activities. And yet special children need to participate in recreational activities as much as any child.

21. Encourage the local YMCA and YWCA, scout troop, or similar group to sponsor special programs for deviant and unwanted children.

22. If you own a summer cottage or a farm, sponsor outings or make facilities available to social workers, therapists, and volunteer groups working with children. (Be sure to make sure that you or the sponsoring group has proper insurance.)

23. Start a toy- and game-lending facility for these children.

24. If you love pets, help start a small "zoo" for children. City dwellers can keep friendly dogs, kittens, birds, or fish. Those in rural areas may want to let children visit and pet other animals.

25. Get the local bowling alley, school or church gym, and other recreational facilities to sponsor special programs for these children.

26. Take a child fishing.

27. Become a member of the Big Brother or Big Sister programs.

28. Start a campaign to make your community accessible to handicapped children. Wheelchair ramps, toilets, playground equipment, sidewalks, and other facilities should be designed with these children in mind.

29. Encourage radio and television stations to run public service announcements supporting groups helping children.

30. Provide local newspapers tips on news stories that involve courage, volunteer service, donations, and programs that help children.

31. Encourage the local paper to look into services for children. Provide them with standards and guidelines that their reporter can use to measure local facilities against.

32. Form a group to decorate a bed-ridden child's room; or to provide a child with books, a radio, magazines, a better bed, whatever the child needs.

33. If you have special training, or know people who do, start a free clinic or family service center. Among skilled professionals that are needed: tutors, lawyers, accountants, dentists, nurses, doctors, social workers, counselors, and family credit counselors. Make these services available to persons with children with problems, those who are on welfare, or with other special needs.

34. Encourage your community to open a human services resource

centers in key sections of town. Ask private and public agencies to staff the center, so parents—often without transportation, and with limited resources—can find help without searching all over the city.

35. Collect and repair toys for children in need and for institutions.

36. Offer your services as a wheelchair repairman; build balance beams, sandboxes, ramps, and other equipment for agencies and institutions that cannot afford to buy them.

37. Provide transportation to mothers who want to visit their children in institutions.

38. Get local merchants to provide clothing, food, and other items they do not sell. In one resort area surplus fruit and ice cream was made available to children on rainy weekends and at other times.

39. Sponsor plays, musical programs, and contests for children who do not participate fully because of problems.

40. From a committee to prepare a community checklist of things every community should have for children. Then call on civil groups, churches, wealthy families, clubs, school groups, and others to help meet the needs of the children in the community.

41. Help establish sheltered workshops in your community. Be sure that they are properly run; that those who work in them are given proper training and care; and that remuneration is fair.

42. Encourage prominent families with handicapped children to become leaders, as the family of the late President Kennedy did. The Kennedys and others like them, by admitting they had a retarded child, helped move retardation out of the Dark Ages and into the twentieth century.

43. Write for literature on children with problems and distribute it to friends and neighbors.

44. Establish a "family of the year" recognition dinner, and reward those who have done the most in the community to help children.

45. Open a gift shop that features work produced by the handicapped.

46. Encourage your local schools to provide *all* children with a full and rounded education. Schools should develop each child to his fullest without prejudice. Use volunteers, if necessary, to cut costs.

47. While nursery school may be available to so-called normal children, the handicapped are often rejected. Special programs should be developed for these youngsters, or special sections of regular preschool programs should be established.

48. Work to close down large state or regional institutions. See that they are replaced with in-home or close-to-home services.

49. Every state should develop reasonable standards for child care. Licensing, inspection, and enforcement are important—but these posts

should not be staffed by small-minded people who hassle those providing services. Avoid the problems that face nursing homes.

50. Fight to increase foster-care payments and funds for small-group homes. Make sure that foster and group homes are properly serviced by professionals.

51. Update child abuse reporting laws so that doctors and other professionals feel free to make reports. Encourage local citizens to report—but avoid big-brotherism and harassment of parents.

52. Fight to keep children out of jails and locked detention facilities. Growing numbers of communities now provide open shelter-care programs for children. No policeman should *ever* make the decision on whether or not a child is locked up. See that a trained person screens every child picked up.

53. The juvenile court operates in secret. Find ways to monitor its activities. Make sure that all children are provided with competent lawyers. Help judges find alternatives to reform school.

54. Open schools during the the evening and on weekends. Provide constructive activities: roller skating, ham radio, swimming, sports with proper instruction, whatever programs interest children.

55. Find ways to hold officials who deal with children accountable. If a facility does not help a child, it should either be improved or shut down. A citizen's group can monitor programs and demand change.

56. Hold a community forum on child-rearing practices. As families scatter, young mothers have no way of knowning how well (or poorly) they are doing. A community-wide forum, followed by weekly or monthly group meetings in local neighborhoods, can help. Involve successful, experienced parents as participants.

57. Encourage your club or study group to look at welfare. Find ways to help welfare families in your community. The goal should be to help the families achieve independence.

58. See that welfare children get special help in school, so that they do not fall into the same patterns as their parents. This should not be stigmatizing. Rather, it should be supportive.

59. Write public officials urging welfare reform. Work to end welfare dependency and its debilitating effects.

60. Offer baby-sitting services and other help to welfare mothers who wish to take classes or training programs to better themselves. Through help, rather than ridicule, those on welfare may be able to break free to their problems. Build on whatever shred of pride the welfare mother may have. Do not destroy this pride unless you want to encourage dependency.

61. Stop isolating those on welfare. Those who receive doles must

believe it possible to move up to higher levels of society. Keep the caste system out of the United States.

62. Develop catch-up programs for battered and neglected children. These youngsters need special help if they are not to repeat patterns set by their parents. We must pay more attention to them, and substitute love for neglect and abuse.

63. Help establish a child-abuse team in your community. This team should provide services to families that abuse children.

64. Encourage the use of retired persons in dealing with families in need and in trouble. The federally sponsored Foster Grandparents program has been a success wherever it has been tried.

65. Stop pitying children who are blind, deaf, retarded, or otherwise handicapped. They do not need pity, which is debilitating. They need encouragement and a helping hand.

66. Fight for "normalization" of all children discussed in this book. If we continue to isolate and limit them, they will continue to be society's little victims. If we accept them as fellow humans, stop making fun of them, give them the love and encouragement they need, and the opportunity to grow to their highest potential, they will be able to lead much fuller, happier lives.

67. Use your imagination. Put your talents, interests, skills, and experience to work. There are thousands of things that can be done if people care. Help is needed now.

There is almost no limit to the things that you can do for children . . . or that children will do for your sense of self-worth. What can be more important in life than helping another human being?

Our goal must be to change our culture. That change must take place first in our own hearts and minds and in our own homes. If each of us takes up the fight for the little victims of this nation, their plight will ease rapidly. It only takes a few people in each neighborhood to produce lasting change.

40

The Little Sparrows

Are not five sparrows sold for two farthings, and not one of them is forgotten before God? But even the very hairs of your head are all numbered. Fear not therefore: ye are of more value than many sparrows.

(Luke 12:6-7)

July. The summer sun beats down on my desk, making me squint. In milder climates the mock orange blossoms browned long ago. Here in the White Mountains the shrubs have not yet finished, and the aroma drifts through my open study window. Near our front door the wild, pink roses are losing their first petals, the iris blooms at the edge of the lawn have begun to shrivel, and the once-pale leaves on the trees that cover our mountains are turning a deeper green. Down on the village common a merry-go-round whirls hour after hour, shouting a single tune, as the perennial July Fourth mini-carnival welcomes in the tourist season.

Sitting at my typewriter I sometimes experience an isolation not unlike that of children in institutions. For days on end my study window becomes my only contact with the world. During prolonged writing periods, seasons slip by. I only look out when sleet rattles against the glass, the wind scatters my papers, when rain spatters through the screen, a cloud spoils the light, or a scent or sound tugs at my senses.

My isolation is hardly the same as the institutionalized child. I am free to come and go as I please. There is a telephone at my elbow. When a few chapters are done I go out to research a new section of the book. In short, my imprisonment is self-imposed. And soon it will end. But how do I finish? What words will make a difference? How can I awaken . . . alert . . . stir . . . even shake a nation?

The carnival music grinds on. It becomes a symbol for a hedonistic, uncaring, wasteful world that ignores deviant and unwanted children. How do you tell Americans, taught to "look out for number one," that there are some who are too small, too weak, or crippled to look out for themselves? I pace the floor . . . stare out of the window . . . run my fingers through my hair . . . look for something to eat . . . boil water for Sanka . . . pace again.

I should sum up what has already been said. Restate basics. Show that *all* unwanted children—retarded, blind, delinquent, abused, crippled —are poorly treated. Isn't that the point of this book? To show what we are doing to *all of them*, rather impartially? That and to encourage change? I pace . . . out of step with the carnival music.

The Biblical passage about sparrows haunts me. If five sparrows are worth two farthings, what value do we put on a retarded child? What is a crippled girl worth to Americans? Or a black, Indian, or Chicano child? What is a delinquent or a cross-eyed kid worth? We love mongrel dogs. Why can't we care more about children who are different?

I recall a social worker who said in his state they pay more to board a dog in a kennel than for foster care. Perhaps a nap will help, but I cannot fall asleep. The carnival music blares on.

Change. I type the word, then type it again with a colon following it. Change: has there really been change? My mind tracks back and forth, trying to weigh the question. Change? We no longer sell children into slavery. Unless one counts hedonism and the easy-credit plan a form of slavery. At least slavery is more subtle now. Child-labor laws have been passed in this century. There are no human sacrifices now. Except, perhaps, abortions—children sacrificed on the altar of self-centered pleasure-seeking. "A kid would ruin my life . . . spoil my happiness." But most Americans cannot buy my view.

I pace again, stopping to reread an editorial in the July issue of *Fortune*. The subject is economics and social change, and it is noted that in the 1960s there was a "fairly sudden change in public sensibilities. Americans generally, and certainly most of those who had any influence on public attitudes and policies, became a good deal less tolerant of certain forms of human suffering—and more disposed to regard various disadvantages and discomforts (not necessarily permanent) as 'suffering.' The persistence of poverty, for example, suddenly came to seem a

360   PART III · SEEKING SOLUTIONS

pressing national problem. And by the same token, high unemployment rates came to seem intolerable."

The *Fortune* editorial is right. There was, briefly, outrage over hunger in America. The War on Poverty passed Congress with little meaningful opposition. Attitudes toward the poor, blacks, Indians, Chicanos, women, homosexuals, and mental patients changed. We are less tolerant of child abuse. Schools, long under attack, try harder.

What caused these changes? We are too close to the events to really know. A nation tormented by the death of a beloved President? Guilt as we became more affluent? Fear of black rioting? Pressure by marchers and demonstrators? Leaders reared by "permissive" parents? Confusion over the Vietnam War? Our growing number of college graduates? Perhaps all and none of these things.

Now we are in an era of economic conflict. This too can produce change. How long will taxpayers put up with soaring welfare costs? How will they react when they at last learn that it costs from $5,000 to $20,000 (and more) to keep one child one year in an institution—with little return on the investment?

I recall the report, written about Harry Vorrath's PPC (Positive Peer Culture) program by a junior high school principal in Omaha. There is a chart on vandalism, showing how it has been reduced since PPC was introduced. In January 1973, a total of thirty-six windows were broken. A year later the number broken: one. In February of 1973 youngsters smashed forty windows. Again only one in February of 1974. The trend continues throughout 1974. It is this reduction of vandalism that has impressed the Omaha school administrators, if I read the report correctly. What if the report had only mentioned a reduction in broken children. Would administrative interest be as high?

Still pacing, I spot a book I found recently in a dusty corner of a bookshop in New York City. *The Economics of Mental Retardation*. It was written by Dr. Ronald W. Conley, and published in 1973 by The Johns Hopkins University Press. With a $15 price tag, written in somewhat scholarly language and filled with statistics, the book, I suspect, is not decorating many coffee tables across the nation.

Without saying so, Dr. Conley argues that we must make the retarded *useful*. He would like to see the American free enterprise system put some 400,000 retarded persons to work. A mildly retarded boy, entering the work force at the age of eighteen in 1970, "could expect lifetime earnings of over six hundred thousand dollars," he says. Every dollar we spend on vocational rehabilitation of such a youth "generates an estimated increase in future earnings of fourteen dollars in present-value terms." It costs some $400,000 to keep one person in an institution for a lifetime.

Prevention of retardation also pays, he says. "For each case of severe retardation among males that is averted, the undiscounted total gain to society is almost $900,000 [1970 dollars]." I tell myself that this should make the politicians take notice—even if they do not have a single shred of human compassion in them.

Dr. Conley also presents a strong case that should appeal to business interests: "It is strange that profit, which has impelled a part of the world's population to spectacular heights, should be viewed with such disdain when made by providing services to people," he writes. (I note that our doctors and lawyers have not totally ignored the profit motive in serving people.) He suggests that the profit motive will help end an era when government runs horrible, inhumane institutions for the retarded. For Americans, "lured by the hope of profit, will seek new and better ways to provide services, hoping to gain business by providing a better service or the same service at lower cost."

Dr. Conley has not forgotten the manufacturer and merchant. He writes of "consumer sovereignty," and how all citizens, including the retarded, have the right to "consume, within the limits of his income, whatever goods and services he chooses." He uses this to bolster his argument that the retarded should be encouraged to earn wages, for they will become excellent consumers.

He is right, I tell myself. The economic issue is politically sound. But there is more than money to consider. Even on this point Dr. Conley does not disappoint me. He suggests that future generations may well consider our neglect and maltreatment of the retarded to be "cruel, incomprehensible, and outrageous."

I put the book down. Perhaps simply being humane is not enough. And yet who would deny that each human life must count for something. Every child, healthy and happy, or retarded, disturbed, delinquent, crippled, or cross-eyed, should be free to live out his life without limitation or restriction. The black child, the victim of abuse, the poor speller in school—all of these children should be able to ride the merry-go-round, sniff the mock orange blossoms, toss pebbles in the brook, run freely across the lawn. Surely each is of "more value than many sparrows." We do not ask sparrows to be eagles or robins or crows. We only ask that they be themselves.

Outside my window the carnival music—that symbol of self-centered hedonism—blares on. But now it is growing dark. The dusky mountains are backlighted by the descending sun. My pacing has ended. My mood mellows. I know that alone I cannot produce change. But I am hardly alone! Seated here in my study for long periods of thought and writing it may seem that I am. Writing a large book requires isolation—a feeling that no one else knows what I know. I understand why I feel burdened. No one can see what I have seen without wanting to press for change. But it is a false sense of burden that I feel.

I know the American people. I have lived through difficult periods in history, and I have seen the people of my nation respond. I know the strength of the American people . . . the depth of the caring. What nation rebuilt Japan, Germany, and much of Europe after World War II? What nation has shared its riches with the world?

We may have become hedonistic. The age of materialism . . . of sensual consumerism . . . may have arrived. But our money . . . our coins and our currency . . . that most tangible symbol of materialism . . . our money still carries the words: *In God We Trust.* That concept may be obscured at the moment, but it has not been erased!

It is easy to become cynical, angry, depressed, indignant when one sees what we have done to children. But there is change all around me . . . in every state . . . in every city and town changes are taking place. The changes are real.

As I consider this, I recall that sociologists often talk of "social forces." For some this has an almost religious connotation. It is my understanding that by *social forces* they mean that when circumstances are right, certain events are inevitable. And yet they do not ignore the importance of the individual effort. I search my shelf and find a college textbook, *Sociology,* by Arnold W. Green (McGraw-Hill, 1952). I find this example, under the heading of *social forces:* "Had Einstein never lived, his theoretical work in physics might have later stemmed from some other man's mind, but this delay would also have delayed the invention of the atomic bomb; this subsequent delay might very well have had incalculable effects upon the entire course of recent history." Green also writes that "the accumulated evidence for a theory of biological evolution was already at hand in the middle of the nineteenth century" and Darwin's theories would have emerged "even if Wallace and Darwin had never lived."

Darwin "discovered" biological evolution. Whether or not we attribute change to a "higher power," to "social force," or to some other source, it seems certain that there also is an evolution of human thought. I can see it in art, music, literature, philosophy, government, the concepts of transportation, communication, and in ecology. The women's movement was produced by such an evolution, and it arrived at the right moment in history to produce change.

There can be little question that we are experiencing changes in the way we think about children . . . in the way we treat them. In less than ten years drastic change has taken place. The United States Supreme Court, in the Gault case, upheld the theory that children are citizens under our Constitution . . . citizens with rights. Since then federal courts have ruled in behalf of deviant, unwanted, and handicapped children. Drastic changes have been made in a number of institutions for the retarded because of this, although not enough has been done. Magazines and newspapers have, in the past three or four years, given more space to the problems of children than in the previous twenty years, I am sure. Books are being published on the subject. Every state has improved its child-abuse laws in the past decade. Youngsters are benefiting from the consumer movement. Groups are fighting to improve television—the progress has been made. Several United States senators have been speaking out loudly, forcefully, clearly for children.

I am hardly alone in this fight. I do not need to produce the words that will move the nation. The nation is already moving! My responsibility—and the responsibility of every person who cares about children—is to join this movement. To help give it shape and direction. To see that it does not stop short of the goal.

Perhaps this book will help those who are not familiar with the problems to see them more clearly, and then to act. That is enough.

The carnival music grinds on.

I consider the concept developed in the previous chapter: community implies the need for unity. But what of the larger community—the community of man? We believe we are living in "civilized" times. And yet millions of children are in pain. Through the agencies and systems we have developed we do things to them (as well as to the elderly and members of minority groups) that stretches the meaning of the word "civilization" to the breaking point.

Bruno Bettelheim, who survived a Nazi prison camp, writes in his book, *The Informed Heart* (Macmillan, 1960), that ". . . the success or failure of any mass society will depend on whether or not man so reshapes his personality that he can modify society into one that is truly human. . . ."

Evolution of thought (or the reshaping of human nature) is a very slow process. At least it has been slow. We are told there have been at least two earlier stages of man—savagery and barbarism. After that came civilization. The change from one stage to another is not quite the same as opening and slamming doors. I wonder if we are not civilized in some ways, yet retain the thought patterns of the savage or barbarian in others?

What qualifies a society to call itself civilized? Among other things, organized government, laws and justice, the growth of science and of problem-solving techniques, expanding technology, literature and the arts, comfort and leisure.

It is possible, after careful research, to date certain changes in civilized society, including the arrival of what we call humanitarian values. *Fortune*, as I have pointed out, notes major changes as recently as the 1960s, or so their editorial would imply. Will some distant generation look back and find that we are living in the early years of *humanitarianism*, the step beyond civilization?

But is humanitarianism the end of the line? Is sympathy or benevolence enough? Will the evolution of thought lead us beyond feeling sorry for (rather than laughing at) those less fortunate than ourselves? Is it enough to try to stop society from inflicting pain on the poor and the weak? Or even to give those who are deviant a fighting chance?

If there is a further step, what is it? *Altruism?* Or is altruism just humanitarianism stretched to the most distant mark? Can we truly become our brothers' keepers? Will this help or hurt our brothers? Can we find happiness in serving others—and in being served?

If altruism is two paces beyond civilization, is that the end of the line? Or will the evolution of thought take us beyond, to an even higher state?

What of *idealism?* At least in one sense, idealism implies the perfectibility of man. In a way, man becomes Godlike—or to borrow from Genesis (Genesis 1:26–27) man has been created in the image and likeness of God.

Savagery. Barbarism. Civilization. Humanitarianism. Altruism. Idealism. It is possible to find shreds of logic in that sequence.

It also is possible to find children being hurt today. Now. At this moment. These children need our help.

The carnival music plays on.

Index

Index

373

guilt and, 54
performed before children, 108
among teen-agers, 54, 56
Sexual involvement, lack of love at home
and, 112, 202
Sexual stimulation, reduction of level of,
59
Skills, 325
living and career, 186
new, mastery of, 187
Slaves, 10-11; young, inhuman treatment
of, 10
Slums, 4, 123, 190, 276. *See also* Ghettos
aged in, 283
elimination of, 32
Social workers, 6, 31, 106, 195, 204, 234,
276-277, 285-292, 294, 297, 303, 327
measuring success rate of, 290
role of, 291
Socialization, for the deaf, 255-257
Society. *See also* Public, the
and the deaf, 257
federal meddling in, 163
and the handicapped, 267, 273, 335
rewards and punishments by, 176
rights of, 134; child bearing and, 310
sex saturated, 69
Solitary confinement, 115-116, 196-197,
211-213
Sons, sexual abuse of, 99
Sports, 166, 168; young children and,
92-93
State governments, 311-312. *See also*
Legislatures
State hospitals, 197, 205-213, 237, 239,
244, 311
State welfare departments, 294
Stepchildren, 122-123
Stepfathers, 25, 30
Sterilization, 132-133, 136
of children, 134-136
of women, 134
Suicides
attempts at, 101
youthful, 40
Superstition, infanticide and, 27
System, the, 40-46
birth of, 45-46
children damaged by, 43-44
cost of, 42
selecting children for, 42-45
and subsystems, 40-42

Taboos, sexual, 99-100
Talent, 85, 166, 176-177, 184, 186-187,
311; of the retarded, 219
Teachers, 48, 81, 106, 164-165, 175-176,

178, 185, 195, 265, 303, 308-309, 311,
349
of the blind, 262, 265, 309
for crippled children, 311
and deaf children, 248, 252, 255-256
legally blind, 262, 309
special education, 31, 183-184, 242, 245,
271, 311
Teen-agers, 122-131, 187. *See also*
Adolescents
and conflict with parents, 124-125
faddishness of, 127
fears of, 126
homogeneity of, 127
as mothers, 7, 30
and premature babies, 61
prolonging childhood of, 129
reasons for bad behavior of, 125-131
role models for, 128
self-concept of, 129
Television, 34-35, 48, 144, 150-160, 190,
193, 363
addictive aspects of, 158
advertising on, 144-147, 153-157, 159
harm to children by viewing, 158, 160
new heroes on, 159
as possible therapist, 157
violence and death on, 6, 17, 152, 158,
194, 290; list of programs showing,
159
Texas, 17, 20, 88, 174, 243, 333, 336;
homosexual murders in, 100
Therapeutic treatment programs, 44, 116,
191, 308
Toddlers
neglect of, 68
unsupervised, 275
Toys, 143-145, 156; dangerous, 143, 147
Tranquilizers for children, 118, 197
Tucson, Arizona, 87, 168, 174, 187,
255-256, 263, 301-302, 313-316,
334-335
Tullos, Olouse and Connie, 249, 253-254

Understanding, average age for, 78-79
United Nations Children's Fund
(UNICEF), 301
United Stand for Children and Youth,
348-350
United States. *See also* Americans
child abuse in, 39
child labor imported into, 9-10
infant mortality rate in, 76, 278
mating system in. *See* American Mating
System
mental illness in, 64
mentally retarded in, 39